The Mammoth Book of Weird Records

Recent Mammoth titles

The Mammoth Book of Undercover Cops
The Mammoth Book of Antarctic Journeys
The Mammoth Book of Muhammad Ali
The Mammoth Book of Best British Crime 9
The Mammoth Book of Conspiracies
The Mammoth Book of Lost Symbols
The Mammoth Book of Steampunk
The Mammoth Book of New CSI
The Mammoth Book of One-Liners
The Mammoth Book of Ghost Romance
The Mammoth Book of Best New SF 25
The Mammoth Book of Street Art
The Mammoth Book of Ghost Stories by Women
The Mammoth Book of Unexplained Phenomena
The Mammoth Book of Futuristic Romance
The Mammoth Book of Best British Crime 10
The Mammoth Book of Combat
The Mammoth Book of Zombies

The Mammoth Book of Weird Records

Jim Theobald

ROBINSON   RUNNING PRESS
             PHILADELPHIA · LONDON

ROBINSON

First published in Great Britain in 2015 by Robinson

A CIP catalogue record for this book
is available from the British Library.

ISBN: 978-1-47211-769-4 (paperback)
ISBN: 978-1-47211-771-7 (ebook)

1 3 5 7 9 10 8 6 4 2

Typeset in Sabon by Hewer Text UK Ltd, Edinburgh
Printed and bound in Great Britain by CPI Group (UK) Ltd, Croydon, CR0 4YY

Robinson
is an imprint of
Constable & Robinson Ltd
100 Victoria Embankment
London EC4Y 0DY

An Hachette UK Company
www.hachette.co.uk

www.constablerobinson.com

First published in the United States in 2015 by Running Press Book Publishers,
A Member of the Perseus Books Group

Books published by Running Press are available at special discounts for bulk purchases
in the United States by corporations, institutions, and other organizations.
For more information, please contact the Special Markets
Department at the Perseus Books Group, 2300 Chestnut Street,
Suite 200, Philadelphia, PA 19103, or call (800) 810-4145, ext. 5000, or e-mail
special.markets@perseusbooks.com.

US ISBN: 978-0-7624-5618-5
US Library of Congress Control Number: 2014952365

9 8 7 6 5 4 3 2 1
Digit on the right indicates the number of this printing

Running Press Book Publishers
2300 Chestnut Street
Philadelphia, PA 19103-4371

Visit us on the web!
www.runningpress.com

CONTENTS

Introduction   vii

Chapter 1: Trivial Pursuits   1
Chapter 2: Fashion Victims   49
Chapter 3: The Body Bizarre   64
Chapter 4: Acquired Tastes   113
Chapter 5: That Sporting Spirit   145
Chapter 6: Pet Projects   226
Chapter 7: That's Entertainment?   272
Chapter 8: Technology and Games   338
Chapter 9: Feats of Strength   362
Chapter 10: Collections and Hobbies   388
Chapter 11: Mind Games   437
Chapter 12: Intrepid Travellers   446
Chapter 13: Unwanted Records   509

Sources   550

Acknowledgements   551

INTRODUCTION

Everyone knows of Usain Bolt, but how many people have heard of Dean Gould? Like Bolt, the Englishman is a world record holder but in the lesser-known sport of beer mat flipping. He is just one of the hundreds of unsung heroes featured in this book chronicling the people who go to bizarre lengths to break records in the weirdest categories. They devote hours of intense training to spitting dung, eating cockroaches, sniffing feet or tossing tuna in the hope of one day being recognized as the best in the world.

Some record-breakers admirably strive to set new goals in order to raise money for charity, but for others it is simply that quest for fame. Not everyone is blessed with the physique or ability to become one of the world's greatest athletes, but with the right dedication, care and a stoic refusal to be embarrassed in public we can all aspire to grow the longest nose hair.

So let us acclaim these intrepid souls – these gladiators of inconsequentiality – who have pushed boundaries further than they were ever meant to have been pushed even though their achievements, often flying in the face of extreme adversity, occasionally reduce the rest of us mere mortals to expressing our emotions in one simple word: WHY?

CHAPTER 1

Trivial Pursuits

LONGEST TIME SITTING IN A BATH OF BAKED BEANS

When, in September 1986, computer worker Barry Kirk sat in a bathtub of baked beans for a record 100 hours, it was to prove a life-changing event. From then on his entire persona was built around the humble foodstuff. He changed his name by deed poll to Captain Beany, started painting his face and bald head orange, and donned a golden cape, pants, gloves and boots to transform himself into the world's only haricot bean superhero. In 2007 he climbed Mount Snowdon while carrying a plate of baked beans on toast, and the following year he took his favourite food around the London Marathon course as the original runner bean. He insists that no beans were harmed or spilt during the twenty-six-mile race. His next half-baked venture was to turn his orange flat in Port Talbot, South Wales, into the Baked Bean Museum of Excellence, complete with a fart alarm to deter burglars. Keeping his finger on the pulse, he entered politics as the founder and sole member of the New Millennium Bean Party. At the 2010 general election, he contested the Aberavon constituency in Wales and received 558 votes, 1.8 per cent of the total vote and over 60 more than the UK Independence Party candidate. When he is not being Captain Beany from the Planet Beanus, he works as a Bono impersonator, although thankfully without the orange face paint or it would look as if the U2 frontman had spent way too long in the tanning salon.

LONGEST TIME BRUSHING TEETH WHILE SPINNING A BASKETBALL ON A TOOTHBRUSH

On 4 October 2011, John West, from Eagle Pass, Texas, managed to brush his teeth while simultaneously spinning a basketball on the other end of his toothbrush for 26.63 seconds. In doing so he was careful to adhere to the strict rules of the challenge – namely that he brushed his teeth in motions approved by the National Dental Association and that he used an accredited brand of toothpaste. He was clearly in a rich vein of form at the time, as the previous day he established a new world record of 45.69 seconds for the longest time spinning a basketball on the tip of a pen held in the mouth.

MOST BEER MATS FLIPPED BLINDFOLDED

When it comes to beer mat flipping, Dean Gould, from Felixstowe, Suffolk, is, frankly, flipping amazing. At the last count he held no fewer than thirteen world records in the category, including speed flipping (1,000 mats in 28.02 seconds), catching from elbow to palm in a row (2,390), flipping blindfolded (71), and what is very much the blue riband event of beer mat flipping, the 360-degree flip (23). To prove he is not just a one-trick pony, Gould has also set world records in such diverse disciplines as coin snatching, pancake tossing, needle threading, stamp licking, egg holding, potato catching, brick catching and winkle picking. He also held the world record for the fastest 301 score in darts, but it was snatched away from him just three minutes later by 1983 world champion Keith Deller. "We each had five attempts to break the record," recalls Gould. "On my last attempt I managed to complete the 301 in 33 seconds, beating the record by three seconds, but then Keith did a 130 check-out, ending with a bullseye in just 25 seconds. One minute I was on this massive high and the next I had really come down with a bump. Someone always wants to beat your record, but that was the shortest time I had ever held one!"

MOST PING PONG BALLS CAUGHT WITH CHOPSTICKS IN ONE MINUTE

Ma Deqi, a forty-year-old farmer from Yuzhou, China, caught forty ping pong balls with a pair of chopsticks in 60 seconds in January 2011, thereby smashing his own previous world record of seventeen. A keen exponent of table tennis, he practises by catching balls spat out from an automatic server. At the time of breaking the record he stated that his next aim was to catch ping pong balls with chopsticks while walking up a flight of stairs and playing a harmonica. We eagerly await news of this development.

LONGEST TIME BURIED ALIVE

Czech magician Zdenek Zahradka (stage name Fakir Ben Ghan) spent ten days buried alive in a coffin without food or water in June 2004. The fifty-year-old beat the previous record by four days, and survived because he was able to breathe through a ventilation pipe. He spent most of his time in the coffin sleeping and meditating, which pretty much covers all you can do when you're alone in a coffin and being constantly monitored. He certainly fared better than Sri Lankan Janaka Basnayake who, in his quest for glory, persuaded friends to bury him alive in a ten-foot-deep trench sealed with wood and soil. He was lowered into the ground on the morning of 3 March 2012 to begin his record attempt and was pronounced dead later that same day.

LONGEST TIME HUGGLING

One day, acclaimed American jugglers Jen Slaw and Michael Karas decided they wanted to combine their passion with another pastime to create a new hybrid discipline. Having perhaps concluded that mugging someone while juggling (muggling) would significantly increase the risk of arrest, they instead chose the safer option of hugging while juggling (huggling). On 16 May 2013, in Philadelphia, Pennsylvania, they established a huggling world record by hugging one other while each success-fully juggled three balls for 33 minutes 43 seconds.

LONGEST TIME HOPPING ON ONE LEG CLOCKWISE WHILE WEARING A PIG HAT WITH ONE EAR FLIPPED UP AND STRUMMING A GUITAR ON BACK

Some cynics might claim that Kyle Matz contrived this event purely so that he could say he had set a world record. We prefer to look on it as a previously undiscovered art. For the record (pun intended), Matz, from Sherwood Park, Alberta, Canada, performed the multitasking routine for 53.6 seconds on 23 February 2013. Keen to ensure that it was being taken seriously, recordsetter.com laid down strict rules for the challenge:

- Must alternate legs when hopping.
- Must hop clockwise.
- Must wear a pig hat with one ear flipped up and the other flipped down for duration of attempt.
- Guitar must be put on back.
- Must strum guitar for duration of attempt.
- Must attempt outdoors.
- Must provide video evidence.

So there. Nothing artificial about it all. Only one thing remains puzzling: why did it have to be done outdoors? Is there some law in Alberta against wearing a pig hat indoors?

LONGEST GRAPE CATCH IN MOUTH

Shortly after noon on 2 September 1988, after about seventy wayward attempts, a large-seeded red grape was dropped from the sixty-storey John Hancock Tower in Boston, Massachusetts, straight into the gaping mouth of Paul Tavilla standing on the street 788 feet below. The record-breaking feat confirmed the fifty-four-year-old Tavilla as the undisputed king of grape catching. Three years later in Boston, this time assisted by professional grape thrower (try telling that to your school careers adviser), James Dedy, he set a new world record for the longest grape catch on level ground by catching Dedy's grape thrown from 327 feet 6 inches away. Tavilla has been catching food since he was a teenager. "Being brought up in the whole-sale fruit and produce business with my family, and being around all kinds of fruits and vegetables, I used to ask different people to throw me a cherry tomato, a strawberry, pieces of bananas and even small plums, and caught them in my mouth at short distances. Everyone always got a big kick out of me doing that." So when he discovered that there was a Guinness World Record for grape catching, he made it his life's ambition to break it. He says he now only uses black grapes because they're big, heavy and easier to see, but the downside is that when a falling one hits him in the cheek or chest at 100 mph, it can sting. At the height of his catching career he had swollen lips from the near misses. "It's very dangerous if you don't know what you're doing,' he once said. 'You could put out an eye. And the neck strain kills me." However, he loved the fame, the only drawback to which came when people would stroll in to his produce company, say, "Here, catch this in your mouth," and throw him an orange.

MOST GRAPES CAUGHT IN MOUTH IN THIRTY MINUTES

Competing in Sydney, Australia, on 16 November 2006, American Steve Spalding (aka The Grape Guy) caught 1,203 grapes in his mouth in thirty minutes – not far short of a grape every second. He discovered he was good at catching things in his mouth at college as his roommates hurled sweets around, but when it came to pursuing a world food catching record he decided to focus on grapes because they don't knock your teeth out.

LONGEST EGG CATCH IN MOUTH

On 3 September 2005, twenty-five-year-old Brad Freeman, from Calgary, Alberta, caught in his mouth a hard-boiled egg thrown by Patrick Breault from a distance of 280 feet. To prove it was no fluke, he caught four out of the twenty eggs thrown by Breault from that distance in his mouth. The other times he ended up with egg on his face.

MOST EGGS BALANCED ON END SIMULTANEOUSLY

In June 2011, Brian "Eggs" Spotts, from Dacono, Colorado, balanced 900 eggs on end simultaneously at a shopping mall in Hong Kong, breaking the world record – but no eggs – by a dozen. His passion for egg balancing dates back to 2003, when he decided to test his mother's assertion (an old wives' tale) that an egg could only be balanced on the equinox. So every equinox he took a few eggs and tried to stand them up, all the while dreaming about the day when, in some huge venue, all he would see before him would be rows and rows of eggs, perfectly balanced. He began practising for half an hour every day, searching for the "sweet spot" on the bottom of the egg and mastering the ideal grip for balancing – with the thumb and forefinger of each hand positioned just at the top of the egg. He soon came to learn that the surface was equally important. "I don't use tables," he says, "because if you bump it, you can lose 100 eggs just like that." His workplace at Denver International Airport was just as unsuitable. Despite its wide concourses, planes flying above and trains rumbling below created a vibration nightmare. Then a Chinese company invited him to showcase his skills on the APM Mall's smooth, level marble floor – and the rest is history.

MOST WEDDING BOUQUETS CAUGHT

As listed in *The Skousen Book of More Amazing Mormon World Records*, which presents "the astonishing, the amazing and the unbelievable achievements of Latter-day Saints from all around the world", Jamie Jackson, from Utah, has caught thirty-eight wedding bouquets since 1996.

MOST TOOTHPICKS ROTATED 360 DEGREES IN MOUTH SIMULTANEOUSLY

New Zealand-based record-breaking enthusiast Alastair Galpin has broken over seventy-five world records for assorted feats, including the most rubber bands stretched over the face in one minute (62), the loudest clap (113 decibels), the longest unbroken potato peel (5 feet 2 inches), the farthest champagne cork spit (16 feet 5 inches), and the fastest time to butter ten slices of bread (52.42 seconds). Few, however, have caused him greater anguish than his 2012 attempt to set a world record for rotating wooden toothpicks in his mouth simultaneously, an experience he likened to having a hedgehog scour out his mouth. "Before I began practising," he says, "I carefully planned what I'd do if a stray toothpick were to lodge in my soft throat tissue or stab me in the nasal canals at the back of my mouth." The answer was: stay calm. He had plenty of opportunity to put the advice into practice. His first attempt before witnesses came to an abrupt end when one toothpick tip stabbed the lining of his throat, causing his windpipe to constrict and forcing him to spit out all of the wooden sticks – along with copious amounts of saliva – into a bowl. On the second attempt, a toothpick got stuck between his teeth and his right tonsil and, unable to loosen it, he once again had to expel the sticks into a bowl. After several more failures, his tongue finally got all the toothpicks to rotate in a single bundle, and he was convinced that he had set a world record, only to discover when he got home that he had only rotated the toothpicks 180 degrees in his mouth instead of the required 360 degrees. The record would not count. Undeterred, a few days later, once his mouth had healed, he tried again and this time he successfully set a new world record by fully rotating thirty-nine toothpicks in his mouth simultaneously. He admitted it was an exhausting exercise, one which he insists he is in no hurry to repeat – unless, of course, someone comes along and breaks his record.

MOST CONSECUTIVE BITES TAKEN OUT OF THREE APPLES WHILE JUGGLING THEM FOR THIRTY SECONDS

On 5 April 2010, Brian Pankey, from Springfield, Illinois, took sixty-five consecutive bites out of three apples (i.e. he did not skip any apples) while juggling the fruit for thirty seconds. He took a bite out of each apple as it passed through the juggling rotation, but happily the rules of the challenge said that he did not need to swallow them. So he stored some pieces in his mouth while others leaked out to form a water-fall of drool, leaving him looking like a rabid dog.

LONGEST TIME BALANCING A JAR OF PEANUT BUTTER ON FOREHEAD WHILE WALKING ON A TREADMILL

There's more to Brian Pankey than just snapping at apples. He has set any number of obscure records – indeed more than you would care to count – including the fastest time to walk 100 yards with a glass of wine balanced on his fist (1 minute 12.13 seconds), the fastest time to walk 100 yards in swim fins while dribbling a basketball (54.61 seconds), the longest time balancing a shopping cart on his chin (30.22 seconds), and the most golf balls balanced on his chin (36) while juggling four other golf balls. But arguably his finest hour came on 19 December 2011 when he spent a record 4 minutes 31.19 seconds balancing a full jar of peanut butter on his forehead while walking on a moving treadmill. That's class!

LONGEST TIME BALANCING A RAW EGG ON A POOL CUE

On 21 July 2011, Doug McManaman, from Nova Scotia, Canada, balanced a raw egg on the handle end of a pool cue, which he held in one hand, for 11 minutes 10.20 seconds. On 26 December in the same year, McManaman set another egg-related record by bending up and down 260 times without breaking the two eggs held inside his pockets. This is just the tip of the iceberg. For the official website of recordsetter.com states that he holds over 700 weird world records, many involving eggs. They include the longest distance walked while balancing an egg on the back of the hand (2,000 yards), the longest time balancing an egg on the back of his hand (59 minutes 13 seconds), the longest time balancing an egg on top of an axe on his chin (4 minutes 20 seconds), the longest time balancing a two-litre bottle of water with an egg on top on his forehead (7 minutes), and, of course, the longest time balancing an egg on a spoon held in the mouth while simultaneously balancing a lacrosse stick on the thumb (9 minutes 22.3 seconds). Doug McManaman is living proof that eggs are versatile.

MOST EGGS BALANCED ON NEEDLE POINTS IN ONE MINUTE

On 19 August 2011, Cui Juguo, from Changsha, China, balanced three eggs on the points of needles in under a minute. A former truck driver, he developed his unique skill just over six years previously to counteract drowsiness at the wheel. "I often take several eggs with me on the road," he says. "Once I felt sleepy, I would pull over and start to stand the egg on the needle point." He can even perform the trick with ostrich eggs – the largest eggs in the world.

LONGEST TIME BALANCING A CHAIR ON FOREHEAD

Without using his hands, Switzerland's Leo Bircher balanced a chair (which he had built himself) on his forehead for 35 minutes 27 seconds in 2004. Bircher has also set world records by balancing a pencil upright on his nose for 2 minutes 33 seconds and by balancing a broom on his nose for 2 hours 1 minute.

LONGEST TIME BALANCING A GOLF BALL ON A TEE ON NOSE

On 3 February 2007, juggler and unicyclist Steve Mills, a member of Ohio's Dazzling Mills Family, balanced a golf ball atop a 2.75-inch tee perched on his nose for 34 seconds.

MOST HAIRS SPLIT

When it comes to splitting hairs, it is no great surprise that no one could top an Englishman. Alfie West was his name and he managed to split a single human hair lengthways into eighteen parts, making all the cuts from the same point. The Londoner, who lived from 1901 to 1985, was a keen amateur cyclist of such proficiency that he went on to represent his country, but it was during World War I that he honed his hair-splitting technique when he worked in a factory making aircraft parts and was taught how to grind the edge of a razor as sharply as possible. He later became a furniture restorer and enthusiastic artist, displaying his hair pieces in a home-made museum.

MOST PEOPLE INSIDE A SOAP BUBBLE

In Krakow, Poland, on 2 December 2012, bubble artist Jakub Bochenek, from Katowice, created a bubble large enough and strong enough to accommodate 193 people, all of whom were over five feet tall and standing upright. This broke the record of 181 people set a few months earlier by Canadian bubble maker Fan Yang, who, using a delicate pulley system and a special secret solution, managed to make a bubble that measured over 160 feet long and 13 feet high.

MOST LAPS WALKED AROUND A TABLE TENNIS TABLE WHILE BOUNCING A BALL ON THE BAT

On 23 March 2011, Thomas McGinnis, from Roscoe, Illinois, completed 174 laps of a table tennis table while continuously bouncing a ping pong ball on his bat. What more could you want from life?

FIRST PERSON TO RUN A COMPLETE LOOP-THE-LOOP

British stunt man, gymnast and wannabe hamster Damien Walters has the distinction of being the first person in the world to run a complete 360-degree loop-the-loop. Scientists at the Massachusetts Institute of Technology in Boston spent four months building a giant, ten-foot-high hamster wheel so that Walters could perform the gravity-defying feat. They calculated that if he ran at a constant speed of 8.65 mph, he would be able to complete a full loop. Sure enough, in February 2014, he finally succeeded in staying on following a series of practice run failures that were only made slightly less painful by the presence of strategically placed mats.

MOST BEER BOTTLES OPENED WITH A HELICOPTER IN THREE MINUTES

German pilot and flight instructor Jan Veen set a Guinness World Record in Dortmund on 26 January 2008, by opening four beer bottles in three minutes with a bottle opener attached to an airborne Robinson R44 helicopter.

FARTHEST DISTANCE TO HIT A PING PONG BALL INTO A STACK OF TEN CUPS WITH A HAIRBRUSH

On 4 January 2012, Joel MacNeil, from New Glasgow, Nova Scotia, Canada, earned himself a place in the recordsetter hall of fame by hitting a ping pong ball with a hairbrush into a stack of ten paper cups from a distance of fourteen feet. Who needs video games when kids can amuse themselves for hours with such inventive pastimes?

MOST LIGHT BULBS LIT BY INSERTING ELECTRICAL WIRE THROUGH NOSE AND TAKING IT OUT THROUGH MOUTH

By inserting an electrical wire through his nose and pulling it out through his mouth, human generator M. Ravikumar, from Namakkal, India, was able to light a total of thirty sixty-watt bulbs at a Tamil Nadu shopping mall on 10 June 2012.

MOST TIMES THREADING A STRAND OF COTTON THROUGH A NUMBER THIRTEEN NEEDLE IN TWO HOURS

In 1993, Om Prakash Singh, a bank employee from Jaunpur, India, set a new world record by threading a strand of cotton through the eye of a number thirteen needle 20,675 times in two hours. In doing so, he beat the existing record by 8,879.

LONGEST TIME SITTING IN A BATH OF MILK

The Record Holders Republic website states that twenty-five-year-old Doris Bray, from Sydney, Australia, sat in a bath of milk for forty-eight hours in May 1989.

LONGEST TIME SITTING IN A BATH OF PORRIDGE

Starting, appropriately enough, on 1 April 1988, Bristol pub landlord Philip Heard sat in a bath tub full of cold porridge for 122 hours 30 minutes.

LONGEST TIME SITTING IN A BATH OF CUSTARD

What would you normally choose to accompany custard? Rhubarb? Probably. Chocolate cake? Sounds good. A fifteen-stone former Army P.T. instructor? Maybe not. Well, fifty-two-year-old Bill Hammond, from Pickering, North Yorkshire, set a new world record in June 1988 by sitting in a bath full of custard for 168 hours in a shop window. That's a whole week sitting in custard and watching the world go by. It is hard to imagine that his presence boosted the sales of either baths or custard.

LONGEST TIME SITTING IN A BATH OF SPAGHETTI

Rob Gordon, twenty-four, from Shrewsbury, Shropshire, sat in a bath of spaghetti for 360 hours (15 days) between 21 September and 6 October 1984. The bath was mounted on a wheeled trolley so that he could be pushed around the streets of Shrewsbury and also continue his disc jockey duties in the evenings.

LONGEST TIME SITTING IN A BATH OF MAGGOTS

Christine Martin, from Horsham, Sussex, sat in a bath containing thousands of squirming maggots for 90 minutes on 30 November 2001. As she ran a fishing tackle shop, she had handled maggots for years but still found bathing in them to be an uncomfortable experience. "You could feel them wriggling against your skin and it was like having pins and needles. They got in a few places they shouldn't have done."

MOST REVOLUTIONS OF A HULA HOOP
WHILE HANGING UPSIDE DOWN

British circus performer Chi Chi Revolver (whose real name is the only marginally less exotic China Olver) achieved a world record 112 revolutions of a hula hoop while hanging suspended upside down in Brighton in March 2012. The twenty-eight-year-old from Worthing started out in the circus at the tender age of three. "When I was little," she says, "I used to dress up as a dog and chase my dad, who was a clown, with a spider on a stick." You probably had to be there to appreciate it.

MOST REVOLUTIONS OF A HULA HOOP
AROUND THE LEG IN ONE MINUTE WHILE
STANDING IN THE ARABESQUE POSE

Adopting the gymnastic arabesque pose, where you stand on one leg and stretch the other leg out behind you at an angle of ninety degrees, nine-year-old Mridula Shanker, of Ann Arbor, Michigan, completed a world record 166 hula hoop rotations in one minute around her non-standing leg on 28 May 2013.

MOST GOLF BALLS HELD IN ONE HAND

On 30 November 2009, Guillaume Doyon held twenty-four golf balls in one hand for 10 seconds at Gatineau, Quebec, Canada. His record was subsequently equalled by Rohit Timilsina in Nepal in 2010 and again by Zachery George in Elkins, West Virginia, in 2011.

MOST BOWLING BALLS STACKED VERTICALLY

In November 1998, Dave Kremer, a production manager for a chemical company in St Louis, Missouri, successfully stacked ten bowling balls vertically without using any form of adhesive. He said the urge first came to him after a few beers when his friends said they had heard of people who could stack four balls. Kremer boldly declared he could beat that and managed five. He soon found that stacking bowling balls was right up his alley, and before long the world record was his. Naturally, he placed the heaviest balls at the bottom of the pile but added that the precise positioning of each ball was equally important. "I always place the thumbhole of the first ball down, which steadies it. The next thumbhole will go on top of the centre of the first ball. There's a weight between the thumb and finger holes, so the thumbholes are always down."

LARGEST BUBBLE GUM BUBBLE BLOWN UNASSISTED

Now you might think that blowing the largest possible bubble gum bubble is the sort of pastime that most people leave behind in the school playground, but Chad Fell, a real grown-up from Haleyville, Alabama, takes it all very seriously. Adopting an earnest tone more appropriate for someone who has climbed Mount Everest carrying a small horse, or crawled to the South Pole on all fours, he has even produced a video offering tips on how to blow big bubbles. He emphasizes the importance of correct tongue positioning and of first chewing the gum long enough to dissolve the sugar, as "sugar will hinder the size of your bubble. It is the worst enemy of the bubble gum blower." But he clearly knows what he's talking about as, on 24 April 2004, he scaled new heights by blowing a twenty-inch-diameter bubble gum bubble without using his hands – a world record that still stands over a decade later.

LARGEST BUBBLE GUM BUBBLE BLOWN

The late Susan Montgomery Williams (aka "Chewsy Suzy"), of Fresno, California, blew a twenty-three-inch-diameter bubble gum bubble in 1996, but, unlike Chad Fell, she used her hands to stretch the bubble while blowing it, which is perfectly legal but comes under a different category in the complex world of international bubble gum bubble blowing.

LARGEST BUBBLE GUM BUBBLE BLOWN FROM THE NOSE

Joyce Samuels, "The Gum Blowin' Granny" from Louisville, Kentucky, has blown from her nose a bubble gum bubble with a diameter of sixteen inches, breaking her own 2000 record by five inches. Like Chad Fell, she first chews the gum for at least an hour to get rid of the sugar before moulding it into a rectangle shape and placing it over her nostrils. Apparently she first came up with the idea of putting gum on her nose and blowing bubbles to entertain her children.

MOST GARTERS REMOVED WITH TEETH IN ONE MINUTE

Using only his teeth, Ivo Grosche of Germany removed twenty-six garter belts from a line of scantily clad ladies in one minute in Berlin on 18 December 2008. The act was performed on the set of Germany's Guinness World Records TV show, so it was all above board, although it would be interesting to know how and where he first identified his unusual talent.

MOST SMOKE RINGS FORMED FROM A SINGLE DRAW OF A CIGARETTE

Jan van Deurs Formann, from Copenhagen, Denmark, set a new world record in August 1979 by forming 355 smoke rings from his lips from a single draw of a cigarette.

MOST LIGHTED CANDLES BALANCED ON MOUSTACHE

Performance artist Rajendra Kumar Tiwari, from Allahabad, India, has grown such a long, bushy moustache that he is able to balance twelve lighted candles on it. He even had two of his teeth taken out in order to make room for more candles. Once the candles are in place, he performs a moustache dance by twirling it to the rhythmic beat of traditional Indian music without moving a muscle in the rest of his body. A born entertainer who often appears under the name Dukanji, he used to amuse neighbours by balancing flowers in his facial growth until one Diwali night in the 1980s he alighted on his new act. "The power was out, it was pitch dark," he recalls. "Out of sheer fun, I placed a burning candle on my moustache. Strangely, I liked it." He made national headlines in 1990 after appearing at a major show in Hyderabad, although he admits he was so nervous his feet moved more than his moustache. To control his breathing he walked to the Allahabad city dump every morning to see how long he could hold his breath amid the foul stench. He says: "I stop eating or drinking anything at least two hours ahead of a moustache dance performance because food makes it difficult to control your breath and that hurts in getting the right balance for the moustache." He has accidentally singed his moustache on a couple of occasions but this has obviously failed to dampen his enthusiasm.

LONGEST TIME HOLDING AN APPLE BETWEEN TEETH

When it came to the crunch, steel-jawed Thomas De Man, from Ghent, Belgium, successfully held a large apple between his teeth for 16 minutes 53 seconds on 18 February 2013.

LONGEST TIME KEEPING TOE IN MOUTH WHILE HOPPING ON ONE FOOT

In October 2011, Dustin Barker, from Clinton, Iowa, managed to keep the big toe of his right foot in his mouth for 1 minute 49.02 seconds while simultaneously hopping on his left foot. Under the rules of the contest, his hopping foot did not stay on the ground for longer than two seconds at a time and no part of his non-hopping foot ever touched the ground.

LONGEST DISTANCE BALANCING A MILK BOTTLE ON HEAD

In April 1998, New Yorker Ashrita Furman balanced a full bottle of milk on his head while walking for 80.95 miles, setting a record that still stands to this day. Appropriately the distance record, which combines endurance, balance and extreme concentration, was first set by a clown, but Furman's single-mindedness quickly made him the cream of the crop. He has practised milk bottle balancing all over the world, to mixed reactions. He says that in Japan people politely pretend that it is nothing unusual, whereas in New York bystanders throw rocks to try and knock the bottle off his head, and in Cancun, Mexicans honk their horns loudly or bark like dogs to unsettle him.

Furman is very much the doyen of weird records, having set around 500 since 1979 in such diverse disciplines as underwater rope jumping, catching a basketball behind the neck and chopstick snapping. He currently holds more than 160 individual records, set on all seven continents and at some of the world's most famous landmarks, including the Eiffel Tower (most sit-ups in an hour), the pyramids (distance pool cue balancing), Stonehenge (longest time standing on a Swiss ball) and Uluru/Ayers Rock (fastest hula hooping for a mile). He has also performed continuous forward rolls along the entire twelve-mile route of "Paul Revere's Ride" in Massachusetts, pausing only to throw up. So what compels the non-driving, celibate bachelor, vegetarian and health food store manager to attempt so many records? "I'm trying to show others that our human capacity is unlimited if we can truly believe in ourselves," he says. To prove his point, the man who has achieved so many remarkable athletic feats reveals: "As a kid I was terrible at sports – I was always picked last at school."

LONGEST TIME BALANCING A CHRISTMAS TREE ON THE CHIN

During the 2001 festive season, David Downes, from Felixstowe, Suffolk, balanced a seven-foot-tall Christmas tree on his chin for 56.82 seconds. And then they found the pot.

FASTEST TIME TO BLOW A GOLF BALL TEN FEET

On 29 January 2011, Scott Evans, a twenty-year-old night-club door supervisor (bouncer in old money) from Norwich, England, set a new mark by lying on the ground and blowing a golf ball a distance of twenty feet in 14.06 seconds. At the same time he laid down new world records for five and ten feet – possibly because nobody had bothered to blow a golf ball along the ground before. Afterwards Evans admitted to feeling a bit giddy from tackling the longer distances, saying: "It took a lot of breath out of me." But he added excitedly: "The fact that you are the only person in the world that has done it is great."

LONGEST IRONING MARATHON

Standing throughout at an ironing board, Janette Hastings ironed for eighty hours in Tumbarumba, New South Wales, Australia, from 1 to 4 April 2012. During that time she ironed 1,157 items, including jeans, shirts and shorts.

MOST POSTAGE STAMPS LICKED AND AFFIXED IN FIVE MINUTES

On 28 August 2004, Thomas Schuster licked and affixed 238 postage stamps to envelopes in five minutes at a demonstration in Ravensburg, Germany.

MOST POSTAGE STAMPS LOOSENED

The Book of Alternative Records states that from 2 to 3 September 1989 French philatelist Henri Pereira successfully loosened 60,171 postage stamps from envelopes in 47 hours 48 minutes. That's two days of his life he'll never get back. As if the record itself wasn't pointless enough, he had already spent fifteen months patiently collecting all the letters he needed just to be able to remove the stamps.

LONGEST TIME JUGGLING A SHUTTLECOCK WITH FEET

Li Huifeng juggled a badminton shuttlecock with her feet non-stop for 4 hours 40 minutes in Beijing, China, on 21 December 2006 – without the shuttlecock ever touching the ground. In doing so, she broke her own world record, set two years previously, by three minutes.

MOST COMPLETED JUGGLES WITH CLUBS WHILE JUMPING ON A POGO STICK

Under his stage name "Phineas", New York entertainer Matthew Lish performed 781 consecutive juggles with three twenty-inch clubs while jumping on a pogo stick.

LONGEST TIME JUGGLING UNDERWATER

Using scuba equipment, Germany's Markus Just juggled three balls underwater for a record-breaking 1 hour 40 minutes in Nuremberg in March 2013. The art of underwater juggling – or gluggling – was developed by Ashrita Furman who inevitably held the record in its infancy. However, his 2006 attempt to break his own record in a Kuala Lumpur aquarium ended prematurely when a large nurse shark appeared on the scene and nudged him off balance, causing him to drop the balls. The aquarium curator later explained that Furman had been unwittingly standing on the shark's favourite sleeping spot.

MOST PING PONG BALL JUGGLES WITH MOUTH

In Akron, Ohio, in June 2013, American entertainer Mark Angelo juggled two ping pong balls using only his mouth for a total of 212 successful spits and catches. His feat of concentration, which took just over two minutes, comprehensively beat the previous world record of 180 spits and catches by China's Jiang Guoying. Angelo was inspired to juggle ping pong balls orally after tossing popcorn into the air and catching it in his mouth. He says: "In my show I do about twenty spits and catches, so it took a bit of training to do the long runs without stopping. You can't swallow while you're juggling." He can also spit and juggle five ping pong balls, although he acknowledges that with all the balls in his mouth he looks like Alvin the chipmunk. He can also balance a golf club on his chin with a golf ball on top of it and another club spinning on top of the ball. "It's nearly impossible," he adds, "but I can do it. Who would think of these things?" Who indeed?

FARTHEST DISTANCE SQUIRTING MILK FROM AN EYE

Back in 2004, Turkey's Mehmet Yilmaz rocked the world of eye-squirting by squirting milk from his eye into a coffee cup positioned 2.7 metres away. The twenty-eight-year-old had perfected the art of sucking milk up through his nose and into his eye before ejaculating it in spectacular fashion across a table.

FIRST PERSON TO SMOKE THROUGH EYES

Alfred Langevin, from Detroit, Michigan, achieved international fame with Ripley's Believe It or Not! in the 1930s for his ability to smoke a cigarette through his eye socket. Making the most of an abnormal tear gland, he could also use his eye to blow up balloons and play the recorder.

MOST PROLIFIC CHAIN-SMOKER THROUGH EARS

Dharmendra Singh, from Bikaner, India, can chain-smoke through his ears, cramming up to twenty cigarettes in a row into his ear-holes. He first discovered his bizarre talent when, while bathing one day, he noticed bubbles coming out of his ear. "I told this to my friend and he told me to try lighting a cigarette in my ear and inhaling the puff. I lit a cigarette and found it clicked. Since childhood I have wanted to do something different and new." He even earned the approval of his father Amar who at first was concerned that his son was promoting an unhealthy lifestyle. "Initially I felt bad," said Amar, "and thought he was doing something wrong. But after talking to people and reading about him in the newspapers, I feel he has done something good. He smokes through his ears. That's a big thing."

LONGEST SPAGHETTI STRAND BLOWN FROM NOSE

When it comes to nasal ejection, Kevin Cole is the man. On 16 December 1998, the twenty-four-year-old resident of Carlsbad, New Mexico, blew a 7.5-inch strand of spaghetti out of his nostril in a single blow, breaking the previous record by two whole inches. Cole said his ability to blow long pieces of spaghetti from his nostril stemmed from his training as a lifeguard, when he learned to push water from his throat and out through his nose. On discovering his rare talent, he started by spraying Ramon Noodles out of his nose before slowly progressing to spaghetti. He can also blow one end of the spaghetti out of one nostril and the other end out of the other nostril to create a "nasal floss" effect. Just the thing for dinner parties.

MOST LIVE FISH SWALLOWED THROUGH MOUTH AND BLOWN OUT THROUGH NOSE IN ONE HOUR

In one hour at Cuddalore, India, on 25 July 2005, G.P. Vijaya Kumar, a twenty-five-year-old yoga teacher, swallowed 509 small fish one by one through his mouth and blew them out alive through his nostrils. Kumar, who moved on to live fish after experimenting successfully with peas and corn, explained his technique: "I swallow the fish and take deep breaths to guide it through my nose. There are times when the fish might glide back to the mouth, but by inhaling hard it can be brought up quickly."

FARTHEST MARSHMALLOW NOSE-BLOW

In Los Angeles on 2 July 2012, Paul Prado blew a marshmallow out of his nose and into the mouth of catcher Sophia Rojas, standing 17 feet 11 inches away. This eclipsed the world record of 16 feet 3.5 inches set back in 1999 by blower Scott Jeckel and his catcher Ray Perisin. As Ms Rojas sagely remarked: "It takes a lot of trust to catch a marshmallow from someone's nostril."

MOST DOMINOES STACKED ON A SINGLE PIECE

Placing the bottom domino in a vertical position and using no form of adhesive, Alexander Bendikov, from Mogilev, Belarus, stacked 1,036 dominoes horizontally on top of it on 5 July 2011. Furthermore, the stack remained standing for over an hour.

MOST MATCHSTICKS STACKED ON THE NECK OF A BOTTLE

In September 2012, Alexander Bendikov again demonstrated what a steady pair of hands he has by balancing 20,270 matchsticks horizontally on the neck of a wine bottle without resorting to glue or any other type of adhesive.

FASTEST TIME TO BREATHE 500 FIREBALLS

Australian extreme circus performer Roy Maloy set a new world record by breathing 501 fireballs in just 23 minutes in Hobart, Tasmania, on 7 December 2012. He is thought to be the first person ever to have breathed that many consecutive fireballs as the previous speed record was 100 in an hour, set by English street artist Dougie Danzig back in 1985. Although there was only a gentle wind on the day of Maloy's attempt, it was sufficient a couple of times to make the fire travel in a direction he wasn't expecting, burning the fringe of his hair, his eyebrows and his goatee. He said: "An hour after the event I still had thick welted lines dividing the bright pink skin from the much fairer non-burned skin. The burning was accompanied by numb lips and stinging eyes even though I wore sunglasses for most of the stunt."

LONGEST DISTANCE RUN WHILE (VOLUNTARILY) ON FIRE

As a general rule, people of sound mind tend to refrain from deliberately setting themselves on fire, but professional stunt man Ted Batchelor does it for fun. In fact he has been setting himself on fire for nearly forty years ever since he won a $400 bet as a high-school student in Chagrin Falls, Ohio, back in 1976. On 20 May that year he lit himself on fire and was ablaze for about 12 seconds before diving into the cooling waters of the falls. The wager won, he proceeded to repeat the stunt for ten consecutive years, but ended up in jail a few times after it was outlawed. Crowds would boo as the human fireball was led away by police officers, but eventually the friendly cops became part of the show. He recalled: "They'd ask me, 'You want the handcuffs on or not?' I'd say, 'Yeah, gimme the handcuffs. It looks good.'" Usually friends bailed him out the same evening, but in 1985 he was fined and put on two years' probation, so he called a halt to the annual jump.

Still fired with a determination to become a stunt man, he studied film production at college, where he set himself on fire at least twenty times and also jumped through glass windows. What some people will do to get out of boring lectures! Eventually the college authorities decided that maybe he should concentrate more on his studies and less on setting himself on fire and banned his extra-curricular activities. Undeterred, he offered his services to Nevada's Burning Man Festival, asking if he could be set on fire before lighting the giant Burning Man effigy, and performed the role before a crowd of 15,000. Then, in 2004, he established a new fire endurance record by staying ablaze for 2 minutes 38 seconds without oxygen. On 4 December 2011, while attending an annual fundraising celebration in Chelsea, Alabama, he was doused with fuels before running a distance of 492 feet 10 inches while on fire, breaking the old Guinness World Record by almost 100 feet.

Batchelor no longer jumps through windows as the recovery time grows longer with the passing years, but he still regularly sets himself on fire, even though he has been burned multiple times in the course of his career. His children are probably relieved to know that he has no desire to see them follow in his footsteps, but he advises everyone to "follow your dream and do something you enjoy" – even if that means setting yourself on fire once a week.

LONGEST TIME PULLED BY A HORSE WHILE ON FIRE

Guinness World Records states that on 12 November 2008 Hungary's Halapi Roland was dragged along the ground by a horse for a distance of 1,551 feet – that's more than a quarter of a mile – while he was on fire.

LONGEST TIME AS A HUMAN TORCH

Austrian stuntman Joe Tödtling kept his cool to stay on fire for 5 minutes 41 seconds in Salzburg in November 2013 and set a new human torch record by 16 seconds. The thirty-three-year-old, who wore a special suit for the challenge, was set alight by his wife Julia. He said: "She always knows how to get me hot, so she was the obvious choice."

MOST LIT FIREWORKS STRAPPED TO BODY AT ONCE

You can usually tell something about a person's character by their nickname, so the fact that Todd DeFazio, from Pittsburgh, Pennsylvania, is known as "The Village Idiot" pretty much tells us all we need to know. Therefore it was entirely within character that on 6 July 2010 DeFazio taped fifteen fireworks to his body – around his clothed chest, legs and bare head – and then had them all lit simultaneously. Although the fireworks were relatively low-powered, meaning that he did not suffer any burns, soar through the air or whizz around in circles on a fence post, it was still a highly dangerous stunt. So please don't try this at home – or anywhere else for that matter.

LONGEST TIME TOSSING TWO COINS

In a worthy demonstration of single-mindedness, India's Mahendra Singh Rajat tossed two coins alternately for 58 hours 5 minutes in 1991. Fortunately best of three is usually enough to settle most wagers.

LONGEST TIME DRESSED AS A GARDEN GNOME

Ron Broomfield quite likes garden gnomes – to the extent that over the course of the past twenty years he has spent more than 10,000 hours dressed as one. Twice a week the retired window cleaner, who keeps 1,700 gnomes at his home in Alford, Lincolnshire, dresses up in full ornamental regalia to visit the village shops or pose in his garden with a fishing rod. "When I dress up as a gnome, I become a gnome," he says emphatically. He began his collection fifty years ago. "I was stressed and someone said get a hobby. Seven gnomes caught my eye at a garden centre so I got them. Then when I started to grow a beard, people said I looked like a gnome. Some people laugh and point at me when I go out in my costume but I don't care. I'm in my own little fantasy land and I raise money for the NSPCC. Anyway gnomes are fantastic. They're always happy-go-lucky with big smiles on their faces." Unsurprisingly his home is called Gnome Cottage and he answers the phone as "Ron the Gnome". He keeps a logbook detailing every gnome he owns and has converted his spare bedroom into a small workshop/hospital where he repairs and paints damaged gnomes. "I'm not married anymore," he adds, "but to be frank there's no room for a woman. You can hardly move for gnomes, but that's the way I like it. They've become my life."

LONGEST TIME DRESSED AS PETER PAN

Randy Constan, of Tampa, Florida, really is the boy who never grew up. Although he is now in his sixties, the six-footer has been dressing up as Peter Pan in green tights ever since he was about twenty. "Being Peter Pan is part of my life," he has said. "When I was eight I told my dad I wanted to be a fairy." His father accepted this – although he strictly forbade Randy from wearing his elf shoes to Christmas dinner – but others were not so understanding and his obsession cost him both his job and his Tinker Bell, first wife Patricia, to whom he was married for twenty-three years. When they first met, he was twenty-two and she loved his outfit, but the novelty slowly wore off. "As we both grew older, she was progressing toward greater normalcy and I was getting more and more outland-ish," he said in 2001. "She'd get mad if I was wearing tights and someone called me Robin Hood. She got tired of the negative attention, I guess." However, his story has a fairy-tale ending, and in 2009 in a magical forest just outside Tampa he married his second wife who goes under the name of Princess Dorothy. Naturally he dressed as Peter Pan and she wore a green dress with wings.

LONGEST TREE SIT

On 10 December 1997, twenty-four-year-old Julia "Butterfly" Hill joined a group of activists near Stafford, California, who were staging a protest against the harvesting of giant redwood trees by sitting on a platform 180 feet above ground up a 1,500-year-old redwood that was subsequently named Luna. She finally came down two years later, on 18 December 1999, after spending a record 738 days aloft. The tree was spared.

LONGEST TIME LIVING UP A TREE

In 2006 it was revealed that eighty-three-year-old Gayadhar Parida, from India's Odisha state, had spent the previous fifty years living up a tree following a trivial argument with his wife. He first took refuge fifteen feet up a mango tree in 1956, and enjoyed the peace and solitude so much that, even after his tree house was destroyed by a storm, he chose to move to another nearby tree rather than go back home and face his wife. He only came down from the tree to drink water from a pool but happily accepted offers of food from family members.

MOST CONDOMS SUCKED THROUGH NOSE AT ONCE

In March 2012, Ryan Stock, from Edmonton, Alberta, inhaled three empty condoms simultaneously through his right nostril and pulled them out through his mouth.

MOST TIMES TO PASS THE BODY THROUGH A TENNIS RACKET IN THREE MINUTES

Nepalese contortionist Thaneswar Guragai passed his body through the head of a tennis racket (after the strings were removed) ninety-six times in three minutes in February 2012. He said he did it for the fame.

FASTEST TIME TO PUT ON A DUVET COVER

On the face of it, fitting a duvet cover over a duvet should be a routine task. There are four corners to the duvet and four corners to the cover. What could be easier? Except that when you seek to impose your will on them, these supposedly inanimate objects develop lives of their own and frequently end up tying you in knots. You think you have all four corners sorted, only to realize that the fourth corner is in fact your left foot. Climbing inside to remedy the situation is rarely a good idea. Like a Burmese python with a pig, a duvet cover can swallow a human whole. In extreme cases a person has been officially reported missing by worried relatives, only to be discovered several hours later trapped under the duvet cover. Clearly the man to turn to in such circumstances is Irish TV presenter Alan Hughes who, on 17 September 2008, in Dublin, fitted a double duvet cover in a rapid-fire 42.97 seconds, ensuring that all four corners of the duvet were in the four corners of the cover and all of the fastenings were done up correctly. In doing so, he broke his own world record of 1 minute 0 seconds set in 2004.

MOST BANANAS DROPPED DOWN A PAIR OF PANTS

Wearing an extra-large pair of trousers that would not have looked out of place on a clown, Shaun McManus, a radio DJ at Nova 93.7 in Perth, Australia, crammed 273 bananas down his pants in February 2012 to break the old record (set by Texan Henry Mazza in 2010) by 125. McManus began dropping fruit down the left leg before switching to the right and the back where he was pleased to report that the trousers were so roomy there was no need to fit any of the bananas internally.

MOST PENCILS SHARPENED IN ONE MINUTE

Demonstrating commendable speed and an eye for a nicely shaped pencil, Jeremy Riley, of Providence, Rhode Island, set a new world record by sharpening twenty-one pencils in a minute on 18 September 2011.

LONGEST CHAIR SPIN WHILE HOLDING A PENCIL WITH UPPER LIP

On 9 October 2011, Kevin LaForest, from Chelsea, Michigan, spun around in a chair for 28 minutes 13.9 seconds while holding a pencil between his nose and upper lip. The video of his achievement shows him spinning around a lot until, with the half-hour mark tantalizingly within reach, the pencil tragically slips from his grip. It would be pleasing to think that he won't rest – unless, of course, you count sitting in a chair as resting – until he finally breaks through that 30-minute barrier.

FASTEST TIME TO TIE A KNOT USING LEFT FOOT

On 8 June 2013, compulsive Canadian record breaker Doug McManaman took 1 minute 38.9 seconds to tie a knot in a piece of string using only the toes of his left foot – at a time when he had two perfectly good hands and even a right foot available.

MOST PENCILS FITTED IN MOUTH

Adam Gronewold, from Galena, Illinois, managed to cram 105 number 2 size pencils in his mouth at once in May 2013. Blessed with a peculiarly elastic mouth, he has also managed to fit 240 playing cards in there . . . but not at the same time as the pencils.

MOST DRINKING STRAWS FITTED IN MOUTH

On 26 July 2013, Dinesh Upadhyaya, a teacher from Mumbai, India, squeezed 1,001 drinking straws into his mouth and held them there without any external support for ten seconds. Although he stands six feet six inches tall, Upadhyaya does not possess an overly large mouth, but by massaging his facial muscles and using his fingers to stretch his lips and cheeks, he has developed a reputation for being able to fit just about anything into his gob, including seventy-nine seedless grapes, sixty-five mini onions, six table tennis balls, five golf balls, three pool balls and a 3.5-inch ceramic cup. "Maximouth", as he is known, says: "After practice or during record attempts I usually experience swellings in my mouth, especially in the lips and gums area, for about an hour. But I always take precautionary measures to avoid choking. My dream is to break all mouth-stuffing records as soon as possible."

MOST SEATS SAT ON IN FORTY-EIGHT HOURS

Jim "Mouth" Purol has been setting weird records for nearly forty years even though his first challenge – in 1976 when he played the drums non-stop for twelve days – nearly drove him crazy. "I could write a book on hallucinating after that experience," he said. "I would never, ever do that again. I saw the Last Supper. My girlfriend thought I had lost my mind." Seeking a less demanding percussion record, the Detroit native played the drums underwater for an hour in 1977. He may have been wet but at least he still had his sanity – sort of. Courtesy of a jaw that he could dislocate at will, he then earned his nickname by cramming different objects into his mouth – 41 lit cigars, 41 pipes, 180 French fries, 18 hot dogs, a dozen slices of pizza – and even changed his stage name to Jim Mouth. On one occasion he stuffed 151 lit cigarettes into his mouth and smoked them for five minutes, leaving him feeling violently sick.

More recently he has taken to sitting down a lot. Back in 1984 he sat in all 107,701 seats at the University of Michigan's football stadium. It took him over four days and he wore through four pairs of jeans. Apparently eager to recapture that sensation of buttock numbness, in July 2008 the fifty-six-year-old sat in a record 39,250 seats in forty-eight hours at the Pasadena Rose Bowl, California, helped by an umbrella-hat to shield his face from the sun and a pad to cushion his aching backside. Battling blisters, he went on to sit down for another three days until he had sat in all 92,542 seats at the stadium. It was, he proclaimed, a dream come true, which is a lot better than a hallucination.

MOST JUMPS OVER A PARKING METER

One of Jim "Mouth" Purol's more bizarre accomplishments took place on 25 October 1983, when he vaulted over the same five-foot-high parking meter in Farmington, Michigan, 5,000 times non-stop. He remembers twice not quite jumping high enough and being unable to walk for three days afterwards.

LONGEST TIME STANDING MOTIONLESS

Most of the weird records in this book involve some form of physical exertion, but in 2002 Akshinthala Seshu Babu, from Andhra Pradesh, India, broke the world record for standing motionless. Adopting Mahatma Gandhi's pose with a stick, he stood perfectly still for 35 hours, the rules stipulating that "no facial movements are allowed other than the involuntary blinking of the eye" and "deep breathing is permitted provided it does not involve observable movement notably greater than that in normal breathing." Dispensing with the stick, which, by virtue of helping his balance, was viewed by some purists as an illegal prop, he then managed to stand motionless for 30 hours 12 minutes in 2003. To acquire the necessary concentration and stamina, he practised yoga and ran about eight miles a day. He was probably glad just to be able to stretch his legs.

BIGGEST NETWORK OF TUNNELS DUG UNDER OWN HOUSE

Over a period of forty years, William Lyttle dug a secret network of tunnels sixty feet long and up to twenty-six feet deep under his house in Hackney, London, excavating an estimated 100 cubic metres of earth, which sounds an awful lot. His motives were vague. Sometimes he told reporters that he had been digging a wine cellar and that he simply had "a big basement". Even Oliver Reed's wine cellar wasn't that big! When the tunnels were finally discovered after a large hole appeared in the street, "Mole Man", as he had been christened by the media, was evicted by the local council over safety concerns. In 2009, he was re-housed in a top-floor flat where he would find it considerably more difficult to burrow underground. He died there in 2010, having already knocked a huge hole from the kitchen to the lounge.

OLDEST PERSON TO SKYDIVE WHILE CARRYING HIS DEAD WIFE'S ASHES

Ninety-three-year-old Jack Hake, from Wimborne, Dorset, skydived from 10,000 feet in November 2013 while carrying the ashes of his late wife Veronica in a bag strapped to his chest. He explained: "My wife and I were married for seventy years and we did everything together."

HIGHEST SKYDIVE BY A TEDDY BEAR

A teddy bear named Babbage plummeted to Earth from a height of 128,000 feet in August 2013 after jumping from a weather balloon. Software programmer David Ackerman fitted Babbage with a computer to take photos of his 200 mph descent, and despite a nasty moment when his parachute yanked his neck back as it deployed, the soft toy made a soft landing in a field in Dorset, England. The only downside from Babbage's point of view was that his insides had been ripped out to accommodate the computer and GPS software.

TALLEST SUGAR CUBE TOWER

On 12 November 2009, Paul Van den Nieuwenhof used 1,753 sugar cubes to build a 6-foot-2-inch-high tower in Zoersel, Belgium. It took him over two hours.

LONGEST UNBROKEN APPLE PEEL

According to the New York apple industry, on 16 October 1976 at Rochester, New York, sixteen-year-old Kathy Wafler Madison created a single apple peel that stretched for 172 feet

4 inches without any breaks. She went on to become a sales manager for an apple tree nursery.

MOST CASHEW NUT JUGGLES IN THIRTY SECONDS

Most jugglers choose to work with balls, clubs or even fire torches that are highly visible to an audience, but American Marc Hartzman prefers smaller objects such as sweets, seeds or nuts, earning himself the title of the world's greatest lightweight juggler. On 31 December 2010, he set a new world record by juggling three whole cashews 80 times in thirty seconds. In that standard time of thirty seconds, he has also set world records by juggling three jelly beans 85 times, three M&Ms 70 times, three roasted pumpkin seeds 68 times, three cheese crackers 86 times, three shelled boiled peanuts 154 times, and three unpopped popcorn kernels 45 times.

MOST CHAINSAW JUGGLES

Milan Roskopf of Slovakia broke his own world record in June 2009 by juggling two running chainsaws and a ball 62 times in a row in Dachau, Germany. His previous record was 35.

MOST CHAINSAW JUGGLING CATCHES WHILE RIDING A UNICYCLE

On 7 December 2012, in Beijing, China, Australian extreme juggler Chayne Hultgren ("The Space Cowboy") made eight successful catches of a running chainsaw while perched atop a ten-foot-high unicycle. In doing so, he beat his previous world record of six catches.

He also juggles axes, machetes and razor-sharp knives (all on a unicycle) and has a nice little sideline in sword swallowing. He swallowed a world record twenty-seven swords simultaneously due to a medical condition known as congenital division of the stomach, whereby part of his stomach sits lower than normal, allowing him to swallow longer objects. His sword routine didn't go down well in New York in 2011, however, when he was arrested while performing on the street for "brandishing a sword in public". He was later released without charge after having his props confiscated. That was hard for him to swallow.

In 2007, he had to undergo emergency surgery to repair the nerves in his hand after a mind-reading stunt in his stage show at Adelaide went horribly wrong. During the performance he asked a member of the audience to hide a sharp blade under one of five polystyrene cups. He then began hitting the cups hard with his bare hand, obviously intending to steer clear of the one concealing the blade, but on this occasion he smashed down on the wrong cup and cut his hand open. Even though blood was flowing freely, he calmly told the audience: "This isn't part of the show; you will have to go now." The following day's newspaper headline read: "Psychic Needs Surgery After Slice of Reality."

MOST CONSECUTIVE AXE JUGGLING CATCHES

Performing at the Green Top Circus in Sheffield, Yorkshire, on 5 November 2013, Chris Marley made a world record 369 consecutive axe juggling catches.

MOST ROPE SKIPS IN ONE MINUTE
WHILE JUGGLING A FOOTBALL

Skipping enthusiast Peter Nestler, from Tulsa, Oklahoma, completed 126 rope skips while juggling a football (soccer ball) in one minute in Juneau, Alaska, on 29 August 2013. He shattered the previous record by 95. The rules of the challenge state that you can use any part of the body a footballer can (in other words, no arms or hands) and the attempt is over as soon as the ball touches the ground. Nestler practised almost every day for six weeks to nail the necessary rhythm.

MOST RUNGS CLIMBED ON A LADDER WHILE KEEPING A FOOTBALL AIRBORNE

On 8 September 2002, Swiss juggler Paul Sahli juggled a football while climbing a fire ladder for 111 steps. On 21 March 2008, he set another new record by juggling a tennis ball for 53 steps while climbing a fire ladder. He boasts more than sixty world records, mostly to do with juggling balls. They include juggling a billiard ball with his feet for 51 minutes 55 seconds on 10 February 2002 and juggling a 6.6-pound medicine ball with his feet for 1 hour 6 minutes on 16 July 1995, touching the ball 8,107 times in the process. Now for the science bit: apparently that is equivalent to a total weight change of 24 tons. Or on the celebrity scale: 470.5 Kylie Minogues.

MOST GNOMES POSED IN "HEIL HITLER!" SALUTE

As a satirical protest at lingering fascist tendencies in German society, German artist Ottmar Hoerl posed 1,250 fifteen-inch-tall black plastic garden gnomes in Straubing town square, in October 2009, with their arms outstretched in the stiff-armed Hitler salute. As Hitler salutes and Nazi symbols have been illegal in Germany since the end of World War II, prosecutors debated whether the display might be against the law, but Hoerl argued that the gnomes were ridiculing the Nazis, not promoting them.

MOST TENNIS BALLS HELD IN ONE HAND

Narayan Timalsina, a twenty-seven-year-old from Palpa, Nepal, held a stack of twenty-four tennis balls in his right hand for 1 minute 30 seconds in April 2013. He had apparently been practising for over two years. He's clearly got a lot of balls.

MOST WINE GLASSES HELD IN ONE HAND

In October 2012, British sommelier Philip Osenton held fifty-one wine glasses in one hand at a hotel in Beijing. On his first attempt he managed forty-five glasses (still enough to shatter the 2007 record of thirty-nine), but on his second try he achieved fifty-one by stacking the glasses on their side on top of each other in his left hand. Luckily he did not feel the urge to sneeze. He learned the art of glass balancing while working at some of London's top hotels. "The carrying of glasses is a sommelier thing," he told the *Daily Mail*. "When I was head sommelier at the Ritz Hotel, I had a 140-cover restaurant to set up in the morning between breakfast and lunch, so basically with two glasses per setting I had to put out 280 glasses in a very short amount of time."

MOST MUGS HELD IN ONE HAND

Darlington teenager Chris May proved that he was no mug, in February 2012, by setting a new world record . . . accidentally. Recalling his moment of glory, the sixteen-year-old said: "I was just in the kitchen unloading the dishwasher, hanging mugs off my fingers, not even thinking about it, when my friend Max Wheatcroft said: 'How many mugs have you got there?' I think I had about ten and he said: 'Keep going, keep going; see how many you can get.' In the end I got up to sixteen and Max said: 'It's got to be a record.'" It was good enough to be recognized by the World Record Academy, but in any case Chris must surely have set a record for being the only teenage boy ever to have unloaded a dishwasher.

FARTHEST DISTANCE CLIMBED INVERTED UP A POLE IN ONE MINUTE

If climbing a pole isn't your idea of a fun afternoon, then the chances are that climbing a pole while hanging upside down is even less so. Germany's Nele Bruckmann thought differently, however, and on 1 September 2007 she adopted an inverted position and set a world record by climbing 31 feet 11 inches up a pole in one minute.

MOST BIRD SONGS IMITATED

A Nepalese man, Gautam Sapkota, can mimic the calls of more than 150 species of birds. He was said to be planning an album of popular Nepali folk songs remixed in the sounds of different birds (including the heron), and his impersonation of monkeys is so uncannily accurate that he can start a fight between two animals. He is available for bookings.

LONGEST TIME HULA HOOPING UNDER WATER

This is another record held by Ashrita Furman who, in August 2007 at the Nassau County Aquatic Center, New York, hula hooped underwater non-stop for 2 minutes 38 seconds. Explaining his choice of event, he said: "I have a record for underwater jump rope and underwater juggling and I was thinking what else could I do and I came up with the idea of trying to hula hoop underwater."

LARGEST UNDERWATER WEDDING

The Guinness World Record for the largest underwater wedding was set by 303 divers who attended the nuptials of Ewa Staronska and Pawel Burkowski at a flooded open pit mine in Jaworzno, Poland, on 27 August 2011. The wedding ceremony lasted around eighteen minutes and was conducted by Father Pawel Wrobel, himself a licensed frogman. The couple and the priest communicated underwater by a combination of waterproof texts and sign language. Afterwards, the newlyweds said the most difficult moment was the underwater kiss, but it could hardly have come as a surprise since they also got engaged underwater.

MOST FOLDS OF TOILET PAPER

Until 2002, the world's most eminent scientists and mathematicians were united in their conviction that the maximum number of times a piece of toilet paper could be folded in half was seven. However, that year California high-school student Britney Gallivan blew their theories and formulae out of the toilet water by calculating that, if the paper was long enough, it could actually be folded eleven times. She worked out that, instead of folding in alternate directions, better results could be achieved by continuously folding in the same direction – provided you had a roll of toilet paper 4,000 feet long. That seemed to be the final word on the matter until, in January 2012, as the culmination of seven years of exhaustive research and experimentation, mathematics students from St Mark's School in Southborough, Massachusetts, managed to fold a piece of toilet paper a record-breaking thirteen times. But if you want to try it at home, the bad news is that you will need ten miles of toilet paper, which is excessive – even after a dodgy curry.

MOST PEOPLE POPPING BUBBLE WRAP

Some things in life are just too tempting to resist – such as licking the lid of an ice-cream container when no one is looking or inspecting your own ear wax. Into the same category comes popping bubble wrap. Whenever you find a sheet, you simply can't help popping a few squares. Some zealots will even pop the whole sheet. It is harmless fun. If, however, you pop fifty or more sheets without stopping for food or toilet breaks, you know you've got a serious problem and should seek medical help.

Bubble wrap was invented in Hawthorne, New Jersey, in 1960 by Marc Chavannes and Al Fielding and has since been elevated to the status of pop culture phenomenon with over two million followers on Facebook. There is also a bubble wrap popper app for an iPhone. Meanwhile, scientists have conducted tests which show that popping bubble wrap relieves stress, much like stroking a cat and a lot less likely to get you scratched. As a mark of the affection in which bubble wrap is held, the last Monday in January has officially been named Bubble Wrap Appreciation Day. This came about in 2001 after a shipment of microphones was delivered to Spirit 95 Radio, a radio station in Bloomington, Indiana. After the microphones were unwrapped and installed, the station inadvertently broadcast the sound of the wrappings being popped. Naturally the "holiday" is celebrated enthusiastically in Hawthorne, where, on Bubble Wrap Appreciation Day 2013 – 28 January – 366 people assembled at the local high school gym to set a new record for the most people popping bubble wrap simultaneously. Using hands, feet and any other part of the body that did not offend common decency, they popped more than 8,000 square feet of the packaging material.

MOST PEOPLE HUGGING TREES

On 20 July 2013, 951 people hugged trees at the same time at Hoyt Arboretum, Portland, Oregon, to establish a new world tree hugging record. The previous record of 702 huggers had been set in Delamere Forest, Cheshire, in 2011.

LONGEST BOUNCY CASTLE MARATHON

A team of eight workers from the Tesco supermarket in Wincanton, Somerset, established a new world record by bouncing on a bouncy castle for 37 hours 14 seconds in August 2013, beating the old record by an hour.

MOST BOUNCES ON A SPACE HOPPER IN ONE MINUTE

Nine-year-old Ethan Fisher, from Worksop, Nottinghamshire, managed to do sixty-two bounces over a line on a space hopper (a hippity hop in the US) in one minute at Butlin's holiday camp, Skegness, in February 2011. Ethan had already made his name as something of a virtuoso on the handled rubber balls by taking part in – and winning – the world's biggest ever space hopper race, a 200-metre event at Sheffield in July 2010.

MOST BOUNCES OF A SOAP BUBBLE

Wearing a glove on his hand to soften the impact, Taiwan's Kuo-Sheng "Andy" Lin bounced a soap bubble 195 times in Taipei on 17 April 2012. The previous December he had also set a record for the most soap bubbles blown inside a larger soap bubble – 152.

LARGEST SAME NAME SOCIETY

Founded in 1969 with just three people, the Jim Smith Society now boasts nearly 2,000 members all called Jim Smith (or a close variation). There are even at least five female Jim Smiths! The society's founder, the late Jim Smith, came up with the idea when he was working for a newspaper in Harrisburg, Pennsylvania, and kept coming across other people with the same name, especially while typing up police reports. Now the group has an annual gathering in July where, to avoid confusion, each Jim Smith is addressed by his or her hometown. There are over 38,000 Jim Smiths in the United States, making it the commonest full name. It is the name that appears most on the Vietnam Wall, 3,800 Jim Smiths fought in World War II, and a Jim Smith has held every elected office in the US apart from President or Vice President. The most famous Jim Smith was the representative of Pennsylvania who signed the Declaration of Independence in 1776.

MOST PEOPLE CRAMMED INTO A PHONE BOOTH

Long before anti-social behaviour orders were introduced, young people got their kicks by squeezing themselves into phone booths. The pastime was particularly popular on university and college campuses, and in 1959 twenty-five students from Durban, South Africa, managed to cram at least half of their bodies into a single phone booth. Shortly afterwards a Canadian school forced forty people into a booth, but their claim was rejected after it was discovered that they had used an extra-large booth, which they had turned on its side to make stacking easier. As a result, official rules were drawn up stating that the booth must be of standard size and must remain upright. England introduced even more stringent regulations, insisting that an actual phone call was either made or received from inside the full booth. Despite repeated attempts, the South African feat still remains unsurpassed. The reason why this record has stood for so long may partly be down to the so-called obesity epidemic but more likely because nobody nowadays can find a public phone booth.

MOST PEOPLE CRAMMED INTO A STANDARD OUTHOUSE

On 7 April 1959, thirty-seven male students in Brookings, South Dakota, crammed themselves into a standard-sized toilet cubicle, although none was in a position to make use of the facilities should the need have arisen. To save space inside, they first placed the essential bum-wiping magazine on the roof.

MOST PEOPLE CRAMMED INTO A HOLLOW TREE

In 1961, male and female students at the University of Maine challenged each other to a tree-stuffing contest, where they attempted to squeeze as many people as possible into a hollow tree on the campus. After removing their shoes, the girls managed thirteen but the boys, with no busts to get in the way, beat them with fifteen to set a new world record.

LARGEST PILLOW FIGHT

During a concert by Swedish DJ duo Dada Life in Chicago, Illinois, on 27 October 2013, 3,813 people became involved in a mass pillow fight. The good news is that the pair (Olle Corneer and Stefan Engblom) had actually organized the fight – it wasn't an expression of audience unrest.

LARGEST SNOWBALL FIGHT

To celebrate Seattle's Snow Day on 12 January 2013, 5,834 people threw snowballs at each other to break the world record for the largest snowball fight. St Paul, Minnesota, had hoped to set a new record on 27 January 2014, but ironically it was wrecked by cold weather. Some 10,000 people attended the annual Beer Dabbler Winter Carnival and it was anticipated that most would stay on to take part in a mass snowball fight, but the freezing temperatures meant that only around 2,000 hung around. The rest went home to get warm.

LARGEST WATER BALLOON FIGHT

On 27 August 2011, 8,957 people from the Christian Student Fellowship at the University of Kentucky in Lexington took part in the world's largest water balloon fight. In the course of the soggy battle they got through more than 175,000 water balloons.

LARGEST TOMATO FIGHT

Back in August 1945, a scuffle broke out during a carnival in the small Spanish town of Buñol, during which fruit stalls were overturned and unruly young revellers started hurling tomatoes at each other. From such inauspicious beginnings grew La Tomatina, an internationally renowned tomato-throwing festival, which, in 2010, attracted a record 45,000 participants pelting each other with around 100 tons of ripe tomatoes. For the first few years of its existence, the tomato fight was strictly unofficial and those taking part were liable to imprisonment. The country's dictator, General Franco, repeatedly tried to have the event banned, and it was not until 1957 that it was finally made legal and a list of rules was drawn up – the main one being that all tomatoes should be squashed beforehand to avoid injury. It is also forbidden to throw any other type of fruit, particularly if it is still in its can. These days Buñol truly embraces La Tomatina, not least because on the last Wednesday of August each year, thousands of tourists from all over the world arrive by special trains to swell the town's population of 10,000. Buñol spends around $115,000 annually on the one-hour fruit fight, including providing the tomatoes, which are dumped by a fleet of trucks in the centre of town. The battle commences at the sound of a firecracker. Many participants wear goggles and gloves and at the end of the contest they use water hoses to wash the tomato paste off their bodies. Some violate the "tomatoes only" rule by hurling their wet T-shirts at each other. In 2013, it was announced that in future the fight would be limited to 20,000 paying revellers (5,000 locals and 15,000 visitors), so the 2010 record is unlikely to be broken. La Tomatina has become such a respectable way of indulging in a food brawl that it has spawned similar tomato fights in other parts of the world, including Colombia, China, Chile and Colorado, USA.

LARGEST ORANGE FIGHT

What Spain does with tomatoes, Italy does with oranges. The annual Battaglia delle Arance (Battle of the Oranges) in Ivrea has its origins in the twelfth century when a miller's daughter reputedly rejected the advances of the town's evil lord by cutting off his head. As well as making her the envy of many a woman on a Singles' Night, this unambiguous act led to a violent revolution by the townspeople that freed them from tyranny and as such was commemorated by an annual procession, initially involving the throwing of beans or apples. In the 1930s, local girls started throwing oranges along with flowers and confetti from their balconies onto the carnival parade carriages below, in an attempt to get boys to notice them. The boys responded by lobbing the oranges back up to them, and in time this gesture of affection degenerated into a full-scale fruit fight. That explains why every year people in Ivrea dress up in medieval costumes to re-enact the twelfth-century hostilities by pelting each other for three days with 500,000 pounds of citrus, the orange representing the tyrannical oppressor's head. The battle of February 2012 attracted a record 650 participants, making it the biggest orange fight in the world.

LARGEST MARSHMALLOW FIGHT

At the end of the academic day on 2 December 2011, 473 students and adults from Eisenhower Junior High School, Taylorsville, Utah, gathered on the school playing field to throw 2,000 pounds of marshmallows at each other. During the course of the fifteen-minute battle, the two lines of rival throwers, who wore protective eyewear, no shoes and were separated by a "no man's land" of twenty feet, threw a total of 140,280 marshmallows. The school has form for setting weird world records, including the tallest tower of pencils, the fastest human conveyor belt and the largest wobble board ensemble.

LARGEST CUSTARD PIE FIGHT

Even though it was not necessarily made of custard, the custard pie was as much an integral part of any circus clown's act as a red nose, a pair of baggy trousers and the misguided belief that the combination of all three was somehow entertaining. So it was inevitable that there would be a clamour to stage the world's biggest custard pie fight, and in 2011 that honour went to the 684 people who took part in a mass pie battle at the Drake University parking lot in Des Moines, Iowa. However, even weird records have to move with the times and when concerns were raised about how much food was being wasted by staging such contests, Guinness World Records changed the category to the world's largest cream pie fight – and for cream, read shaving foam. In Dallas, Texas, on 31 July 2012, 714 participants wearing clown costumes kicked off International Clown Week by setting a new record for staging a mass brawl with synthetically filled pies.

LARGEST FLOUR BOMB BATTLE

Every year at the end of the carnival season, on the ironically named Clean Monday, the Greek village of Galaxidi erupts in a day-long flour war, where participants hurl flour bombs at each other. The 2012 event attracted a record 540 farinaceous fighters from all corners of Greece who threw an estimated 3,000 pounds of flour. Prior to the battle, which is thought to date back to the nineteenth century, historical buildings and boats in the village are covered with plastic sheets. To add to the spectacle, the combatants dye their bags of flour with food colouring before donning goggles and overalls to protect themselves from the flying starch. By the end of the battle, everyone is covered from head to toe in sticky flour, which many then wash off by jumping into the sea, even at the risk of turning themselves into instant pastry.

CHAPTER 2

Fashion Victims

LONGEST WEDDING DRESS VEIL

For her wedding to Ferdinand Pucci in the village of Casal Di Principe near Naples in September 2011, Italian bride Elena De Angelis wore a wedding dress with a veil that was three kilometres long – about twenty-eight times the length of a soccer pitch. The veil, which was designed by Gianni Molaro, took several months to make and had to be carried by 600 people. Experts with time on their hands (or a reporter with a pocket calculator) worked out that it would take Usain Bolt, sprinting throughout at an impossible world record speed, nearly five minutes to run the full length of the dress. So now you know.

GRADUATION DRESS MADE FROM MOST PIECES OF OLD ALGEBRA HOMEWORK

Inventive seventeen-year-old Kara Koskowich decided to put her old algebra homework to good use by turning it into a dress. She wore the garment – made from seventy-five pages of algebraic formulae – for her June 2012 graduation from the Lethbridge Collegiate Institution in Alberta, Canada. Since it was made from homework, it was only fitting that she left it to the last minute, only finishing the design the night before the event. She made her grand entrance alongside friend Dorothy Graham, who fashioned a dress out of old plastic shopping bags. "It was actually funny," said Graham, "because everyone was wearing these elegant dresses and we're in dresses that cost nothing and we were the most popular people there." No doubt all the other girls in their expensive gowns saw the funny side, too.

WEDDING DRESS MADE FROM MOST COW NIPPLES

As part of her "Nippleocalypse" collection at the 2011 London Fashion Week, Liverpool designer Rachel Frere unveiled a dress made of 3,000 real cow nipples, thus undoubtedly breaking the world record for the wedding dress made from the greatest number of cow nipples. Unless you know udderwise.

LONGEST TIME WEARING WEDDING DRESS

After escaping from an abusive relationship, Xiang Junfeng, from Shandong, China, was so delighted to marry Zhu Zhengliang in 2004 that she has worn a wedding dress ever since – a total of more than 4,000 days. Fearing that the original garment would wear thin, she had three more wedding dresses made so that she had something to wear all year round. She explained: "I had only ever known a violent and abusive man and I avoided men until I met my new partner who brought me truly out of my shell and treated me so differently. I couldn't believe it when he asked me to marry him. My wedding day was the happiest day of my life and I never wanted it to end, and that was when I decided I wanted to keep wearing my wedding dress." She even wears it while working in the fields, prompting raised eyebrows from locals who have dubbed her "Sister Wedding Gowns". "I don't even have any other clothes," said Xiang. "I don't care what people say about me. My wedding dresses are part of my life."

LONGEST TIME WEARING BRAZILIAN NATIONAL COLOURS

When Brazil won the 1994 World Cup, soccer-crazy Nelson Paviotti promised to wear nothing but the national colours of yellow, green, blue and white for the rest of his life. In 2014, the fifty-seven-year-old lawyer marked twenty years of going to work each day in a bright yellow jacket, green shirt, yellow pants and a blue hat. His patriotic devotion does not end with his clothes, because his office and home are also decorated in the national colours, as are his two Volkswagen Beetle cars, which for good measure are fitted with speakers that play Brazil's national anthem on his way to work. His wife adds that 90 per cent of the food he eats on international match days is green and yellow. Luckily he likes sweetcorn, although after Brazil lost 7–1 to Germany in the 2014 World Cup semi-final he was apparently seen tucking into humble pie.

LONGEST TIME WEARING SAME FOOTBALL SHIRT

After receiving a Brett Favre Green Bay Packers' football jersey for Christmas 2003, schoolboy David Witthoft, from Ridgefield, Connecticut, became so attached to it that he wore it every day for the next 1,581 days. He finally shunned the No. 4 jersey on his twelfth birthday – 23 April 2008 – because by then he had grown to the extent that it barely reached down to his waist. During those four years and four months, his mother Carolyn had faithfully washed it every other day and mended it when necessary.

LONGEST TIME WEARING SAME SHOES

In October 2003, eighty-one-year-old Jusuf Sijaric, from Novi Pazar in southern Serbia, announced that he had been wearing the same pair of shoes for the past sixty years. He said he bought what he calls his "good shoes" six decades ago from a shop in Bosnia and planned to leave them to a museum when he dies. By then they could probably walk there by themselves.

LONGEST TIME FOR A COUPLE WEARING MATCHING OUTFITS

Mel and Joey Schwanke, who run a flower shop in Fremont, Nebraska, have been wearing matching outfits every day for over thirty-five years. They had already been married for thirty years when they suddenly had the idea for matching wardrobes while on holiday. Now they own 146 custom-made matching outfits, which they wear whenever they go out together, and never leave the house unless they are dressed in the same pattern. "Every day my tie matches her dress," said Mr Schwanke proudly, before hinting that the careful colour coordination was at least partly responsible for their long marriage.

MOST DRESSES BOUGHT BY A HUSBAND

Let's be honest: if a man buys his wife one dress in the course of their marriage, she can count herself lucky. But during his fifty-six years of being married, Paul Brockmann, of Lomita, California, has bought his wife Margot 55,000 dresses (no, that's not a misprint), sometimes purchasing as many as thirty a day. Since they first met on the dance floor, he likes to buy her ballroom-style dresses that swish around but he never wanted her to have to wear the same one twice. "Every time I saw a nice dress, I had to have it," he explained. "Whether it fitted or not I always thought maybe someday she'll grow into it. Some people collect automobiles, some people like stamps, I got into dresses." Not literally, he was quick to add.

DRESS MADE FROM MOST CONDOMS

In November 2012, Nguyen Minh Tuan, a former student at Van Lang University in Ho Chi Minh City, Vietnam, exhibited a dress made from 2,000 condoms. He designed the glowing dress, which also contained 1,000 LED lights, to raise awareness of safe sex among the Vietnamese population. There were no plans to recreate the dress in retail stores because it was felt that the vast majority of women would be reluctant to wear such a garment, although it should be pointed out that all of the condoms were at least empty.

MOST ROLLS OF DUCT TAPE USED TO MAKE A PROM OUTFIT

For her high school's 2013 prom, student Kristen Calfee, from Gretna, Louisiana, made a dress for herself and a tuxedo for her date, Cody Hunter, from seventy rolls of duct tape. It took her a year and a half to make the dress, which weighed thirty pounds and was covered in dozens of hand-made blue, green and white butterflies. The downside was that it was difficult to put on, she couldn't sit down or dance in it (so possibly not great for a school prom), and when she walked she sounded like a walking plastic bag. But, hey, it was different.

MOST HUMAN HEARTS KEPT IN A SKIRT

Marguerite de Valois (1553–1615) was one of the most reviled women in French history. Even her mother, Catherine de Medici, said she must have been born on an evil day. Marguerite's problem was her voracious sexual appetite, which led her to take a string of lovers even though she was married to Henri, King of Navarre. Although it was perfectly acceptable – indeed almost compulsory – for Henri to take any number of mistresses, sexual equality was unheard of in sixteenth-century France and Marguerite's lovers had a tendency to meet violent deaths, often by hanging, beheading or dismembering. As a memento, she had the hearts of all of her ill-fated lovers – thirty-four in total – embalmed and placed in gold boxes which she kept in little pockets that had been specially sewn into her voluminous skirt.

MOST DRESSED MAN

On 21 November 1996, American entertainer Jim "Mouth" Purol appeared on *The Jerry Springer Show* wearing sixty shirts and thirty pairs of pants. He had to be rolled out on stage in a hand cart.

MOST T-SHIRTS WORN AT ONCE

Watched by a crowd of people in a public park in Colombo, Sri Lanka, Sanath Bandara wore 257 T-shirts simultaneously in December 2011. It took him nearly an hour to pile on the layers of clothing, which weighed a total of 145 pounds and left him with aching joints but happy.

MOST PAIRS OF UNDERPANTS WORN AT ONCE

Gary Craig, a fifty-three-year-old architect from South Tyneside, squeezed himself into 302 pairs of underpants in September 2012 to reclaim his world record for the most underpants worn simultaneously. Craig was a man on a mission. He had previously held the record with 211 pants, only for it to be broken by an American woman, Janine Keblish, with 252 items of underwear. The jubilant father-of-three said afterwards: "I wanted to be the first person to put on over 300 pairs and I did it. I think I'm also the first person to hold the record twice – probably because no one else is daft enough to do it twice."

MOST SOCKS WORN ON ONE FOOT

In March 2011, Fiona Nolan managed to wear 152 socks on one foot in Shannon, County Clare, Ireland. Luckily she didn't have to walk very far afterwards.

MOST SOCKS SORTED IN ONE MINUTE

When it comes to sorting pairs of socks at speed, it is no great surprise that the record was set by a woman. After all, most men consider that wearing matching socks to work is a bonus rather than a necessity. According to Guinness World Records, the champion sorter is Joanne Wright who, in Cincinnati, Ohio, in April 2011, matched up ninety pairs of different socks in sixty seconds.

MOSAIC MADE FROM MOST PAIRS OF SOCKS

In July 2012, Israeli artists Anat and Ehud Shamai created a huge mosaic in a Netanya city square from 12,000 donated socks. Residents were encouraged to bring along their old footwear for the project, the only stipulation being that the socks had to be clean. The Shamais' efforts also allow them to lay claim to the little-known record for the world's largest temporary collection of socks, narrowly beating that of Southport foot fetishists Steven Bain and Steven Gawthrop who collected more than 10,000 socks from unsuspecting members of the public in the 1990s. However, whereas the Shamais received a Guinness World Records certificate, Bain and Gawthrop got eighteen months in jail.

BIGGEST SOCK MONKEY

Looking for a hobby in 2009, Canadian Cherylle Douglas, from Merritt, British Columbia, stitched together an 8-foot-10-inches-tall sock monkey named Oscar. It had a 54-inch

tail, weighed over 50 pounds and was made from thirty-
two pairs of socks. Originating in North America in the
1950s, sock monkeys were traditionally given to bring luck
to a newborn baby. This giant would have scared the hell
out of one.

LONGEST SKI HAT

With the aid of a programmed knitting machine, in 1977,
Gini Woodward, from Bonners Ferry, Idaho, knitted a ski hat
that measured 700 feet long and weighed 80 pounds. The hat,
which remains in mint condition, has 539 advertising panels
promoting local businesses, so was probably not intended for
everyday wear on the slopes.

FASTEST TIME TO TIE THE WINDSOR KNOT

India's "Tie-Man", Dr Deepak Sharma, from Bhopal, set a
new world record by tying a Windsor knot in 17.91 seconds
on 28 December 2013 – more than two seconds faster than
the old record. A bank official, he has a collection of over
3,000 ties, which means he'll never be short of one to wear to
work. And it won't take him long to get ready.

MOST GLOVES WORN ON ONE HAND

South African-born Alastair Galpin loves gloves and he loves
breaking records, so since 2006 he has actively combined the
two, regularly looking to raise the bar in terms of the world
record for the most gloves worn on one hand. His fourth
successful quest took place on 28 October 2012 in Waipu,
New Zealand. Using different sizes of cream latex glove, he
broke his previous record of forty-four by comfortably
managing to squeeze sixty onto his hand – or to be more accurate, uncomfortably. For although you might think that
wearing gloves is not the most arduous of tasks, try wearing

sixty on your hand at the same time. Galpin says that, towards the end, the pain of the constricting layers was quite intense and so he was hugely relieved not only to have set a new record but also to be able to tear the gloves off in bunches and finally get some feeling back into his hand. This is not his only glove-related world record. In Auckland, New Zealand, on 12 November 2009, he managed to put thirteen gloves on one hand in one minute.

MOST SWIMMING CAPS WORN AT ONCE

Defying the fear that his skull might burst under the sheer pressure of so much rubber, Alastair Galpin wore twenty swimming caps on his head simultaneously at Dargaville, New Zealand, on 30 August 2012. The first dozen caps went on easily enough, but as the pressure on his skull intensified, he just wanted to get it over with as quickly as possible. After keeping all twenty on his head for the requisite few seconds, he set about removing them, but with his head wobbling under the weight and his eyelids feeling as if they had "been pulled upwards to the point of tearing open", that was easier said than done. On his website, worldrecordchase.com, he describes the pain of tearing off the caps in one fell swoop as like "having my hair glued into a single lump and then ripped off my head without mercy. It was no laughing matter, but the witnesses didn't agree."

MOST PEOPLE IN A SINGLE PAIR OF UNDERPANTS

This may sound hard to believe but 169 people crammed into a single pair of underpants at Thorpe Park, Surrey, in March 2012 – the achievement made possible largely because the custom-made, outsize Y-fronts were over 33 feet wide and 11 feet high.

LONGEST TIME SPENT WEARING A NAMETAG

Scott Ginsberg, of St Louis, Illinois, has voluntarily worn a nametag every minute of every day since 2 November 2000 – and before you ask, he even has a nametag tattooed on his chest for certain occasions. He came up with the idea in the hope that it would make him more approachable, and it has certainly paid off as he has managed to turn his simple concept into an award-winning business. More importantly, perhaps, he is now regarded as the world's foremost expert on nametags.

LARGEST T-SHIRT

At the 2011 Country Music Association Festival in Nashville, Tennessee, Gildan Activewear paraded a T-shirt that measured 281 feet 4 inches long by 180 feet 10 inches wide – the equivalent of 12,000 standard-sized T-shirts. The company said it had already received a number of orders from professional darts players.

LONGEST SCARF

A 33.74-mile-long scarf was knitted over a period of three years from 2002 to 2005 by a team of more than 2,000 volunteers in aid of a Welsh hospice. The world record for the longest scarf knitted by an individual is held by Norway's Helge Johansen who, after thirty years of studious knitting, unveiled a 3.1-mile-long scarf in 2013. It took him four hours to roll it out just so that it could be measured. He learned to knit from his mother when he was seventeen. "I asked her if she could teach me. She asked me why, and I said that I would knit the world's longest scarf." He accomplished that feat back in 2006, but has carried on out of habit. "I just can't put it down," he says. Nor can he pick it up, since it weighs about 1,100 pounds.

LONGEST TIE

A neck tie measuring 2,650 feet – about half a mile – long and 82 feet wide at its broadest point was made by members of the Academia Cravatica organization and wrapped around the Pula Arena, Croatia, in October 2003. When marauding seagulls threatened to splatter the world's longest tie, the world's largest owl – a seven-foot model – was brought in to stand guard.

LARGEST LEDERHOSEN

Having previously created the world's smallest lederhosen – a 38-millimetre pair which he often wore attached to his hat – Walter Sinnhofer, from Henndorf, Austria, went to the other extreme in 2010 by creating baggy lederhosen that measured 16 feet high and 13 feet wide. They weighed 100 pounds, and it took him nearly two months to make them from seventy-seven square metres of cow hide.

MOST MONEY SPENT ON CUSTOMIZING CAR TO MATCH HANDBAG

Janette Benson, of Macclesfield, Cheshire, paid an extra £10,000 (over $16,000) in 2004 just to have her Mini Cooper car customized to match her £20 ($32) pink Kookai handbag. As a final touch of class she hung a pair of pink fluffy hand-cuffs on the rear-view mirror. "Lots of people wave and beep at me," she told the *Sunday Mirror* excitedly. "They must think there's a movie star inside."

MOST EXPENSIVE HAT WORN BY A KILLER

The fedora hat worn by Jack Ruby when he shot and killed John F. Kennedy's assassin Lee Harvey Oswald at Dallas Police Headquarters, on 24 November 1963, sold at auction for $53,775 in 2009. At the same auction, the 60-inch-long leg shackles used by doctors to secure the dying Ruby to his Parkland Hospital bed in 1967 sold for $11,054. The shackles were not primarily intended to stop the convicted Ruby from escaping, but to prevent over-zealous memorabilia hunters from stealing his body when he died.

LONGEST TIME WITHOUT REMOVING HAT

Al Elderkin, who lived in a small hut on Wright's Fen, Cambridgeshire, in the late nineteenth century, didn't take off his battered hat for forty years. This allowed his unkempt hair to grow through the brim and crown. Throughout that time he never washed, changed his clothes or trimmed his nails, allowing them to curve like an eagle's talons over the ends of his fingers. His only tragedy was that he was born before the advent of online dating.

MOST T-SHIRTS REMOVED WHILE HEADING A FOOTBALL

At São Paulo, Brazil, on 24 April 2009, in a virtuoso exhibition of dexterity and bodily contortion, Marcelo Ribeiro da Silva managed to take off twenty-one T-shirts while simultaneously keeping a football in the air using only his head.

LONGEST CONGA LINE OF PEOPLE WEARING GUMBOOTS

As part of Welly Week in October 2008, 208 students and staff from Bicton College, Devon, danced around a field in a conga line while wearing gumboots. Those in the know state that never before in the history of welly wearing have so many people donned gumboots while doing the conga. There may be a good reason for that.

MOST PEOPLE WEARING SUNGLASSES AT NIGHT

To kick off the fourth annual LaughFest at Grand Rapids, Michigan, on 6 March 2014, 1,675 people pushed back the boundaries of comedy by wearing sunglasses at night. Just to remind the participants that they were meant to be having fun, the sunglasses were bright yellow. The previous three years of the festival of mirth saw record-breaking attempts for donning false moustaches, wearing chicken beaks and tossing rubber chickens.

MOST PEOPLE DRESSED AS PENGUINS

In November 2013, 325 people dressed as penguins gathered at London's Canary Wharf. Under the rules for forming the world's largest human penguin colony, each participant needed to be dressed from head to toe as a penguin in an outfit consisting of a beak, a black-and-white bodysuit and webbed feet.

MOST PEOPLE DRESSED AS COWS

In June 2013, 470 people wearing black-and-white cow costumes gathered at the George Mason University Field House in Fairfax, Virginia. As would be expected, there were strict rules about what constituted a cow and each participant was instructed to wear a one- or two-piece cow suit, with a head piece or decorated hood. Furthermore, all shoes had to be either black or white to match the cow suit. Presumably the cow costumes were provided by the organizers, a local restaurant chain, because otherwise it would have placed an enormous strain on Fairfax's fancy dress shops. They might reasonably stock one cow costume but to be asked for 470 would constitute a stampede.

MOST PEOPLE DRESSED AS TURKEYS

At the 2011 Dallas Turkey Trot, a record 661 runners turned up dressed as turkeys. The event, which celebrates Thanksgiving, was first staged in 1967. One of the organizers declared proudly: "Spain has the running of the bulls, but Dallas has the running of the turkeys."

MOST PEOPLE DRESSED AS TREES

In September 2013 at One Tree Hill, South Australia, 407 people donned leaves and twigs to set a new record for the most people dressed as trees in one place. To be honest, the human forest was not exactly lifelike, but, just in case, all dogs were banned from the event.

MOST PEOPLE DANCING WHILE DRESSED AS MOBILE PHONES

It's always a dilemma deciding what to wear to a school dance. Do you choose something smart or casual, sexy or modest, or do you throw caution to the wind and make yourself look a complete idiot by going dressed as a mobile phone? Well, 330 people decided on the last course of action when they turned up at Caterham School, Surrey, in July 2012. It would have been even more embarrassing had they not been attempting to set a new world record for the most people dancing while dressed as mobile phones. Since it was for charity, they got a good reception.

MOST PEOPLE WEARING UNDERPANTS ON THEIR HEADS

For an appearance by *Captain Underpants* author Dav Pilkey on 8 September 2012, 270 people stood outside Anderson's Bookshop in Naperville, Illinois, wearing underpants on their heads.

MOST PEOPLE WEARING ONESIES

Drayton Manor Theme Park in Staffordshire claimed the world record for the most people wearing onesies when 3,152 people gathered there on Sunday 13 April 2014 wearing one-piece jumpsuits. In anticipation of the event, the fashion police had cancelled all leave.

MOST PEOPLE DRESSED AS KATE BUSH

As part of the 2013 Brighton Festival Fringe, 300 Kate Bush fans gathered in Stanmer Park wearing red dresses, long black wigs and bright lipstick to set a new record for the most people dressed as Kate Bush. For the event, which was organized by performance group Shambush, the fans spent the afternoon perfecting the iconic dance moves from the video for Kate Bush's 1978 single "Wuthering Heights".

MOST BRIDESMAIDS AT A WEDDING

The fashion these days is for increasingly lavish weddings, but Sri Lankan bride Nisansala took things to extremes by having 126 bridesmaids when she married Nalin on 8 November 2013. The surfeit of bridesmaids was apparently the idea of her sister-in-law, bridal gown designer Champi Siriwardana, who helped plan the wedding and was hellbent on breaking the existing world record of 96 bridesmaids. Nisansala also had twenty-three flower girls in attendance while, not to be outdone, the groom was assisted by twenty page boys and no fewer than twenty-five best men. The speeches are due to finish any day soon.

CHAPTER 3

The Body Bizarre

BIGGEST PENIS

New York-born actor and writer Jonah Falcon boasts a penis that has been measured at 9.5 inches long when flaccid and a whopping 13.5 inches long when erect. Falcon, who says he is bisexual, has enjoyed media attention on both sides of the Atlantic and has appeared in a documentary titled *UnHung Hero*. He claims to be able to envelope a doorknob completely with his foreskin, and in 2012 the large bulge in his pants led to him being stopped by security officers at San Francisco International Airport, who thought he might be concealing a bomb down there. Falcon, who is a modest 5 feet 9 inches tall and has size 10 feet, realized from a young age that he was different from other boys. "I went to a mostly Jewish school, and I was the only one who was uncircumcised so I always thought that was what my classmates were fascinated by." He admits to playing to the public by wrapping his penis around his leg and wearing tight cycling shorts but has turned down numerous offers to appear in porn films. While he is proud of his special appendage, he can't help feeling that it has hindered his acting career. "I worry that it has cost me work. I mean as an actor do you think I'd ever work for Disney?"

LARGEST VAGINA

The largest vagina in history is reputed to have belonged to Scottish giantess Anna Swan (1846–88) after giving birth to the world's biggest baby. On 18 June 1879, she gave birth to a mini monster measuring 34 inches long and weighing 26 pounds. Tragically, the infant's 19-inch-circumference head became stuck in its mother's birth canal and although it was eventually extricated with the use of forceps and belts, the newborn died as a result of the trauma. Based on the baby's huge head size, medical experts have calculated the minimum dilation of Anna Swan's passage as six inches – 50 per cent wider than the normal dilation for childbirth. That Swan should have had such a big baby is hardly surprising as she stood 7 feet 8 inches tall at the age of 19, and her husband, Captain Martin Bates, was also over 7 feet tall.

BIGGEST BOOBS

German model Beshine (aka Mayra Hills) has had numerous saline implants to give herself a top-heavy 59-28-36 figure and, as she so joyously puts it, "the largest augmented breasts on the planet". Since the thirty-two-year-old's bra size has ballooned from a modest 32B to 32Z, each breast now weighs roughly twenty pounds and is considerably larger than her head. They are so big they almost warrant their own post code. She undergoes a strict exercise regime to avoid back problems but struggles to find clothes that fit and, unsurprisingly, she can no longer sleep on her stomach. She says: "It is always an adventure to be in public with such big boobs. Sometimes you hear a wonder, a giggle, or just staring." Mostly staring.

LONGEST TIME FOR MAN TO WEAR
FEMALE BREAST IMPLANTS

In 1996, Canadian professional gambler Brian Zembic accepted a US$100,000 bet that he wouldn't wear female breast implants for a whole year. Not only did he win the bet but he liked his new 38C breasts so much that he is still wearing them nearly twenty years later, his decision possibly influenced by the fact that as part of the wager he receives an additional $10,000 for each year he keeps them in. He describes them as a normal part of his life but worries that, now that he is in his late forties, the ageing process might cause them to sag. "I don't want them to start sagging too much because they'll really get disgusting. On the other hand, when I take them out they are going to look like wet socks with nipples in them and that's what I'm more afraid of. So for now they stay. I've grown too attached to them." His teenage daughter Mika seems to have no problems with her father's outsized man boobs. "It gets the bills paid," she says frankly. "It's a little weird obviously but I guess you could say now he's like my mom and my dad."

BIGGEST TONSILS

When twenty-one-year-old Justin Werner, from Topeka, Kansas, underwent a 2011 tonsillectomy, his larger tonsil measured 2.1 inches long, 1.1 inches wide and 0.7 inches thick and his smaller one was 1.9 inches long, 1 inch wide and 0.7 inches thick, crushing the previous record by 0.8 inches. Although his monster tonsils had caused him years of chronic sore throats and major league snoring, Werner was proud of achieving the record. "I put it on my résumé before I applied for my last job," he said. "What can I say? I got the job!"

LONGEST TIME SPENT MASTURBATING

At the 2012 World Masturbate-a-thon in San Francisco, US porn star Sonny Nash bashed the bishop for 10 hours 10 minutes non-stop to win a trophy in the shape of a hand. It is arguably the only contest where coming first results in instant disqualification as under the rules of competitive masturbating the man must stay aroused for as long as possible without ejaculating. Nash's masturbatory mastery wrestled the world record from Japan's Masanobu Sato, who had held the world title since 2008. Sato practises his hobby in the presence of his girlfriend who helpfully times him on an app while she is busy sewing or cooking. "I make love to her only a few times a year," he says, "as she's not really into making love with me." A representative for a sex toy company, Sato trains by watching DVDs and likes to keep in shape by taking himself in hand for two hours every morning. Ultimately, however, he says he owes his impressive staying power to using sex toys which prevent his penis from becoming paralyzed and to his "abundant imagination".

LONGEST FEMALE ORGASM

A woman known only as Liz from Seattle appeared on the 2014 US TV show *Sex Sent Me to the ER* to describe how she had once endured rather than enjoyed a three-hour orgasm following sex with her boyfriend Eric. At first everything was wonderful but when her orgasm became a gift that kept on giving, she began to get concerned. "I started hopping up and down to see if that would do anything," she said. "I started trying to drink wine to see if that would calm down my system. I tried just about every possible thing I could do to stop having an orgasm." When her ecstasy extended to a second hour, she was admitted to hospital where confused medics, seeing her panting and short of breath, thought she was in labour. It took another hour of painful pleasure before her climax finally subsided, by which time even Eric's initial pride had turned to anxiety. "There were eyes on me," he said, "and I was feeling very tense and uptight about what was going on." He added that he was definitely not for hire.

MOST ORGASMS IN TWENTY-FOUR HOURS

Amanda Gryce, a shop worker from Altamonte Springs, Florida, has experienced up to fifty orgasms a day for nearly twenty years because of a rare medical condition called Persistent Genital Arousal Disorder. She said in 2013: "It's something I've been living with since I was about six. Different things can trigger it like vibrations, riding in cars and riding with a loud bass", by which she was referring to music rather than a particularly vociferous fish. "It can happen anywhere and sometimes I'll have five back to back. It can happen when I'm with my friends or out in public and it's very embarrassing. It's not pleasurable – it's become like torture, but I just have to put on a smile and pretend that nothing's wrong." After struggling for years with doctors who had no idea how to treat her, she met one who has at least been able to relieve the intensity of her orgasms. He gave her medication to numb the areas and advised her to exercise more in a bid to take her mind off being constantly aroused. He also banned her from having sex with her boyfriend.

LONGEST ERECTION

Let's make one thing clear, we're not talking about the longest erection in inches because that would go to a blue whale, an elephant or a pornstar donkey, but the longest erection in duration . . . by a human. Many have laid claim to the record but few have been able to provide the necessary proof until in 2014 doctors at the Tallaght Hospital in Dublin revealed that a twenty-two-year-old man had a continuous erection for seven – yes, seven – weeks after injuring himself on the cross-bar of his mountain bike. The man, a competitive cyclist, had fallen astride the crossbar, suffering acute pain and swelling.

He put up with his unusual condition for five weeks before finally deciding it was too much of a good thing and seeking medical help. When doctors first examined him, he "revealed no signs of injury, but his penis was erect." He was found to be suffering from a priapism, where an erection occurs without sexual stimulation for a prolonged period. Medics inserted gel foam and four platinum coils between an artery and a vein that supplied blood to the man's penis, thereby steadily reducing the flow. The cyclist preferred to remain anonymous, presumably for fear of receiving too many hospital visitors, not to mention proposals of marriage.

STRETCHIEST SKIN

James Morris, a nineteenth-century Rubber Man, could stretch his skin as much as eighteen inches from his body, apparently without suffering any pain. Contemporary photographs show him pulling the skin on his neck right over his nose so that it resembled an elephant's trunk. It must have been a sure-fire hit with the ladies. Born in Copenhagen, New York, in 1859, Morris suffered from Ehlers-Danlos Syndrome, a condition that gave him exceptionally soft, stretchy skin. He first worked in a cotton mill, where he would pull his epidermis to amuse his co-workers. On joining the army, he demonstrated this trick to officers, who were so impressed they invited reporters to witness the feat, and the resultant publicity led to Morris being recruited by the Barnum & Bailey Circus in 1882 on a reported $300 a week. He travelled the world with the circus and became a major attraction, but by the last years of the century his appeal had started to wane. His salary was halved and that, coupled with drinking and gambling problems, stretched his finances and forced him to take on a secondary job as a barber.

LONGEST HUMAN TAIL

Chandre Oraon, a tea estate worker from West Bengal, India, has a 14.5-inch-long tail protruding from his back, the result of being born with a form of spina bifida. Combined with the fact that he has to climb trees in his job, the tail has led local people to believe that he is an incarnation of Hindu monkey god Hanuman and they travel for miles to worship him. His mother did chop off his tail when he was young but he immediately developed a high fever and almost died, so since then he, too, has become convinced that his tail is divine and has resisted all suggestions to have it surgically removed. He does concede that it has proved something of a turn-off for the opposite sex. "Almost twenty women have turned down marriage proposals," he lamented in 2006. "They see me and agree, but as soon as I turn around, they see my tail and leave." However, in 2007, he did finally land a bride, although his wife Maino's words were hardly a ringing endorsement. "He doesn't look good," she admitted. "My brothers wanted me to get married, so I had to compromise and marry him."

MOST EYEBROWS WAXED IN THREE HOURS

Gemma Barrow, owner of the Beauty with Pure Indulgence salon in Wollaston, Northamptonshire, set a world record by waxing 104 eyebrows in three hours in aid of the 2009 Children in Need appeal. "There is no set style for each person as each eyebrow is different," she explained. "I even had eight men turn up, for which I was grateful."

MOST FEET SNIFFED

For fifteen stinking years Madeline Albrecht, of Cincinnati, Ohio, was employed by the Hill Top Research Laboratories – a testing lab for Dr Scholl – to smell human feet and armpits. In the course of her career she got up close and personal to an estimated 5,600 feet and an unknown quantity of armpits to set a record that is definitely not to be sniffed at.

FASTEST TALKING FEMALE

In Las Vegas, Nevada, on 5 June 1990, New York comedian Fran Capo was recorded speaking 603 words in 54.2 seconds – an average of 11 words per second. Guinness officials tried to congratulate her on breaking the world record but they couldn't get a word in. She can read the story of the *Three Little Pigs* in 15 seconds flat, which doesn't give the Big Bad Wolf much time to recharge his batteries between blows. No wonder he keeps failing.

LARGEST PIECE OF PRESERVED HUMAN EXCREMENT

The oldest lump of human poo currently on display anywhere in the world is believed to be the 1,200-year-old Lloyds Bank Coprolite, so named not as a reflection of the characters who run the banking industry but because it was discovered in 1972 during an archaeological dig on land in York later occupied by a branch of Lloyds TSB. The seven-inch-long faecal specimen is also considered to be the largest complete example of preserved human excrement ever found. Paleoscatologist Andrew Jones hailed it as "the most exciting piece of excrement I've ever seen. In its way, it is as valuable as the Crown Jewels." No doubt the Queen is pleased that's where the similarity ends. Examination of its content revealed that its former owner had a diet high in meat and low on vegetables, which contributed to its impressive length and girth. "Whoever passed it probably hadn't been for a few days," said expert Gill Snape. The presence of several hundred eggs in the faeces also indicated that his or her stomach and intestines would have been full of worms. Ms Snape added ominously: "This person had very itchy bowels." Before moving to the city's Jorvik Viking Centre in 2008, it was the pride and joy of York

Archaeological Resource Centre, where it was a popular exhibit with visiting school parties. Alas, in 2003, its display stand collapsed in the hands of a teacher, and the rock-hard lump broke into three pieces as it crashed to the floor. There is no record of what the unfortunate teacher said, but the chances are that it was a four-letter exclamation entirely descriptive of the dropped exhibit. Whatever, the cherished excrement had to be repaired with glue, making it also the stickiest poo ever passed.

MOST GENITAL PIERCINGS

Rolf Buchholz, from Dortmund, Germany, has 278 genital piercings. The fifty-five-year-old computer expert first got into body piercing in 2000 and now has over 450 covering his entire body. Undoubtedly the most impressive thing about his genital piercings is that he had room for so many – a fact that should surely lead to him being nicknamed "The Stud". "I'm often asked why I've done this," he says, "but I don't know. There's no real reason behind it." Thanks for clearing that up, Rolf.

TALLEST TRANSSEXUAL

The honour of being the world's tallest transsexual goes to Ohio's Lindsey Walker who used to be a seven-foot-tall basketball player named Greg. Until the age of twenty-one, Walker had muscles, a "manly" tattoo and dated a string of pretty girls, and with size seventeen feet appeared to be the stereotypical American college sportsman. Yet all the while he longed to be a woman, a situation that finally came to a head in 2007. "I just snapped," said Walker. "I was playing basketball, it was my third season at college, but I ended up quitting the team halfway through. I didn't come out right away. I just didn't know if I could be seven feet tall and transition into being a woman. But then I started wearing women's clothes and later turned to female hormones to suppress the testosterone in my body." Now as Lindsey, with a curvaceous body and 38B bra size, she admits that one of her toughest challenges is finding clothes that fit. "It was difficult as a boy to find clothes and now it's ten times harder. Shoes are bad. There are a couple of fetish stores that have something my size but otherwise I have to get them custom made." On the plus side, her intimidating height deters people from abusing her in the street. "People occasionally shout stuff at me, but they do it at a distance. I mean, I don't blame them – I wouldn't want to say anything to my face."

MOST COSMETIC SURGERIES

Retired Los Angeles government worker Monique Allen has undergone more than 200 plastic surgeries, including twenty-three nose jobs and nine breast augmentations, taking her to a whopping 38FFF. Twice-married Monique, fifty-eight, reflected ruefully in 2013: "In my twenties and thirties, as soon as I had a couple of hundred dollars I would head to Tijuana to have illegal silicone injections. The doctor would numb you, then attach a funnel to whichever part of your body you wanted, then screw a vial of silicone on and pump it in. I was so reckless but I was obsessed with having more even though my family begged me to stop. I've ended up destroying the good looks I had when I was younger. Even now I would like another nose job, but doctors turn me away, and I understand why." Monique also holds the record for having been the longest-serving transgender state employee in US history.

PERSON WHO HAS GONE TO GREATEST LENGTHS TO BECOME HUMAN BARBIE DOLL

Weirdly there are quite a few adult women in the world who believe their ideal role model is Barbie, a character whose main features are that she is materialistic, plastic and comes in a box. Most of these women focus their time and money on desperately trying to look like the doll, but one, Blondie Bennett, has gone the extra mile by having weekly hypnotherapy sessions to make her as brainless as Barbie. Bennett, who unsurprisingly hails from California, worshipped Barbie from a young age, bleaching her hair to look like her heroine and later driving the same car as Barbie – a Corvette. When she was eighteen, she took on promotional work at toy stores as a real-life Barbie and then decided to have plastic surgery to turn herself into a living doll. She has spent around $40,000 on five boob jobs to take her to size 32JJ and has regular spray tans, Botox and lip fillers to give her a distinctly artificial appearance. However, that was not enough to complete the total transformation, and in 2014 she revealed that she was having hypnotherapy to become more stupid. She said: "I've had twenty sessions and I'm already starting to feel ditzy and confused all the time. Recently I went to pick a friend up at the airport and couldn't remember if I needed to go to departures or arrivals. I also got lost for three hours driving to my mum's house – the house where I grew up. When people ask why I want to be Barbie, I think, 'Who wouldn't want to be?' She has the best life. All she does is shop and make herself look pretty. She doesn't worry about anything. Some other women pretend they are human Barbie dolls but I take it to the next level. I want people to see me as a plastic sex doll and being brainless is a big part of that. People can criticize me but this is who I am: I want my transformation to be head to toe, inside and out."

MOST MONEY SPENT ON COSMETIC SURGERIES TO LOOK LIKE KEN DOLL

Rodrigo Alves, a thirty-something Brazilian air steward living in the UK, loves Barbie's boyfriend Ken so much that he has undergone more than twenty cosmetic surgeries in the hope of looking like him. Over the course of ten years, Alves has spent $160,000 on a range of procedures designed to transform himself into Ken's doppelganger, including Botox, nose jobs, abdominal and pectoral implants, liposuction, laser comb hair treatment and even calf shaping. "With Ken, everything is in the right place," he coos, "his back, his biceps, his jawline. So of course I'd like to look like him. He's perfect." One slight drawback with modelling yourself precisely on Ken is that the doll famously has no genitalia. As far as we know, Alves has drawn the line at that particular procedure.

MOST IDENTICAL TWINS

Born just a minute apart, identical twins Anna and Lucy DeCinque, from Perth, Australia, share everything – a Facebook account, a house, a job, a car and even a boyfriend. And as if being naturally identical wasn't enough for them, they have spent more than $200,000 on plastic surgery just to look even more like each other! The two sisters are so similar that their own father used to struggle to tell them apart. For the record, Lucy has a small mole on her cheek while Anna has a scar on her forehead, but don't rule out surgery that gives Anna a mole and Lucy a scar.

The only time either showed a streak of rebellion was when they were twelve and Lucy had her hair cut short while Anna decided to keep hers long. However, that was just a blip and now both have long hair. When the girls were twenty-four they had their breasts enlarged from a BB cup to a DD, and they follow the same diet and exercise regime so that their bodies look identical. Their tastes in clothes are also identical, to the point that they stopped buying each other gifts because they would both buy the same thing. They also feel each other's pain. "If Lucy's at the dentist, I will feel her pain," says Anna.

In 2014, they revealed that their indistinguishable tastes also extend to boys. "We used to swap boyfriends if we were bored," admitted Lucy. "Like, if I didn't want to talk to my boyfriend on the phone, Anna would take the phone and pretend to be me. We would play games like that, and the other person never realized. We currently have one boyfriend and all of us share the same bed. It's not really weird to us. We have the same taste in everything, so obviously we're going to like the same boy, too. We're all together when we have sex, and if we like the same guy, so be it. For guys, in their hearts and dreams, they want two girlfriends."

Running a close second to the DeCinques are Los Angeles identical twins Amy and Becky Glass who have never been apart for more than thirty minutes over the past fifteen years. Now in their forties, they share a Facebook profile, a bedroom, a mobile phone and a marketing business, where their desks sit facing each other. To make sure they look identical, they wear the same outfit every day – in slightly different colours – and they, too, monitor their diets so that they weigh the same. Amy says: "At one point I weighed a little more than Becky, so people would say I was the bigger twin and we hated it. We decided to go on diets and we have both weighed the same ever since. It's really like we're one person in two bodies."

IDENTICAL TWINS WHO LED THE MOST IDENTICAL LIVES

Born in 1940, identical twins Jim Lewis and Jim Springer were adopted by separate families in Ohio and grew up within forty-five miles of each other. Both were independently named James by their adoptive parents. Both excelled at maths but were bad at spelling and both had childhood dogs named Toy. Both worked as sheriffs. Both owned light blue Chevrolet cars and had carpentry workshops in their garages. Both took vacations at Pas Grille beach in Florida. Both drank Miller Lite beer and smoked Salem cigarettes. Both suffered from migraines. Both married women named Linda, divorced them and married again to women named Betty. Both men had sons. Jim Lewis named his son James Alan, and Jim Springer named his son James Allan. Their parallel lives were finally revealed when they were reunited in 1979 after thirty-nine years of separation.

LONGEST MALE BEARD

When Norwegian-born Hans Langseth died in Barney, North Dakota, in 1927 at the age of eighty-one, he had cultivated a beard that was 18 feet 6 inches long. Affectionately known as "King Whiskers", he used to exhibit his beard in a travelling sideshow until he tired of people tugging it to see if it was real. Since his beard was more than three times longer than his body, it looked like a bridal train when left to hang loose, so to keep it clean, he used to roll it up and tuck it into his coat. Before he was buried, his family decided to cut off all but a foot of his beard (which probably would not have fitted in the coffin anyway), and forty years later the severed section was donated to the Smithsonian Institution in Washington, DC.

Back in the sixteenth century the title was held by an Austrian, Hans Steininger, whose 4-feet-6-inches-long beard literally brought about his downfall. One day in 1567 there was a fire in his home town of Braunau, but in his hurry to escape he forgot to roll up his beard (which he used to stuff into a leather pouch) and as a result he tripped over it, broke his neck and was killed.

LONGEST FEMALE BEARD

At the height of her fame, Grace Gilbert – the Redheaded Bearded Lady – boasted a beard that measured eighteen inches long, giving her a more luxuriant set of whiskers than any woman before or since could wish for. Born on 2 February 1876 on a small farm near Nettle Lake, Ohio, Gilbert was the youngest of four children and the only one in the family whose body was covered in a fine layer of hair. This hair quickly became thicker, and by the time she was eighteen months old the hair on her head was a foot long and four-inch-long whiskers were sprouting from her face. One reporter sent to meet her described her as "the greatest living curiosity we have ever seen". She soon developed a full beard, and by the age of eighteen, with her marriage options somewhat limited, she was being exhibited full-time with the circus as a bearded lady, initially bleaching her beard to form a golden mane before concluding that it was too much trouble and reverting to her natural ruddy shade.

Her sturdy build, love of manual labour and total lack of femininity helped fuel rumours that she was really a man, although she was also fond of lacemaking. Perhaps in a bid to silence the gossips, she married her childhood sweetheart, Giles Calvin, in South Bend, Indiana, in 1910, but when it emerged that Calvin was actually her cousin, many thought that the wedding was just a publicity stunt. When the judge who married them mistook the beardless Calvin for the bride and Grace for the groom, it did little to stifle the wagging tongues. Grace became so irritated by the speculation that she announced her retirement shortly after the wedding and went to work on her husband's farm in Kalkaska, Michigan. There, she used to wear a veil around town so that her appearance wouldn't startle pregnant women who might be walking along the street with her. However, a few years later she returned to show business for financial reasons, exhibiting herself at Coney Island until the winter of 1924 when she was taken ill. She died on 11 January that year after complaining of a sore throat.

Grace Gilbert's closest modern-day equivalent is sixty-five-year-old Vivian Wheeler, from Lawton, Oklahoma, who has a beard that has grown to eleven inches long. She was born with both male and female reproductive organs, and even after the removal of the male parts at birth (because her parents wanted a girl), her hormones allowed her to grow a beard. She also suffers from hypertrichosis, or werewolf syndrome, which results in an abnormal amount of body hair, and had to start shaving at the age of seven. Her horrified father sold her to travelling sideshows where she appeared for the next fifty-five years, often under the stage name Melinda Maxie. During that time she sometimes shaved to placate the men she dated "because of their low self-esteem. It didn't bother me." She stopped shaving entirely in 1990 following the death of her mother. "I let it grow back to be myself," she said. "Without my beard, I'm not me. I'm pretending to be someone I'm not."

MOST TYPEFACE LETTERS CREATED FROM A BEARD

New York graphic designer Mike Allen spent two years creating a twenty-six-letter typeface, encompassing every letter of the alphabet, from his own facial hair. After carefully sculpting his beard into the shape of the required letter, he would then have to shave it off and wait two weeks before attempting the next. Unveiling the Alphabeard in February 2014, he said: "I've been amused by the huge beard trend in the last couple of years and by interesting and irregular facial hair styles. The idea came from a joking conversation among friends until I started thinking of it as a real design problem. The first letter I tried was the upper-case A. I found it so amusing, I had to try another on my next shave. A few weeks later, I carved in stages the O, C and L from a single beard. Each shave was tested on my young son who was asked if he could recognize the letter I had created. Or I'd ask my wife if she'd like me to wear that letter for the day. She didn't like them all. Sometimes I'd ask her for a kiss and she'd refuse."

LONGEST MOUSTACHE

When measured in 2010, fifty-eight-year-old Ram Singh Chauhan, from Jaipur, India, had a moustache that was fourteen feet long – well over twice his height. He had been growing it for thirty-two years and groomed it religiously for two hours every day. "Growing a moustache is like taking care of a baby," he explained. "You really need to nurture it. Once I get up in the morning, the first thing I do is massage my moustache using coconut, olive or almond oil. Then I comb it and neatly roll it up." Describing his whiskers as a symbol of manhood, he added proudly: "Whenever I go out to the market or anywhere else, I become the centre of attention. People look at me in complete awe. They ask me all sorts of questions." Like why don't you have a shave?

LONGEST EAR HAIR

Patience was the key to success for Radhakant Bajpai, from Uttar Pradesh, India: that and not being worried by people staring and pointing at him in the street because it looked as though a small forest was growing from each of his ears. Back in 2005, having never trimmed his ears since the late 1960s, he held the world record for the longest ear hair with a comparatively modest tuft of about four inches. He was quite happy with that until a rival Indian, Anthony Victor, snatched his crown with a five-and-a-half-incher. Lesser mortals would have conceded defeat and moved on to try for a less embarrassing record, but Bajpai was determined to persevere. He just kept that ear hair growing and growing – way beyond the magic 20-centimetre mark, until by 2010 it had reached 28 centimetres or 8.5 inches. One of his relatives enthused: "This is a great achievement. At first the society used to taunt him that why is he growing his ear hair. I used to tell them that one day he will get some result out of it. Now he has the record and the same people say that he has really achieved something in his life." It seems that his poor wife's pleas for him to get it cut will fall on . . . well, deaf ears.

LONGEST NOSE HAIR

Vernon Frenzel, Sr, from Waynesville, Missouri, plucked an eighteen-millimetre-long hair from his left nostril on 8 October 2011 to claim the recordsetter.com crown for the world's longest nose hair pulled out using tweezers.

LONGEST ARM HAIR

Having carefully nurtured one particularly long arm hair throughout 2012, hirsute sixty-three-year-old Kenzo Tsuji was delighted when it was officially measured by Guinness at a world record breaking 7.44 inches, in Tokyo, Japan.

LONGEST LEG HAIR

A leg hair attached to Wesley Pemberton, a medical student from Dallas, Texas, was measured at six-and-a-half inches long in 2008. As it grew and he started to realize he was on to something special, he began washing it regularly with conditioner to keep it healthy and strong. "It's a great conversation piece," he said of the record-breaking follicle, "but a lot of people are grossed out about it." Pemberton's record might have been challenged by Taiwanese student Lin Kuan-wei who spent a year nurturing a leg hair to an impressive length of over five inches, until one day tragedy struck when he accidentally pulled it out.

LONGEST EYELASH

A single white hair grown and nurtured for a year on the left upper eyelid of Stuart Muller, a university student from Gainesville, Florida, reached a length of two-and-three-quarter inches when measured in 2007. Muller attributed his ability to develop such a long eyelash to a "mutant follicle" and revealed that he first let it grow as a child. At the age of eleven he saw it grow before his very eyes to a length of three-and-a-half inches, but there were no officials around to measure it. Over the years, the rogue eyelash has been accidentally singed to its roots while he was drinking a flaming alcoholic shot called a Psychopath, and on another occasion someone sat on his chest and cruelly plucked it out as a trophy. So when Muller set his sights on the world record, he often took the precaution of wearing sunglasses in public to prevent helpful strangers trying to pull it out. "People were usually very apologetic when they realized the importance of the lash," he said, "and then they'd get 'weirded out' by it. People started to associate me as the guy with the freaky eyelash." Once the record was set, Muller happily let it be plucked. "It's done its duty, and even if someone breaks my record, I have no intention of ever growing it that long again." Ha! That's what they all say.

FASTEST HAIRCUT

Forty-four-year-old hairdresser Ivan Zoot cut a full head of hair in just fifty-five seconds on 22 August 2008 at a salon in Austin, Texas, trimming sixteen seconds off the previous record. On the same day, Zoot, who has been described as the Michael Phelps of barbering, also set world records for the most haircuts in an hour (34) and the most haircuts in twenty-four hours (340). What made his achievement all the more remarkable is that he got through the entire twenty-four hours without once asking a customer where they were going on holiday.

MOST HEADS SHAVED IN AN HOUR

On 9 April 2014, barber David Alexander set a new world record by shaving the heads of seventy-three people in an hour on New York City's Rockefeller Plaza.

LONGEST HAIR EXTENSION

A team of students and employees from South Gloucestershire and Stroud College created a hair extension in November 2012 that stretched for 1,185 feet (361.4 metres) – nearly a quarter of a mile. It took seven hours to make and was attached to twenty-two-year-old Jade Bryer who had to lie on the floor for it to be measured. The idea to fashion an extension so long it almost needed planning permission was that of Jade's mother Sally Hathaway. She said: "I wanted to attempt this challenge a couple of years ago when the record was 30 metres. When I discovered the record had increased to nearly 300 metres, it came as a bit of a shock."

TALLEST MOHAWK

Japanese fashion designer Kazuhiro Watanabe boasts a Mohawk hairstyle that defies gravity by standing 3 feet 8.6

inches tall. It took him fifteen years to grow, and to get it suitably erect required the combined efforts of three stylists, three canisters of hair spray and a bottle of gel. Without the gel and the hair spray, his locks reach his knees. "It's too expensive to do the Mohawk every day," he admits, "so I only do it for special occasions and parties." And only then if they're held outdoors or in rooms with extra-high ceilings.

LARGEST AFRO

Guinness World Records says that the head of Alan Edward Labbe, of Waltham, Massachusetts, is covered in an afro that is 5.75 inches high, 8.5 inches wide and with a circumference of a fraction over 5 feet. In terms of sheer size, it is the equivalent of wearing two large curly bowling balls on his head.

MOST EXPENSIVE CHEST HAIR

In 2008, singer Sir Tom Jones had his chest hair insured for a reported $7 million, thus protecting the abundant curls that seem to drive women of a certain age crazy. Lloyd's of London were initially concerned that at sixty-seven the Welsh knight might suddenly start moulting, but when you've also insured food critic Egon Ronay's taste buds, Australian cricketer Merv Hughes's moustache, the fingers of Rolling Stone guitarist Keith Richards and comedian Ken Dodd's protruding teeth, you tend to take these things in your stride.

LONGEST DANDRUFF-RELATED PUNISHMENT

Catherine the Great, the Empress of Russia from 1762 to 1796, was an enthusiastic collector of toy boys and as such dreaded the onset of old age. In a bid to delay the ageing process, she employed two dwarfs to look after her beauty products but was particularly sensitive about her hair, having seen it fall out on more than one occasion. So when she found a few flakes of dandruff on her collar, she was so horrified that she imprisoned her hairdresser in an iron cage for three years, partly as a punishment but also to stop the news from spreading around the royal court. Catherine also holds the world record for the longest physical guard of a wild flower. Gazing from her window one spring morning, she spotted the year's first primrose and, to deter anyone from picking it, she posted a sentry to guard the plant day and night. The sentry and his descendants continued to patrol the lawn long after the death of both Catherine and the primrose, for the simple reason that nobody had countermanded the order. In fact it was some fifty years before Count Bismarck finally identified the chronic waste of human resources and decided that the manpower could be employed more gainfully elsewhere.

LONGEST FINGERNAIL

Shridhar Chillal, from Pune, India, stopped cutting the finger-nails on his left hand in 1952, and by 2000 the thumbnail measured a mind-boggling 4 feet 9 inches long. Had it been straight it would have been almost as tall as Chillal himself but instead it coiled around in ever-increasing circles like a Danish pastry, but chewier. Even so, when he sat in a chair, the other nails on his hand, which sprouted in a more Medusa-like fashion, scraped along the floor. "I decided to start growing them when I was sixteen after reading a story about a Chinese saint's long and uncut nails. My family told me I would never get a job, but that didn't deter me." For nearly half a century as his nails spiralled out of control, he was unable to sleep properly at night and could not hug his chil-dren. Living in constant fear of breakage, he nervously guarded his personal space, and when venturing out he wrapped his nails in what looked like a golf bag. The sheer weight of the nails damaged his hand and also caused him to lose his hearing in one ear – but he maintained that was the result of body imbalance rather than an itch that he could not resist scratching.

WIDEST MOUTH

Francisco Domingo Joaquim, a twenty-year-old from Sambizanga, Angola, won the World's Widest Mouth title at a 2010 Big Mouth competition in Rome by fitting a Coca-Cola can *sideways* into his mouth. Dubbed the Angolan Jaw of Awe, he boasts an elastic mouth that is 6.7 inches wide at full stretch, meaning that he comfortably outshone rival contestants who were fitting mere cups or saucers into their mouths. To maintain his elasticity and newfound fame, he started putting a Coke can into his mouth every day.

LONGEST TONGUE

Nick Stoeberl, a twenty-four-year-old from Monterey, California, currently boasts the world's longest tongue, measuring an alarming 3.97 inches – long enough to accommodate five doughnuts. This proved bad news for Britain's Stephen Taylor who had been able to dine out on his 3.86-inch-long tongue since 2002.

FARTHEST ROTATION OF HEAD

German sideshow performer Martin Laurello (1885–1955) was billed as the "Human Owl" or sometimes "Bobby the Boy with the Revolving Head" because of his remarkable ability to turn his head 180 degrees. He was born, as Martin Emmerling, in Nuremburg, with a slightly bent spine. This enabled him to dislocate several neck bones so that, in the words of fellow freak show performer "Monkey Girl", he "could put his head all the way around". To sum up, he could look backwards while his body was facing forwards. When his head was turned, his spine assumed the shape of a question mark because of its twisted nature. He was apparently so relaxed in that position that he was able to drink a pint of beer. Even so, he is reported to have practised rotating his head for three years before finally being ready to go public. Arriving in the United States in 1921 with a selection of other European novelty acts, he was soon snapped up to appear with Ringling Bros. and Barnum & Bailey, and in the 1930s he played to huge crowds at the popular Ripley's Believe It or Not! Odditoriums. His last recorded performance was in 1945 with Ripley's before his untimely death a decade later from a heart attack.

FARTHEST EYE POPPING

John Doyle, a thirty-year-old internet marketer from Liverpool, can pop his eyes fourteen millimetres out of their sockets. It may not sound much but when you're talking about eyeballs, it really is a long way, like popping them out on stalks. In fact it is so impressive that, in September 2013, two professional optometrists, who were given the task of determining whether he had beaten the previous record of twelve millimetres, were unable to give an official ruling because their measuring equipment wasn't long enough. John, who is known as "Mr Zoom" rather than "Popeye" Doyle, has been honing his craft since 2011, having discovered his eye-bulging talent at his local pub. "I started doing it just for fun," he says, "and put it on YouTube one day. Suddenly it had a hundred views, then the figure kept going up and up and I was getting dozens of emails every couple of hours. It just took off." Soon he was appearing on US TV and performing in Japan. His act really is a sight for sore eyes – and probably a recipe for them, too.

MOST EAR WIGGLES IN ONE MINUTE

From Orlando, Florida, dermatologist Dr John "Lucky" Meisenheimer is a man of many talents. As well as being a noted physician, author, actor, director and athlete, he wrestles bears, is a rifle-shooting champion and a world-class swimmer. Oh, and he collects yo-yos, too – over 4,000 of them. But all of these accomplishments paled into insignificance on 8 December

2010 when he set a new world record by wiggling his ears 153 times in a minute.

MOST WRIST CRACKS IN ONE MINUTE

On 2 July 2011, thirty-year-old Rajiv Sharma, from Delhi, India, cracked his wrists 182 times in sixty seconds.

MOST FINGER SNAPS IN ONE MINUTE

On 24 December 2013, Raymond Gustavo, from Kiev, Ukraine, snapped his fingers 292 times in sixty seconds, beating the record of 278 set by Sweden's Jens Gudmandsen in 2008.

LONGEST KNUCKLE CRACKING SESSION

A young American, Edwin Browder, cracked his knuckles non-stop for thirty-two seconds in 2013 – a grand total of 64 consecutive cracks.

MOST NEEDLES IN HEAD

Looking like a metal hedgehog, thirty-seven-year-old Sri Lankan-born Mohanathas Sivanayagam stuck 2,100 acupuncture needles into his head and the sides of his face at a banquet hall in Markham, Ontario, Canada, in September 2012. He inserted each needle to a depth of 1.5 centimetres so that they wouldn't fall out and spoil the record bid. It took him forty-eight hours, during which time he ate only sparingly because whenever his jaw moved, the needles did too. His triumph followed a couple of failed attempts to work his way into the Guinness World Records. In 2005, he glued 12,000 pennies to the wall of a pizza shop in Markham, presumably with the intention of setting a world record for the most pennies glued to the wall of a pizza shop by a Sri Lankan living in Canada. He intended calling his restaurant Penny Pizza, but when Guinness told him the record was not acceptable he abandoned the whole project without selling a slice. His next attempt was a seashell collection. On beach holidays in Malaysia, Cuba and Mexico he picked up what he considered to be interesting shells and had collected 1,200 when he discovered that record wouldn't count either. That was when he remembered the old proverb: if at first you don't succeed, stick needles in your head.

LONGEST CONTINUOUS KISS

Husband and wife Ekkachai and Laksana Tiranarat locked lips for 58 hours 35 minutes 58 seconds non-stop at the World's Longest Continuous Kiss Competition in Pattaya, Thailand, in February 2013. They were not allowed to sit or snooze, had to drink through straws while kissing, and even had to continue kissing when they went to the toilet. Ironically, kissing in public is frowned upon in Thailand and all entrants had to submit written proof that they were either married or in a proper relationship. The happy couple walked away with $3,300, two diamond rings and chapped lips.

MOST HUGS GIVEN IN TWENTY-FOUR HOURS

Under the guise of his alter ego Teddy McHuggin, fifty-one-year-old Jeff Ondash, from Youngstown, Ohio, hugged 9,236 people individually in twenty-four hours in February 2013, on the strip in Las Vegas, Nevada. In the process "Teddy" became the first person to break three Guinness hugging records and promptly set himself a target of hugging a quarter of a million people in the course of the year.

MOST CHILDREN FATHERED

Moulay Ismaïl Ibn Sharif, the Sultan of Morocco from 1672 to 1727, sired a confirmed 867 children (525 sons and 342 daughters) by various women, although some sources claim the figure to be as high as 888. It must have been difficult for him to keep count, and a nightmare when it came to remembering birthdays. However, his prodigious sex drive did not stop him living well into his eighties. An honourable mention should also go to Augustus II, King of Poland, who lived from 1670 to 1733, during which time he fathered an estimated 355 children – one for nearly every day of the year. Incredibly, only one of these children – a boy, Frederick Augustus – was born legitimate. Inevitably, Augustus struggled to keep track of his legions of offspring, with the result that at least one of his daughters went on to become his mistress. There is no evidence to suggest that he was overly troubled by this.

LONGEST TIME WITHOUT A WASH

Amou Haji, an eighty-year-old man from the village of Dejgah in Southern Iran, revealed in 2014 that he had not washed for over sixty years, thus making him the world's dirtiest man. He hates contact with water so much that the mere suggestion of a bath makes him angry. He does drink the stuff – but only from a large rusty can – and mainly to wash down his favourite meal of rotten porcupine meat. You see, Haji isn't too keen on fresh food either. Whether his diet has affected his skin is hard to tell since it is encrusted in decades of dirt and grime. To emphasize his alternative lifestyle, he smokes a pipe filled with animal faeces rather than tobacco and trims his hair by burning it off over an open flame. He lives in a hole in the ground – unsurprisingly, there isn't a Mrs Haji – or in an old shack built for him by sympathetic villagers, who view him as a kindly, if unhygienic, figure.

LONGEST HANDSHAKE

Two actors shook hands continuously for forty-three hours in Tbilisi, Georgia, in December 2013 in a bid to improve relations between Turkey and Armenia. Turkey's Deniz Banş and Armenia's Hovhannes Hajinyan held hands through rain, wind and freezing temperatures to beat the existing world record, set in New York in 2011, by twenty-five minutes. The exercise was designed to help foster peace between the two countries who are long-time foes, although the prolonged handshake could also have been interpreted as an instance of keeping your enemies close. The whole event – nearly two days of it – was broadcast live on the internet. That must have made for gripping viewing.

LOUDEST BURP (FEMALE)

Measured from a distance of 2.5 metres and a height of 1 metre, thirty-eight-year-old Jodie Parks, from St Louis, Missouri, emitted a burp that registered 107.7 decibels in Madrid in 2008. The self-styled Queen of Burps was thus louder than the roar of a motorbike and a snowmobile and nearly as loud as a power saw. In releasing her gas to a world-wide audience she proved once and for all that burping is not an all-male domain.

LOUDEST BURP (MALE)

Paul Hunn from Waltham Abbey, Essex, has always taken great pride in his breathtakingly loud burps, and in 2009 at Butlin's, Bognor Regis, he let one out that measured 109.9 decibels and probably sent the campers running for cover. The Burper King prepares for a challenge by not eating on the day so that his stomach is empty when he takes in deep breaths of air and a fizzy drink to assist in the build-up of internal gases. As a tip for budding burpers, he says that eating spicy foods the day before can also help pump up the volume. On a cautionary note, he adds that he suffers for his art, experiencing very bad sore throats and problems at the other end, in the form of upset stomachs. When he is not burping, Hunn works as an accounts clerk for a firm of solicitors who, perhaps unsurprisingly, prefer to remain nameless.

LONGEST BURP

Italy's Michele Forgione Savignano sul Panaro (aka Rutt Mysterio) produced a burp that lasted an eye-watering 1 minute 13.6 seconds at the 2009 Ruttosound contest at the Reggiolo Beer Festival. Nearly 20,000 people attend Ruttosound to hear performers in four sections – burp long, burp power, burp spoken and burp freestyle.

LOUDEST SCREAM

At a screaming contest inside London's Millennium Dome in 2000, teaching assistant Jill Drake, from Tenterden, Kent, set the Guinness World Record for the loudest scream by an individual when she registered an ear-piercing 129 decibels. Her scream was as loud as a pneumatic drill and only 10 decibels lower than a jumbo jet taking off, making her a force to be reckoned with in the classroom. Her unusual talent earned her a trip to Los Angeles where she was required to scream for an hour to promote Disneyland's new white-knuckle ride, Twilight Zone Tower of Terror.

LONGEST JET OF WATER EXPELLED ANALLY

Joseph Pujol was the toast of Parisian entertainment around the start of the twentieth century – not for singing, dancing or even playing a musical instrument, (unless you count the sphincter as a musical instrument), but because he could fart to order. Under the stage name of Le Pétomane, he reduced audiences to tears by demonstrating his extraordinary ability to fart in five keys, extinguish candles and expel water from his backside over a distance of up to 15 feet. It was said of him that "he could wash your walls with just a bucket and a squat". Pujol used his anus the way other people use their mouths. By constricting or loosening it, he could vary the pitch of the air he expelled, and by controlling his abdominal contractions he could also vary its volume from a gentle whisper to the roar of a cannon or a clap of thunder. As a result he was able to make music – although it was rarely described as sweet.

Pujol discovered his rare gift after a disconcerting boyhood experience. Playing in the sea one day, he was holding his breath and ducking under water when he suddenly felt an unwelcome rush of cold water enter his bowels. He went to find his mother but was embarrassed to find that water was flowing freely from his body. He had become a veritable water butt. He maintained a discreet silence about the episode until he was called up for military service by the French army when, as a party piece to amuse his fellow soldiers, he once again succeeded in taking in water and letting it out, producing an impressive jet that travelled several yards. Their response was so enthusiastic that Pujol sensed he could be on to something and so he began practising muscle control and adding air to his liquid repertoire. A star was born.

Upon discharge from the army, he returned to his job as a baker in Marseilles but supplemented his income by working part-time in music halls as a singer, trombone player and occasional performer of comic routines. But it was when friends encouraged him to include the farting impressions with which he had delighted them in private that things really took off. His anal mimicry included the delicate fart of a young girl, the loud slide of a mother-in-law and the demure gas passed by a bride on her wedding night followed by the unbridled ripper she lets out the morning after.

Taking his talents to Paris in 1892, he became an instant sensation at the famous Moulin Rouge, remarking that the building's big red windmill sails would be a marvellous fan for his act! Always dressed immaculately to inject an air of decorum into proceedings, this patron of the farts would often insert a rubber tube into his rectum to facilitate the blowing out of the gas-fired footlights. He even used to slip a flute into the tube so that he could accompany his own singing and could also smoke on a cigarette from both ends of his body at the same time. For his finale, he would invite the audience to fart along with him, which they invariably did with great gusto. His anal version of "La Marseillaise" always went down a storm and soon he was the country's highest-paid entertainer. As Le Pétomane's fame spread, King Leopold II of Belgium travelled incognito to Paris to see, hear and, if he was unlucky, smell the fabled flatulist, although for the most part Pujol's act was odour-free. Sigmund Freud also came to see a performance, which must have made for an interesting conversation in the bar afterwards.

Of course, nothing in show business lasts forever and, horrified by World War I, Pujol retired from the stage and went back to his bakery. He died in 1945 at the age of eighty-eight, whereupon his family rejected an offer by the Medical Facility of the Sorbonne, who were willing to pay 25,000 francs to examine his body after his death in the hope of discovering the anatomical secret behind Le Farteur Extraordinaire.

FASTEST CLAPPER

Bryan Bednarek clapped his hands 804 times in one minute (which works out at over 13 claps per second) at Arlington Heights, Illinois, on 1 February 2014 to beat the previous world record of 802. He deserves a round of applause.

MOST BLINKS IN THIRTY SECONDS

Most adults blink about 12 times a minute, but on 3 December 2012, Samantha Falin blinked 207 times in thirteen seconds in Austin, Texas, for no reason other than to set a world record.

MOST WHISTLES IN ONE MINUTE

Using only her mouth and with no artificial aids, Taylor Wolfe, of Fresno, California, whistled 296 times in one minute on 30 June 2013.

HIGHEST WHISTLER

Walker Harnden, a nineteen-year-old oboe student at the North Carolina School of Arts, achieved a new world record for the highest whistle when he hit the note B7 – the second to top note on the piano – on 7 November 2013. He says his incessant whistling used to drive his family and friends crazy until, by practising five hours a day, "I got good enough that it became a pleasant sound." If he goes much higher, only dogs will be able to hear him.

LOWEST WHISTLER

At the Impossibility Challenger in Dachau, Germany, on 6 November 2006, Jennifer Davies, from Ottawa, Canada, whistled the F below middle C – the lowest whistled note ever recorded. At the same event, she whistled the second E above middle C to create a record for the highest note until Walker Harnden snatched it from her. However, she does also hold the world record for the longest whistling marathon – 25 hours 30 minutes 5 seconds, set at the 2010 Impossibility Challenger. Her repertoire incorporated 125 tunes, whistled in rotation, no doubt to the delight of her audience.

LOUDEST WHISTLER

Marco Ferrera set the record for the loudest whistle when he reached 125 decibels at Santa Monica, California, on 5 March 2004 – a volume level equivalent to an air-raid siren.

BIGGEST BLONDE PARADE

Latvia's annual Go Blonde Festival prides itself on hosting the world's biggest blonde parade, which, it should be explained, is a big parade of blondes as opposed to a parade of big blondes. The 2011 event in Riga attracted over 500 blondes, all dressed in pink and cheered along the parade route by a crowd of around 1,000, mostly men. Event organizer Marika Gederte, head of the Latvian Association of Blondes, said: "It is hard for one blonde woman because there will always be some jokes. When there are 10 of them, there are no jokes already, but if there are 100 then it turns into great power."

MOST SPECTACULAR WEIGHT LOSS

The heaviest man in history, American Jon Brower Minnoch (1941–83), weighed 1,400 pounds – 100 stone – at his peak, although that was only an approximation because he was too large to fit on a set of scales. He suffered from a condition called edema, where the body accumulates excess fluid, and already weighed twenty-one stone by the time he was twelve. His weight continued to balloon, but in 1978 he set a new world record for the greatest difference in weight between a married couple when he wed 110-pound Jeannette with whom he subsequently managed to father two children. As doctors sought to cure his condition, he was admitted to hospital in Seattle where it took thirteen people just to roll him over in bed so that the sheets could be changed. He was discharged sixteen months later, having lost 924 pounds (66 stone) – the largest weight loss ever documented. However, he was readmitted in 1981 after putting on 200 pounds in seven days, and died less than two years later.

FATTEST CONTORTIONIST

Convention dictates that contortionists should possess slim, supple bodies, thereby enabling them to squeeze their torso into a small suitcase or pass their body through the head of a tennis racket. However, circus performer and comedian Matt Alaeddine, from Edmonton, Canada, flies in the face of convention because even though he can weigh up to thirty-two stone at the height of the candy season he is able to press the soles of his feet to the cheeks of his face by doing the "Sumo splits" and dislocate his shoulders to escape from a straitjacket. He is therefore officially the world's fattest contortionist. For "Fat Matt", as he is known to his fans, obesity pays.

SHORTEST POLICEWOMAN

Despite standing a mere 2 feet 8 inches tall, thirty-one-year-old Aisha Al Hamoudi has been serving as a sergeant with Al Bidya Police in Fujairah, United Arab Emirates, since 2010. The eldest of seven siblings, she knew she would never grow beyond the height of a three-year-old after being diagnosed with growth hormone deficiency. This did not stop her having big ambitions – notably to join the police force, following in the footsteps of her father and two younger brothers. So she took a course in maintaining records and documents and landed a job at her local police station compiling reports. She sits in a small chair at a small desk and the office door handles have been adjusted so that she can reach them.

SHORTEST FIREFIGHTER

When 4 feet 2 inches tall Vince Brasco went for his physical exam in 2007 to join his local fire department at Carbon, Pennsylvania, the doctor tried to talk him out of it. However, Brasco, who was born with achondroplasia, a form of dwarfism that affects bone growth, and has had fourteen surgeries on his left leg, was not to be denied his dream and became a volunteer firefighter. "I'll never let achondroplasia stop me from doing anything," he said in a 2011 interview. "I wanted to be a fireman as a child so as soon as I was old enough to volunteer at sixteen I did it. I work out a lot, as much as I can at the gym. I can bench-press over three times my own weight. It really helps on the job because you need to be strong. Because I can lift so much, I'm handy at salvage jobs where we have to move heavy bits of metal debris, like after car accidents. And it means I can be part of a line of men using a hose. If you aren't strong enough, it would fly out of control."

MOST PROLIFIC REGURGITATOR

The Great Waldo, a twentieth-century, German-born sideshow entertainer, could swallow and regurgitate watches, rings, keys, coins, eggs and even live animals. Known as "The Human Ostrich", his most celebrated routine saw him swallow a live white mouse, smoke on a cigarette and then, to the amazement of the audience, regurgitate the rodent unharmed, physically if not mentally. He always dressed as a distinguished gentleman in a tuxedo, and his concern about animal welfare was such that when swallowing fish or frogs he would first swallow large amounts of water so that they could swim around happily inside him! Born Dagmar Rothman in 1920, he loved the circus as a child and, desperate to join the performing ranks, began to train his stomach muscles to regurgitate items that he swallowed. In time his muscular control was so precise that he was able to swallow several different coloured balls and regurgitate them in the order the audience demanded. He could also swallow a locked padlock, then the key, and unlock the padlock. If a member of the audience questioned the authenticity of his act, Waldo would invite the person on stage, swallow their watch and tell them to listen to the ticking coming from his stomach. As a Jew, Waldo fled to Switzerland in 1938 as the Nazi menace began to ravage Europe. He was spotted there by an American talent agent who took him to the United States where his career blossomed with Ringling Bros. and Barnum & Bailey. Alas, although The Great Waldo was lucky on stage, he was continuously unlucky in love. He found one rejection particularly hard to swallow and committed suicide in 1952 by gassing himself in his home.

LONGEST TIME SPENT WITH RIGHT HAND RAISED

Since 1973, Indian holy man Sadhu Amar Bharati has kept his right hand raised in the air in a currently unsuccessful bid to achieve world peace. The exertion has reduced his hand to a useless piece of skin and bone, and since clipping his nails would have meant lowering the limb, he has not trimmed them in decades so that they now curl around his fingers. More alarmingly, perhaps, a number of disciples have decided to follow his example and have also held their hands up for over ten years.

GREATEST HUMAN LIGHTNING CONDUCTOR

Roy C. Sullivan, a ranger at Shenandoah National Park, Virginia, survived a record seven lightning strikes in the course of his lifetime – no mean feat considering that the chances of being struck just once by lightning are around 10,000 to 1. He was first hit in April 1942 while sheltering from a storm in a fire lookout tower, and sustained a burn the length of his right leg and the loss of the nail on his big toe. In July 1969, he was knocked unconscious by a strike which burned off his eyebrows, eyelashes and much of his hair, and in July 1970 another lightning strike seared his left shoulder. On 16 April 1972, his new hair was set on fire by lightning and the same fate befell him on 7 August 1973 in a strike which also burned his legs. The next strike, on 5 June 1976, injured his ankle. On 25 June 1977, he was hit for a seventh time, while fishing. The lightning hit the top of his head, singed his hair and travelled down his body, burning his chest and stomach. As he headed for his car, a bear suddenly appeared on the scene and tried to steal the trout from his fishing line. Despite his injuries, Sullivan still had sufficient strength to fight off the bear with a tree branch. Possibly in search of another world record, he later recalled that it was the twenty-second time he had fended off a bear with a stick. Since Sullivan had now been hit by lightning six times in eight years, and seven times in total, it was perhaps no great surprise that people started avoiding him. This saddened him, and on 28 September 1983, the great survivor committed suicide at the age of seventy-one by shooting himself in the stomach, apparently over an unrequited love.

Sullivan's record is under threat from Melvin Roberts, of Seneca, South Carolina, who in 2011 was struck by lightning for the sixth time. One strike in 2007 put him in a wheelchair for more than a year. Roberts must be in two minds as to whether this is a world record he really wants to have.

LONGEST TIME TO COME OUT OF A COMA

A Canadian woman, Annie Shapiro, fell into a coma in 1963 on the day that John F. Kennedy was assassinated and finally awoke twenty-nine years later in 1992, shocked to find that she was a seventy-nine-year-old grandmother. "I was staring at a stranger," she said a couple of days after coming round. "When I went to sleep I was a darn good-looking woman. But when I awoke and looked into a mirror, I saw an old woman with bags under her eyes and grey hair." Shapiro had been going about her business as usual in Hamilton, Ontario, on 22 November 1963 when she suffered a massive stroke while watching TV reports of Kennedy's death. For the next two years, she lay totally paralyzed with her eyes wide open – a condition known as "Doll's Eyes" – and remained asleep through the Moon Landing, the Vietnam War, Watergate, the fall of the Berlin Wall and her children's weddings. Then suddenly, on 14 October 1992, she snapped out of her coma. Her devoted husband Martin was stunned. "I was laying beside her in bed when she sat up and said, 'Turn on the television. I want to see *I Love Lucy*.' It was like a dead person come to life." Her first surprise was discovering that TV shows were in colour instead of black and white. Then when she tried to call her son, she was afraid to speak on the phone because it was cordless. "The phone didn't have any wires attached to it," she recalled. "A voice was coming out of it and I thought it must be magic." Gradually the woman who had become known as "Mrs Rip Van Winkle" caught up with her family and the new technology, and before her eventual death in 2003 she was the subject of a movie *Forever Love* starring Reba McEntire.

PRISONER WHO SURVIVED MOST HANGING ATTEMPTS

Despite protesting his innocence, John Lee, a nineteen-year-old petty thief, was convicted of murdering his employer Emma Keyse, a former maid to Queen Victoria, at her home in Babbacombe, Devon, on 14 November 1884 and was sentenced to hang. The execution was scheduled to take place at Exeter Prison on 23 February 1885, but three times Lee was placed on the hangman's trap and each time the trap failed to drop, even though it had been thoroughly tested beforehand by the executioner, James Berry. The official explanation was that the gallows mechanism had been assembled incorrectly, preventing the hinges from opening when the trap door was weighted. Others suggested that rain may have caused the trap door to swell. Whatever the cause of the failure, it saved Lee's neck because his death sentence was commuted by Home Secretary Sir William Harcourt to life imprisonment. The man they couldn't hang was released after serving twenty-two years in jail and later emigrated to Milwaukee, USA, where he died in 1945.

MOST TEETH REMOVED

Most adults have thirty-two teeth, but Ashik Gavai, a seventeen-year-old Indian boy, underwent a seven-hour operation on 21 July 2014 to remove 232 of his teeth! He had been complaining to his parents for eighteen months about a painful swelling in the right side of his lower jaw, and when doctors investigated they were in for a shock. Sunanda Dhivare-Palwankar, head of dentistry at Mumbai's JJ hospital, said: "Ashik's malaise was diagnosed as a complex composite odontoma where a single gum forms lots of teeth. It's a sort of benign tumour. At first, we couldn't cut it out so we had to use the basic chisel and hammer to take it out. Once we opened it, little teeth started coming out, one by one. Initially we were collecting them – they were really like small white pearls – but then we started to get tired. We counted 232. According to medical literature available on the condition, it is known to affect the upper jaw and a maximum of 37 teeth have been extracted from such a tumour in the past. But in Ashik's case the tumour was found deep in the lower jaw and it had hundreds of teeth." The doctors kindly left him with a more manageable twenty-eight teeth.

MOST EXPENSIVE TOOTH

In November 2011, Dr Michael Zuk, a dentist from Alberta, Canada, paid $31,000 for John Lennon's rotten molar, thereby breaking the record for the world's most expensive tooth, which had previously belonged to the upper right canine extracted from Napoleon's mouth in 1817 and which sold at auction for $19,140 in 2005. Lennon had given the discoloured tooth (described by the auction house as "rather gruesome, yellowy, browny with a cavity") to Dot Jarlett, his housekeeper during the 1960s, advising her either to get rid of it or to give it to her daughter as a souvenir. She chose the latter course of action and the tooth stayed in the family. Zuk is apparently an aficionado of celebrity teeth and has written a book on the subject. He said that when he heard about the auction for Lennon's tooth he simply had to buy it. "Some people will think it is gross," he said, "others will be fascinated by it." Rather alarmingly, Zuk said he planned to use the tooth as the first step towards cloning the dead Beatle from DNA, in the same way that scientists hope to be able to clone a woolly mammoth. "Many Beatles fans remember where they were when they heard John Lennon was shot," he said. "I hope they also live to hear the day he was given another chance. To say I had a small part in bringing back one of rock's greatest stars would be mind-blowing." Imagine.

MOST EXPENSIVE DENTURES

A pair of false teeth worn by Winston Churchill was sold at auction in Norfolk in 2010 for £15,200 ($23,700). As the BBC put it: "Never has so much attention been paid by so many, to so few teeth."

Churchill was unusually attached to his partial upper dentures, and had several sets specially constructed to preserve his lisp and accentuate his slightly slurred diction – familiar to all who listened to his rousing wartime broadcasts. Indeed he lived in such fear of losing his falsies that his private secretary always had a spare set to hand in the event of emergencies. Churchill's teeth were made by dental technician Derek Cudlipp whose role was considered so vital during World War II that he was not allowed to join up. His son Nigel recalled: "When my father's call-up papers came, Churchill personally tore them up. Churchill said that he would be more important to the war effort if he stayed in London to repair his dentures. Churchill used to flick out his dentures when he was angry and throw them across the room. My father used to say he could tell how the war was going by how far they flew." Churchill memorabilia has always been big business. One of his half-smoked cigars sold for £4,500 ($6,750).

MOST EXPENSIVE KIDNEY STONE

Canadian online casino GoldenPalace.com went where no bidder had gone before by paying $25,000 for *Star Trek* actor William Shatner's kidney stone in 2006. For their money, they also got the surgical stent and string that had been used to facilitate the passage of the troublesome stone. "This takes organ donors to a new height, to a new low, maybe," said Shatner, who donated the money to charity and described the stone as so big "you'd want to wear it on your finger".

MOST EXPENSIVE FALSE FINGERNAIL

An acrylic fingernail belonging to Lady Gaga and retrieved by a crew member sold for over $12,000 on an internet auction site in May 2013. The black nail, decorated with tiny gold beads, was apparently worn by the singer at her concert in Dublin, Ireland, in September 2012. To show that the false nail was genuine, it was accompanied by a photo of Lady Gaga performing on stage with – wait for it – a missing fingernail. Listed as an item "expected to have broad appeal from Lady Gaga's ardent fans who want something personal for their collection," it was bought by an unnamed fan in the UK.

MOST EXPENSIVE CHEST X-RAYS

Three chest X-rays of Marilyn Monroe taken during a 1954 hospital visit sold for $45,000 at a 2010 Las Vegas auction. She had been admitted under her married name of Marilyn DiMaggio to the Cedars of Lebanon Hospital in Florida to undergo surgery for endometriosis, a painful womb condition.

MOST SPOONS STUCK TO BODY

In December 2013, Etibar Elchiyev, a forty-two-year-old kickboxing coach from Tbilisi, Georgia, balanced fifty-three metal spoons around his neck and chest at the same time. In doing so, "The Magnet Man", as he is known, broke his own record of fifty spoons set in 2011. He claims his body is naturally magnetic.

MOST POWERFUL HUMAN MAGNET

Human magnet Aurel Raileanu, a forty-year-old hospital worker from Bucharest, set a new world record in 2011 by making a fifty-seven-pound TV set stick to his chest without any outside aids. Arguably the most attractive man in the world, he says he can make metal items cling to his body just by concentrating and releasing his magnetic powers, which means he has to be very careful when visiting his local hardware store. It is said he can clear a table of cutlery faster than an army of waiters. "I might have had a sort of magnetism since I was a child," he told the *Sun* in 2007, "but it wasn't until about six years ago that I realized the objects would stay as if glued on to me. At the time I was wearing a fairly heavy necklace and the clasp broke. I saw it in the mirror – it was open and yet still stuck to my neck. I became curious about this and tried it with other objects – spoons, lighters, electric irons and even the TV set. They all stuck to me." His magnetism only works on bare skin, and when he visits the doctor in an attempt to find an explanation for his curious ability, it invariably creates a new problem because the stethoscope gets stuck to his chest.

MARRIED COUPLE WITH GREATEST
HEIGHT DIFFERENCE

When Al Tomaini married fellow sideshow performer Berniece Smith, known as Jeanie, on 8 September 1936, the only way they could fit into the same wedding photo was for him to pick her up and hold her with one arm. For due to an overactive pituitary gland, Al stood 7 feet 4 inches tall (although for publicity purposes he claimed he was 8 feet 4 inches), while Jeanie, who was born without any legs, measured just 2 feet 6 inches in height. They toured for decades as the 'World's Strangest Married Couple'.

LONGEST TIME STAYING AWAKE

Between 5 and 15 February 1964, Toimi Soini stayed awake for 276 hours – a total of eleven-and-a-half days – in Hamina, Finland, to break the world sleep deprivation record of 264 hours set by seventeen-year-old Californian high-school student Randy Gardner less than a month earlier. In 2007, forty-two-year-old Tony Wright, from Penzance, Cornwall, used a Stone Age diet of raw food to help stay awake for 266 hours, in the belief that he had set a new world record. He thought he was outdoing Gardner but unfortunately he had never heard of Soini, so his eleven days of suffering were all for nothing.

LONGEST TIME PLANKING (FEMALE)

Sixteen-year-old Gabi Ury, from Denver, Colorado, set a new women's world planking record on 19 April 2014 by holding the position for 1 hour 36 minutes 58 seconds. By planking for over 80 minutes, she obliterated the existing record of just under 37 minutes set in 2011 by seventy-one-year-old Betty Lou Sweeney, from Plover, Wisconsin. For the benefit of those who are allergic to any form of exercise, planking involves lying face down on the floor and propping yourself up on elbows and toes and keeping the body in a straight line. Gaby's achievement is all the more remarkable because she was born with Vater Syndrome, a muscular condition for which she has already undergone fourteen major surgeries. Planking was not her first crack at a world record. She had previously tried to break the record for the most socks on one foot, but struggled to get beyond sixty.

LONGEST TIME PLANKING (MALE)

George Hood planked for 3 hours 7 minutes 15 seconds in a shopping mall in Newport, Kentucky, on 20 April 2013. In the process, the fifty-five-year-old former marine from Aurora, Illinois, easily beat his own world record of 1 hour 20 minutes 5 seconds, set in 2011. His only moment of concern came when he finally realized how long he had been there. "Nobody is allowed to tell me the time unless I ask for it," he said. "When I first called for it, we were at one hour and 57 minutes. I damn near lost my balance because I didn't think we were that far."

HIGHEST ALTITUDE PLANK

The internet craze of extreme planking – where participants lie flat on their stomach in precarious locations with their arms by their sides – has already claimed a few victims, including a twenty-year-old Australian man, Acton Beale, who was killed planking on a seventh-floor Brisbane balcony while his friend was photographing him. The carefree quest to go ever higher reached its peak in 2011, when Kristen Evans planked on the summit of her namesake, Colorado's Mount Evans, 14,265 feet (4,348 metres) above sea level. Recalling her moment of triumph, she said: "I had no intention of planking Mount Evans. In fact, I had never planked before that day. But somebody just suggested, 'Hey, why don't you plank that?' So I climbed over [the summit] and everyone was screaming, 'No, no, don't do it!' But I just got down and planked for my life."

MOST PEOPLE PLANKING SIMULTANEOUSLY

A total of 1,549 students from King George V School in Hong Kong took to the school playing field on 16 December 2011 and planked for two minutes on undersized chairs to smash the old world record of 260 simultaneous plankers. Luckily they did not smash any of the chairs, which were being retired from duty after four decades of service. The school's business manager said: "Our aims were to give a fitting farewell to the chairs that have caused so much discomfort for 45 years, set a record and have some fun."

MOST PEOPLE TEBOWING SIMULTANEOUSLY

When National Football League quarterback Tim Tebow started marking his team's victories by getting down on one knee, resting an arm across the upright knee, bowing his head and praying, he unwittingly sparked a wave of imitators. A picture of him in the pose spread like wildfire on the internet in 2011 and, before long, Tebowing was recognized as a word by the Global Language Monitor. Then on 13 July 2012, over 500 fans of minor league California baseball team the Lake Elsinore Storm set a new record by Tebowing simultaneously to celebrate a 4–1 comeback victory over the High Desert Mavericks.

LIVING THE LONGEST WITH A BULLET IN THE HEAD

William Lawlis Pace died in his sleep aged 103 at a Turlock, California, nursing home on 23 April 2012 – ninety-four years and six months after his older brother Marvin accidentally shot him in the head with their father's .22-calibre rifle, in 1917, while they were playing a game of "stick-up". The wound damaged one of Pace's eyes and his facial nerves but doctors in his native Texas decided to leave the bullet in his skull for fear that surgery might cause brain damage. Thus he was able to claim the world record for the person who lived the longest with a bullet in his head. Having cheated death, Pace went on to work as a cemetery custodian.

BIGGEST McDONALD'S RECEIPT TATTOO

When it comes to choosing a tattoo, most people opt for something meaningful like a dedication to a loved one. However, Stian Ytterdahl, an eighteen-year-old from Lørenskog, Norway, knew where his affections lay and so decided to pay homage to his favourite fast-food joint by having the receipt of the meal he had eaten at his local McDonald's on 24 March 2014 tattooed on his right forearm. As well as the date and time, the tattoo featured his full order, including three cheeseburgers, a Coca-Cola and a McFlurry. Although his parents were apparently far from impressed, Ytterdahl was unrepentant. "It's fun to think I have a tattoo that no one has seen before. Maybe it won't be as fun when I'm 50 or 60 years, but it's my choice."

BIGGEST BREAKFAST TATTOO

In 2007, nineteen-year-old Dayne Gilbey, from Coventry, had a colourful tattoo of a full English breakfast inked on the top of his shaved head. It took tattoo artist Blane Dickinson six hours to complete the body artwork, which consisted of bacon, eggs, sausages, beans and even cutlery. Gilbey said he answered the call for a volunteer because he wanted to do something different, although his mum was so unimpressed she threatened to throw him out. Dickinson confirmed: "I first had this idea four years ago, so I'm glad to have finally found someone brave, or perhaps unhinged enough, to do it."

FIRST WOMAN WITH A PERMANENT
HEAD TATTOO ADVERTISEMENT

For some people – namely men – the forehead is simply one of those parts of the body that gets bigger with age, sometimes even reaching down to the back of the neck. But others see it as a potential advertising space. Forehead advertising first hit the headlines at the start of the twenty-first century with companies paying volunteers to promote their product for a month or so in the form of a temporary forehead tattoo. However, in June 2005 Kari Smith took things a step further by auctioning her forehead space permanently to bidders on eBay. It was eventually bought by internet company GoldenPalace.com who matched her asking price of $10,000. The thirty-year-old mother, from Bountiful, Utah, wore the GoldenPalace.com tattoo with pride and announced that she would be using the money to send her son Brady to a private school.

MOST DISNEY TATTOOS

George C. Reiger, a postal worker from Easton, Pennsylvania, had 2,200 tattoos of Disney characters on his body, including 103 Dalmatians on his back after the tattoo artist lost count. He also owned 40,000 items of Disney memorabilia – accumulated over forty years – but in 2010 he decided to sell them all. With part of the money raised from the sale, he also set about having most of the tattoos removed. "I'm telling everybody the 'Disney Tattoo Guy' is dead," he said. "I don't want to be that person anymore."

MOST HOMER SIMPSON TATTOOS

Lee Weir, of Auckland, New Zealand, has a record forty-one Homer Simpson tattoos on his left arm. Yet when he was growing up he wasn't allowed to watch *The Simpsons*. "My dad was a real Ned Flanders," he says. "He wouldn't let me watch as it depicted the father and the head of the household to be a buffoon. Holding the world record hasn't made me a better person but I definitely think it has made me a slightly cooler one."

MOST WORDS TATTOOED ON HEAD

Montreal male model Vin Los has twenty-four random words tattooed on his head, including FAME, LICK, PLAY, SCREAM, WORLD and GUILTY, as part of the twenty-five-year-old's modest ambition to become the most famous man in the world. He also has SEX BOMB inked on his neck and his own name tattooed in large letters across his stomach, presumably in case he forgets it. The man who has been described as having put the "dick" into "dictionary" says he makes his word selections by going on YouTube and selecting key words from hit songs. "I want to be an image for people to look at," he gushes. "Everybody who sees me is bound to ask questions." Yes, like, "What were you thinking?"

MOST LEOPARD TATTOOS ON A SCOTSMAN

Forget the Surrey Puma or the Beast of Bodmin, for nearly twenty years a leopard stalked the Isle of Skye off the west coast of Scotland. The difference was that this was a two-legged beast in the form of Tom Leppard, who had spent $8,000 on getting 99.2 per cent of his body covered in leopard spot tattoos. Only his nose, the skin between his toes and the insides of his ears are spot-free. He used to live in a remote hut made of sticks and stones, sleeping on a bed made from blocks of polystyrene, washing in a river and travelling by canoe once a week to the mainland to pick up supplies and his pension. By 2008, however, the seventy-three-year-old former soldier (whose real name is Tom Woodbridge) decided that he was getting too old for that kind of primitive lifestyle and the Leopard Man of Skye moved into a nice one-bedroom house. "I've loved every minute," he said, "and when you're covered in leopard tattoos you certainly get noticed. I became a bit of a tourist attraction on Skye." He is not the world's only leopard man. A Texan tattoo artist calling himself Larry Da Leopard has covered every inch of his body with more than 1,000 spots to become half man, half cat.

BIGGEST BALL OF SNOT

Over a period of two years, from 2002 until 2004, London artist James Robert Ford doggedly collected his nasal mucus until it formed a giant ball of snot some two inches in diameter. He came up with the idea while studying at Nottingham Trent University. "I was having a conversation with a friend who didn't like contemporary art, and he said: 'You might as well pick your nose and display that as art.' The little flakes of mucus took a long time to start piling up and I kept them in a Tom and Jerry egg cup. It took around two years for the 'bogey ball' to reach the same size as a Brussels sprout." Ford went on to show his snot ball at four separate art exhibitions before announcing that he was willing to sell it for £10,000 ($15,000). His optimism was admirable.

MOST TESTICLES GRABBED IN PUBLIC

In November 2013, French hand sanitizer company Merci Handy sent three women out onto the streets of Paris to grab unsuspecting men by the testicles in order to increase awareness of prostate cancer. Each successful grab of a stranger's privates raised €10 (and probably more besides), and fifty feels later the trio had collected around $650.

MOST HAEMORRHOID SURGERIES PERFORMED IN ONE DAY

Surgeon Dr Sudershan Chugh operated on a record 137 cases of haemorrhoids in a single day on 28 October 2007 at a special free piles clinic at Khanna, India. He started at 8.52 a.m. and finished at 11.53 p.m., pioneering his own technique that he called MISP (Minimal Invasive Surgery for Piles).

OLDEST WOMAN TO HIRE A STRIPPER FOR HER BIRTHDAY

Whereas most centenarians prefer to mark the occasion with a quiet family gathering, Doris Deahardie celebrated her hundredth birthday in January 2014 by hiring a male stripper for a party at a North Nottinghamshire pub. The perky pensioner, who travelled to the venue by limousine, even brought along her own bottle of baby oil. She had originally intended booking a helicopter ride in a repeat of her ninetieth birthday celebration but went off the idea after learning that the pilot would not be prepared to strip off while in the air. Her daughter-in-law Sharon explained: "We told her that no, pilots don't do that, we'll have to get you a real stripper. So she chose one herself from an online directory, saying: 'He looks like he's been looked after!' I told the lad he might have to be careful with her because of her age, but then she told me she wanted the full monty! It was a brilliant night. You should have seen her face when he straddled her. I don't think she'd believed he would do the whole lot."

CHAPTER 4

Acquired Tastes

MOST COCKROACHES EATEN

Retired Manchester ratcatcher Ken Edwards ate thirty-six cooked cockroaches in one minute on the set of *The Big Breakfast* TV show in 2001. Less successful was Edward Archbold, thirty-two, of Broward County, Florida, who choked to death in October 2012 after eating dozens of live cockroaches in a contest to win a python. He joined thirty other competitive eaters at a pet store in Deerfield Beach but collapsed and died shortly after devouring the insects. The local medical examiner's office stated that Archbold had died of "asphyxia due to choking and aspiration of gastric contents" after his airway had become obstructed with "arthropod body parts".

MOST COW BRAINS EATEN

Japan's Takeru Kobayashi ate fifty-seven pink, slimy cow brains, weighing a total of 17.7 pounds, in fifteen minutes at the 2002 Glutton Bowl contest. Kobayashi, who ruled the world of competitive hot dog eating from 2001 to 2006 with relish, expands the capacity of his stomach with water rather than food. He is famous for his trademark body wiggle

– known as the "Kobayashi Shake" – which he uses to force food down his oesophagus and to help it settle more compactly in his stomach. Although his tastes away from the speed-eating table are quite conservative, he says he will eat just about anything, which is probably a good philosophy to have if you are about to tackle a bucketful of cow brains. One of his rare fast-food defeats came on the 2003 US TV show *Man vs. Beast* when he was beaten by a 1,089-pound Kodiak bear. Kobayashi wolfed down thirty-one bunless hot dogs in 2 minutes 36 seconds but the bear managed fifty.

FASTEST HARD-BOILED EGG EATER

Rising competitive eater Adrian "The Rabbit" Morgan, from Baton Rouge, Louisiana, devoured twenty hard-boiled eggs in 84 seconds in August 2011 aboard the USS *Fitzgerald*. He had first shown that his stomach was a force to be reckoned with the previous year when he consumed eighteen-and-a-half peanut butter and banana sandwiches in 10 minutes.

MOST STINGING NETTLES EATEN IN ONE HOUR

It remains a mystery why anybody would choose to eat something with the word "stinging" in its name but, since 1987, the world's most accomplished stinging nettle eaters have converged on The Bottle Inn near Bridport, Dorset, for an annual event that sees around fifty competitors eat nettles non-stop for an hour. The nettles are cut into two-foot lengths, and every leaf has to be cleared and eaten from the stem for that length to count. The person who clears the most lengths is declared the winner. Experienced practitioners roll up the leaves to reduce the stinging sensation and wash them down with copious amounts of beer, but nothing prevents their tongues and lips quickly turning black. Bottle Inn landlord Chris Thomas said: "Apparently after the first few minutes your tongue and mouth become numb, which is how people can do it." The current world record holder is the aptly-named Philip Thorne who, making his debut at the 2014 event, consumed eighty feet of nettles in the allotted time to beat the previous best of seventy-six feet set back in 2002.

MOST MARS BARS EATEN IN FIVE MINUTES

Chicago's Patrick "Deep Dish" Bertoletti ate thirty-eight Mars Bars in five minutes at the 2010 Mars Bar Eating World Championship – nearly twice as many as his closest rival. Bertoletti, who has held eating world records in more than twenty-five categories ranging from corned beef and cabbage to peanut butter and jelly sandwiches, made his name in 2007 by becoming the first person to complete the Sasquatch Burger Contest at Big Foot Lodge Café in Memphis, Tennessee. Previously, 679 people had tried and failed to finish the giant meal of burger and fries, but Bertoletti polished off the lot in eleven minutes.

MOST CRICKETS EATEN IN ONE MINUTE

In 2012, American magician Richie Magic ate sixty-one crickets in 60 seconds to break the previous world record of thirty-seven set in 2009 by Don "Inferno the Dragon" Wilson. Magic did not particularly enjoy the experience, describing their taste as bitter. "I guess they're like sunflower seeds," he said, "but the legs got stuck in my teeth. On the plus side, a healthy diet consists of around 50 grams of protein a day. The crickets I ate in one minute were 25 per cent of my protein requirement for the day – and without as much fat as a hamburger."

MOST ICE CREAM EATEN IN TWELVE MINUTES

In his five-year career as a competitive eater, from 2001 to 2006, during which he expanded by over eleven stone, Long

Island real estate agent Ed "Cookie" Jarvis won thirty-three titles. He practised by attacking all-you-can-eat buffets with such enthusiasm that by the end of his visit the only thing left on the table was the tablecloth. "The buffet places hated me," he says. "I'd come in and eat 300 chicken wings, and they didn't like that." You can see their point. He set several world records, his first being when he forced down 1 gallon 9 ounces of vanilla ice cream in twelve minutes at the inaugural Max & Mina's Ice Cream Open in New York on 26 October 2001. To avoid immediately setting another world record for the longest ice cream headache, he came up with a cunning plan. He explains: "When you put the spoon in your mouth, typically the spoon faces up, meaning the ice cream is touching the top of your mouth, and I realized right away that if you turn the spoon upside down, the top of your mouth doesn't get cold because the spoon hits your mouth and not the ice cream." So that's a handy tip for anyone with half a mind to pig out on ice cream.

MOST PEAS EATEN IN TWELVE MINUTES

Eric "Badlands" Booker, a competitive eater from New York who says he has been hungry and focused since 1997, set the benchmark for international pea-eating by consuming 9.5 one-pound bowls of peas in twelve minutes. He has also devoured a record 8.5 ounces of Maui onions in a minute – a feat which, unsurprisingly in view of the state of his breath, earned him an appearance on *Wife Swap*.

MOST MEALWORMS EATEN IN ONE MINUTE

In 2009, an American man, Ray "Buster" Brabant, ate nineteen live mealworms in one minute, leaving just five tasty morsels wriggling around on the plate.

MOST REINDEER SAUSAGES EATEN IN TEN MINUTES

When serial eater Dale Boone, the self-proclaimed "Mouth of the South" from Atlanta, Georgia, decided to tackle sausages in 2002, he wasn't content to settle for any old sausages – he wanted to try his hand at reindeer sausages. So it was that at an Alaskan speed-eating contest, Boone, who lists his favourite foods as gravy and biscuits, gobbled down twenty-eight reindeer sausages in the allotted time of ten minutes to set a new world record. It would seem that Boone is the bad boy of speed eating, having served a suspension in 2006 for unspecified reasons. Indeed his entry on the International Federation of Competitive Eating website states that he "has maintained a reputation as a combative competitor who has disrupted some eating events with verbal excess." Perhaps it's just indigestion.

MOST RAW SAUSAGES EATEN

Even more than thirty years after his death, Latvian-born strongman Walter Cornelius remains something of a legend in his adoptive home town of Peterborough, England. Locals remember the gentle giant bending old pennies in his teeth, allowing motorbikes to be ridden over his chest, pushing a double-decker bus half a mile with his head, and walking on his hands up a flight of steps with a tray of tea balanced on his feet. One of his most famous stunts was his attempt to fly off the roof of a local supermarket across the River Nene. He knew he would fail but was tempted by the prize of £300 (nearly $500) plus a year's groceries. After a particularly ignominious failure in 1970 left him with a broken nose, he lamented: "The elastic broke on my wings. A friend of mine who knows about herons tells me that next time I'll need a 20-foot wingspan. These 10-foot wings are just not enough." Then there were his eating exploits. He claimed to live on a diet of raw eggs and grass "because cows eat grass, and look how strong they are!" Apparently he used to eat onions like they were apples and he seemed to have a particular penchant for eating raw sausages. To this day, he holds two world records for raw sausage eating – admittedly not the most keenly contested category in competitive eating. He once ate 47.2 ounces of raw sausages in 8 minutes 30 seconds, and on another occasion he devoured a 17.5-foot-long chain of raw two-ounce sausages in 5 minutes 34 seconds.

MOST LIZARDS EATEN IN TWENTY YEARS

Mukesh Thakore first became addicted to eating live lizards when he was five. Spotting a lizard while playing in 1986, the boy from India's Saurashtra region popped it in his mouth out of curiosity and enjoyed the taste so much that he went on to eat another 25,000 live lizards over the next twenty years. He would eat up to twenty-five a day for breakfast, lunch and dinner, and apparently suffered no adverse effects. He even started to experience withdrawal symptoms if he didn't get his regular lizard fix. Attending a local wedding, he refused the offer of sweets and other delicacies and instead went off to catch a few lizards before gulping them down. That's a photo you don't see in many wedding albums.

FASTEST TIME TO DRINK A GALLON OF MILK

On 18 July 2013, Takeru Kobayashi drank a whole gallon of milk in nineteen seconds at Upper Saddle River, New Jersey. The Japanese competitive eating champion had just set a record by eating thirteen cupcakes in a minute, so he "needed to wash it down". To put his achievement into perspective, milk chugging's "gallon challenge" usually requires competitors to down a gallon of milk in under an hour – 180 times slower than Kobayashi – without vomiting.

FASTEST TIME TO EAT THREE JACOB'S CREAM CRACKERS WITHOUT DRINKING

On 9 May 2005, British boxing promoter Ambrose Mendy set a new world record by eating three dry Jacob's cream crackers – including crumbs – in 34.78 seconds without taking in any liquid.

FASTEST TIME TO EAT SIX POUNDS OF SPAM

Eating it straight from the can, competitive eater Richard LeFevre, from Henderson, Nevada, scoffed six pounds of Spam in twelve minutes at the annual Spamarama event in Austin, Texas, on 3 April 2004.

FASTEST TOMATO KETCHUP DRINKER

In 1999, Dustin Phillips of California earned the title of the world's fastest ketchup drinker when he drank more than 90 per cent of a fourteen-ounce bottle of ketchup through a straw in thirty-three seconds . . . without throwing up.

FASTEST TABASCO SAUCE DRINKER

In Sydney, Australia, on 8 May 2005, stuntman Andrew Hajinikitas drank two bottles (4.2 ounces) of Tabasco sauce in thirty seconds without taking in any water. Just a few minutes earlier, on the same live TV show, he had eaten seven jalapeño peppers in under a minute. As one observer noted: "His intestines must be lined with asbestos and his asshole made of pure steel."

MOST SPIDERS EATEN BY A PERSON FOR LUNCH

When Raju Handi, from Assam, India, was bitten by a spider at school one day, he ate one as an act of revenge. He enjoyed the taste and, because he suffered no ill-effects from his arachnid snack, he has continued eating spiders for the next two decades, regularly munching his way through as many as 100 at lunch. In 2009, the thirty-year-old revealed that, rather like wine, every spider tastes a little different – some are bitter, some are sweet, some are juicy and some have a definite milky taste. That's something to bear in mind the next time you see one running out from under the sofa.

MOST CLOVES OF GARLIC EATEN IN ONE MINUTE

On 1 December 2009 in Kathmandu, Nepal, Deepak Sharma Bajagain set a new world record by eating thirty-four cloves of garlic in one minute. This was a remarkable display of garlic gobbling because when Oliver Farmer won the inaugural World Garlic Eating Competition, in Dorset in 2013, he did so by eating forty-nine cloves of garlic in *five* minutes.

MOST JELLY EATEN WITH
CHOPSTICKS IN ONE MINUTE

Damien Fletcher, a reporter on the UK's *Mirror* newspaper, got his name into the record books on 4 October 2006 by managing to eat 180 grams of jelly in one minute with chopsticks, thereby totally obliterating the previous world record of 45 grams. Afterwards he told colleagues: "They say dedication's what you need [to be a record breaker] but I'd also suggest a total lack of dignity."

MOST SMARTIES EATEN WITH
CHOPSTICKS IN THREE MINUTES

Kathryn Ratcliffe, from Whitley Bay, North Tyneside, set her first chopstick world record in 2002 at the age of just twelve when she shovelled 108 Smarties into her mouth with chopsticks in three minutes. "I don't eat Chinese food very often," she said at the time, "but I learned to use chopsticks at my aunt and uncle's house. They used to live in Hong Kong." The experience has served her well because over the next decade she has repeatedly broken the record, eventually raising the bar to 175 Smarties in three minutes in November 2013. Although she says she doesn't get sick of Smarties because she swallows them so quickly that she can't actually taste them, she briefly diversified in 2008 to eat 96 individual grains of rice in two minutes with chopsticks, smashing the existing record of 64 grains in three minutes. She also holds the world record for separating jelly beans by colour into pots with a straw, managing 30 beans in 17.69 seconds on Guinness World Records Day 2010.

MOST COTTAGE CHEESE EATEN IN FOUR MINUTES WITH A TABLESPOON

Dr Peter Altman, from Edgware, Middlesex, wolfed down three pounds of cottage cheese with a tablespoon in four minutes on 4 March 1984. Three years later, the good doctor set the thirty-second cottage cheese record, consuming half a pound of it on a TV talk show.

MOST LIVE SCORPIONS EATEN IN A SINGLE MEAL

Majid al-Maliki, a civil servant from Saudi Arabia, has eaten fifty live scorpions in a single meal. Al-Maliki, who also set a new Guinness World Record in 2009 for holding twenty-two live scorpions in his mouth simultaneously, has been eating scorpions since 1987. Much like wine gums, he says the yellow ones are best. He claims he has never been poisoned, but to reduce the potency of the sting he cuts off part of the scorpion's spike before putting it in his mouth. If scorpion is off the menu, he has been known to tuck into snakes, small crocodiles and lizards.

MOST BAKED BEANS EATEN WITH A COCKTAIL STICK IN FIVE MINUTES

On 18 March 2011, Gary Eccles, a Sainsbury's supermarket worker from Coventry, ate 258 baked beans – one by one – with a cocktail stick in five minutes. His workmates were then able to experience, albeit second-hand, the sensation of eating so many baked beans approximately every thirty seconds for the rest of the day.

MOST CATS EATEN IN A YEAR

Born in Poland around 1778, Charles Domery was one of nine brothers, all of whom had what could be termed hearty appetites. However, to the dismay no doubt of Mrs Domery, it was young Charles who stood out, eating virtually everything that crossed his path. At the age of thirteen he joined the Prussian Army and became part of a force besieging the French town of Thionville during the War of the First Coalition. Food supplies were scarce among the Prussian military and Domery quickly showed he knew which side his bread was buttered by surrendering to the French commander in return for a melon, which he swiftly devoured, rind and all. So impressed was Domery with the French cuisine that he defected to their side and, although of no more than average build, was granted double rations. Nevertheless he remained voraciously hungry, and while based at an army camp outside Paris his fellow soldiers noted that he ate 174 cats in a single year, leaving only the skins and bones. A French soldier named Picard stated: "Sometimes he killed them before eating, but when very hungry, did not wait to perform this humane office." When times were hard and the local cats kept their distance, he had to settle for eating five pounds of grass a day.

He preferred raw meat to cooked and wasn't fussy if it was human. While on board the French frigate *Hoche*, an unfortunate sailor had his leg shot off by cannon fire, whereupon Domery grabbed the severed leg and began to eat it until a crew member wrestled it from him and threw it into the sea. In 1798, the *Hoche* was captured by the Royal Navy off the coast of Ireland and Domery was imprisoned near Liverpool. The guards were shocked by Domery's insatiable appetite and his rations were steadily increased until eventually he was granted enough for ten men on a daily basis. This did not prevent him snacking on anything that took his fancy, including the prison cat, at least twenty rats which had strayed into his cell and a number of candles. In September 1799, Domery's case was brought to the attention of Dr Johnston, the Commissioner of Sick and Wounded Seamen, who conducted an experiment to test his eating capacity. Over the course of a day, Domery was fed sixteen pounds of raw cow's udder, raw beef, twenty-four large tallow candles and four large bottles of porter, all of which he ate and drank without defecating, urinating or vomiting at any time. That evening he was observed to be of good cheer and the following morning he awoke at four o'clock, eager for his breakfast.

Dr Johnston wrote: "The eagerness with which he attacks his beef when his stomach is not gorged, resembles the voracity of a hungry wolf, tearing off and swallowing it with canine greediness. When his throat is dry from continued exercise, he lubricates it by stripping the grease off the candles between his teeth, which he generally finishes at three mouthfuls, and wrapping the wick like a ball, string and all, sends it after at a swallow. He can, when no choice is left, make shift to dine on immense quantities of raw potatoes or turnips; but, from choice, would never desire to taste bread or vegetables."

MOST SNAKES EATEN IN A MONTH

Over the course of a month in 2002, Bangladeshi snake-charmer Dudu Mia ate nearly 3,500 baby snakes that he had captured from two houses in a two-day period, all of which suggests he hasn't quite grasped the concept of snake charming: you're not supposed to eat the act.

MOST BANANAS FORCE-FED TO SUSPECT TO RETRIEVE STOLEN GOODS

After twenty-eight-year-old Damu Gupta was arrested for stealing and swallowing a train passenger's gold chain, in December 2013, Indian police forced him to eat ninety-six bananas so that they could retrieve the jewellery. Gupta snatched the chain on the Vidarbha Express from Mumbai to Gondia and when his female victim screamed, he put the eleven-gram piece of jewellery in his mouth and swallowed it. An X-ray showed the chain in his stomach, so police officers fed him eight dozen bananas over a three-day period until it finally came out with his stool.

MOST BURNING PIECES OF CHARCOAL SWALLOWED

In April 2013, twenty-three-year-old Ridip Saikia, from Assam, India, swallowed 150 pieces of burning charcoal in 3 minutes 22 seconds apparently without needing to be rushed to intensive care.

MOST PIZZA EATEN

Dan Janssen, a thirty-eight-year-old woodworker from Ellicott City, Maryland, revealed in 2014 that he had eaten virtually nothing but pizza for the past twenty-five years. He eats two 14-inch pizzas every day, with the result that he has consumed more than 18,000 pizzas . . . and counting. As a teenager he actually decided to become a vegetarian for ethical reasons but quickly realized that he hated vegetables and so he turned to pizza. Now he eats pizza for breakfast, pizza for lunch and pizza for dinner – and nearly always the same variety: plain cheese. He will occasionally eat a bowl of raisin bran once a week if he's on a health kick, but otherwise it's just pizza and coffee. "I never get sick of it," he says. "If I go to a different pizza shop or try a new brand, it's like eating a completely different meal. Pizza is like sex; even when it's bad, it's good. But I do see a day in the future when I get a little more adventurous. I remember about four years ago I ate a peach and it was amazing."

FASTEST TO DRINK EIGHT PINTS OF MILK WHILE STANDING UPSIDE DOWN

Before his retirement in 2011, Peter Dowdeswell, from Earls Barton, Northamptonshire, held more than 350 eating and drinking records. Not satisfied with just guzzling stuff down as fast as possible, Dowdeswell liked to perform these challenges while standing on his head. So it was while being held in an upside-down position that he set world records by downing eight pints of milk in 42.4 seconds, eight pints of beer in 55.6 seconds and a pint of champagne in 2 seconds. The burp resulting from the champagne challenge must have registered on the Richter scale. Sadly it was while trying to break the record for sinking a pint of beer upside down that the seventy-one-year-old was forced to retire, with back and shoulder injuries reportedly sustained after the two men who were supposed to be holding his legs twice dropped him. Mortified at having to retire after a forty-year career, which saw him eat twenty-four pickled onions in a minute and drink thirty-four pints of beer in an hour (perhaps to get rid of the taste of the pickled onions), he bowed out with one final record attempt, by trying to eat twelve sausages in ten seconds while lying on a bed of nails balanced on a friend's head. What a trouper!

MOST EARTHWORMS EATEN IN THIRTY SECONDS

C. Manoharan, a twenty-three-year-old hotelier from Madras, India, swallowed 200 earthworms, each at least four inches long, on 15 November 2003, to smash the previous world worm swallowing record of ninety-four held by aptly-named

American Mark Hogg. Manoharan, who spent a year training for the feat, prefers to be called "Snake Manu" because when he is not eating worms he likes to relax by threading live baby cobras through his nostrils and pulling them out through his mouth.

LONGEST PIECE OF CLOTH SWALLOWED

In 2011 at Madhya Pradesh, India, yoga practitioner Mr G.P. Katiya was able to swallow a piece of cloth that was 18 feet long and 2.5 inches wide.

MOST LIGHT BULBS EATEN

American magician and sideshow performer Todd Robbins is famous for sword swallowing, hammering a nail into his nostril, and eating glass items such as wine glasses and light bulbs. He estimates that he has eaten more than 5,000 light bulbs throughout his career, sometimes devouring over twenty a week. He took his first bite of glass over thirty years ago when he started to develop his own magic act after moving to New York City from his native California. "To say I didn't have some trepidation about eating glass would be lying," he admits, but when he suffered no ill-effects he began to incorporate it regularly into his act. At first he used to step on a bag of glass to shatter it into smaller pieces, making it easier to digest, before he graduated to eating an entire light bulb in the same way that anyone else would eat an apple. He follows a strict diet of herbs and fibre, which, he says, helps his system process the glass he swallows. However, he acknowledges that eating so much glass over the years has taken its toll. A number of his teeth have cracked from the pressure of grinding up broken shards, and the risk of bodily injury is ever-present. "The danger of glass eating is the lack of control," he says. "When I swallow it, I don't know where it will go. It's like Russian Roulette for about two days."

FASTEST TESTICLE EATER

Patrick Bertoletti swallowed 3 pounds 11.75 ounces of bull calf testicles in ten minutes at the 2010 World Rocky Mountain Oyster Eating Championship in Colorado, earning himself a prize of $1,500. Masquerading under the slightly more appetizing name of Rocky Mountain Oysters, calf, pig or sheep testicles are a popular novelty dish in parts of North America where they are usually deep-fried and served with a sauce dip. Lest anyone should think that these poor creatures have sacrificed their gonads purely for human consumption, it should be pointed out that the main reason for castration is medical rather than culinary. Bertoletti says the most disgusting thing he ever had to eat was in Thailand. "The dish contained a raw cured egg that spends a month buried under ashes until it hardens to a translucent black-green. I almost puked when I put the eggs in my mouth, and since in the past I've put nearly four pounds of bull balls into my system in 10 minutes, that's saying something."

FASTEST TIME TO EAT A JAM DOUGHNUT WITHOUT USING HANDS OR LICKING LIPS

Guinness World Records notes that Philip Joseph Santoro ate a three-inch-diameter jam doughnut in 9.86 seconds in San Francisco on 27 April 2014 without using his hands or licking his lips. He did it by devouring the doughnut in three mighty gulps.

FASTEST TIME TO DRINK FOUR PINTS OF COLD CUSTARD

The Book of Alternative Records states that Yorkshireman Alan Newbold drank the entire contents of four pint mugs of cold custard in 1 minute 36 seconds in April 1986.

MOST YEARS EATING ROADKILL

To most people, owl, badger, fox, rabbit, toad and mole might sound like characters from a gentle children's woodland story, but for Jonathan McGowan they constitute a menu. For when it comes to stocking up on ready meals, he ignores the supermarket in favour of scavenging the highways and byways for creatures that have come off second best in an encounter with road vehicles. The Bournemouth taxidermist has been eating roadkill for more than thirty years, ever since as a fourteen-year-old he found a dead adder by the side of the road and decided to cook it. Although he confesses that the taste left a lot to be desired – "a bit like bacon rind" – it did not deter him from scraping up fur and feather from the tarmac. Rabbits, badgers and pheasants are his most common finds, but he has also sampled, among others, mole, mouse, stoat, weasel, crow, gull and cormorant, and has earned rave reviews from his friends – yes, he does have some – for his owl curry. Comparing the relative merits of roadkill, he says: "Rabbit is actually quite bland. Fox is far tastier; there's never any fat on it, and it's subtle, with a lovely texture, firm but soft. It's much more versatile than beef, and has a salty, mineral taste rather like gammon. Squirrels are delicious. Not many animals taste like what they eat but squirrels do have a fantastic, nutty flavour. Frogs and toads taste like chicken and are great in stir-fries. Rat, which is nice and salty like pork, is good in a stir-fry, too. Mice have a very bitter flavour, badger is not nice, hedgehogs are very fatty and moles are horrible with a rancid taste. I've only had mole once – and never again."

MOST GOLDFISH SWALLOWED

At a contest in Oakland, California, on 14 October 1975, Leonard McMahan swallowed 501 goldfish in four hours to become the world's undisputed goldfish eating champion. To mark his achievement, which smashed the previous record of

300 set the previous year by twenty-four-year-old John Parker in Los Angeles, McMahan was presented with a 240-gallon aquarium worth $1,000 – a somewhat ironic choice of prize.

MOST LIVE MINNOWS SWALLOWED

Chicago's Shane Williams swallowed 350 live minnows in under an hour at The Aquarium Bar and Grill at Fox Lake, Illinois, in February 2002 to smash the existing record of 280 set four years previously. Consuming live minnows has been a tradition at the bar since 1963.

MOST PIGEON FOOD EATEN BY A HUMAN

In 2003, fifty-eight-year-old Gerben Hoeksma, from Veendam, the Netherlands, revealed that he had been eating pigeon food three times a day for the past eleven years. He said his meals were nutritious, healthy, appetizing and cheap. "I let the food soak in water for a night and then cook it the next day to get it softer," he said. "Since I started to eat pigeon food I never felt so good."

MOST PET FOOD EATEN BY A HUMAN

For one month in the summer of 2014, Dorothy Hunter, the owner of Paws Natural Pet Emporium stores in Richland and Kennewick, Washington State, ate only dog, cat and bird food to demonstrate their nutritional value. She had the idea when, too busy to go out for a snack, she grabbed a bag of dog treats from the counter and was amazed how good they tasted. She developed a particular fondness for a brand of tinned cat food, which she said gave her increased energy and helped her lose weight. There was no indication as to whether the extra energy included a newfound ability to climb trees or whether the weight loss allowed her to lick her own butt-hole.

MOST BRUSSELS SPROUTS EATEN

On average most people eat Brussels sprouts no more than four times a year – once at Christmas dinner and three times during periods of intense constipation. Assuming five sprouts per portion, that works out at a lifetime's consumption of about 1,600 sprouts, which sounds an awful lot until you learn that James Hucheon, from Basingstoke, Hampshire, has already eaten over 50,000 sprouts – by the age of seventeen. He has been hooked on sprouts since he was a child and now eats them every day, even as an accompaniment to fish and chips or chicken tikka masala. He has a bag of 100 delivered with his weekly food shop and has been known to have sprout sandwiches for lunch. He works as an apprentice aero engineer, so his bizarre diet could come in handy if they need to do any wind testing.

MOST BIG MACS EATEN IN A LIFETIME

Don Gorske, from Fond du Lac, Wisconsin, has eaten over 26,000 Big Macs since 1972 and estimates that they constitute 90 per cent of his solid food intake. He says that after getting his first car at the age of eighteen, he went straight to a McDonald's where he bought his first Big Mac. He was so impressed that he ended up eating nine that day. He proceeded to devour 265 Big Macs in the course of the following month – averaging over eight a day – and kept all the boxes in the back of his car. He also keeps every McDonald's receipt, and records when and where he eats his Big Macs in a notebook which travels everywhere with him. So it will come as no great surprise to learn that he met and proposed to his wife, Mary, at a McDonald's – in 1973. Passing the 25,000 milestone on 17 May 2011, Gorske revealed that there had only been eight days over the previous thirty-nine years when he didn't eat a Big Mac – the day when his mother died, a "snow day" when McDonald's remained closed due to blizzards, a Thanksgiving Day when he was travelling and couldn't find a McDonald's (hard to imagine, we know), and days when he had to work past midnight in his job as a prison guard. He has since started keeping an emergency stash of Big Macs in his freezer for snow days and other unforeseen circumstances. "I plan on eating Big Macs until I die," says Gorske, and, perhaps surprisingly, that could be some time off as he has been given a clean bill of health. "I have no intentions of changing. They're still my favourite food and I look forward to them every day. But my wife warns that when she has to put them in a blender, it's over."

MOST CANS OF DIET COKE DRUNK PER DAY

Jakki Ballan began drinking Diet Coke when she was fourteen to help lose weight, but became so addicted to the stuff that at one point she was drinking fifty cans a day. "This addiction is taking over my life," said the forty-two-year-old mother-of-five from Ellesmere Port, Cheshire, who has spent about £150,000 ($225,000) on her Coke habit. "I can't even go out of the house without making sure I've got enough Coke on me. I won't do the school run unless I have at least two bottles in my bag." If no Diet Coke is to hand, she starts to panic and begins sweating, shaking, and pacing up and down. She has even had hallucinations, probably due to the caffeine overload. "It was really scary as at first I didn't know what was going on. I see strange things like oranges flying across the room. I am constantly tired, but all the caffeine I consume means I have trouble sleeping. So I end up sitting awake at night and drinking even more Coke. It's a vicious cycle." By 2014 she had managed to cut down to thirty cans a day and was hoping to break the habit altogether with the help of hypnotherapy.

LONGEST MEAT-SLICING SESSION

In December 2013, Paris-based Spanish butcher Noé Bonillo Ramos sliced thirty hams during a twenty-five-hour marathon chopping session in the French capital, beating the old record by just under six minutes. Ramos, who had trained for the event in thirty-hour sessions, which suggests that he could go on for longer if his record is challenged, was aided in his successful attempt by being ambidextrous, allowing him an all-important 360-degree ham rotation.

FASTEST SANDWICH MADE USING FEET

Using just his feet, Texan comedian Rob Williams, a founder member of The Flaming Idiots, entered the Guinness World Records by making a Bologna, cheese and lettuce sandwich, complete with olives on cocktail sticks, in 1 minute 57 seconds on 10 November 2000. The effort required him to use his feet to take two slices of bread out of the packet, remove the rind on the Bologna sausage, remove the plastic on the slices of processed cheese, slice tomatoes and pickles, add lettuce, mayonnaise and mustard, and finally cut the bread in half with a knife and present it on a plate. Both Jay Leno and Donny Osmond have eaten Williams's foot-made sandwiches and lived to tell the tale, although you would want to make sure that any corn in the sandwich was sweet rather than crusty with a taste of plaster.

BIGGEST GINGERBREAD HOUSE

Using more than 7,000 eggs and nearly a ton of butter, a team of volunteers in Bryan, Texas, built a 60 feet by 42 feet gingerbread house in 2013. The 36-million-calorie dwelling was large enough to accommodate a family of five.

LONGEST CURLY FRY

When Kim Medford asked a co-worker to pick up some large fries for lunch from an Arby's restaurant in Waynesville, North Carolina, in February 2013, she expected it to be like any other standard fast-food fare. Instead she found it contained a curly fry that was so large she felt obliged to take it home and carefully measure it. Stretched out on a table, it came to a record-breaking thirty-eight inches long. She then had it photographed for posterity and presumably refrained from eating it, partly on account of its cultural significance but also because by then it would have been cold.

LONGEST SAUSAGE

A sausage made by J&J Tranfield on behalf of Asda Stores at Sheffield, in October 2000, measured 36.75 miles long. It took over two days to prepare, weighed nineteen tons, equated to the length of 166,320 sausage dogs and would have stretched nearly all the way to Doncaster and back. All that was needed was a 36.75-mile-long grill.

HEAVIEST CAULIFLOWER

Peter Glazebrook doesn't grow ordinary-sized vegetables; he grows ones that are big enough to feed an entire village. In more than thirty years of gardening, Glazebrook, from Newark, Nottinghamshire, has held almost a dozen world records for his freakishly large vegetables, including the heaviest potato (11 pounds), longest beetroot (21 feet), longest parsnip (19 feet) and an 18-pound onion that brought tears to the eyes of his rival growers. In 2014, he surpassed himself by raising a monster cauliflower, which measured 6 feet wide and tipped the scales at 60 pounds, making it twenty times heavier than the average supermarket cauliflower and around the size of a sheep. It was also the heaviest cauliflower to have been grown anywhere in the world since 1999, when Sheffield's Alan Hattersley had set the old record with his 54-pound specimen. Glazebrook is the doyen of giant vegetable growers, although he says he has had to stop growing pumpkins because they have become too big to handle and has also given up on giant cabbages because he can no longer fit them in his car to take to shows. As for the champion cauliflower, it provided meals for Glazebrook and his wife Mary for weeks on end. "We don't have a freezer," she says. "I don't believe in them, so we ate cauliflower twice a day. It tasted just like an ordinary cauliflower, only a bit bigger."

HIGHEST PIZZA TOSS

Mark Patton, from Virginia Beach, Virginia, tossed pizza dough 27 feet into the air in 2012, setting a new record for the highest pizza base toss. There is no indication as to whether the dough was fit for purpose when it eventually landed.

LARGEST PIZZA ORDER

To celebrate American Independence Day 2012, Illinois-based Pizzas 4 Patriots arranged for the delivery of 30,000 twelve-inch pizzas to US military service personnel in Afghanistan. The ready-to-bake pizzas weighed a combined total of over twenty-three tons and were transported in a Boeing 777 freighter. To make sure they arrived in pristine condition, they were packed in eleven tons of dry ice.

LONGEST PIZZA DELIVERY

On 22 March 2001, Bernard Jordaan of Butler's Pizza, Cape Town, South Africa, hand-delivered a pizza to Corne Krige, the captain of the Fedsure Stormers rugby team, at the Bondai Hotel in Sydney, Australia – a distance of 6,861 miles. This broke the distance record set by a New York pizzeria that delivered to Tokyo.

MOST BRUSSELS SPROUTS IN A MINI CAR

With commendable single-mindedness, Lawrence Jones, a greengrocer from Slough, Buckinghamshire, managed to squeeze 38,182 Brussels sprouts into a Mini in December 2013. The vegetables weighed the equivalent of twenty-nine festive reindeer and, if laid out end to end, would stretch for a mile.

FIRST SANDWICH CONTAINING FOOD FOR EVERY LETTER OF THE ALPHABET

In 2014, aptly named food fan Nick Chipman created a towering sandwich with twenty-six fillings – one for every letter of the alphabet. Chipman, from Milwaukee, Wisconsin, said his biggest problem was finding a food starting with the letter X. "I eventually settled on xylocarp, which is defined as 'a hard, woody fruit that grows on trees', or, in other words, a coconut." His full list of ingredients was: avocado, bacon, cheese, Doritos, egg, fish sticks, garlic bread, ham, Italian sausage patty, jalapeño peppers, Krispy Kreme doughnut, lettuce, macaroni and cheese, noodles, onion rings, pepperoni, queso blanco dip, ramen noodles, spinach, turkey burger, Usinger's bratwurst, veal parmesan, waffle, xylocarp, yams and zucchini. He added: "I have no idea how many calories are in it, but I'd guess it's somewhere in the thousands. I ate it, but it was over the course of an entire day and I had to disassemble it and eat it in pieces."

HIGHEST POPPING TOAST

Using a specially built supertoaster powered by high-pressure carbon dioxide gas and a mechanical ram, London art student Freddie Yauner propelled a slice of toast 8 feet 6 inches into the air in June 2008. Before his record-breaking pop, he tested the "Moaster" at home where its impressive thrust meant that he was forced to scrape crumbs off the ceiling.

LARGEST CUSTARD CREAM BISCUIT

Nottingham chef Paul Thacker and his cousin, Simon Morgan, spent eleven-and-a-half hours making the world's biggest custard cream biscuit in November 2010. The behemoth biscuit measured nearly two feet long and sixteen inches wide, making it more than 140 times the size of a standard custard cream.

LARGEST GRAND PIANO CAKE

In April 2010, workers from Confection Bakery in Kalamazoo, Michigan, made a 300-pound cake that looked like a baby grand piano. The record-breaking cake, which was supported on wooden legs, measured four feet wide, six feet long and five feet high, and had to be transported in sections. It took three weeks of planning and 183 hours to make.

MOST EXPENSIVE SLICE OF TOAST

A ten-year-old stale toasted cheese sandwich sold on eBay for $28,000 in November 2004 because the bread was said to bear an image that resembled the Virgin Mary. To be honest, it could just as easily have been Marilyn Monroe but Catholicism sells better. The sandwich was made by Diane Duyser, from Hollywood, Florida, who noticed the burned image as she was about to tuck into it in 1994. She told reporters: "I went to take a bite out of it, and then I saw this lady looking back at me. It scared me at first." For the next decade she carefully preserved the bread in a plastic box before deciding to auction it online, although she warned potential buyers that the sandwich was "not intended for consumption". After frenzied bidding, it was bought by internet casino GoldenPalace.com whose CEO, Richard Rowe, praised the slice of toast to the heavens, saying: "We believe that everyone should be able to see it and learn of its mystical power for themselves."

MOST EXPENSIVE PIECE OF HALF-EATEN FRENCH TOAST

An unfinished piece of French toast that had been briefly munched on by Justin Timberlake sold on eBay in 2000 for $3,154 – less than twenty-four hours after being put up for auction. Timberlake had been appearing with *NSYNC on the *Z Morning Zoo* radio show, but only took one bite out of his breakfast. Seeing this, an enterprising employee retrieved the remaining toast and put it up for sale, along with the fork Timberlake had apparently used. You know you're a star when you eat toast with a fork. The partly chewed toast was bought by rabid *NSYNC fan Kathy Summers, a student at the University of Wisconsin, who said she would "probably freeze-dry it, then seal it . . . then put it on my dresser."

MOST EXPENSIVE PIECE OF USED CHEWING GUM

A wad of used gum said to have been chewed by serial masticator Sir Alex Ferguson during his last match as manager of Manchester United in May 2013 sold almost immediately on eBay for nearly $640,000. The listing read: "Used chewing gum: RARE. Recovered from The Hawthorns. Clear Perspex/wooden case. Unofficial merchandise, rumoured to belong to Sir Alex. After 1,500 games of intense chewing as manager of Man Utd, here lies Fergie's last piece of chewing gum." There was no confirmation as to how the saliva-infused item of memorabilia was obtained – although it is hard to imagine it being prised from Ferguson's mouth – or indeed whether it was genuine, but all proceeds from the sale were supposed to be going to charity, so that's fine. In neighbouring Yorkshire, elderly locals talk about the sale to this day and can often be heard muttering "eBay gum".

MOST EXPENSIVE CORN FLAKE

Sisters Melissa and Emily McIntire, from Virginia, sold a corn flake shaped like the state of Illinois for $1,350 on eBay in 2008. It was bought by Texan Monty Kerr as part of his Americana collection. He had previously bought a corn flake billed as the world's largest, but by the time it was delivered it had crumbled into three pieces. The sisters' success prompted a wave of copycat items for sale, including corn flakes shaped like Hawaii and Virginia and a potato crisp shaped like Florida.

MOST EXPENSIVE CHEESE SANDWICH

Michelin-star chef Martin Blunos, from Bath, unwrapped a £110.95 ($170) cheese sandwich at the 2010 Frome Cheese Show in Somerset. It used bespoke Cheddar cheese blended with white truffles, quail eggs, black tomato, epicure apple and fresh figs. Furthermore it was dressed with 100-year-old balsamic vinegar and the sour dough bread was sprinkled with edible gold dust. But at heart it was still a cheese sandwich – and a bloody expensive one at that!

MOST EXPENSIVE BRUSSELS SPROUT

A Brussels sprout named Nicholas that was left over from Christmas dinner was sold by Teesside teenager Leigh Knight for $2,100 on eBay in 2006 to raise money for a cancer charity. Knight explained: "I was washing up on Christmas Day and there's always something left in the pan. I just thought it would be a fun idea to put the sprout on eBay."

MOST EXPENSIVE WATER

A few tablespoons of water left in a plastic cup from which Elvis Presley sipped while introducing his backing band at a concert in Greensboro, North Carolina, in 1977, sold on eBay in 2004 for $455. Fan Wade Jones, then thirteen, saw Presley drink from the cup and kept it after a guard had handed it to him as a souvenir. He lovingly stored the water in a freezer until 1985 before placing it in a sealed vial. However, he refused to sell the Styrofoam cup. Some things are just too precious to part with.

OLDEST HOT CROSS BUN

A hot cross bun baked on Good Friday 1821 has been kept in a box as a family heirloom for 193 years – and it still has the cross on top, has retained its smell and shows no sign of mould. It has been passed down through five generations and is currently (or should that be currantly?) owned by Nancy Titman, from Deeping St James, Lincolnshire, whose great-great-great-grandfather William Skinner originally made the bun at his London bakery in the same year that Napoleon died, George IV was crowned King, and John Constable painted *The Hay Wain*. Nancy said: "It is rock hard like a fossil and the currants have disintegrated, but it still smells and looks like a hot cross bun. It was given to me by my mum who said bakers used to believe that buns baked on Good Friday didn't go mouldy, which this has proved. It's a rather unusual family heirloom, but I'm proud of it and we still get the bun out of its box every Easter." A rival claimant to the title recently emerged in the form of a hot cross bun kept by Andrew and Dot Munson in a cardboard box at their home near Colchester, Essex. They were given it over thirty years ago by a neighbour, along with an envelope claiming that the bun was baked as far back as 1807, which, if verified, would make it the world's oldest hot cross bun. It could develop into a bunfight between the two.

OLDEST FRUITCAKE

The world's oldest fruitcake was baked in 1878 by Fidelia Bates and is still in her family today. She always baked a cake for Thanksgiving, but when she died before the 1878 holiday, her family could not bring themselves to eat it and decided to keep it instead. In 1952, the care of the cake passed into the hands of her great-grandson, Morgan Ford, of Tecumseh, Michigan, who took it to a class reunion, a funeral, and on board a plane. In 2003, he took the cake onto Jay Leno's TV talk show, where Leno was brave enough to take a small bite. He said it smelled good but tasted crystallized, which is about the best you could expect from a 125-year-old cake.

OLDEST WEDDING CAKE

A wedding cake baked in 1898 and which is on display at the Willis Museum, Basingstoke, Hampshire, is still complete and even moist. The icing on the ornate, four-tier cake has turned brown where sugars have seeped through to the surface and there is a crack down the side due to vibration from a World War II bomb blast, but tests with a syringe have revealed the rich fruit cake beneath the icing to be moist, if no longer edible. The cake was originally displayed in the window of family bakery C.H. Philpott until the shop closed in 1964, and was then kept in an attic by the baker's daughter, Ruby Philpott, before being given to the museum. Miss Philpott, who was unmarried, donated the cake towards the end of her life because she was worried that someone might discover it in her attic and think that she had been jilted at the altar.

OLDEST EDIBLE HAM

In 1993, Oxford butcher Michael Feller paid £900 (nearly $1,500) at auction for a ham that was 101 years old. He said it looked "rather yukky" but apparently remained edible although, in deference to its longevity, he decided against cutting into it and putting his mouth where his money was. Today the ancient ham hangs in the shop window, unnibbled, at the ripe old age of 123. A rival meat, cured in 1902 before being donated to the Isle of Wight County Museum in Smithfield, Virginia, lays claim at 113 to being the world's oldest edible cured ham. Although a special casing has protected it from bugs and mould, those who have seen the American ham say it looks like a piece of old leather and doubt whether it would actually be edible. As the BBC patriotically points out: "To most people 'edible' means more than the ability to eat something without it killing you." Ultimately the only way of determining which is the oldest edible ham is to have a transatlantic taste-off – with teams of paramedics standing by.

OLDEST TUB OF LARD

When student Hans Feldmeier, from Rostock, Germany, was given a tin of Swift's Bland Lard in 1948 as part of an American aid package sent to the war-ravaged country, he chose to put it to one side and save it for an emergency. The emergency never arose, and in 2012 Feldmeier, by now an eighty-seven-year-old retired pharmacist, decided to send the sixty-four-year-old tin of lard, which had no expiry date, to be tested by food safety experts. They pronounced it fit for consumption – if a little gritty and tasteless. Feldmeier said: "I just didn't want to throw it away."

OLDEST SURVIVING McDONALD'S

Built in 1953, the oldest surviving McDonald's restaurant is located in Downey, California, and as such attracts visitors from all over the world. It was only the third McDonald's ever built, the previous two having been demolished. It still has the towering presence of McDonald's original mascot "Speedee" (before he was brutally ousted by the scary Ronald

McDonald in 1967), who embodied the chain's goal of fast service. Staff there also wear 1950s-style uniforms with paper hats, and the menu retains old-fashioned hamburgers, cheeseburgers and milkshakes, but naturally the prices are bang up to date.

FASTEST AEROPLANE EATER

French showman Michel Lotito (aka Monsieur Mangetout – "Mr Eat Everything") ate metal and glass for around forty years, regularly munching his way through two pounds of metal a day – and with no ketchup! He was born at midday on 15 June 1950 – halfway through the middle day of the middle month of the middle year of the twentieth century – and became convinced that this gave him superhuman powers. His idiosyncrasy first manifested itself at the age of nine when he started eating parts of the family TV set, and by 1997 he had swallowed nearly nine tons of metal, each meal invariably preceded with a drink of mineral oil and washed down with copious amounts of water. These acted as a lubricant to help the metal slide down his throat. He claimed to suffer no ill-effects nor did he experience any problems passing the material at the other end.

In the course of his career he devoured eighteen bicycles (including the spokes), fifteen shopping trolleys, seven TV sets, six chandeliers, two beds, countless plates, razor blades, cutlery, vinyl records and coins, a pair of aluminium skis, a computer, a 400-metre-long steel chain and a coffin (handles and all). This is believed to be the only instance of a coffin ending up inside a man rather than the other way around. But Lotito's greatest claim to fame came in 1978 when, in Caracas, Venezuela, he set about eating a Cessna 150, his theory being that a light aircraft would make a light snack. Eating a few pieces each day, it took him two years to finish the entire plane. Mystified by his ability to eat absolutely anything, medical experts discovered that the lining of his stomach and intestines was twice the thickness of the average person. As a result, while he could merrily eat usually indigestible objects, his digestive system was unable to cope with soft foodstuffs such as eggs and bananas, which made him sick. He died in his home city of Grenoble in 2007, aged fifty-seven, of natural causes.

MOST SOFAS EATEN

Mother-of-five Adele Edwards has not so much a sweet tooth as a suite tooth. For whereas most people get their sugar fix via biscuits or ice cream, Edwards, from Bradenton, Florida, gets hers by eating cushions. She estimates that over a period of twenty years she has munched her way through eight sofas and five chairs, consuming sixteen stone of lovely foamy cushions in the process. "I was ten years old when I was first introduced to cushion," she said in a 2011 interview. "At first I thought it was strange but after sucking it for a while I came to like the texture. To me, the foam tasted like sweets." Soon she began eating large chunks of foam "as though it was candy floss" with the result that she eventually had to undergo an emergency operation to remove lumps of cushion from her intestines. When her supply of cushions is temporarily exhausted, she tucks into other household items, such as elastic bands and rubbers. That's erasers, not condoms – that would be too weird.

FIRST PEOPLE TO TAKE TEA ON TOP OF A HOT-AIR BALLOON

In 2001, Australian stuntmen Julian Saunders, Ross Taylor and Rob Oliver gave a new meaning to the term "high tea" when they became the first people to sit down for a cuppa on top of a floating hot-air balloon. Before they could brew up, they had to climb on top of the balloon as it soared 500 feet above Melbourne, and afterwards they calmly abseiled down the side of the balloon and back into the basket.

FIRST RESTAURANT STAFFED ONLY BY TWINS

On 14 November 1994, twin sisters Lisa and Debbie Ganz (and actor Tom Berenger) opened a New York City restaurant called Twins, which is staffed by thirty-seven pairs of identical twins who work the same shift in identical uniforms.

LARGEST UNDERWATER DINNER PARTY

On 22 September 2007, 500 people set a world record for the largest underwater dinner party when they dined on a three-course meal of smoked salmon, crab with asparagus, and hazelnut praline while sitting at tables four feet below the surface of the swimming pool of London's Park Club. Everyone dressed up for the occasion in formal dinner jackets or ball gowns, although the fashion statement was compromised somewhat by the heavy belts they were obliged to wear to keep them in their seats and stop them floating away. The food was prepared in jelly to prevent it disintegrating in the water, but even so each bite was quite a performance with the guests having to remove their aqua lung from their mouth, insert the food, then replace the aqua lung and press a button that purged water so that they could breathe and swallow. Consequently each course consisted of just one ice cube-sized chunk of food, which meant that most people's first impression of underwater dining was that it leaves you hungry.

CHAPTER 5

That Sporting Spirit

FASTEST MARATHON AS A PANTOMIME HORSE

Disguised in their alter ego of Bonzo the pantomime horse, Surrey brothers Bill and Tom Casserley trotted around the 2012 London Marathon course in 4 hours 49 minutes. "The heat was unbearable and Bill's neck was very sore," said Tom, a PE teacher at Reigate College, who formed Bonzo's front quarters. "We went out at a ten-minute-mile pace and did the first half quite quickly. We really started to struggle in the second half and the last five miles was just sheer grit to get through. Not being able to see was one of the hardest things because we kept bumping into people." Seconds after crossing the finish line, the horse's back half (Bill) collapsed from exhaustion but was later reported to be in a stable condition.

LONGEST SCARF KNITTED WHILE RUNNING A MARATHON

Forty-one-year-old David Babcock completed the 2013 Kansas City Marathon in 5 hours 48 minutes while knitting a 12-feet-2-inch-long scarf, thereby shattering Susie Hewer's record of knitting a comparatively modest 6-feet-9-inch scarf while running that year's London Marathon. Asked what possessed him to combine the two disciplines, Babcock said: "I thought distance running and knitting could go together well. They both take a long time and they are both kind of tedious. I thought it would be a fun challenge."

FASTEST MARATHON ON CRUTCHES

Michael Milton, a one-legged Australian athlete, completed the 2013 Gold Coast Marathon on a pair of custom-made, carbon-fibre crutches in a time of 5 hours 28 minutes 59 seconds, breaking the previous world record for a full marathon on crutches by over an hour. A six-time Winter Paralympic gold medallist in skiing, it was his first ever attempt at a marathon.

FASTEST MARATHON ON STILTS

In October 2013, Neil Sauter set a new benchmark for speed stilt walking when he completed the 26.2-mile course at the Grand Rapids Marathon in Michigan in a time of 5 hours 56 minutes 23 seconds, breaking his own world record by over half an hour. Sauter suffers from a mild case of cerebral palsy but finds that this actually helps him with stilt walking. "The leg muscles in my calf are constricted, causing my feet to turn inward, and my heels to raise when I walk. Because of this, I'm pretty clumsy. But when you wear stilts, your feet are strapped in tight, which keeps my heels down and my feet turned straight. For most people, walking on stilts would be harder than regular walking; for me, I'm much more coordinated on stilts than on my own two feet." Even so, it took him a lot of practice – and quite a few falls – to get it right. One day he hopes to break the five-hour barrier. It could be a tall order.

FASTEST MARATHON WHILE SKIPPING

Thirty-year-old Chris Baron, from Oakville, Ontario, Canada, ran the 2007 ING Ottawa Marathon in 4 hours 28 minutes 48 seconds while skipping with a rope. In doing so, he broke his own world marathon skipping record by over 20 minutes.

FASTEST MARATHON WHILE TOSSING A PANCAKE

After his proposal to run fifty miles with a python around his body was rejected by Guinness for being "a little too unique", Mike Cuzzacrea from Lockport, New York, decided to pursue the world record for running a full marathon while tossing a pancake. The reasoning was that there was almost certainly less risk of being crushed to death by a pancake than by a python. He broke the existing record at his fifth attempt in 1990, but it was nine years later, on 24 October 1999, that "The Pancake Man", as he had become known, completed the Casino Niagara International Marathon from Buffalo, New York, to Niagara Falls, Canada, in a time of 3 hours 2 minutes 27 seconds, a record that stands to this day. As fresh pancakes proved too fragile to survive the rigours of a twenty-six-mile run, he instead used two microwaved pancakes which he stuck together with a combination of clingfilm and glue.

FASTEST MARATHON WHILE WEARING A DEEP-SEA DIVING SUIT

In 2002, Lloyd Scott, a former goalkeeper with Blackpool, Watford and Leyton Orient, walked the London Marathon course in 5 days 8 hours 29 minutes wearing a 130-pound 1940s deep-sea diving suit. He removed the glass from the helmet to enable him to breathe and made slits in the suit so that he could go to the toilet. He wore out one set of lead boots, each weighing 22 pounds, halfway round the course and was forced to replace them. In terms of the race, he finished 32,875th.

FASTEST MARATHON CRAWLING AS BRIAN THE SNAIL FROM *THE MAGIC ROUNDABOUT*

The intrepid Lloyd Scott also crawled the entire length of the 2011 London Marathon course in twenty-six days dressed as 1960s children's television's most famous mollusc. Coincidentally his average speed of one mile per day also earned him the record for the world's slowest marathon. Inside the nine-foot-long snail costume was a sledge on which Scott lay face down while propelling himself along – inch by inch – with his knees and toes. On the way he suffered cramp, a bout of vomiting and a trip to Accident and Emergency for a severe nosebleed. He said afterwards: "I kept being sick in the snail. The big problems have been the weather because it gets very, very hot inside, and then there are the deposits that are left on the pavement – glass, nails, takeaway meals, dog poo . . ." Scott has also completed the London Marathon as St George pulling a 200-pound dragon and as Indiana Jones pulling a 350-pound boulder which was so unstable it almost dragged him into the River Thames. When awarded the MBE in 2005 for his services to charity, he said it should stand for "Mad, Bonkers and Eccentric".

FASTEST MARATHON DRESSED AS ELVIS

British-born Ian Sharman is generally regarded as the world's fastest Elvis for his achievement in running the 2012 Napa Valley Marathon in California in a time of 2 hours 40 minutes 53 seconds while wearing a black Elvis wig and a white jump-suit. It was Sharman's fourth record-breaking run as Elvis. An accomplished athlete in his own right (Sharman, not Elvis), he reckons that wearing a costume adds around two minutes to his race time and notes that the Elvis outfit in particular is "not good for sweating". He has also run marathons as Santa Claus, Maximus from the movie *Gladiator* (with a costume that included a mask, a sword and knee-length sandals), and Spider-Man. "It's basically whatever costume I happen to have from parties," explains Sharman. In one race as Spider-Man, he had to cut a hole in his mask so that he could take on nourishment, and on at least two occasions it has rained, something this particular spider does not appreciate. "It's like being waterboarded," he says, "because the Spider-Man mask is just covering your face and your nose, and you're trying to breathe while running fairly hard. But the crowd's reaction makes it worthwhile because when you're the first costumed runner to come through, you always get a huge cheer."

FASTEST MARATHON DRESSED AS AN EYEBALL

Emma Denton, a thirty-seven-year-old musician from Cam, Gloucestershire, gave new meaning to the term "roving eye" by running the 2014 London Marathon in 3 hours 52 minutes dressed as a human eyeball. In doing so, she not only became the world's fastest-ever eyeball but she also beat the previous record for the quickest marathon by a female body organ by 36 minutes.

FASTEST MARATHON DRESSED AS A VEGETABLE

Twenty-seven-year-old Edward Lumley completed the 2012 London Marathon in 2 hours 59 minutes 33 seconds while dressed as a carrot. To claim the record, he beat five other athletes dressed as vegetables, including, appropriately, one man dressed as a runner bean.

FASTEST MARATHON DRESSED AS A FRUIT

Patrick Wightman, a twenty-three-year-old financial consultant from Sevenoaks, Kent, ran the 2011 Barcelona Marathon in 2 hours 58 minutes 20 seconds dressed as a banana. He said he chose a banana costume because it was the most streamlined fruit shape he could find.

FASTEST MARATHON DRESSED AS A FAIRY (MALE)

While dressed as a purple fairy, complete with wings, tutu and a rather fetching wand, thirty-eight-year-old Martin Hulbert, an insurance manager from Wigston, Leicestershire, ran the 2012 London Marathon in 2 hours 49 minutes 44 seconds. He said afterwards: "It's a real honour to be the world's fastest fairy."

FASTEST MARATHON DRESSED AS A BABY (MALE)

Competing in his sixth marathon, thirty-one-year-old lawyer Ali King, from London, ran the 2014 London Marathon dressed as a baby in 2 hours 51 minutes 18 seconds.

FASTEST MARATHON IN A WEDDING DRESS

Bearded Lee Goodwin, from Stoke-on-Trent, set a new record for the fastest marathon in a wedding dress when he ran the 2014 London Marathon in a time of 3 hours 0 minutes 54 seconds. He bought the dress for £20 ($30) from a charity shop and his biggest concern was that the obligatory veil might wrap itself around his neck in windy conditions. Before the event he predicted: "If I'm not the quickest bride on the day, I will certainly be the quickest bride with a beard." In the same race, Londoner Sarah Dudgeon, displaying markedly less facial hair, set a women's world record by completing the course in 3 hours 16 minutes 44 seconds while wearing an ankle-length wedding dress (including veil).

FASTEST MARATHON DRESSED AS A LEPRECHAUN

Wearing a leprechaun costume, Kent's Ben af Forselles finished the 2010 London Marathon in a time of 3 hours 9 minutes 40 seconds to become the world's fastest leprechaun. It was no small feat as he had to beat four other leprechauns in the race to claim the record.

FASTEST MARATHON DRESSED AS A VIKING

Having set his leprechaun record, forty-three-year-old Ben af Forselles went from one end of the intimidation scale to the other at the 2011 London Marathon by setting a new world record for the fastest marathon run by a Viking. He completed the course in 3 hours 12 minutes 11 seconds wearing full Viking regalia, including horned helmet, furry leggings and cape and carrying a plastic axe. He did, however, wear trainers, which, as some historians might point out, is not strictly authentic Viking costume.

FASTEST MARATHON DRESSED AS A GIRAFFE

Twenty-one-year-old Jean-Paul de Lacy, from Wokingham, Berkshire, was head and shoulders above the rest of the field as he ran the 2010 London Marathon in a time of 5 hours 55 minutes 11 seconds strapped to a twenty-three-foot-tall giraffe costume (mostly neck). The outfit was made using a carbon fibre pole attached to a small inflatable swimming pool at the base while the head was made of papier-mâché. De Lacy said: "The previous record for the tallest outfit in a marathon was 14 feet, so I wanted to beat that, but when making the giraffe with my friends it just got out of hand and kept getting bigger and bigger. I had to start the race from the back because they were worried about me falling over, and tunnels along the route were also a problem. I had to crawl through a couple of them as the outfit was about 10 feet too tall!"

FASTEST MARATHON IN A GAS MASK

Reservist Lance Corporal Andy MacMahon, from Inverness, Scotland, completed the 2012 London Marathon in 3 hours 28 minutes 38 seconds while wearing a gas mask. In doing so he broke the world record for the fastest marathon wearing a functioning gas mask that was set by US Staff Sergeant Marc Dibernardo, from Clarksville, Tennessee, who ran Hawaii's

2011 North Shore Marathon in 3 hours 49 minutes 42 seconds. Dibernardo has been running in shorts, T-shirt, shoes and a gas mask since 2003 to raise money for soldiers who have been wounded in combat. In January 2014, he took things a step further by completing a 235-mile bike ride from Fort Campbell to Frankfort, Kentucky, while wearing his trusty gas mask.

FASTEST MARATHON WHILE JUGGLING A FOOTBALL

Dr Jan Skorkovsky ran the 26.2 miles of the 1990 Prague City Marathon in 7 hours 18 minutes 55 seconds while juggling a football the whole way. The following year, on 6 April, the good doctor, evidently in a rich vein of form, set another world record by walking 2 miles 90 yards with a table tennis ball balanced on his head, in Zurich, Switzerland. It took him 34 minutes 36 seconds, but in fairness he would have been a lot quicker without the table tennis ball.

FASTEST MARATHON WHILE DRIBBLING A BASKETBALL

American chemistry professor Mark Ott ran the 2010 Martian Marathon in Dearborn, Michigan, in 3 hours 23 minutes 42 seconds while dribbling a basketball the entire way. He first came up with the idea of the basketball to relieve the monotony of doing endless laps around an indoor gym.

FASTEST THREE-LEGGED MARATHON

After an accident left him with a broken back, Irish solicitor Colin Carroll established himself as a sporting icon by becoming Ireland's first sumo wrestler and winning a gold medal at the 2005 World Elephant Polo Championships in Nepal, in the process becoming the first left-hander to play elephant polo. His interest in non-mainstream sports then led him to found the Paddy Games, an alternative Olympics featuring events such as bathtub races, backwards running, the high dive belly-flop and the 100 metres egg-and-spoon race.

In June 2008, Carroll and running partner John Meade, a civil engineer, broke the three-legged marathon world record by completing the Cork Marathon in 3 hours 25 minutes 22 seconds. This shaved fifteen minutes off the time set by identical twins Alastair and Nick Benbow at the 1998 London Marathon. What made the Irish duo's performance all the more remarkable was that they had only met six weeks before the race, after Carroll's original running partner pulled out with an injury. On a mission to take silliness seriously, Carroll appealed for a replacement and found Meade's stride a perfect match for his. Their exploits were captured in a documentary, *A Tale of Three Legs*.

FASTEST MARATHON BACKWARDS ON ROLLER SKATES

Germany's Jörn Seifert completed the full 26.2 miles of the 2005 Berlin Marathon backwards on roller skates in a time of 1 hour 43 minutes 29 seconds.

FASTEST MARATHON UNDERWATER

This is another record for Lloyd Scott who, in 2003, walked 26.2 miles along the bottom of Loch Ness wearing his antique diving suit. It took him twelve days, and at one point when he felt something grab his foot he thought he may have stumbled across Nessie. Therefore it was something of an anticlimax when he realized he had merely caught his foot in an oil drum.

MOST RUBIK'S CUBES SOLVED WHILE RUNNING A MARATHON

Germany's Uli Kilian solved 100 Rubik's Cubes while completing the 2011 London Marathon in 4 hours 45 minutes 43 seconds. As it was too heavy to carry 100 cubes in a rucksack, he had friends and family placed strategically around the course to give him twenty unsolved cubes at a time and collect the solved cubes. When not running, he can solve a cube in 31 seconds.

FASTEST MARATHON RUN BACKWARDS

Germany's Achim Aretz ran a full marathon backwards in 3 hours 42 minutes 41 seconds at Frankfurt/Main in 2010. Germany is very much the hotbed of backwards running – or retro running as the sport prefers to be known. Aretz first got into it when he woke up with a hangover one day and went jogging with a friend. His friend ran backwards because Aretz – with his sore head – was so slow, and soon the two of them started running backwards all the time. "When I am running alone," he said, "I have to look back maybe every 10 metres, but when I am running together with my friends, they tell me what lies behind me and they can warn me." He went on to set a new world record for running the half marathon backwards, finishing 123rd at a race in Essen, apparently undeterred by the fact that the other 463 runners were running forwards. However in 2012, at the height of his fame, the twenty-seven-year-old geosciences student announced that he wanted to head in a new direction because he was tired of being mocked by children and chased by dogs. The retro running world held its breath when Aretz heretically declared that in future he would only be running forwards.

MOST PEOPLE TO FINISH A MARATHON TIED TOGETHER

A group of thirty-four friends tied together by bungee cord formed a giant green caterpillar that completed the entire 2010 London Marathon course in 5 hours 13 minutes. The caterpillar convoy included Princess Beatrice who, wearing a bright green tutu, became the first member of the Royal Family to run the London Marathon.

FASTEST RUNNING WAITER

Swiss-born Roger Bourban holds no fewer than five world records for being the fastest running waiter. He has run a marathon in 2 hours 47 minutes (London, 9 May 1982), 20,000 metres in 1 hour 14 minutes 58 seconds (Paris, 18 October 1981), 10,000 metres in 36 minutes 56 seconds (Beverly Hills, 9 December 1979), 5,000 metres in 17 minutes 44 seconds (Beverly Hills, 5 December 1982), and 1,000 metres in 2 minutes 59 seconds (Beverly Hills, 4 December 1983). In each instance he had to be dressed as a waiter and carry an open bottle of mineral water on a tray. Even though he was not allowed to touch the bottle during the race, not once did he spill so much as a drop. A restaurateur and chef whose hobby is sport, he began running competitively in 1976 when the first annual waiters' races were held in California. He went on to win more than 200 international waiters' races while his 1982 record-breaking marathon time would have won the first four Olympic marathons, where runners were not encumbered with carrying a tray and bottle.

FASTEST HALF-MARATHON WHILE PUSHING A VACUUM CLEANER

In October 2013, baked bean aficionado Captain Beany (aka Barry Kirk) completed the thirteen miles of the Cardiff Half

Marathon in 4 hours 1 minute 57 seconds while pushing an upright vacuum cleaner, setting a new record for a vacuum-a-thon.

FASTEST 10K RUN WHILE PUSHING A PRAM

New Zealand distance runner Dougal Thorburn pushed a three-wheeled child carrier containing his two-year-old daughter Audrey over a distance of ten kilometres in a time of 32 minutes 26 seconds in a race at Outram in October 2012, slicing almost two minutes off the previous world record. While Dougal lapped up the plaudits, his wife Amy was quick to praise young Audrey's role, pointing out that if she had needed a nappy change at any point during the run his time would have been considerably slower.

FASTEST 5K RUN WHILE DRESSED AS A PENGUIN AND JUGGLING

In March 2013, Pete "The Juggler" Moyer, from Hillsboro, Illinois, ran a five-kilometre race in a time of 24 minutes 41 seconds while wearing a penguin costume and juggling three balls. He has held a number of other juggling world records, including the longest time juggling while hula hooping (1 hour), the longest time juggling three raw eggs while lying down (13 minutes 26 seconds) and the most hatchets juggled while hula hooping next to a statue of Abraham Lincoln (3).

FASTEST MILE ON A POGO STICK

New Yorker Ashrita Furman hopped a mile on a pogo stick in 12 minutes 16 seconds at Iffley Fields, Oxford, in July 2001 – close to the track where Roger Bannister had run the first four-minute mile (without a pogo stick) back in 1954. Furman also holds the record for the fastest mile on a pogo stick while juggling three balls. He completed that particular challenge in 23 minutes 28 seconds in his home city in September 2007.

FASTEST MILE HOPPING ON ONE FOOT

Joseph Scavone, Jr, a thirty-year-old truck driver, hopped a mile on one foot in 23 minutes 15 seconds at Hamburg, New Jersey, on 23 June 2012, knocking over four minutes off the world record set by Ashrita Furman in 2006. Scavone started hopping as a means of rehabilitation after seriously rupturing his Achilles tendon in an indoor soccer game in 2009, and said the fatigue from hopping over such a long distance meant that it was a constant struggle to keep his balance and stop falling over. So he could not understand why so many people treated his feat as a joke. "It's a kind of comical thing," he admitted, "but it was extremely hard to do. People knew that, but they'd still joke about it." Maybe it has something to do with the hopping.

FASTEST MILE HOPPING ON ONE LEG AND JUMPING ROPE

Describing it as one of the most painful things he had ever done in his life, Peter Nestler hopped a mile on one leg while skipping rope in 24 minutes 44 seconds at Tulsa, Oklahoma, on 4 December 2013. He said: "This event is torture! Pick your least favourite leg and get ready to beat it up because once you start, you can't touch the other foot to the ground at all. Seriously, I would not suggest *ever* trying this. Now that I've done this record, it will go in the dustbin of history and will not be attempted again."

FASTEST TIME TO HOP TWENTY METRES
WITH A TENNIS BALL BETWEEN TOES

At Wollongong, New South Wales, on 12 July 2011, Paul Burleigh hopped for twenty metres with a tennis ball between his toes in a time of 12.5 seconds. In case you're struggling to grasp the concept, he hopped on his right foot and held the ball between the toes on his left foot. Gripping the ball with the hopping foot would prove challenging to the point of nigh on impossible, which means that as you read this, someone, somewhere in the world, is probably attempting to do exactly that.

FASTEST MILE RUN IN A SACK

The good old sack race that used to be a staple of school sports day inspired the indefatigable Ashrita Furman in May 2007 to see how see how long it would take him to run a mile in a sack. Since he was in Mongolia at the time and thought an animal opponent would make the race more interesting, he decided to race a mile in a sack against a yak! "As with all my records I had been practising for some time," he recalls, "but on the day the high altitude started to affect me. I was huffing and puffing but then I realized the yak was having a tougher time than me." In fact, the yak had to be replaced by a substitute yak at half distance, but even so Furman held on to win by a nose in a time of 16 minutes 41 seconds. Another world record was in the bag – or rather, the sack.

FASTEST MILE RUN ON TWO STOOLS

On 10 October 2004, Germany's Nico Kloos established a new world record in one of sport's lesser-known disciplines, the stool run. Using two bar stools and placing one in front of the other as he walked along the tops, he managed to cover one mile in a time of 5 hours 41 minutes 50 seconds without his feet ever touching the ground.

FASTEST 1,000 METRES WHILE KEEPING A TENNIS BALL AIRBORNE

In 1986, Josef Lochman played keepy-uppy with a tennis ball while running 1,000 metres in 6 minutes 51 seconds at Valašské Meziříčí in what is now the Czech Republic.

FASTEST TRIATHLON WHILE JUGGLING

Combining swimming, cycling and running, the triathlon is seen as one of sport's toughest events. However, the challenge still wasn't stiff enough for Joe Salter who decided to do the whole thing while juggling. In April 2012, in a triathlon at Perdido Key, Florida, the thirty-one-year-old from Pensacola swam a quarter of a mile backstroke while juggling three balls, then cycled 16.2 miles while juggling two balls in one hand and finally ran four miles also while juggling. He completed the course in 1 hour 57 minutes, even beating ninety-nine non-juggling competitors. During the race he made nearly 20,000 throws and catches and only dropped a ball three times – all on the swim. "Swimming was the hardest part," he said, "because I had to swim just using my legs. Plus, swimming in open water makes it harder – it's not like in a pool. Cycling was also quite a challenge. I was going about 17 mph, surrounded by other competitors, and had to toss the balls from one hand to the other when it was time to switch gears." Salter first got into joggling – the act of juggling while running – in 2008 and soon became obsessed with becoming the first man to complete a triathlon while juggling. "For a long time it's been a joke among the joggling community," he admitted, "but after 10 months of training I have shown that it can be done!"

FASTEST 4 x 100 METRES RELAY RUN BACKWARDS

The German quartet of Sebastian Krauser, Stefan Siegert, Roland Wegner and Gene Allen ran the 4 x 100 metres relay backwards – complete with reverse baton changeovers – in a time of 1 minute 2.55 seconds at Neustadt an der Waldnaab in August 2007. Their time was nearly half a minute slower than the world record for running in a more conventional manner, but was much more fun.

FASTEST 100 METRES IN HIGH HEELS

In July 2013, eighteen-year-old Julia Plecher, from Rückersdorf, Germany, ran the 100 metres in 14.53 seconds while wearing shiny golden shoes with 7-centimetre-high heels. Her time was just four seconds outside Florence Griffith-Joyner's world 100 metres record – and Flo-Jo was wearing shoes more suited to the occasion. Plecher has also won a Berlin stiletto race in tottering 8.5-centimetre-high heels after which she advised: "You need shoes which ideally are closed in the front because you run on the front part of the foot. You have to be careful not to slip out. I think sandals would not be too appropriate."

FASTEST 100 METRES IN HIGH-HEEL ROLLER SKATES

Marawa Ibrahim, from Melbourne, Australia, completed the 100 metres wearing a pair of high-heeled roller skates in 26.1 seconds. The multi-talented performer, who operates under the stage name of "Marawa the Amazing", can also twirl 160 hula hoops around her body simultaneously and it is her expertise with hoops that has seen her rise from managing a branch of Topshop to performing before the King of Sweden.

FASTEST 100 METRES ON ALL FOURS

Japan's Kenichi Ito ran 100 metres on his hands and feet in 16.87 seconds in November 2013, basing his distinctive style on the movements of the African Patas monkey. He spent more than a decade perfecting his technique by studying videos of monkeys and making regular trips to the zoo. He has even started walking on all fours in everyday life in the hope that it might one day become a recognized sport. Before he gets too excited, however, he should remember that he is by no means the fastest creature on all fours, a cheetah having been timed at 5.95 seconds for the 100 metres.

FASTEST 100 METRES EGG-AND-SPOON RACE

Australian Olympic champion Sally Pearson broke Ashrita Furman's world record for the 100 metres egg-and-spoon race by clocking a time of 16.59 seconds in Sydney in September 2013. Pearson, who won gold in the women's 100 metres hurdles at the London Olympics, said: "I honestly never thought my first world record would be in the egg and spoon!"

FASTEST 100 METRES HURDLES IN FLIPPERS

In September 2008, Germany's Christopher Irmscher ran the 100 metres hurdles in 14.82 seconds while wearing flippers – or swim fins – on his feet.

FASTEST 100 METRES ON A SPACE HOPPER

While Guinness lists the ubiquitous Ashrita Furman as the current record holder with a time of 30.2 seconds set in New York on 16 November 2004, *The Book of Alternative Records* begs to differ. It states that on 16 November 1985, eleven-year-old Tony Smythe, from Birmingham, England, bounced down a 100-metre course on a space hopper in 28.5 seconds at the Birmingham Students Carnival. Whoever is the true record holder, they both deserve our undying gratitude for selflessly promoting the all-too-frequently overlooked sport of space hopping.

FASTEST 100 METRES WHILE HULA HOOPING

While twirling a hula hoop around his waist, Austria's Roman Schedler ran the 100 metres in 13.84 seconds on 16 July 1994.

FASTEST 100 METRES BY A PANTOMIME HORSE

With Paul Donaghy as the front end and Jared Deacon as the back end, the equine duo galloped to 100-metre glory in a time of 13.23 seconds at Gateshead International Stadium on 6 July 2009 – the fastest-ever sprint by a pantomime horse. Deacon, who has won European and Commonwealth gold medals (as an athlete rather than as a horse), said frankly: "We looked ridiculous, but the training we had to do was tough. We only just broke the record. One thing I do know: the record will be going straight on my CV!"

FASTEST 100 METRES PUSHING AN ADULT IN A WHEELBARROW

On 15 May 2005 at a park in Mareeba, Queensland, future Australian national sprint champion Otis Gowa pushed a wheelbarrow containing forty-one-year-old Stacey Maisel along a 100-metre course in 14 seconds. Injury would eventually curtail his career without him being able to realize his dream of representing his country at the Olympics, but at least he had the (small) consolation of knowing that nobody in the history of world sprinting had ever pushed a wheelbarrow faster.

FASTEST 50 METRES AS A HUMAN WHEELBARROW

Guinness World Records states that the fastest fifty metres by a human wheelbarrow team is 14.87 seconds by Josh McCormack (the wheelbarrow) and Arjuna Benson (the pusher) in Melbourne, Australia, on 9 September 2008.

SHORTEST FUN RUN

A total of 390 people, ranging in age from 3 to 93, took part in a 55-yard fun run around the UK's smallest park on 6 May 2013, making it the world's shortest event of its kind. The 150-year-old Prince's Park in Burntwood, Staffordshire, measures just 30 feet by 15 feet – approximately the size of a traffic island – but that did not stop competitors, including a miniature Darth Vader and a couple of Elvises, from jogging around its triangular course. The fastest finished in just seven seconds and even the slowest took under a minute.

MOST PANTOMIME ANIMALS IN A RACE

More readily associated with the Grand National, Liverpool's Aintree racecourse played host to less elegant four-legged creatures on 15 September 2013 when forty-two pantomime animals – horses, reindeer, bulls, zebras and camels – took part in a charity race. As with the National, there was no shortage of fallers (even though it was on the flat), with one competitor breaking a rib. Senior accounts executive Andrew Thompson, who was the front half of runner-up Viewsonic the Camel, revealed: "It was hot, sweaty and quite difficult to see where we were going. The other handicap was that the back legs were quicker than the front legs."

LARGEST RACE FEATURING COMPETITORS IN KILTS

A total of 1,764 competitors – all wearing kilts – took part in the annual five-mile Perth Kilt Run, staged at Perth, Ontario, Canada, on 23 June 2012. The winner, for the third consecutive year, was nineteen-year-old Kieran Day. The event was first staged in 2010 to mark the 800th birthday of its sister city of Perth, Scotland, where a rival kilt run is held over a distance of five kilometres.

FASTEST HUMAN CRAB WALKER

For the uninitiated, crab walking is the discipline of moving forwards, backwards – or, to be truly authentic, sideways – while sitting with your hands and feet on the ground and your bottom raised off it. In August 2011, teenager Cameron Jones, from Issaquah, Washington, crab-walked a twenty-metre course in 7.84 seconds, smashing his own world record.

LONGEST DISTANCE RUN ON A TREADMILL IN FORTY-EIGHT HOURS

For sheer monotony this record is hard to beat. In August 2008, Irish ultra-distance runner Tony Mangan ran 251.79 miles on a treadmill over a period of two days, thereby eclipsing his own world record, set five years earlier, by 20 miles. Forrest Gump would have been proud of him.

LONGEST DISTANCE WALKED ON BROKEN GLASS

In August 2009, Yorkshire sports coach Nigel Jardine, fifty-six, walked for 27.5 hours on broken glass, covering a world record distance of eighteen miles. Curiously the record walk took place in a local restaurant, and Jardine admitted: "I'm used to walking on broken glass but I suppose the customers at the restaurant weren't used to watching someone do it as they tucked into their meals." For fear that he might suddenly collapse into a diner's sticky toffee pudding, he was allowed a five-minute break every hour to recharge his batteries. Not that he works on batteries; it's just an expression.

LONGEST DISTANCE WALKED WHILE BALANCING A FOOTBALL ON HEAD

On 22 October 2011 in Dhaka, Bangladesh, Abdul Halim walked 9.4 miles while balancing a soccer ball on his head.

LONGEST HANDSTAND WALK ON CRUTCHES IN ONE MINUTE

On 14 April 2013 at the National Stadium in Addis Ababa, Ethiopian athlete Tameru Zegeye performed a handstand walk of 249 feet (76 metres) in one minute while his hands were resting on crutches. Zegeye was born disabled and could not walk for the first fifteen years of his life.

GREATEST HEIGHT CLEARED ON A SPACE HOPPER

According to *The Book of Alternative Records*, the greatest height ever cleared on a space hopper was thirty inches by Janina Pulaski, on BBC television on 26 May 1975.

MOST RUNNERS DRESSED AS GORILLAS

In October 2013, 1,161 competitors wearing gorilla suits assembled at the start line for a five-kilometre fun run in Denver, Colorado. Entry cost up to $99.95 (including gorilla costume) but the runners did get to keep their outfits, which ranged in size from small baby gorillas to extra-large silver-backs, meaning that they would never again be short of something to wear to a fancy dress party. Besides, the annual Denver Gorilla Run is all in a good cause as it aims to raise money for the Mountain Gorilla Conservation Fund.

MOST RUNNERS WEARING INFLATABLE SUMO SUITS

On 28 July 2013, 150 competitors wearing inflatable suits took part in the annual five-kilometre Sumo Run in London's Battersea Park.

FIRST RUNNER TO BEAT HORSE IN
MAN v HORSE MARATHON

When landlord Gordon Green overheard a discussion between two men in his pub, the Neuadd Arms in the mid-Wales town of Llanwrtyd Wells, as to whether a man could beat a horse in a long-distance cross-country race, he decided to test the theory by staging a public event. Thus in 1980 Green organized the first Man v Horse Marathon, where runners competed against riders on horseback over a twenty-two-mile course. In that inaugural race, the first horse home beat the first runner by nearly an hour, a pattern that was repeated every year right up until 2004. With the prize money to any runner who finished ahead of the fastest horse increasing by £1,000 a year, the pot then stood at £25,000 (over $40,500) and, to the amazement and delight of spectators, it was finally claimed by Huw Lobb from South London whose time of 2 hours 5 minutes 19 seconds beat the first horse by over two minutes. That ground-breaking 2004 race also saw a record number of entrants: 500 runners and 40 horses. Gordon Green was particularly excited. "I've always thought someone would do it one day," he beamed, "and today it happened." Three years later, a second human, Florian Holzinger, also won the race by beating the fastest horse, but his time of 2 hours 20 minutes 30 seconds was 15 minutes slower than that of Lobb, whose name will forever be written large in Man vs Horse history.

MOST CONSECUTIVE BOUNCES ON A POGO STICK

On 29 July 2011, James Roumeliotis, from Boston, Massachusetts, set a new world record by bouncing 206,864 times on a pogo stick at Costa Mesa, California – a marathon effort involving 20 hours 13 minutes of non-stop bouncing (apart from the five-minute break every hour allowed by Guinness). Such luxuries were not afforded to an earlier trailblazer, Sussex golf professional Charlie Macey, who, in December 1953, set out to make 1,000 consecutive pogo hops in order to win a £1 bet. Instead he pogoed 12,000 times, starting in the street at Crowborough but, when it started to rain, moving indoors to a pub where he covered about seven miles bouncing around the tiny wooden floored room, all the while singing his theme song "Charlie boy is slightly mad, Charlie boy is crazy, Charlie boy is hopping mad, That's poor Charlie Macey." In the circumstances it is difficult to argue with the veracity of the lyrics.

MOST CONSECUTIVE BACKFLIPS ON A POGO STICK

In Montpellier, France, in May 2013, sixteen-year-old professional Xpogo (extreme pogo) athlete Dmitry Arsenyev, from St Petersburg, Russia, achieved fifteen consecutive backflips on a pogo stick.

MOST TEDDY BEARS THROWN ONTO THE RINK DURING AN ICE HOCKEY GAME

Since the 1993–94 season, fans of Canadian ice hockey teams have celebrated the pre-Christmas period by bringing teddy bears to games and hurling them onto the rink when the home team scores its first goal. The toys are then collected from the ice and given to charity. The Teddy Bear Toss, as it is known, has been warmly embraced by fans of the Calgary Hitmen in particular, and on 2 December 2007 they set a new world record by launching 26,919 teddies onto the ice when Ian Duval scored against the Prince George Cougars.

SHORTEST CRICKET MATCH

A supposed friendly game of cricket between a team of Fijians and Europeans, the latter under the captaincy of the Honourable J.A. Udal, on the island of Taveuni in 1906, was abandoned after just one ball had been bowled. It had dismissed the local high chief who was so irate at being out that it was deemed prudent not to proceed further with the game.

LONGEST RUN-UP FOR A BOWLER AT CRICKET

There were times when legendary Australian fast bowler Dennis Lillee used to start his run-up perilously close to the boundary, but Jason Rawson of Salesbury Cricket Club in Lancashire beat him out of sight in March 2010 with a 1.6-mile run-up. Rawson's run-up began at the Shajan Indian restaurant on the A59 and continued to the Ribchester Road ground, where umpires and players had been in position for twenty minutes. After all that effort, batsman Ian Riley scrambled through for a leg-bye.

LONGEST KICK OF SOCCER BALL

A wayward shot by a ten-year-old boy during a playground soccer match in 2002 sent a football on an unlikely twelve-mile journey. He could only watch in despair as the ball sailed over the seven-foot-high wall at Wilberlee Junior School, Huddersfield, West Yorkshire, and began rolling down a steep hill. A helpful motorist stopped the ball and attempted to return it with a drop-kick, but accuracy deserted him and the ball ricocheted off a wall and into the back of a passing truck, which disappeared into the distance with the driver unaware of his newly acquired cargo. Luckily he discovered the ball at his next stop and, guessing what had happened, returned it to the school half an hour later.

FIRST TEA LADIES TO MANAGE A SOCCER TEAM

Following a spat with the Manchester County Football Association over the eligibility of players, Droylsden FC manager Dave Pace put the club's two tea ladies, Stella and Julia, in charge for all of the team's 1999–2000 Manchester

Premier Cup ties. They guided Droylsden all the way to the final where they beat Mossley, prompting their fans to chant '2–1 to the tea ladies'.

FASTEST SOCCER GOAL SCORED WHILE GOALKEEPER WAS ON HIS KNEES PRAYING

Playing for Corinthians of São Paulo at the Bahia Stadium in the 1970s, Brazilian ace Roberto Rivelino scored a goal from the halfway line after just three seconds . . . while the opposing goalkeeper was on his knees in the goalmouth finishing his customary pre-match prayer. The unfortunate goalkeeper was Isidore Irandir of Rio Preto whose religious ritual was clearly well known to Sr Rivelino. So when the referee blew the whistle to start the match, Rivelino unsportingly shot for goal with his trusty left foot and the ball whistled past Irandir's ear on its way into the net.

SHORTEST SOCCER INTERNATIONAL

Estonia and Scotland were scheduled to play a World Cup qualifying tie in Tallinn's Kadrioru Stadium on the night of 9 October 1996, but when the Scots trained at the stadium on the eve of the match, they were unhappy with the floodlighting and protested to FIFA who decreed that the kick-off should be brought forward from 18.45 EET to 15.00. However, the Estonian FA were unhappy with the late switch and flatly refused to change their plans. So when the Scotland players lined up on the pitch at the revised kick-off time of three o'clock, they found they had no opponents. While the Scottish fans chanted "One team in Tallinn, there's only one team in Tallinn", the Scots kicked off and referee Miroslav Radoman promptly blew his whistle to abandon the game after only three seconds. The Estonian team, who had been having lunch at a hotel, arrived at the stadium later that afternoon to prepare for the original kick-off time. The tie was eventually replayed in neutral Monaco on 11 February 1997 and ended in a 0–0 draw, having arguably featured less action than the curtailed match.

LONGEST SOCCER GOAL SCORED

Just thirteen seconds into the Premier League fixture with visiting Southampton on 2 November 2013, Stoke City goal-keeper Asmir Begović launched a clearance from deep inside his own penalty area. In ordinary circumstances, the twenty-six-year-old Bosnia and Herzegovina international would have expected his effort to reach a little beyond the halfway line but this was an exceptionally windy day, even by Stoke standards, and the tailwind sent the ball sailing ever onwards before bouncing in the Southampton penalty area and flying over the head of opposing goalkeeper Artur Boruc and into the net. The distance was subsequently measured at 100.5 yards and acclaimed the longest goal ever scored. As his jubi-lant team-mates swarmed all over him, Begović had the good grace to look sheepish, explaining afterwards: "It's a cool feeling, but it was a fortunate incident. I felt a bit bad for Boruc. It is a long ball that got caught in the wind and it took a wicked bounce. It's not nice to be on the receiving end of those things as a goalkeeper. It does not make a goalkeeper look good and after it I did not want to celebrate out of respect for him." It was the first goal of Begović's career.

LONGEST HEADED GOAL IN SOCCER

Jone Samuelsen, a midfielder with Odd Grenland, scored a headed goal from a world record distance of 63.5 yards against Tromsø in a Norwegian League match on 25 September 2011. In the last minute of the game with Tromsø trailing 2–1 and pushing desperately for an equalizer, they sent their goalkeeper forward for a corner. The ball was cleared upfield by Odd, then headed back into Odd's half by a Tromsø defender. Standing a couple of yards inside his own half, Samuelsen instinctively headed the ball forward in the general direction of one of his team mates, only for it to bypass everyone and roll on into the unguarded Tromsø net, as the visiting goalkeeper raced back in vain.

SHORTEST BASEBALL PLAYER

Bill Veeck, owner of the St Louis Browns, was one of baseball's great showmen, someone who never rejected a publicity gimmick on the grounds that it might be too tacky. With attendances in decline, his fertile imagination went into overdrive for the 1951 season as he attempted to woo back fans with a succession of free gifts, ranging from cakes to Cadillacs, and orchids to live lobsters. He also introduced an exploding scoreboard which marked every Browns' score by erupting in a dazzling display of fireworks to the strains of Handel's "Messiah". However, his masterstroke was to employ 3 feet 7 inches Eddie Gaedel, who had dwarfism, as the team's secret weapon in the second game of a doubleheader against the Detroit Tigers on 19 August. The rules of baseball stipulate that the ball must be pitched in the zone between the batter's knees and armpits, usually a space of around 2 feet 6 inches, but when Gaedel assumed a tight crouch at the plate, the legal area amounted to only 1.5 inches, making it virtually impossible for the pitcher to hit the target. And lest Gaedel should be tempted to open up his body by swinging at a pitch, Veeck warned him that he had taken out a $1 million insurance policy on his life and would be standing on the stadium roof with a rifle ready to shoot Gaedel if he even looked like he was going to swing. He was probably joking.

While Detroit pitcher Bob Cain was struggling to keep a straight face, his catcher, Bob Swift, was in a kneeling position advising his team-mate to "keep it low". Inevitably Cain didn't manage to keep it low enough and delivered four high balls, allowing Gaedel, wearing the number 1/8 on his back, to move to first base where he was replaced by pinch-runner

Jim Delsing, but not before the 18,369 fans had given the little man a standing ovation. Tigers went on to win 6–2 and the next day American League president Will Harridge voided Gaedel's contract, saying that Veeck had made a mockery of the game, and banned all little people from playing. Veeck responded by claiming that the League's action amounted to discrimination against little people. At first, Gaedel's single-game, Major League record was expunged, but it was reinstated the following year and Veeck went on to use him in further promotions, including selling mini hot dogs at the stadium. Gaedel died in 1961 at the age of thirty-six following a violent mugging in Chicago. His autograph is so rare that it now sells for more than Babe Ruth's.

FIRST ONE-ARMED MAJOR LEAGUE BASEBALL PLAYER

Despite losing his right arm in a childhood accident, Pete Gray played for the St Louis Browns in 1945 – one of only two one-armed men (the other was Jim Abbott) to play Major League baseball. Gray learned to bat and field one-handed, catching the ball in his glove and then quickly removing the glove before transferring the ball to his hand in a single motion. A successful minor league outfielder with the Memphis Chicks, he was named the Southern Association's Most Valuable Player in 1944, earning him a contract with the Browns for whom he played seventy-seven games.

However, even though this was six years before the publicity-crazy Bill Veeck owned the Browns, Gray always harboured the suspicion that he had been employed more as a novelty turn to bring in the crowds. Sure enough, when pitchers exploited his inability to change his timing once he had started his swing – because he had no second hand to check the swing – and began throwing him curve balls, he returned to the minor leagues, plying his trade with, among others, the peculiarly named Toledo Mud Hens. He died in 2002 and his glove is kept in the National Baseball Hall of Fame and

Museum at Cooperstown, New York. Asked once how good he could have been had he not lost an arm, Gray replied: "Maybe I wouldn't have done as well. I probably wouldn't have been as determined."

FASTEST TIME TO VISIT ALL THIRTY MAJOR LEAGUE BASEBALL STADIA

From 6 to 28 April 2012, Chuck Booth visited all thirty Major League baseball stadia and watched the entire game at each venue in just twenty-three days, beating his previous world record by a day. He started in Phoenix, Arizona, and finished in Baltimore, Maryland.

HIGHEST BASEBALL CATCH

In 1939, on his thirty-seventh birthday, Joe Sprinz, who played for the San Francisco Seals at the time, tried to set a new world record for the highest baseball catch by holding on to a ball dropped from a Goodyear blimp hovering 800 feet up in the sky. Sprinz missed the first four balls, but for the fifth he angled his catcher's mitt in perfect position to catch the ball as it hurtled down on him at over 150 mph. The ball did indeed slam into his gloved hand but with such force that it broke his upper jaw in twelve places, fractured five of his teeth, broke his nose and knocked him unconscious. To add insult to extensive injury, he dropped the ball. Given that the hapless Sprinz spent the next three months in hospital, it was perhaps understandable that there was no great rush by anyone else to try and succeed where he had failed. However, an enthusiast by the name of Zack Hample has recently taken up the mantle, and on 13 July 2013, he successfully caught a baseball dropped from a helicopter flying 1,050 feet up at Lowell, Massachusetts, to establish a new record. And because he was wearing full protective gear, he managed to avoid the misfortune that befell poor Joe Sprinz.

FIRST US PRESIDENT TO THROW FIRST PITCH AT A BASEBALL GAME

Two years after Japanese Prime Minister Ōkuma Shigenobu had become the first person to throw a ceremonial first pitch at a baseball game, the ample figure of US President William Howard Taft repeated the feat before the game between the Washington Nationals and the Philadelphia Athletics on 14 April 1910. Realizing that Taft was on to a potential vote-winner, his successors in the White House have maintained the tradition with varying degrees of success. In 1940, Franklin D. Roosevelt's wayward pitch hit a *Washington Post* photographer's camera.

FIRST *STAR WARS* CHARACTER TO THROW FIRST PITCH AT A BASEBALL GAME

Cheered on by Princess Leia and Han Solo, Chewbacca (okay, a man in a Chewbacca costume) threw out the ceremonial first pitch before the Boston Red Sox played the Toronto Blue Jays at Fenway Park on 28 September 2005. Darth Vader similarly tried his hand before the Oakland Athletics' game with the Detroit Tigers on 16 September 2011, but his rather limp pitch suggested that his demonic powers were on the wane. Either that or the gravitational pull in California that night was considerably different from long ago in a galaxy far, far away.

FIRST DINOSAUR TO THROW FIRST PITCH AT A BASEBALL GAME

Baby T, a human-powered miniature Tyrannosaurus Rex from the stage show *Walking With Dinosaurs*, threw the first pitch before the baseball game between the San Diego Padres and the Kansas City Royals on 7 May 2014. Apparently the pitch came up a little short but everyone was willing to overlook that because, after all, it had been thrown by a dinosaur.

FIRST CAT TO THROW FIRST PITCH
AT A BASEBALL GAME

After Tara the tabby cat made international headlines by bravely chasing off a ferocious dog that was attacking her owner, four-year-old Jeremy Triantafilo, in California, she was invited to throw the first pitch before the baseball game between the Bakersfield Blaze and the Lancaster Jethawks on 20 May 2014. Since a cat couldn't really be expected to master the art of pitching a baseball, the ball was pulled along with fishing wire to give the illusion that it was flying – albeit very slowly – through the air. Nobody was exactly fooled, but at least it was a real cat and not some guy in a cat costume.

BIGGEST BASEBALL

On 1 January 1977, house painter Mike Carmichael, of Alexandria, Indiana, took a regulation nine-inch baseball and asked his three-year-old son Mike, Jr to paint it – and as is the way with these things the family has kept on painting it ever since, applying at least one coat every day. By 2013, Mike, Sr and various invited luminaries had added a staggering 23,400 coats, with the result that the ball had ballooned to a circumference of over 125 inches and weighed more than 4,000 pounds, making it both the world's largest ball of paint and the world's largest baseball.

He created his first giant ball of paint in the 1960s after accidentally spilling a tin of paint over the baseball he was playing with. Seeing the paint-covered ball the next day sparked an idea to add more coats, and when he got to 100, he donated it to a children's home. However, the restless artistic spirit kept gnawing away at him and he knew he would have to start another, but on an even grander scale. "Before I knew it, the ball was enormous," he says. "Then I didn't want to stop." As its fame has spread, people come from all over the world to add a layer, the only stipulation being that each new coat must be a different colour to the last. "I have absolutely no idea what I'm going to do with it," he admits, "but have no plans to stop painting it. My grandchildren have expressed an interest in it, so maybe it could become a family heirloom."

FASTEST ROUND OF GOLF

Guinness World Records credits the fastest-ever round of golf to Irishman Jim Carvill who, on 18 June 1987, played the 6,154-yard Warrenpoint Golf Course in just 27 minutes 9 seconds. The rules of the challenge dictated that after each shot, the ball had to come to a complete stop before the next stroke could be played. Carvill, who had trained for the feat by running six miles a day on the course for a year, teed off at 7.30 p.m. and was back in the clubhouse by 8. "I had a pacer who ran with me," he recalled in a 1993 interview. "If I was going slow, he'd push me to go faster. I used 14 clubs, though I didn't carry a bag. Volunteers in the crowd ran 20 yards ahead and handed me the club I needed. I used a 4-wood to stay in the fairway, instead of a driver. I couldn't afford the risk of wasting time looking for a wayward ball." He went round in a creditable eighty-one but was sure that someone would soon break his record, although he warned: "That person had better be on a motorbike to do it!"

MOST HOLES OF MINIATURE GOLF
PLAYED IN TWENTY-FOUR HOURS

Rocky's Fun House indoor miniature golf facility in Waukegan, Illinois, may be a far cry from the historic links of St Andrews, but in March 2011 it was the setting for one of golf's most remarkable achievements. For that was when that staple of a British seaside holiday, miniature (or crazy) golf, found a new devotee in Mick Cullen who set a world record by playing 5,040 holes in twenty-four hours, breaking the previous record of 4,729 with three hours to spare. In effect, the thirty-four-year-old played 280 eighteen-hole rounds during which he managed 570 holes-in-one. Even eighteen hours in, he was still averaging four minutes per round and was helped by having a solid plan, which included taping spots on the course that he needed to hit for bank shots. They tend to frown if you try that at Scotland's home of golf.

LONGEST GOLF PUTT HOLED ON TV

This qualifies as a weird world record not because of the nature of the feat but because of the identity of the holder. You would have thought that the longest putt sunk on TV would have been by one of the all-time greats – maybe Arnold Palmer, Jack Nicklaus or Tiger Woods. Instead the player in question was not even a professional golfer, but US Olympic swimming champion Michael Phelps. In October 2012, playing at Kingsbarns in Scotland, Phelps holed a monster 153-foot putt – a shot which was only slightly shorter than the length of an Olympic swimming pool and which took a full seventeen seconds to reach the hole. Phelps said afterwards: "It was the longest putt I've ever had, and to see it go in was a pretty cool feeling. I will never forget it. I just tried to get it to the top of the rise in the green and I couldn't believe it when it ran down the other side and all the way into the hole." The putt smashed the previous record – also set by a non-golfer, broadcaster Terry Wogan. In 1981, competing in a pro-celebrity contest at Gleneagles in Scotland, Wogan holed a 99-foot putt – a shot so improbable that, as he stood over the ball, commentator Peter Alliss had predicted that the Irishman would need four shots to get down from there.

HIGHEST ALTITUDE GOLF SHOT

On 6 February 1971, *Apollo 14* astronaut Alan Shepard hit two golf balls on the surface of the Moon using the head of a six-iron attached to a lunar sample scoop handle. Due to the constrictions of his space suit, he had to play the shots one-handed. The balls are still up there somewhere, the lack of atmosphere having allowed them to fly, according to Shepard, "for miles and miles and miles".

BEST ROUND OF GOLF WHILE WEARING A SUIT OF ARMOUR

On St George's Day, 23 April 1912, singer and actor Harry Dearth played nine holes at Bushey Hall Golf Club in Hertfordshire while wearing a full suit of armour. Dearth had worn the armour on stage for the role of St George in a production of *The Crown of India*, and for a wager he agreed to lumber onto the golf course in it. The only concession was that he didn't have to wear the visor. His opponent, one Graham Margetson, was more conventionally attired, but despite his heavy metal handicap Dearth played remarkably well, only losing two and one.

LOWEST GOLF SCORE WHILE BLINDFOLDED

On 7 August 1954, Laddie Lucas proved that not seeing is believing when he shot a round of eighty-seven at Sandy Lodge Golf Course, Hertfordshire, while blindfolded.

LOWEST GOLF SCORE AT NIGHT

On the night of 27 December 1930, Rufus Stewart, the golf professional at Kooyonga, Adelaide, played the full eighteen holes of his home course in seventy-seven strokes, guided only by a torch shone by a friend. He teed off at 9.15 p.m. and finished just an hour-and-three-quarters later. He only landed in one bunker – at the unlucky thirteenth – and incredibly he didn't lose a single ball. His driving in the dark was said to be so accurate and his knowledge of the course so profound that he knew within a few yards where the ball would come to rest.

LONGEST USABLE GOLF CLUB

Michael Furrh, a golf professional from Arlington, Texas, drove a ball 146 yards in December 2012 using a club that measured 14 feet 2.5 inches long. Revealing the technique for hitting such an unwieldy club, he said: "Because the club is so heavy and so long with so much width, you really have to wait for it to finish its coil in order to start your downswing. You have to be very patient." On the same day, Furrh hit a drive off a 6-foot-high tee while standing on a ladder.

FIRST HOLE-IN-ONE CAUSED BY AN EARTHQUAKE

A spot of natural assistance is always welcome on the golf course to compensate for all those occasions when trees run out into the middle of the fairway and deflect your ball. James Cash, Jr certainly had the gods on his side while playing the sixteenth hole at Belmont Springs Country Club, Massachusetts, on 18 November 1929. His beautifully struck tee shot came to rest on the very rim of the cup, but just as he was starting to curse his luck, there was a sudden earth tremor and the ball dropped in for an unexpected hole-in-one.

FIRST HOLE-IN-ONE CAUSED BY A BUTTERFLY

Playing at the Bay of Quinte Club, Belleville, Ontario, in 1934, golfer Jack Ackerman was dismayed to see his tee shot stop on the lip of the hole. However, just then a butterfly landed on the ball, causing it to drop in for a hole-in-one.

LONGEST HOLE-IN-ONE

Brett Melson, a twenty-three-year-old student at the San Diego Golf Academy's Hawaii campus, aced the 448-yard, par-4 eighteenth hole at the Ko'olau Golf Club in Oahu, Hawaii, on 1 December 2006. "I knew the ball had reached the green," said Melson afterwards, "but when my friends and I got up there, we couldn't find it. We looked for 15 minutes and I was totally shocked to find it at the bottom of the cup." His shot snatched the longest hole-in-one record away from two-handicapper Robert Mitera who, with the assistance of a 50 mph tailwind, had holed his tee shot at the 446-yard tenth at the aptly named Miracle Hill Golf Club, Nebraska, back on 7 October 1965.

MOST EXTREME PAR-3 GOLF HOLE

Whereas the nineteenth hole at most golf courses is a seat at the club bar lamenting the catalogue of inexplicable misfortunes that bedevilled your round, at the Legend Golf & Safari Resort in Limpopo Province, South Africa, it is a genuine hole that gives new meaning to the term "a tricky par-3". The hole is 641 yards from tee to green, but it is downhill all the way, as the tee, which can be accessed only by helicopter, is perched high on a cliff on Hanlip Mountain and is 400 metres above the green. There is a $1 million prize for any golfer who hits a hole-in-one, but the fact that when you land at the tee you are handed six balls fitted with tracking devices suggests that it is a tall order. Since it costs $1,060 for a foursome to play the hole, the challenge is beyond the reach of most players, but a number of celebrities have tried their luck, including Hollywood actor Morgan Freeman who became one of the first to record a par.

MOST SOUTHERLY GOLF COURSE

Scott Base Country Club, run by the New Zealand Antarctic Programme, is located just thirteen degrees above the South Pole, and players are required to wear full survival gear. As the course is made of solid ice, the players use orange golf balls, which are frequently stolen by skua birds. Under a strange local rule, this incurs a one-shot penalty. Perhaps as compensation, another local rule states that a ball hitting a skua counts as a birdie.

FARTHEST GOLF SHOT CAUGHT IN A MOVING CAR

Ex-Scottish Formula One driver David Coulthard teamed up with young professional golfer Jake Shepherd in May 2012 to set a distinctly unusual world record that combined their respective skills. Shepherd smashed a golf ball at 178 mph off a makeshift tee at Dunsfold Aerodrome in Surrey and Coulthard, at the wheel of an open-topped Mercedes-Benz SLS AMG Roadster, raced down the runway in hot pursuit and caught the ball in the car 300 yards from the tee. Coulthard was still travelling at 120 mph when the ball landed in the car's front seat. Note: most golf clubs will not be happy if you try to break this record on their course.

LOWEST GOLF SCORE THROUGH THE STREETS OF LONDON

In 1939, Tony Milibanke bet London stockbroker Richard Sutton £5 and a set of golf clubs that he couldn't play golf through the heart of the city, from the south side of Tower Bridge to the front steps of White's Club in St James's Street off Piccadilly – a distance of about three-and-a-half miles – in under 200 strokes. On 23 April, Sutton teed his ball up on a bus ticket and, using a putter, smashed the ball forty yards down Tooley Street. Reporting the challenge, the *Daily Mail* noted that Sutton "kept to the gutter" throughout and averaged forty yards a stroke with his trusty putter. Wisely he refrained from using any other club, thereby avoiding the ignominy of a wayward iron shot sailing through an open window and leaving him with an unplayable lie from behind a sofa. By this method he safely crossed the Thames at Southwark Bridge and, despite experiencing a "bit of bother" on the turn from Pall Mall into St James's Street, he arrived at White's in a more than respectable 102 strokes. It then took him another 40 to get up from the gutter to the pavement, giving him a final round of 142 and a successful wager.

FASTEST TIME TO PLAY GOLF FROM SAN FRANCISCO TO LOS ANGELES

Californian teenagers Bob Aube, seventeen, and Phil Marrone, eighteen, played golf in 1974 all the way from San Francisco to Los Angeles – a round of 500 miles. It took them sixteen days and they lost more than 1,000 balls.

FIRST PERSON TO PLAY GOLF ACROSS MONGOLIA

After visiting Mongolia in 2001, New Hampshire civil engineer Andre Tolme's chief impression of the country's barren landscape was that it would make a perfect golf course. So the fifteen-handicapper set about planning eighteen holes that would take him 1,234 miles (a total fairway distance of 2,171,505 yards) right across the country from east to west, bypassing the world's biggest bunker, the Gobi Desert. On 4 June 2003, armed with two clubs, 500 balls, a radio receiver and compass, he teed off on the 138,889-yard first "hole" at Choybalsan near the Chinese border. He completed the first nine in 854 shots, losing 352 balls in the process, but his progress was then blocked by a sea of impenetrable, knee-high vegetation, forcing him to postpone the remainder of his round for a few months. He finally holed out at the eighteenth in the western city of Khovd on 10 July 2004. He had taken 12,170 shots (290 over par), lost 509 balls and played golf for ninety days.

FIRST GOLFER TO PLAY FIVE ROUNDS IN FIVE COUNTRIES IN ONE DAY, BREAKING 80 EACH TIME

Ernest Smith, the thirty-two-year-old professional at Davyhulme Golf Club, Manchester, was bet the princely sum of £100 that he could not play five rounds of golf in five different countries in a single day, scoring under eighty each time. So on 12 June 1939, Smith and his companion Sidney Gleave, a racing motorcyclist and former TT winner, set off on their golfing marathon. At first light at 3.45 a.m., Smith teed off at Prestwick (Scotland) and scored a round of seventy in 1 hour 35 minutes. Then, with Gleave at the controls, Smith flew to Bangor (Northern Ireland), where he teed off at 7.15 a.m. and raced round in seventy-six in 1 hour 30 minutes. Next they flew to Castletown (Isle of Man), teeing off at 10.15 a.m. Here, Smith went round in a score of seventy-six in 1 hour 40 minutes. Then it was on to Stanley Park, Blackpool (England), where they teed off at 1.30 p.m. Smith took seventy-two shots and completed his round in 1 hour 55 minutes. The final port of call was Hawarden (Wales), where they teed off at 6 p.m. With time on his side, Smith took 2 hours 15 minutes to post a course record score of sixty-eight. His average for the five rounds was a remarkable seventy-three. In total, the pair travelled 1,000 miles by plane and car and walked nearly thirty miles around golf courses – sustained solely by a couple of ham sandwiches and a glass of beer.

LONGEST GOLF HOLE

Father-of-four and keen golfer David Sullivan, from Oxted, Surrey, walked the length of Britain – from John O'Groats to Land's End – in 2005, hitting golf balls all the way. He completed his 1,100-mile journey in seven weeks and, having adhered to the rules of golf by hitting each ball from the spot where it landed, promptly claimed that he had therefore played the world's longest golf hole. It took him 247,000 strokes and he lost 293 balls. On the way he played through a wedding party and putted through the centre of Glasgow while hundreds of youngsters queued to see American rapper 50 Cent in concert. After completing the marathon hole, he said: "I've been up mountains, in gardens, chased by bulls . . . you name it. My feet are killing me."

However, his record was smashed in 2013 by Fishers, Indiana, law student Luke Bielawski who played a 2,928-mile hole coast-to-coast across the United States from the beach at Ventura, California, to the shore of Kiawah Island, South Carolina, where he finally "holed out" by hitting a biodegradable ball into the Atlantic Ocean. Like Sullivan before him, he hit each ball from wherever it landed, be it on a mountain, desert or swamp. His preferred surface was a sand and dirt road, and on one ideal track he managed to log sixty-two miles in a single day. Playing for up to fourteen hours a day, he took ninety-three days and an impressively modest (at least compared to Sullivan) 46,805 strokes, although he did lose 5,540 golf balls en route.

MOST HOLES OF GOLF PLAYED IN A YEAR

Between 1 January and 31 December 2012, Canadian-born Chris Adam played a world record 14,625 holes of golf – all at the King Kamehameha Golf Club in Wailuku, Hawaii. Averaging forty holes a day, the 6-feet-6-inch former University of Manitoba basketball player never went more than two straight days without picking up his golf clubs, and on one manic day he somehow played ten rounds. In total he played 809 full rounds and seven half rounds over the course of the year, his fastest round being a whirlwind forty-three minutes. "The thing that kept me going was my pure stubbornness," he said at the end of his mission. "When I put my mind to something I just keep going until it's done. Looking back, it must be the craziest, if not the dumbest, thing I've ever done."

MOST GOLF BALLS HIT IN TWENTY-FOUR HOURS

Simon Jones, a twenty-year-old golf tutor from Hastings, Sussex, hit a world record 10,610 golf balls in twenty-four hours – one every six seconds – at Tonbridge Golf Centre on 21 July 2012. For each ball to count towards the record it had to travel at least 100 yards and land within a thirty-degree arc. In doing so, he broke the record of 10,392 set by Californian David Ogron in 2002. However, Ogron, with the help of his faithful ball-setter Scott "Speedy" McKinney, still holds the record for the most golf balls hit in one minute – 102 on 30 May 2007.

HIGHEST BASKETBALL SHOT

A group of young Australian basketball stars calling themselves How Ridiculous travelled to Rotterdam in the Netherlands in 2013 to land a basket from a height of 321 feet into a hoop on the ground below. Following sixty-two failed attempts from the observation deck of the city's Euromast tower, twenty-year-old Kyle Nebel finally managed to net the record-breaking basket.

FASTEST TIME TO SCORE A BASKET IN THE FORTY-EIGHT CONTIGUOUS US STATES

Three basketball fanatics from Southern California – retirees Richard Paff, John Baker and Jack Davis – embarked on a madcap dash around the United States in April 2010. Their goal was to drive to all forty-eight contiguous (adjacent) states in the fastest possible time and to land a basket in each before swiftly moving on to the next state. Aided by pre-planning on a military scale, they accomplished their 7,000-mile mission in 8 days 5 hours 33 minutes. They found courts in church parking lots, school gyms and city parks and shot hoops day and night, their nocturnal efforts often helpfully illuminated by the car headlights of well-wishers. "I love basketball," said Paff afterwards, "and I love travelling, too. It was a great way to combine my passions."

MOST CONSECUTIVE BASKETS BY HEADING A BASKETBALL

At the 2001 Saxonia Record Festival in Dessau, Germany, Poland's Jacek Roszkowski headed 17 consecutive baskets with a basketball, breaking the previous record of 15 held by Israel's Eyal Horn. During Roszkowski's feat of sporting concentration, the ball did not touch the ground or any part of his body other than his head.

LONGEST BASKETBALL PUNT
INTO A BASKETBALL NET

Seemingly unaware of the rules of the sport, Christian Bullard drop-kicked a basketball from a distance of ninety-six feet straight through a basketball hoop in Beaufort, North Carolina, on 7 June 2012. It may not have earned him any points but it brought him a world record on recordsetter.com.

MOST BASKETBALL BOUNCES IN ONE MINUTE

Nepal's Thaneswar Guragai bounced a basketball a record 444 times in one minute in 2010. In case you're wondering, he trained for it by bouncing a basketball.

LONGEST BASKETBALL DRIBBLE

Pawan Kumar Srivastava, a thirty-two-year-old teacher, dribbled a basketball for 55 hours 26 minutes at Lucknow, India, from 10 to 12 December 2007.

LONGEST SUCCESSFUL BASKETBALL
SHOT WHILE SITTING DOWN

On 23 February 2010, Orlando Magic basketball player Vince Carter landed a basket from 85 feet while sitting down, thereby snatching the world record from team-mate Dwight Howard who had managed a distance of 52 feet 6 inches from a seated position just ten days earlier. Maybe there's a lesson for basketball stars everywhere. Forget all the unnecessary running around, you can do equally well sitting down.

FIRST MALE BOXING CHAMPION TO BE KNOCKED OUT BY A WOMAN

John L. Sullivan, the "Boston Strong Boy", held the world heavyweight boxing title from 1882 to 1892. During that time, he earned a reputation for being able to withstand the most powerful of punches, which makes it all the more remarkable that, when he was finally knocked out for the first time, it was by a woman. By early 1892, Sullivan was just about the most famous boxer in the world. Supplementing his title fights, he toured the theatres of the United States performing in exhibition sparring contests that proved hugely popular with the crowds.

One of his advisers was Charles Converse, who ran a boxing school in Worcester, Massachusetts. Converse was married to an imposing woman by the name of Hessie Donahue who, at her husband's suggestion, was brought in to spar with Sullivan and add a spot of merriment to the roadshow. Sullivan and Hessie came up with an act whereby the champion would insist that he could beat any member of the audience and would offer money to anyone able to defeat him. After seeing off all comers, he would then announce that he had been challenged by a woman, at which point the ample form of Hessie – weighing 160 pounds and close to six feet tall – would climb into the ring wearing boxing gloves, blouse, flowing skirt, long stockings and bloomers. The act went down well until one night, in March, Sullivan made the mistake of not pulling his punches, with the result that he caught Hessie full in the face with a blow. Although her physical presence was such that her pride was hurt more than her cheekbone, the bruiser in bloomers reacted angrily and, completely forgetting the script, lashed out with a right to the jaw, sending the world heavyweight champion tumbling to the canvas, where he remained stunned for the best part of a minute. She later recalled: "John L. Sullivan was out cold as a corpse! He could hear the birdies singing. They were chirping a sweet, sweet song for Big John."

The knockdown became the talk of boxing and created such interest that Sullivan, realizing it was good for business, decided to keep it in the act. Six months later, on 7 September

1892 in New Orleans, he returned to the prizefighting ring for a serious contest, a world title defence against Gentleman Jim Corbett, but in round twenty-one Sullivan was knocked out – for the first time by a man. Hessie Donahue had obviously softened him up.

LONGEST TENNIS RALLY

German professional Frank Fuhrmann and his son Dennis played a tennis rally that lasted for 50,970 strokes at Bayreuth on 20 July 2013. The rally, which went on and on for the best part of seven hours, must have left the adjudicators with very sore necks.

TENNIS GAME WITH MOST DEUCES

On 26 May 1975, a game in the Surrey Grass Court Championships at Surbiton between Keith Glass and Anthony Fawcett contained a world record thirty-seven deuces. Glass had won the first set and the score stood at 2–2 in the second when he began serving the interminable game. Speaking to the *Guardian* in 2010, he recalled: "Judy Dawson – I think she was Judy Taggart at the time – a women's player whom I knew quite well, came on the next court and I nodded to her but carried on serving. And I continued serving . . . and serving. Then I noticed she was shaking hands on the next court, and I thought: 'That's funny, someone must have been injured.' But she had won 6–0, 6–0, and I was still serving the same game!" Glass eventually won that game – no one thought to time it – but the exertion of serving for so long had taken its toll and he went on to lose the set and, fairly quickly, the match.

LONGEST BOWLING STRIKE

On 4 May 2014, Joey Augustine, manager of Seaside Lanes Bowling Alley in Virginia Beach, Virginia, made a strike from 120 feet – double the length of a standard bowling lane. At only his sixth attempt to bowl the fourteen-pound ball from the alley entrance, right across the carpeted floor and down the lane, he succeeded in knocking down all ten pins. Having discovered that he couldn't curve the ball on the carpet, his biggest concern was making sure the ball bypassed a table and ottoman.

HIGHEST SCORE MADE WHILE BOWLING BACKWARDS

Bowling facing the pins is too boring for Andrew Cowen, of Rockford, Illinois. So he started bowling with his back to them and on 2 January 2014 he recorded a score of 280 points in a single game that included ten straight strikes and broke the previous world backwards bowling record of 278 set by Jim Cripps in 2006. Cowen has actually bowled a 300 maximum facing the right way, but decided to change tack partly for the pleasure of doing something different but also to protect his knees. "My knees aren't in the best shape," he says, "but when I throw backwards it doesn't really affect them because there's no knee bend. But the best thing about bowling backwards is it's a lot of fun. A lot of people come up to me and say, 'Hey, that's really neat.'"

FIRST FORMULA ONE DRIVER TO PUSH HIS CAR TO THE WORLD CHAMPIONSHIP

Approaching the final race of the 1959 Formula One season, the United States Grand Prix at Sebring on 12 December, three drivers were still in with a chance of taking the World Drivers' Championship – Australia's Jack Brabham and Britons Stirling Moss and Tony Brooks. Championship leader Brabham appeared to be coasting to the title with a comfortable lead in the race until, with barely a mile to go, his usually reliable Cooper-Climax suddenly started to run on only two cylinders. Then the engine went dead, and the awful truth dawned on him – he had run out of fuel, having resisted his team's pleas to start on full tanks because he thought he could obtain more speed from a lighter car.

As Brabham slowed to a crawl, his young team-mate, New Zealander Bruce McLaren, who had been running second, slowed down to see what the problem was, but Brabham waved him on, knowing not only that any outside assistance would result in disqualification but also that Brooks could still snatch the title if he won. Brabham's car finally came to a halt some 500 yards from the finish, and he knew he had no option but to get out and push. To make matters worse, it was a hot, sunny Florida day and the finish straight was uphill.

Up at the finish, spectators were puzzled by Brabham's non-appearance until in the distance someone spotted a figure in blue overalls hunched over the car and pushing it. As Brabham inched nearer to the finish line, the crowd went wild and police motorcyclists had to hold them back. Meanwhile, the man with the chequered flag waved it to encourage the thirty-three-year-old Australian. After five minutes that must have seemed like five hours, Brabham pushed the stricken car across the line in fourth place and promptly collapsed with exhaustion. However, he had the satisfaction of knowing that, with Brooks only finishing third, the points he had earned had been enough to clinch his first world championship.

FIRST FORMULA ONE DRIVER WITH THREE EARS

Many sportsmen carry strange items in their pockets, usually to bring them good luck, but the needs of charismatic French racing driver Jean Behra (1921–59) were more practical. In 1955, his right ear was severed by the lens of his goggles in a crash during the Tourist Trophy race at Dundrod, Northern Ireland, and thereafter he had to wear a plastic ear in its place. And, just in case history should happen to repeat itself, Behra always kept a spare plastic right ear in his pocket. As a party piece, he used to enjoy scaring the mesdemoiselles by removing his ear at an opportune moment – a chat-up line which is surely unique in the annals of civilization.

MOST DRAG RACING EVENTS ATTENDED BY A DEAD MAN IN ONE YEAR

When Californian drag racer "Wild" Willie Borsch died of lung cancer in 1991, it was by no means the end of his participation in the sport. For every year after that, his best pal and former mechanic, Al "Mousie" Marcellus, would attend at least thirty races carrying Borsch's cremated remains in a foot-high silver urn. "Some people think it's morbid, but it's not," said Marcellus in a 2004 interview. "He goes to the races all the time and people come up and give him their respects, pat him on the urn and say hello. I see no harm in that."

LOWEST HEIGHT CLEARED WHILE LIMBO SKATING BLINDFOLDED

In May 2009, nine-year-old Rohan Ajit Kokane, from Belgaum, India, did the splits so that he could roller-skate underneath a car with a clearance of just 6.75 inches while blindfolded. In 2011 in Mumbai, he also set the world record of 126 feet 11 inches for the longest distance limbo skated underneath vehicles (without a blindfold) when he flattened his body to pass under a line of twenty cars. However, that record has since been broken, most recently in July 2014 by six-year-old Gagan Satish, from Bangalore, India, who roller-skated under thirty-nine cars, covering a distance of almost 230 feet.

LONGEST BACKWARDS LIMBO SKATING

In July 2009, another boy from Belgaum, flexible seven-year-old Abhishek Navale, limbo skated backwards for a distance of sixty-two feet under a series of bars that were just 8.7

inches above the ground. In the same month, he also roller-skated backwards under a line of ten Tata Sumo Jeeps. Practising his skills for two-and-a-half hours every day, he had previously skated 335 miles from Bangalore to Belgaum in six days. "He can skate with his body almost touching the ground," said his proud father Sanjay, a local bus conductor.

LONGEST PIROUETTE IN FIGURE SKATING

Swiss ice skater Nathalie Krieg pirouetted for an impressive 3 minutes 32 seconds for a German TV show on 11 October 1992. She said she only stopped because she was worried that viewers would find it too boring if she carried on.

MOST CONSECUTIVE DAYS SKIING

It's one thing to enjoy skiing, but fifty-year-old Rainer Hertrich, a German-born snowcat operator at Copper Mountain, Colorado, is so committed to the sport that he skied every single day for eight years, two months and ten days. He skied for 2,993 consecutive days, covering 98 million vertical feet in that time, until the diagnosis of a dangerously irregular heart-beat stopped him in his tracks on 10 January 2012. Having previously defied a separated shoulder, bruised ribs and count-less days of sickness to take to the slopes, he was distraught at having to end his unbroken run. "I was shooting for 3,000 days," he said, "which was only a week away. Or what I really wanted to do was hit 100 million vertical in 100 months, which would have been February 29. It's a bummer."

MOST CONSECUTIVE DAYS SURFING

Every day since 3 September 1975, Dale Webster has made it his mission to surf at least three waves in Bodega Bay, California. He had originally planned to call it quits on 29 February 2004 after 10,407 consecutive days, but he found that he simply couldn't stop and in September 2014 the sixty-five-year-old notched up thirty-nine years of surfing – 14,245 days straight.

During the original record-breaking stint up to 2004, he battled hurricanes, sharks and kidney stones, went through thirty boards and twenty-eight wet suits, never took a vacation, accepted poorly paid night jobs so that his days would be free for surfing and postponed his wedding for ten years. He found time to attend the birth of his daughter (he went surfing in the morning and she was born in the afternoon) but regretted never being able to visit his in-laws in Utah, although some might see that as a blessing. "I feel so funny sometimes being this complete creature of habit," he said in 2011. "I remember coming home one night from some midnight job I had and there was this ad on the TV describing OCD symptoms. This infomercial nailed me; I'm this surfer that has to do this routine every day. It'll die when I die." And his recipe for success? "I always take a shit before I go surfing." Thanks for sharing that with us, Dale.

MOST SANTAS SURFING SIMULTANEOUSLY

More than 210 surfers dressed as Santa Claus took to the waves off Cocoa Beach, Florida, on Christmas Eve, 2013. It was the fifth year of the Surfing Santas event, which had begun in 2009 when organizer George Trosset went surfing by himself dressed as Santa. He quickly realized that if you're going to make a fool of yourself, it is no bad idea to surround yourself with other fools.

MOST SANTAS SCUBA DIVING SIMULTANEOUSLY

Also on Christmas Eve 2013, 175 Santas (quite probably different Santas from those in Florida, even allowing for the speed of sleigh travel) took to the freezing waters on the other side of the Atlantic at Vobster Quay, in Avon, England, to set a new record for the most scuba-diving Santas.

FARTHEST TARGET HIT BY A CONTORTIONIST ARCHER FIRING AN ARROW WITH FEET

Just as Ginger Rogers was said to be able to do everything Fred Astaire did backwards and in high heels, so Inka Siefker can do everything Robin Hood did, but with her feet and while doing a handstand. In August 2013 on the Los Angeles set of a Guinness World Records TV show, Siefker, a twenty-six-year-old contortionist based in San Francisco, got into a handstand position and, firing the bow with her feet, burst a four-inch balloon attached to a target twenty feet away . . . with her first shot. Although she has hit a target thirty feet away in practice, she was relieved to burst the balloon at the first attempt in front of Guinness officials and a live audience – particularly because, unable to look down the line of the arrow as it is positioned a couple of feet above her head, her normal strike rate is only one in four.

LONGEST BOOMERANG THROW

Although the boomerang was originally designed for hunting birds or mammals as large as a kangaroo, these days it is generally used for sport. On 15 March 2005, British-born David Schummy set a new distance record by hurling a boomerang 1,401.5 feet at Murarrie Recreation Ground, Queensland, Australia. "It wasn't really a boomerang throw," admitted Schummy, "as it didn't come back. But it was enough to set a Guinness World Record."

LONGEST THROW OF A RETURNING BOOMERANG

Boomerangs come in two types: returning and non-returning. When you hurl one into the distance, it is useful to know which type you have. In 1999, Switzerland's Manuel Schütz threw a boomerang a world record distance of 780 feet out and the same distance back.

MOST CONSECUTIVE CATCHES OF A BOOMERANG

Japan's Haruki Taketomi made 2,251 consecutive catches of a boomerang in March 2009. It took him 11 hours 41 minutes.

SMALLEST RETURNING BOOMERANG

At the 1997 Australian National Championships, Sadir Kattan flew a tiny boomerang measuring 1.9 inches long and 1.8 inches wide a distance of 66 feet before it returned to him.

FIRST STREAKER AT A MAJOR SPORTING EVENT

The first recorded streaker at a major sporting event was Michael O'Brien, a twenty-five-year-old Australian, who ran stark naked across the pitch during the rugby international between England and France at Twickenham on 20 April 1974. He was apprehended by PC Bruce Perry who promptly tried to spare TV viewers' blushes by covering O'Brien's genitals with his helmet. The helmet – the policeman's, not the streaker's – is on display at Twickenham's World Rugby Museum.

FARTHEST KUDU DUNG SPIT

Kudu dung spitting – or Bokdroel Spoek – is such a popular sport in South Africa that it has its own national competition, and in 2006 Shaun van Rensburg spat a lump of kudu dung a world record distance of fifty-one feet. Contestants use either kudu or impala dung pellets and can spit them from a stationary position or with a run-up, the distance being measured according to where the dung finally comes to rest rather than where it first hits the ground. Before the spit, competitors traditionally drop the dung in a shot of alcohol to help sterilize the bacteria. Experts say the secret is to find a nice hard pellet and not to let it melt on your tongue.

Even so, the whole experience of Bokdroel Spoek can leave a nasty taste in your mouth.

FARTHEST CHERRY PIT-SPIT

Football had the Charltons, cricket had the Chappells, and Formula One had the Hills, but when it comes to world-class cherry pit-spitting, the Krause family have always been the ones to beat. Rick "Pellet Gun" Krause was a sixteen-time champion, and when the years of spitting cherry stones finally took their toll, his son Brian "Young Gun" Krause took it to a new level with a spit of 93 feet 6.5 inches at the 2004 International Cherry Pit-Spitting Championship at Eau Claire, Michigan. Later that day, and away from the strict rules that govern the sport, the twenty-six-year-old managed to spit a pit an astonishing distance of 110 feet 4 inches in the freestyle event, but it was not recognized as a true world record because he did not remain flat-footed when launching his spit.

Each contestant gets three tries and has one minute between spits to eat the fruit off the cherry. As height is considered an advantage in cherry pit-spitting – except on windy days – taller competitors have to stand further back. The championship was first staged in 1974, and Rick Krause made his mark in 1980, picking up his first title. Brian, then aged three, made his debut the following year. For the next three decades, the Krauses pretty much reigned supreme, until in 2012 first-time unknown Ronn Matt, a Chicago delivery driver, rocked the sport to its foundations by lifting the title. It was like a Shetland pony winning the Grand National. Brian Krause was heard to mutter: "Every squirrel finds a nut once in a while."

In 2013 the natural order was restored, however, with a third Krause – Brian's younger brother Matt "BB Gun" – claiming the crown. As he went up to accept the world championship belt and trophy for the first time, his father yelled: "Now I can stop telling everyone you're adopted!" It can be tough being part of the world's most famous cherry pit-spitting dynasty.

FARTHEST TOBACCO SPIT

Randy Ober, from Bentonville, Arkansas, was a seven-times winner of the annual Calico Tobacco Chewing and Spitting Championships, held near Barstow, California, and set a world record distance of 47 feet 7 inches on his first attempt in 1982. He went on to break that record in 1986 with a spit of 53 feet 3 inches during a charity fundraiser with the Los Angeles Rams football team. He explained the secret behind good gobbing in a 2008 interview. "I would roll my [tobacco] wads up and dry them out on the windowsill, so they would be real hard. They wouldn't come apart that way. Most of the spitters would just pull a wad out of a pack and press it together and spit it, and heck, it would just fly apart when they'd spit." Eventually Ober decided that spitting tobacco, even as a world record holder, did little for his image, and so he retired gracefully from the sport.

FARTHEST GOLF BALL SPIT

On 12 February 2010, Brian Jackson spat a golf ball a distance of 18 feet 6.75 inches at Tahlequah, Oklahoma. His motto in life is "I believe I can do anything", a claim he chose to illustrate on 17 June 2012 by setting the fastest time to burst a balloon through a 100-metre-long fire hose (53.2 seconds). You can't help thinking that if he really can do anything, finding a cure for the common cold might be more useful.

FARTHEST SNAIL SPIT

It is no great surprise that the hotbed of snail spitting is France, home to the World Snail Spitting Championships, an event which in 2004 attracted more than 2,000 spectators and 100 participants from fourteen countries. Competitors roll the live snails around in their mouths, take a twenty-metre run-up and then spit the creatures as far as they can. How many snails survive the ordeal is not known. The winner that year was forty-three-year-old fisherman and seaweed collector Alain Jourden with a spit of 30 feet 9 inches, although unfavourable wind conditions on the Brittany coast meant that he was unable to break his own world record distance of 34 feet 1 inch, a spit which broke the all-important ten-metre barrier. Jourden said he always trained hard for a week before the competition, carrying out several spits a day. Hopefully not in company.

FARTHEST CRICKET SPIT

Cricket spitting made its debut on the sporting calendar in 1997 thanks to the foresight of Tom Turpin, an entomologist at Purdue University in West Lafayette, Indiana, who devised it as a competition for the university's annual Bug Bowl, a feast of insect-related events. Dead brown house crickets weighing between 45 and 55 milligrams are the insect of choice in cricket spitting, having been frozen and thawed specially for competition. Contestants must spit the cricket within twenty seconds of placing it in their mouth, although it is hard to imagine that this is a rule that many would try to break. Even so, some unscrupulous individuals have been known to bite off the odd leg or wing in order to make the cricket lighter and therefore travel farther, but Turpin warns them against such underhand practices because "it's not cricket". Therefore to maintain the integrity of the sport, judges check each spat cricket to make sure that it is intact. Only spat crickets with six legs, four wings and two antennae are counted as legal.

The official world record is held by Danny Capps, of Madison, Wisconsin, who spat a dead cricket a distance of 32 feet 0.5 inches on 26 June 1998. He has recorded a spit of 47 feet in competition but it was wind-assisted. His trick of the trade is to coat the cricket with saliva while it is in his mouth and then expectorate it head-first in a spiral. However, in a 2001 interview he admitted that really it was just a question of blowing hard. "We're talking about a limp, dead thing that doesn't give you any assistance. It isn't very aerodynamic."

MOST SKIPS OF A STONE ACROSS WATER

Most people who turn their hand to skipping stones across a lake or the sea can consider themselves lucky to muster half a dozen skips, but on 19 July 2007, Russ Byars, a forty-three-year-old test engineer from Franklin, Pennsylvania, blew his rivals out of the water with a record-breaking fifty-one skips. He reckoned that single stone travelled 250 feet from the moment it left his hand. Experts analysed film of his effort frame-by-frame, checking the concentric circles left in the water by each hop – or, as stone skippers say, by the plinks and pitty-pats. "I actually threw 40 stones that day," said Byars, explaining that patience and perseverance are key weapons in the stone skipper's armoury, "but that was the first skip that I threw."

He favours smooth, round stones, between three and four inches across, which he grips with his thumb and forefinger curving around the perimeter. He prefers not to bend down in the traditional crouch. Instead he takes a one-step run-up and then stands and delivers the stone with a sidearm release and an abundance of spin and follow-through. Those who have investigated the science of stone skipping have calculated that an angle of twenty degrees to the horizontal is ideal for a skipping stone to enter the water. For Byars, who was inspired to enter his first stone skipping contest solely by the prospect of winning fudge, there was only one downside to his record skip – the absence of Renee, his wife, muse and "only groupie". She turned up late and missed the vital throw. It's no way to treat a world champion.

LONGEST PEA THROW

If pea shooting requires a little too much skill, why not try the alternative sport of pea throwing? The World Pea Throwing Championships have been held in Lewes, Sussex, since the 1990s. Each competitor throws three frozen peas (supplied by the organizers) down a lane, the winner being the one whose pea travels the farthest, either along the ground or airborne. The rules state that there shall be no kicking, spitting, blowing, batting, slapping or punching. The current world record, set by local resident Mike Deacon in 2009, stands at 144 feet 4 inches.

LONGEST EGG THROW

The earliest recorded instance of egg throwing in Swaton, Lincolnshire, occurred back in 1322 when the swollen river prevented the local peasants from getting to church to receive their customary egg, forcing the resourceful abbot to lob the eggs across the river instead. As such, the village is the obvious venue for the World Egg Throwing Championship, which, as befits its grand title, attracts teams from far and wide, including Japan, USA, the Netherlands, Australia, Germany, South Africa, the Czech Republic and Brazil. It takes two to play – a thrower and a catcher. The thrower hurls the raw egg as far as possible for the catcher to collect without breaking it. In May 2013, chucker Wild Willie O'Donovan set a new world record at the Irish National Championship in Connacht with a throw of 233 feet 6 inches (71.2 metres). O'Donovan is also an Irish Road Bowling champion (a sport where competitors lob a heavy steel ball along a three-mile road course in the fewest possible throws), and he successfully adapted that underarm lob technique to egg throwing. The distance record was previously held by the Dutch, who take their egg throwing very seriously indeed. When a Dutch pair became the 2012 world champions, it made front-page news back in the Netherlands. Sadly this enthusiasm is not replicated in the UK where in 2011 Sport England rejected a bid by the event's organizers to have egg throwing recognized as an official sport. The WETC's Andy Dunlop complained: "Egg throwing and catching involves three distinct skills – throwing the egg, catching it, and catching it without breaking it. Other so-called sports like javelin and throwing the hammer are just playing."

LONGEST TUNA TOSS

In January 1998, former Olympic hammer thrower Sean Carlin hurled a dead tuna a distance of 37.23 metres (just over 122 feet) at the annual tuna tossing festival in Port Lincoln, South Australia. The town boasts Australia's largest tuna cannery, and the fish used in competition weigh between 8 and 10 kilograms (17 and 22 pounds).

LONGEST FRUITCAKE TOSS

Observing that friends never seemed to want to eat fruit-cakes they had received as Christmas gifts, Michele Carvell, former chamber of commerce director for Manitou Springs, Colorado, came up with a wizard wheeze for disposing of the unwanted foodstuff – a sporting contest. Thus in 1996 was born the Great Fruitcake Toss, an event which, in its heyday, attracted up to 1,000 fruitcakes every January. The world record was set at the 2013 event when Joe Jeanjaquet tossed a ten-pound fruitcake a distance of 415 feet at the local high-school playing field.

There is no subtle way of putting this, but Jeanjaquet is a hand tosser; he propels his cake by hand. However, a separate arm of the contest was latterly opened to mechanical devices, some of which would not have looked out of place at NASA. These were capable of launching fruitcakes far and wide to distances beyond measurement. In 2013, one official distance was recorded as "destination unknown". While these launchers may have enhanced the fruitcake-tossing spectacle, they also contributed to the event being cancelled in 2014. Leslie Lewis of the Manitou Springs chamber of commerce explained: "These more powerful fruitcake launchers had begun to send cakes into residential areas. When you hit businesses and houses it's not a good thing."

LONGEST VINYL DISC THROW

Former German heavyweight boxer Axel Schulz set a sort of record record by hurling a vinyl disc a distance of 477 feet 4 inches – the ultimate long player. Think how much further he would have thrown it if it had been by Justin Bieber.

LONGEST COMPACT DISC THROW

Germany's Kim Flatow managed to propel a compact disc a distance of 119 feet at a festival in Flensburg in 1998 – further proof that CDs are never as good as vinyl.

LONGEST HAGGIS HURL

At the 2011 Bearsden and Milngavie Highland Games, nineteen-year-old Lorne Coltart hurled a one pound eight ounce haggis a mighty 217 feet, shattering the world record of 180 feet 10 inches which had been held by Alan Pettigrew since 1984. In fact Coltart's throw was so huge and unexpected that officials charged with measuring the distance ran out of white tape. Haggis hurling requires a subtle technique rather than sheer brute force as the haggis must still be edible after landing. A split haggis results in instant disqualification. Plans to use a fake haggis in a hurling competition at a Highland festival in Melbourne, Australia, divided the purists from those who were fearful of the mess caused by a high-impacting specimen of Scotland's national dish. The idea was to create a simulated haggis in the form of a bag packed with sand or oatmeal, but as one diehard, butcher Rob Boyle, said witheringly: "If there's no haggis, how can it be haggis hurling? I'm a traditionalist. If you have an egg-and-spoon race you don't use a golf ball."

LONGEST THONG THROW

The English language is fraught with potential hazards depending on what part of the world you happen to be in. Just as Durex in Australia refers to the UK's Sellotape or US's Scotch Tape, so what Australians call "thongs" we in the UK call "flip-flops", which means that you can go up to a girl on Bondi Beach and admire her thong without getting your face slapped. The rules of Australian thong throwing state that the footwear must be a size 10, made of rubber, and weighing 145–150 grams. After a run-up not exceeding ten paces, the shoe is propelled from a circle and must fall within an arc of thirty-five degrees to be deemed legal. The current world thong-throwing record stands at 140 feet 4 inches and was set in Pomona, Queensland, by a local man (whose name sadly seems to have disappeared with the sands of time) at the King of the Mountain Festival.

LONGEST CLOG THROW (BACKWARDS)

Every Easter, hundreds of people flock to the Roebuck Inn in Rossendale, Lancashire, to witness a demonstration of the little-known sport of clog cobbing. Standing on a path next to the pub, competitors throw their clogs backwards over their heads, and whoever hurls their footwear the farthest is declared the winner. The World Clog Cobbing Championships were first staged in the early 1960s and the current record holder is local rugby player Andy "Taff" John who chucked his clog a distance of ninety-three feet in 2006.

LONGEST GUMBOOT THROW

For such a basic sport, the origins of gumboot throwing are shrouded in mystery. Some say it began in rural Finland in the early part of the twentieth century; others claim that welly wanging (as it is known in the UK) was first practised in Yorkshire; and to muddy the waters still further, the town of Taihape in New Zealand, which stages an annual Gumboot Day, calls itself the gumboot-throwing capital of the world. Where there is a sport, there is a world championships and an international organization, in this case the International Boot-Throwing Association (IBTA), founded in 1998. The IBTA stipulates that in competition men must throw a size 43 boot (left or right), women and older children a size 38, and children under ten a size 33. Apart from removing the strap in the top of the leg, the boot must not be tampered with in any way – for example, the leg must not be rolled back on top of the foot. To obtain maximum distance, it is also advisable to remove the boot from the wearer's foot. The target that every competitor is trying to beat is the world record of 214 feet 4 inches set by Finland's Jouni Viljanen on 22 May 1999. The sport has become so popular in Sweden that participants have developed unorthodox styles of throwing, such as between the legs and from behind the back. This has produced a number of personal injuries, resulting in warnings from doctors about the very real dangers of gumboot throwing.

LONGEST COW PAT THROW

As if living somewhere called Beaver was not sufficient to provoke sniggers from the outside world, the Oklahoma town is also home to the World Cow Chip Throwing Championships – the greatest showcase for the noble sport of tossing pieces of dried cow dung. The contest was first held in 1970 and the world record throw of 185 feet was achieved by Robby Deevers back in 2001. Competitors travel from as far afield as Australia, Japan and Germany and, mercifully for airport customs staff, they do not need to bring their own cow pats with them. Instead an official on-site dung wagon supplies the disc-shaped projectiles, which must be at least six inches in diameter. Any competitor who attempts to tamper with a chip to make it more aerodynamic automatically incurs a twenty-five-foot penalty. There are various other cow pat throwing contests in the United States, but any red-blooded male will always head straight for Beaver.

LONGEST FRYING PAN THROW

If Germany's Jürgen Schult thought that the pinnacle of his career was winning gold in the discus event at the 1988 Seoul Olympics, he was probably right. Nevertheless it would be remiss of us to overlook the sensational world record he achieved eighteen years later when he hurled a frying pan a distance of 156 feet 1 inch at a sports meeting in Schwerin.

LONGEST ROLLING PIN THROW

When it was discovered that Stroud, England, and Stroud, USA, both had brickworks, a brick throwing contest was held in 1960 to cement relations between the two towns. Then it emerged that there were two other Strouds – in Canada and Australia – and so the following year they were included in the international brick throwing event. For 1962 the Australian Stroud proposed that while the men threw bricks, women should have a separate contest for throwing something more traditionally associated with them. Since nobody could lay their hands on a tantrum, it was decided that the women should throw a two-pound rolling pin. The pin is usually hurled discus-style, and, even though the contest has now been going for over half a century, the record throw of 156 feet 4 inches was set as far back as 1977 by Sherri Salyer Peckham from the American Stroud. Incidentally, the men's brick throwing record dates right back to 1970 when Robert Gardner from Stroud, England, produced a mighty throw of 142 feet 6 inches.

LONGEST PAPER PLATE THROW

Alan Thomas, from Yeovil, Somerset, set a new world record for paper plate throwing when he achieved a distance of 50 feet 8 inches (without wind assistance) on 10 August 1990. It should be noted that there was no food on the plate at the time as even a cocktail sausage or a leftover cheese and pineapple chunk would have seriously hampered the flight.

LONGEST MOBILE PHONE THROW

When his mobile phone stopped working, New Zealand javelin thrower Ben Langton-Burnell decided that instead of just throwing it away he would try and throw it the length of an athletics field to set a new world record. He promptly hurled the offending Nokia N5 a distance of 395 feet 8 inches in March 2013, breaking the existing record by 60 feet. "It just missed a TV cameraman," said Langton-Burnell, "so I think it's definitely written off now." A rumour recently surfaced that a mobile phone was thrown over 400 feet after going off repeatedly in the quiet coach of the 7.55 from York to London, but this has yet to be confirmed.

LONGEST BILLIARD CUE THROW

For reasons best known to himself, Dan Kornblum threw a billiard cue, javelin-style, a distance of 141 feet 4 inches in Flensburg, Germany, in 1998.

LONGEST PICKLE FLING

The town of Berrien Springs, Michigan, hosts an annual Pickle Festival, the sporting highlight of which is the World Famous Pickle Fling where competitors hurl pickles down Main Street. The record fling of 297 feet was set by local boy Vince Rago in 1995.

LONGEST DWARF TOSS

In the mid-1980s, some of the less enlightened bars in America played host to a controversial new sport – dwarf tossing – where little people wearing protective clothing were hurled as far as possible by patrons who were invariably drunk. As the landing sites were lined with mattresses, none of them were hurt physically, and indeed it was reported that some made over $100,000 a year for the privilege of being thrown around. Nevertheless, the sport was banned in the US in 1989 but has continued surreptitiously in other parts of the world. Not surprisingly, the world record is unofficial, but sources claim that one Jimmy Leonard, a bouncer and truck driver, won the 2002 British Dwarf Throwing Championships by tossing the late Lenny Fowler (aka Lenny the Giant), a 4 feet 4 inches, 98-pound British dwarf, a distance of 11 feet 5 inches at a pub in Surrey. However, in Australia, where they tend to use shorter dwarfs, the record is believed to be nearer 30 feet. In New York, dwarf tossing spawned a spin-off sport, dwarf bowling, where the little person was placed on a skateboard and used as a bowling ball.

LONGEST KNOB TOSS

Every May, more than 5,000 excited onlookers gather in the village of Cattistock, Dorset, to watch others toss their knobs. It should be explained at this point that the knob in question is a spherical savoury biscuit that has been made locally since 1880, and that the object of the exercise is to throw it under-arm as far as possible while keeping one foot on the ground. The world record was set in 2012 by Dave Phillips who tossed his knob a distance of 96 feet. That's something to tell his grandchildren. Or perhaps not.

FIRST PERSON TO JUMP THE GREAT WALL OF CHINA ON A SKATEBOARD

Professional skateboarder Danny Way made history on 9 July 2005 by becoming the first person to jump the Great Wall of China without motorized assistance. Flying down a ramp at 50 mph, he leaped over a sixty-one-foot gap and landed safely on a ramp built on the other side of the wall – even though he had a broken foot after suffering a bad fall the day before. It took the thirty-one-year-old American the best part of a year to plan a jump that was all over in a few seconds. After the successful vault, he was officially presented with a piece of the wall.

MOST JUMPS OVER A CONCRETE HIPPOPOTAMUS

In March 1979, sixteen-year-old John Simpkiss leaped over a concrete hippo statue in Walsall town centre 1,111 times in what was hailed at the time as the Hippo Leaping World Championships. The hippo, which was designed by local architect John Wood at a cost of £500 and unveiled in 1972, is affectionately known as George after the pink hippo on the children's TV series *Rainbow*. There were plans to demolish it in the 1990s and replace it with another piece of art, but by then it had become a popular meeting point, particularly among young people, and the townsfolk demanded that it stay. Recently 3,000 people have joined a Facebook group to post pictures and express their love for the hippo. Group founder Heidi Ashley described the webpage as being "for anyone who ever sat on his back, played around him or chose him as a meeting place, or just damn well loves that funky hippo!"

FIRST PERSON TO WIN THE WORLD'S CHAMPIONSHIP DUCK CALLING CONTEST WITHOUT ARTIFICIAL AID

The inaugural World's Championship Duck Calling Contest was staged on Main Street in Stuttgart, Arkansas, on 24 November 1936 and the first prize – a hunting coat worth $6.60 – was won by Thomas E. Walsh, who raised ducks at his home in Greenville, Mississippi. Rather than use an artificial duck call, Walsh, having evidently studied the birds at close quarters, impressed the judges by creating a lifelike quacking sound from the back of his throat. In the long and distinguished history of the championships, which involves performing a hail call, a mating call, a feed call and a comeback call – all within 90 seconds – he is one of only two people to take the title without resorting to artificial aids. In case you are wondering, the other competitor to go *au naturel* was Herman Callouet, the 1942 duck calling champion. Coincidentally he, too, hailed from Greenville, Mississippi. It must be something about birds of a feather . . .

HIGHEST ALTITUDE IRONING

For the uninitiated, extreme ironing (or EI) is a recently introduced sport in which daredevils take ironing boards to remote and challenging locations where they proceed to iron items of clothing. It is said to combine the thrills of an extreme outdoor activity with the satisfaction of a well-pressed shirt. The story goes that the sport was conceived in Leicester in 1997 by Phil Shaw (or "Steam" as he is known in EI circles) who, fancying an evening out rock climbing but faced with a mountain of ironing, decided to combine the two. As the sport caught on, fellow enthusiasts started ironing across gorges, underwater, and on the ends of bungee ropes. The first world championships were held in Germany in 2002, and the following year antiques dealer John Roberts and heating system designer Ben Gibbons, both from Cheltenham, Gloucestershire, flattened the altitude world record when they steamed up Mount Everest carrying an ironing board and ironed a Union Jack flag at 17,800 feet. They trekked for seventeen days to get to base camp with the board strapped to Gibbons' back and with Roberts carrying the iron. "We ironed in some brilliant locations," Roberts told the *Guardian*. "We'd run out on to a 200-foot rope bridge and get the board out. People didn't know what to make of us. The Nepalese are great fun and understand the British sense of humour. They would join in with the ironing, whereas some of the Europeans thought we were deranged . . . My mum's proud, but I don't think she's sure what she's proud of."

FASTEST TOILET PLUNGER THROWER

Germany's Gerhard Donie is widely created with pioneering the niche sport of toilet plunger throwing. Therefore it is only fitting that Donie set the world speed record by hurling thirty plungers against a board in ninety seconds with such force that they stuck to the board for a minimum of three seconds. Rather like darts, if they don't stick to the board they don't count. As a variation, he hurls toilet plungers at the naked backs of people and has managed to get sixteen to stick in one minute, another world record. In 2012, he took the plunge and performed his routine on *Britain's Got Talent*, prompting Simon Cowell to ask "What the bloody hell was that?"

FASTEST WINDOW CLEANER

To most people, window cleaning is nothing more than house-work, but to a select few it is a highly competitive sport with its own world championships. And the undisputed king of the squeegee is Britain's Terry "Turbo" Burrows who holds the world record for fastest window cleaning. On 9 October 2009, at Blackpool Zoo, the fifty-four-year-old father-of-two from Romford, Essex, broke his own record set four years previously by cleaning three windows, each measuring 45 inches square, and wiping the sills in an incredible 9.14 seconds. The rules of the contest state that each competitor is limited to a maximum squeegee size of 12 inches and that time is deducted for any smears or water marks left on the glass. His finishing time was actually 8.14 seconds but he was penalized a second for leaving two water marks. No quarter is given in the cut-throat world of competitive window cleaning.

Burrows first sensed an unlikely route to fame when he demonstrated his speed cleaning on a 1993 edition of the TV entertainment show *You Bet!* "I knew that this was the start of something much bigger," he says. "It was the opportunity for me to realize my dream: to become the fastest and most famous window cleaner in the world!" Known to his friends as the fastest man with a 12-inch rubber, he has gone on to take part in window cleaning competitions all over the world as well as entertaining audiences by performing – naturally – George Formby's "When I'm Cleaning Windows". A black belt in karate, he attributes his success to "moving the body in sequence. I clean the windows in just 16 moves, and it's pretty intense. Many people try to break my record, but they're just not fast enough. Some of them are still trying to clean the windows after 10 seconds, well I'm finished by then."

FASTEST BOG SNORKELLER

The World Bog Snorkelling Championships have been staged in the Welsh town of Llanwrtyd Wells every year since 1985. Wearing a mask, snorkel, flippers and usually a wet suit, more than 150 competitors a year (from as far afield as Australia and New Zealand) snorkel two lengths of a specially dug 60-yard trench which runs through a weed-infested peat bog. Conventional swimming strokes such as the breaststroke and crawl are banned, so the participants must rely on flipper power alone. It has been described as like swimming through pea soup. The world record was set in 2013 by Dineka

Maguire from Northern Ireland who navigated the mud and water of the stench trench in a time of 1 minute 23.13 seconds – several seconds faster than the bog standard. Perhaps understandably there was no great rush to congratulate her.

FASTEST HALF-MILE SWIM WITH ONE FOOT IN MOUTH

Yo-yo collector and ear wiggling champion Dr John "Lucky" Meisenheimer first found fame on 14 February 1979 by swimming half a mile with his left foot in his mouth in a time of 30 minutes 14 seconds. Then a competitive Kentucky college student, the idea for the unorthodox swim came to Meisenheimer as the result of a chance remark. He remembers: "One day I was standing in the water stretching and someone said, 'Ew, don't put your foot in your mouth!' So, of course, I did. Then someone said, 'I bet you can't swim that way.' I said, 'I'm sure I can.'" He wrapped a sock around his toe, bit down, swam around a bit, and got a friend to take a photo, which was published in the swimming team newsletter.

To Meisenheimer it was all a joke, but it prompted such enthusiasm from his fellow students that he decided to try and swim half a mile with his foot in his mouth, practising that way on his mornings off and even inventing a little toe snorkel so that he could breathe. "I asked the coach several months in advance if we could arrange a time to set this record, but when the date came around he had forgotten about it. But the guys had gone out and put up fliers everywhere. The story got picked up by TV and radio stations. The stands started filling up. My coach asked: 'Does anyone know why the stands are filling up with people?' My team-mates were like, 'Well coach, don't you remember? You told Lucky he could swim the half-mile with his foot in his mouth and set a world record.' The coach just said: 'Oh my God!' But by the end of it he was happy because we had more people there than at any swim meet. In fact he was so happy he paid for the 20 pizzas the team had ordered in his name.'

LONGEST SWIM WHILE TOWING A TON OF BRICKS

Jim "The Shark" Dreyer, a forty-nine-year-old extreme swimmer, swam twenty-two miles across Lake St Clair, Michigan, in August 2013 while towing a ton of bricks. The swim took him 51 hours – two days and nights – and 21 hours longer than he had anticipated after he encountered a series of problems along the way, including losing a hand paddle, falling asleep, getting lost, suffering hallucinations, and needing to abandon one of the two rubber boats containing 1,000 pounds of bricks 18 hours into the adventure. Speaking through an oxygen mask on finally reaching the shore, Dreyer told reporters: "When you're getting tired of being pounded by the waves, when you get tired of your dingy filling up with water and you've got to bale it, when you're trying to stay awake with everything you can do and you keep falling asleep while you're swimming, you think, 'Why do I do this?' But I would never change it; I would never think of quitting. It's not in my vocabulary. There was no way I was not going to deliver those bricks." Well, half of them anyway. He may not have finished with all 334 bricks but he still achieved his goal because, unsurprisingly, there was no previous world record for swimming any distance whatsoever with a ton of bricks.

FIRST PERSON TO SWIM ACROSS THE DARDANELLES WITH HANDS AND FEET TIED

Seeing someone tossed into a river with their hands and legs tied might sound like the opening sequence from an episode of *CSI*, but in the world of weird records just about anything goes. In fact it is a recognized swimming discipline called Colchian, a form of Georgian swimming that was once practised by the nation's soldiers as part of their military training to improve their physical strength. It was revived in the twenty-first century by Henry Kuprashvili, a Georgian professor. In 2002, with straightened legs together, arms at the side, and bound at the chest, hips, thighs and ankles, Kuprashvili completed the 7.5-mile swim across the Dardanelles in Turkey in a time of 3 hours 15 minutes – the first person to achieve the feat Colchian-style.

HIGHEST SHALLOW DIVE

Darren Taylor, from Denver, Colorado, specializes in diving from great heights into a tiny inflatable children's paddling pool containing just 12 inches of water – almost the equivalent of diving from a fourth floor window into a puddle on the street below. On 8 April 2012 in São Paulo, Brazil, the fifty-year-old known as "Professor Splash" broke his own world record with a successful dive from a height of 36 feet 10 inches, hitting the water at around 33 mph. His bellyflop technique may not be one for the stylists, but by stretching his body as he falls he is able to reduce the impact on his torso when he hits the water. "The real big trick," he says, "is to land flat and try and get as much water out of the pool as I can. I want to dissipate as much water as possible for a cushion effect." Even so, the splashdown invariably leaves his lower ribcage covered with bruises that take weeks to heal and make laughing extremely painful.

LONGEST TIME SMOKING A PIPE WITHOUT RELIGHTING

On 4 May 2003 at Savigliano, Italy, Gianfranco Ruscalla, a forty-five-year-old professor of philosophy and member of the Cerea Pipe Club of Turin, set a new world record by smoking his pipe without relighting for 3 hours 18 minutes 15 seconds. International pipe smoking championships are held annually, the aim being to discover which smoker can make their allotted amount of tobacco burn the longest without having to relight their pipe. Inevitably in the past this has tended to be a male-dominated sport, but the 2013 world champion was a woman – Jennifer Spaniola, from Swartz Creek, Michigan, who outlasted her closest male rival by 20 seconds. A member of the Arrowhead Pipe Club, she hails from a distinguished family of puffers – the pipe smokers' answer to the Kennedys. Even so, if anyone had said that a woman hoped one day to be world champion, it would have been dismissed as just a pipe dream.

MOST ARMPIT FARTS IN ONE MINUTE

If armpit farting ever becomes an Olympic sport – as will surely be the case one day – the USA has a budding gold medallist in Ryan Nielsen, from Mesa, Arizona. In December 2011, adopting the traditional stance of left hand pressed into the right armpit, Nielsen gave a virtuoso display of armpit farting to record an unsurpassed 318 in one minute at an average speed of more than five farts per second.

MOST WATERMELONS SMASHED WITH THE HEAD IN ONE MINUTE

At the 2007 Chinchilla Melon Festival, John Allwood, a twenty-nine-year-old melon picker from Queensland, Australia, smashed forty-seven watermelons with his head (using no hands) in sixty seconds. The record smash left him with a badly bruised nose and facing a couple of days off work, but otherwise he told a local TV reporter he felt "good as gold, mate". The biennial festival, one of the biggest social events on the Queensland bush calendar, regularly draws crowds of 10,000, but for 2013 health and safety concerns forced organizers to drop the head-smashing contest. Instead they announced that they were replacing it with melon punching, where competitors have to shatter the fruit with their fist. The existing world record stood at seventy and naturally Allwood was up for the challenge. "I'll give it a bloody good go, mate," he said. "It beats whacking your head against a melon anyway." Spoken like a true sporting icon.

LONGEST DISTANCE FOR FIRING A PUMPKIN

A team led by Pennsylvania-based Ralph Eschborn and his sons Eric and Alex used their 90-foot-long "Big 10" compressed air cannon to fire a pumpkin a record distance of 5,545 feet 5 inches at Moab, Utah, on 9 September 2010. In doing so, they attained the "holy grail" of the sport by breaking the elusive one-mile barrier that had squashed the hopes of the world's pumpkin chuckers for so long. The team used a dozen La Estrella variety pumpkins, which are known for their roundness and tough outer skin, and which were presoaked in a bath of ale. This was done either to harden the skin or to get the pumpkins so drunk they would happily agree to be blasted out of a cannon. Each pumpkin was then fired skyward at speeds of up to 700 mph, their passage through the air helped by the warm, dry weather and a slight tailwind – perfect conditions for creating pumpkin-chucking history.

LONGEST DISTANCE FOR FIRING A RUBBER BAND

Have you ever wondered how far you could fire a rubber band just with your fingers? No, thought not. But American Leo Clouser did, and he managed to shoot one a distance of 99 feet at Wyomissing, Pennsylvania, on 18 June 1999 – a world record that still stands more than fifteen years later.

LONGEST DISTANCE PUSHING A PEA WITH NOSE

On 14 August 1978, twenty-three-year-old Helga Jansens pushed a pea with her nose for more than 1.25 miles along a riverbank in Peterborough, Cambridgeshire. It took her 8 hours. Nursing a scratched nose from the ordeal, she said: "It all started as a joke, but once I got behind that pea it became deadly serious. But now it's very painful and I'm sick of the sight of peas." The estimable Record Holders Republic website also states that Ms Jansens, presumably spurred on to even greater heights, subsequently pushed a pea with her nose for a distance of 2 miles in 15 hours 28 minutes, by which time she must have looked alarmingly like Rudolph.

LONGEST DISTANCE PUSHING A MONKEY NUT WITH NOSE

Under the headline "Nut Reaches Downing Street", thirty-seven-year-old London performance artist Mark McGowan used his nose to push a monkey nut seven miles through the streets of the capital from New Cross to 10 Downing Street. He set off on 1 September 2003 and completed his journey eleven days later, pushing an average of eight hours a day and overcoming a number of potentially fatal wide cracks in the pavement. Afterwards he said: "It's been a long two weeks. A lot of people treated me shamefully and sometimes I thought I was going to give up. I felt like a dog down there on the pavement, on my hands and knees with people laughing and jeering. It was really hard and lonely work. The kerbs and pavements were very tricky. You have to get your nose right under the nut to get through all the nooks and crannies. My nose is throbbing, my back hurts and my knee caps are in a terrible state. The streets were dirty. There was hair and spit and bird poo and some unmentionable things." He admitted that the nut he finished with was not his original. He wore out eleven others and one was stamped on by yobs.

FASTEST TIME TO PUSH AN ORANGE ONE MILE WITH NOSE

Ashrita Furman – who else? – took just 22 minutes 41 seconds to push an orange a distance of one mile with his nose at a New York mall in November 2007. This may sound like a gentle pursuit, but pictures of Furman after the event show him looking as if he had just gone fifteen rounds with Mike Tyson. Whacking an orange repeatedly with your nose can prove a painful experience, particularly as firmer, less ripe oranges travel faster and are therefore the fruit of choice in competition. During one training session Furman looked down and thought he was pushing a blood orange. It took him a few moments to realize that the red stuff on the orange was actually his own blood.

FASTEST TIME TO PUSH A CANNONBALL ONE MILE WITH NOSE

Using only his nose, Reg Morris took forty-two minutes to push a 16-pound cannonball around Walsall, West Midlands, for a distance of one mile on 1 March 1986. In what could only be termed a varied career, the fearless Reg also set world records by lying on a bed of nails for thirteen days, lying on a bed of four razor-sharp swords for four days and nights, carrying a 9.75-pound engineering brick between his finger and thumb for 63.5 miles, and living in a beer barrel on top of a pole for six-and-a-half weeks. The only way he could be pigeon-holed was if he was trying to squeeze his body into one for another record.

FIRST PERSON TO PUSH A SPROUT UP MOUNT SNOWDON WITH NOSE

On 2 August 2014, forty-nine-year-old Stuart Kettell, from Balsall Common, West Midlands, stood proudly on the 3,560-foot summit of Mount Snowdon in North Wales, having spent four days painstakingly pushing a Brussels sprout all the way up with his nose. He trained for the feat by pushing a sprout around his garden, and deliberately chose large sprouts for the actual climb because they were less likely to fall down a rock crevice. Even so, he still got through twenty-two sprouts during the ascent. He wore a special face-guard to protect his skin but by the end his entire body hurt like hell. Not surprisingly, he got plenty of strange looks.

"People definitely think I'm mad," he gasped, "and I'm beginning to think it myself."

LONGEST TIME SITTING ON A POLE

Daniel Baraniuk, an unemployed twenty-seven-year-old from Gdansk, Poland, set the modern world record for pole-sitting by perching on top of an 8-feet-2.5-inches-high pole for 196 days and nights to win the 2002 World Pole-Sitting Championship and nearly $23,000 in prize money. The competitors mounted their poles at a fun park in Soltau, Northern Germany, on 15 May and were only permitted to leave the 16-inch by 24-inch platform for ten minutes every two hours. Baraniuk finally gave up on 26 November, his closest rival having fallen off the pole a month earlier. The championship was inspired by St Simeon the Stylite who, in an attempt to be nearer to God, spent thirty-seven years on top of a stone pillar in Syria right up until his death in AD 459 – a record that is unlikely to be broken.

LONGEST TIME SITTING IN A SAUNA

Held annually in Heinola, Finland, the Sauna World Championships were an extreme endurance contest to find the competitor who could remain in a hot, sweltering sauna the longest. Dressed in swimsuits, the competitors had to sit with their buttocks and thighs on the bench, elbows on their knees, and arms raised. If they touched their skin at any time, they were disqualified. The starting temperature inside was 110°C – already 10 degrees above the boiling point of water – and every 30 seconds half a litre of water was thrown onto the stove to crank up the heat. The winner was the last person to stay in the sauna and be able to walk out without needing assistance. It was not a sport for the faint-hearted. The championships were first held in 1999 and soon attracted contestants from more than twenty countries. Many lasted only a minute or two, and even those with the toughest skin often gave up after six minutes, but in 2003 Finland's Timo Kaukonen somehow managed to stay in the sauna for a world record 16 minutes 15 seconds. Kaukonen went on to win the title on four more occasions, but then in 2010 the event reached a tragic climax. Kaukonen himself and Russia's Vladimir Ladyzhensky passed out after spending six minutes in the sauna, both suffering from terrible burns. Ladyzhensky died from his injuries and Kaukonen was rushed to hospital, where thankfully he eventually recovered. The Sauna World Championships were suspended indefinitely.

MOST SUCCESSFUL TOE WRESTLER

Alan "Nasty" Nash is the Tiger Woods of toe wrestling – but with a much less complicated private life. The fifty-three-year-old father of four from Weston Coyney, Staffordshire, was crowned world champion for the tenth time in 2013 after going toe-to-toe with twenty other competitors at the annual World Toe Wrestling Championships at the Bentley Brook Inn in Ashbourne, Derbyshire. The championships were introduced to the sporting calendar in 1976 when regulars at the Royal Oak in nearby Wetton wanted to invent a sport at which the British could be the best in the world. Unfortunately a Canadian won and took the trophy home with him, so the contest was dropped for eighteen years until the Brits had regrouped.

Following the opening call to remove shoes and socks, competitors sit barefoot facing each other and lock their big toes together, the object being to pin their opponent's big toe on the platform (or toedium) for three seconds in a best-of-three contest, using alternating feet. While putting their best foot forward, they must keep their hands flat on the floor and their non-fighting foot in the air. Shifting position to gain leverage is strictly prohibited. As the referee warns: "The crack of your bottom must remain flush with the line at all times." Psychology plays a key role for these podiatric gladiators. Contests begin with a blood-curdling chant as the rivals get themselves into the zone, sometimes threatening "I'll break your ankle" or delivering the ultimate toe wrestling insult "Lick my verruca!"

Nash, the bald beast, lifted the title at his first attempt in 1994 and has dominated the event ever since. His finest hour came in 1997 when, after suffering four broken toes in the semi-final, he rested them in an ice bucket before simply snapping them back into place and winning the final. "I just don't like losing," he said with a degree of understatement. He trains at the gym three times a week and owes his toe strength to a diet of raw meat. He growls: "I don't eat fruit or vegetables. If it was meant to be eaten, it wouldn't be buried in the ground." In more serious vein, he adds: "The sport is like arm wrestling, but you use your legs instead. However, it is harder than arm wrestling because you need to have strength in your whole body to be good at it." Nor are Nash's toes just for wrestling ... and walking on, of course. He can also crack forty-nine eggs between them in a minute. And he claims that he can hypnotize chickens, but that's probably not with his toes.

FARTHEST VAULT OVER A CANAL

In the popular Dutch sport of canal jumping (or fierljeppen), competitors sprint up to a tall pole positioned on one side of a canal and climb up it as quickly as they can while it tips to the other side and dumps them in a sand pit. In 2011, Bart Helmholt set a new world record of 21.51 metres during the Dutch Championships and promptly celebrated by jumping into the very canal he had fought so hard to avoid. The sport dates back to the eighteenth century and is thought to have originated with farmers who used poles to jump over drainage channels in order to reach otherwise inaccessible plots of land. The latest figures indicate that there are over 500 registered active canal jumpers in the world, almost half from the Netherlands.

FASTEST WIFE CARRYING

At the 2000 World Wife Carrying Championships in Sonkajärvi, Finland, Estonia's Margo Uusorg carried compatriot Birgit Ullrich over a 253.5-metre obstacle course in a record time of 55.5 seconds. The race was inspired by the legend of a local brigand, Herkko Rosvo-Ronkainen, who, in the late nineteenth century, made a habit of snatching women from villages in the region. As Rosvo-Ronkainen was apparently not fussy who he picked up, competitors do not necessarily have to carry their own wife – it can be someone else's wife or indeed any woman provided she is over the age of seventeen. She must also weigh a minimum of 49 kilos (nearly 108 pounds). If she tips the scales at less, she must carry a rucksack containing extra weight. The world championships have been staged annually since 1992 and the victorious man wins the wife's weight in beer. Several types of carry are permitted, including piggy-back, fireman's carry (over the shoulder) and the more intimate Estonian style, where the wife holds onto her husband's waist while hanging upside-down with her legs around his shoulders. If competitors were not in a relationship before the race, there is a good chance that they will be by the time they cross the finish line.

FASTEST COAL CARRYING

If you were to ask the good folk of Gawthorpe in Yorkshire whether they are impressed with Mo Farah's athletic feats, they would probably grumble that all his victories are essentially worthless because he never has to carry a sack of coal around with him. For since 1963 Gawthorpe has been the venue of the grandly titled World Coal Carrying Championships, an elite event where men and women run just over 1,000 metres through the former mining village carrying on their shoulders a sack of coal weighing 50 kilograms (110 pounds) for men and 20 kilograms (44 pounds) for women. As with all the best ideas, the race stemmed from a chance remark in a local pub when Lewis Hartley cast aspersions on the fitness of another man, Reggie Sedgewick. That amounted to fighting talk in Reggie's language, so, fortified by ale, he challenged his rival to a race with a bag of coal on their backs. Sensing the opportunity to make a spectacle of the duel and draw in crowds from all over the area, the secretary of the village Maypole Committee suggested they stage it on Easter Monday. And it has been raced on Easter Monday ever since. The men's world record was set by Huddersfield's Dave Jones in 1991 with a time of 4 minutes 6 seconds, a mark he achieved again in 1995. In total, he won the event six times. The women's record holder is Batley police fitness instructor Catherine Fenton (née Foley) who blitzed around the course in 4 minutes 25 seconds in 2011 to complete a hat-trick of victories in the event. She trained for the race by carrying a bag of gravel that was five kilos heavier.

MOST WORMS CHARMED

The brainchild of John Bailey, deputy headmaster of Willaston County Primary School in Cheshire, the World Worm Charming Championships have been held annually in the village since 1980, the winner receiving a trophy in the shape of a golden rampant worm. It has grown into such an international event that the rules are printed in over thirty languages, including Tibetan. The inaugural champion, farmer's son Tom Shufflebotham, charmed 511 worms out of his three-metre square plot in the allotted time of thirty minutes. This record stood until 2009, when ten-year-old local girl Sophie Smith charmed an incredible 567 worms from her plot. Most competitors lure worms to the surface by hand vibrating a four-tine garden fork inserted approximately six inches into the turf – a method known as twanging – although others prefer to use cricket stumps or knitting needles or even to tap dance on a plank to the *Star Wars* theme. Digging is strictly banned, as is the use of water, which for the purposes of worm charming is considered an illegal stimulant. Competitors who do not wish to handle worms may appoint a second – or "Gillie" – to do so, and to ensure that no worms are harmed in the pursuit of sport, the charmees are released that evening after the birds have gone to roost.

LONGEST TIME WITH A FERRET DOWN TROUSERS

The quaint sport of ferret legging – an endurance test where two live ferrets are placed down a man's trousers – seems to have originated among Yorkshire coal miners in the 1970s. The rules stipulate that trousers must be belted at the waist, tied at the ankles and be loose enough to "allow easy ferret access between the legs". No underpants are permitted and male competitors "whose families are not yet complete" must have written permission from their partner. The ferrets must have a full set of teeth and must not be sedated. Competitors can attempt, from outside their trousers, to dislodge the ferrets, but as the animals can maintain a strong hold for long periods their removal is no easy matter. The goal is to survive for as long as possible and to emerge from the ordeal with one's dignity and manhood intact.

Former world champion Reg Mellor used to wear white trousers so that he could show spectators the blood from the wounds caused by the ferrets. In 1981, Mellor, a retired Barnsley miner who attributed his success to ensuring that the ferrets were well fed before they were inserted into his trousers, set a new world record of 5 hours 26 minutes at the annual Pennine Show in Holmfirth, after which he set about breaking the magical six-hour barrier – the four-minute mile of ferret legging. In 1986, he was well on his way to doing just that until, after five hours, most of the 2,500 crowd became bored and started to drift away. Even though he protested that he was on his way to setting a new world record, workmen arrived to dismantle the stage. Disillusioned at such apathetic treatment of a national sporting icon, he retired on the spot. Nevertheless his 1981 record stood until 2010 when sixty-seven-year-old retired headmaster Frank Bartlett and

Christine Farnsworth managed to last for 5 hours 30 minutes at a ferret-legging contest in Whittington, Staffordshire. Afterwards a euphoric Bartlett took time to praise one of his ferrets, White Fang, as a "gentle little girl", adding: "The very baggy trousers I used had been used by my ferrets as a bed for the last couple of weeks. They like nothing better than a warm, dark tunnel. They usually curl up and fall asleep once they find themselves safe." Inevitably there were mutterings about Ms Farnsworth's right to be named as a joint world record holder as quite clearly she had less to lose in the contest. Incidentally an attempt to introduce a female version of the sport, ferret busting, in which women placed ferrets down their blouses, had previously proved unsuccessful.

CHAPTER 6

Pet Projects

FARTHEST DISTANCE SKATEBOARDING BY A GOAT

In March 2012, Melody Cooke's Nigerian dwarf cross goat Happie skated thirty-six metres in twenty-five seconds around a parking lot in her home town of Fort Myers, Florida – the farthest distance ever travelled by a goat on a skateboard. And she could have gone even farther had she not run into the parking barrier. Cooke says once Happie learned to get on a skateboard the rest was easy. "I realized Happie was a talented goat when she was following me around and trying to do tricks just to get treats out of me. She tried jumping on a bicycle while I was riding it and I thought, 'Whoa! This goat has potential.'" Sadly Cooke fears that fame may have gone to Happie's head, admitting: "She has this attitude, this look in her eye that says, 'Look at me'. She's a little bit of a diva now."

LONGEST JUMP BY A GUINEA PIG

Gravity-defying guinea pig Truffles sensationally recaptured his world long jump record in 2013 with a mighty leap of forty-eight centimetres (that's nearly 1 foot 8 inches) from box to box, beating his previous personal best by eighteen centimetres. The daredevil rodent's owner, fourteen-year-old Chloe Macari, from Rosyth in Fife, Scotland, revealed that the marked improvement in Truffles' performance was down to kale, his favourite snack. For a nibble of cucumber, he had never leaped beyond thirty centimetres, but replacing it with kale made him pull out all the stops. However, Chloe's mother Angela warned: "Truffles is starting to age now. He's four years old, so he's in retirement." There could be room for a new pig on the block.

FIRST WATER-SKIING SQUIRREL

American TV audiences were first introduced to Twiggy the water-skiing squirrel on a 1979 NBC show titled *Real People*. Chuck and Lou Ann Best had found the orphaned grey squirrel in the wake of Hurricane David and raised it as a family pet that would happily sit on their shoulders even when they were in the pool. When Chuck bought a remote-controlled toy boat for his daughter Lalainia, he saw the potential in teaching Twiggy to water-ski behind it. And so an animal novelty act was born. Over thirty-five years later, Twiggy is still going strong, explained by the fact that the Bests have since trained several squirrels to don the miniature life vest and ski around a small heated pool. Just as there were more Lassies than you could shake a stick at, there have been at least four Twiggys. The sporty pet has even made a splash in Hollywood, appearing in the movies *Dodgeball: A True Underdog Story* and *Anchorman: The Legend of Ron Burgundy*. Although audiences predictably went nuts about her, rumour has it she is worried about getting typecast as a squirrel. Even so, surely an Animal Oscar beckons.

MOST ACCOMPLISHED WATER-SKIING ELEPHANT

A water-skiing elephant sounds as unlikely as a skateboarding carp or a bungee-jumping hamster, but in the 1950s and early 1960s a Florida tourist attraction actively promoted "The World's Only Water-Skiing Elephant". Her name was Queenie, and she was an Asian elephant born in Thailand in 1952. She was soon imported to the United States where she was purchased from a New York City pet store by Bill Green and housed in his private zoo in Vermont. She was later introduced to water-skiing by Marj and Jim Rusing, owners of De Leon Springs, an entertainment park in Florida, as a replacement for the world's first water-skiing elephant, Sunshine Sally. Queenie's water skis came in the form of two pontoons welded together and she performed her routine with Green's teenage daughter Liz Dane for over a decade, taking to it like a very large duck to water. Dane said: "I always had to be careful that Queenie didn't get too rambunctious. She loved rocking the skis, getting water in her trunk and squirting it. I just stood beside her, kept my balance and made sure she was paying attention." The elephant's only mishap of note occurred in June 1959, during a personal appearance in Pittsburgh, when waves from a passing towboat caused her to fall off her skis. Bill Green, who had been water-skiing next to her, held her trunk above the water so that she could breathe until a crane was able to lift her clear. Queenie, who could also play the harmonica and hopscotch (but maybe not simultaneously), went on to make a number of TV appearances before being sold to a circus. She retired in 2003 and was finally put down in 2011 at the age of fifty-eight because of health problems. Countering accusations that Queenie was exploited, Marj Rusing pointed out that there was little possibility of physically making an elephant do something it didn't want to do.

FASTEST THIRTY METRES ON A SCOOTER BY A DOG

On 12 July 2013, Norman, a three-year-old briard dog from Canton, Georgia, set a new world record by riding a scooter unassisted for thirty metres in 20.75 seconds, making him the fastest pooch on four wheels. "Norman the Scooter Dog", as he is known to his legions of YouTube fans, gripped the handlebar with his front paws and propelled himself across the school gymnasium with his hind legs. He even found time for a spot of showboating by putting both hind legs on the scooter as he coasted over the finish line. Although at least one observer remarked that it looked like a small man in a dog costume, Norman is the genuine article. His owner, Karen Cobb, started training him to ride a scooter when he was a puppy. "We wanted to introduce him to all new objects," she says, "so we just happened to have the kids' scooter in the backyard and thought it would be fun to put him on there and get him used to it, and he loved it. He just wouldn't get off." He mastered it in only a few weeks and can also pedal a bicycle and ride a skateboard – feats that have launched him into canine superstardom with his own Facebook page and Twitter account plus frequent appearances on US TV shows such as *Saturday Night Live* and *The Late Show with David Letterman*. If there was a talent show for dogs – *Bone Idol* – Norman would surely walk it, or at least ride it.

LONGEST SURFBOARD RIDE BY A DOG

Abbie Girl, an Australian kelpie, set the world record for the longest surf ride by a dog in open water when she caught a wave and travelled sixty-five yards at the Surf City Surf Dog competition at Huntington Beach, California, in September 2011. A veritable sporting superhound, former rescue dog Abbie has also gone skydiving with her owner, Michael Uy. Meanwhile, the annual dog surfing contest has been a welcome addition to the Californian canine calendar since 2009, with over forty pooches taking to the water, no doubt watched over by their owners, their therapists and their owners' therapists, and even coping with conditions that could best be described as "ruff".

FASTEST TIGHTROPE-WALKING DOG

Balancing exquisitely on his hind legs, Osbert Humperdinck Pumpernickle (or Ozzy for short), a four-year-old border collie/ kelpie crossbreed, negotiated an 11.4-foot-long rope in 18.2

seconds at a Norfolk animal rescue centre in 2013, to claim the official title of the world's fastest tightrope-walking dog – quite possibly in the face of zero competition. Ozzy lives in Norwich with his owner, carpenter Nick Johnson, who, despite having no formal dog training experience, has taught his pet a number of tricks, including balancing on street signs and saluting Nick while standing on his hind legs. The proud owner of the collie who never wobbles revealed his technique: "Old-style dog trainers say you should never look at the dog, but I bring him into my eyes and that helps him balance. I use a lot of sign language with him. I use my eyebrows to encourage him, but the most powerful command is me wagging my little finger. That means 'Come on' when he is right on the edge of what he can do. Even so, he only practises his tricks when he's finished doing the things that dogs do naturally, like sniffing around other dogs."

FASTEST DOG ON A SKATEBOARD

Tillman, an English bulldog, travelled 100 metres along a parking lot in 19.68 seconds during the 2009 X Games in Los Angeles to set a world canine skateboarding record. Encouraged by his owner, Ron Davis, Tillman started skateboarding when he was nine months old and his exploits have drawn more than 20 million views on YouTube. He has since expanded his sporting range to encompass snowboarding, soccer and surfing, and in 2013 he took first place in the large dog category at the prestigious Loews Surf Dog Competition in California. He keeps his energy levels high by eating apples, and between laying claim to being the world's sportiest dog, he also found time to appear in an iPhone commercial. Naturally he has his own blog, Facebook page and Twitter feed.

MOST SUCCESSFUL FRISBEE-CATCHING DOG

Alex Stein, a student at Ohio State University, first introduced his pet whippet, Ashley, to Frisbees as a puppy by using them as dishes for the dog's food and water. Soon Ashley was demonstrating an extraordinary ability to leap high into the air and catch the flying discs, much to the amusement of Stein's fellow students. By the age of six months, Ashley Whippet was attracting large audiences on campus. "Ashley loved to perform in front of a crowd," said Stein. "He'd jump up and twist and contort his body on a catch because he knew that's what people liked."

Sensing that Ashley could become a doggie superstar, Stein moved to Hollywood and began contacting agents. They were universally disinterested. Their tales did not wag. They just could not recognize a good novelty act when they saw one. Desperate to get his dog noticed, on 5 August 1974 Stein smuggled Ashley Whippet into Dodger Stadium during a nationally televised baseball game between the Los Angeles Dodgers and the Cincinnati Reds. Just before the Dodgers came to bat in the bottom of the eighth inning, Stein jumped the fence, went onto the field with Ashley and hurled Frisbees for the whippet to catch. The spectators were left open-mouthed as Ashley sprinted at speeds of 35 mph, over distances of ninety yards, and leaped nine feet into the air to catch the discs with the grace of a ballet dancer. So captivated were the baseball fans that the game was held up for eight minutes before Stein was eventually escorted from the field, arrested, and fined $250 for trespassing.

However, it was a small price to pay because Ashley's performance had captured the public's imagination, and the following year Stein helped organize the inaugural Frisbee Dog World Championship. Unsurprisingly, he and Ashley won the first three championships – in 1975, 1976 and 1977. The event was later re-named the Ashley Whippet Invitational in his honour. Meanwhile, Ashley appeared on TV shows, performed at half-time at Super Bowl XII, and also at the White House for a young Amy Carter. He had retired from competitive sport by 1980 but still served as spokesdog for a dog food company. Upon his death in 1985 at the age of thirteen, Ashley received a glowing tribute in the pages of *Sports Illustrated* where he was described as "the creator of a sport and its greatest practitioner . . . the surest jaws on all four paws."

DOG WITH MOST SKYDIVING JUMPS

Wearing a custom-made harness and special "doggles" to protect his eyes, Otis, a pug owned by Will DaSilva, completed his sixty-fourth tandem skydiving jump in the skies above California in August 2011. Otis, who died in his sleep in 2012, made his first jump at Lodi Parachute Centre in Los Angeles as a puppy in 2002 and, according to his owner, he loved every minute of every jump. "He was totally aware of what was happening when he was free falling," said DaSilva. "Just like any first-time jumper, he got all excited about it and got nervous at the door. Once he was out, though, he was just having a ball like a dog with its head out of the car window."

DOG THAT WALKED FARTHEST TO RETURN HOME

While on a family trip to Indiana, in 1923, Bobbie, a two-year-old collie mix, became separated from his owners, Frank and Elizabeth Brazier, after they stopped the car at Wolcott to fill up with petrol. He was last seen being chased around a corner by a pack of dogs. After a lengthy search, the distraught family reluctantly drove back to their home in Silverton, Oregon – 2,551 miles away – never expecting to see their beloved dog again. To their amazement, however, six months later Bobbie turned up outside the family restaurant in Silverton, mangy, hungry and with paws worn to the bone. He immediately bounded up to their youngest daughter and was readily identified by three scars and a missing tooth, legacies of previous adventures. Although he was unable to offer his own version of events, he looked to have walked every yard of the way – negotiating rivers, deserts and mountains, all in the depths of winter. Bobbie's story made him an overnight star and saw him labelled "The Wonder Dog of Oregon". He received hundreds of letters from people all over the world and was honoured with ribbons, a jewel-encrusted harness and collar, and the keys to cities. The following year, he played himself in the silent movie *The Call of the West*. Following Bobbie's untimely death in 1927, no less a figure in the canine world than Rin Tin Tin laid a wreath at his grave.

LONGEST TIME SPENT BY A DOG GRIEVING AT THE GRAVE OF ITS DEAD OWNER

After Edinburgh night watchman John Gray died in 1858, his faithful Skye terrier is said to have guarded his grave at the city's Greyfriars Kirkyard for the next fourteen years, giving rise to the legend of Greyfriars Bobby. According to most sources, Bobby spent the rest of his life sitting on his master's grave until he, too, died in 1872, but even though the devoted dog is commemorated by a local statue, some authors have questioned the authenticity of the story. One claim is that the original Bobby died in 1867 and was secretly replaced with a younger animal. The lengths to which some people will go in order to break a record!

MOST STEPS WALKED BY A DOG BALANCING A GLASS OF WATER

Sweet Pea, an Australian shepherd/Border collie mix owned by Alex Rothacker, a professional dog handler from Illinois, walked down ten steps while balancing a five-ounce glass of water on her head at the Sport and Schau Show in Verden, Germany, on 5 January 2008. Sweet Pea also walked backwards up the same ten steps while balancing the same glass of water – again without spilling a drop. Rothacker has even taught her to perform the same tricks while she is blindfolded. He spent five years training her to do the balancing act. He said: "I spent two to three hours a day working with Sweet Pea. We worked with different staircases and in various locations. I also got her to balance other items on her snout – things that were harder to balance than a glass of water."

MOST NAZI SALUTES BY A DOG

Sometime in the 1930s, Finnish merchant Tor Borg's Dalmatian mix Jackie was trained to raise a single paw whenever the name "Hitler" was mentioned, thereby mimicking the Nazi salute. In 1941, shortly before the German invasion of the Soviet Union, an anonymous source tipped off the Nazis about Borg's dog. Borg was summoned to the German embassy in Helsinki where he admitted that his wife Josefine, a German citizen with anti-Nazi views, had occasionally called the dog "Hitler" and that it had responded with a raised paw. However, he tried to play down the accusations and assured the Nazi diplomats that neither he nor Jackie had ever done anything "that could be seen as an insult against the German Reich."

The zealous diplomats did not believe him and wrote back to Berlin that "Borg, even though he claims otherwise, is not telling the truth." They were convinced that the dog was mocking Hitler. Over the next three months, the German Foreign Office, the Economy Ministry and Hitler's Chancellery all investigated the dog and actively looked for ways of bringing Borg to trial for insulting the Führer. Meanwhile, they attempted to sabotage his business. In the end, none of the witnesses was prepared to repeat their accusations in front of a judge and no charges were pressed. Historian Klaus Hillenbrand described the episode as "completely bizarre", adding: "The dog affair tells us the Nazis were not only criminals and mass murderers but silly as hell. There were two or three dozen people discussing the affair of the dog rather than preparing for the invasion of the Soviet Union. They were crazy."

LONGEST MARATHON RACE COMPLETED BY A DOG

A stray dog ran 1,100 miles across China with a team of cyclists who were taking part in a marathon ride to Tibet after one of them threw her a bone. Five days after leaving Chengdu in 2012, one of the cyclists, twenty-two-year-old Xiao Yong, spotted the small white mongrel by the roadside and threw her a chicken drumstick. The dog proceeded to follow the riders for the next twenty days, climbing twelve mountains higher than 13,000 feet and braving violent storms. A number of the cyclists dropped out exhausted by the steep climbs and the thin air of the Tibetan plateau, but the little dog kept going, running with the pack for over fifty miles a day. The riders took her to their hearts, naming her Little Sa, feeding her their rations of custard tarts, boiled eggs and sausages, and allowing her to sleep on their raincoats at night. At the end of the marathon, Xiao Yong adopted her and had her flown back to Chengdu after a vet in Lhasa had given her a clean bill of health. As news of her exploits spread, internet users in China nicknamed her "Forrest Gump".

MOST STAGE PERFORMANCES BY A DOG

Danny, a soft-coated wheaten terrier owned and trained by Rita Mansell, from Telford, Shropshire, played Sandy, Orphan Annie's faithful pet companion, for ten years, racking up over 1,400 performances. Danny joined the cast of the UK production of the stage musical *Annie* as a seven-month-old puppy, and despite his retirement being announced in 2011, he missed the limelight so much that he decided to reprise his role two years later in a comeback worthy of Sinatra. Mansell, who rewarded the four-legged thespian after each performance with a plate of cheese and sausages, revealed: "When the *Annie* tour went to Singapore, I thought the travel would be too much for Danny and so he retired. He kept his paw in with a few amateur productions, but I could tell he was itching to get back on a bigger stage again."

DOG WITH LONGEST TONGUE

Brandy, a boxer owned by John Scheid in St Clair Shores, Michigan, had a tongue that was seventeen inches long – twice the length of most dogs. She was born with a tongue that was already the size of an adult boxer and it just kept on growing until her death, at the age of seven, in 2002. "We were told that Brandy would grow into her tongue," said Scheid, "but it became very apparent that was not going to happen." Although her enormous tongue made her famous, she sometimes struggled to fit it in her mouth. Meanwhile, her patient owner had to deal with food and water flying everywhere at mealtimes, as well as copious amounts of drool.

FIRST DOG TO BE VOTED UGLIEST IN THE WORLD THREE YEARS IN A ROW

Staged annually in California, the World's Ugliest Dog contest offers $1,000 to the winner's owner and is therefore as keenly contested as Miss World. But whereas the stated ambition of Miss World contestants is usually to travel the globe spreading peace and goodwill, the World's Ugliest Dog contestants have more modest travel goals – about as far as the nearest lamp post or fire hydrant. Since its inception in the 1970s, a variety of mangy mutts have been named the least photogenic in the world, but between 2003 and 2005 the event really became a no-contest as Sam, a blind Chinese Crested hairless dog, owned by Susie Lockheed of Santa Barbara, swept all before him. With wild eyes, no fur and hideous, protruding teeth, Sam was the stuff of nightmares, a canine Freddy Krueger. As a result of his appearance he was considered unadoptable until Lockheed picked him up from a rescue pound in 1999, only for her then-boyfriend to be so repulsed by Sam that he broke up with her. Love me, love my dog proved a tall order in Sam's case. Rival owners at the contest were soon muttering that Sam was simply too ugly for their dogs to stand a chance, and indeed his reign of supremacy was ended only by his death on 18 November 2005, just before his fifteenth birthday. The *Milwaukee Journal Sentinel* carried the story beneath the headline "HEART FAILS HIDEOUS DOG", not exactly the obituary Sam had dreamed of as a puppy. Then again, he did get to appear on TV and radio all over the world and to meet Donald Trump, an encounter which must have made Sam realize that being hairless was not such a bad thing after all. "I don't think there'll ever be another Sam," said Lockheed shortly after his death. "Some people would think that's a good thing."

MOST ANARCHIC DOG

A stray mongrel named Loukanikos (which is Greek for "sausage" even though, confusingly, he's not a sausage dog) attended more than twenty anti-austerity protests in Athens in the years from 2008. Virtually every time rioters took to the streets, Loukanikos appeared on the front line. Braving tear gas and flares and barking menacingly at riot police (and passing cabs), the dog quickly became a symbol of the protest movement. In September 2011, when striking police officers marched through the Greek capital, Loukanikos, according to eyewitnesses, was initially confused by the sight of the opposing ranks of uniformed policemen, but when the riot police unleashed their weapons on their striking colleagues, the dog instinctively sided with those who were coming under attack. The following year, it was reported that he had finally been given a home and had officially retired as a protester to live out his remaining years in peace and quiet.

WEALTHIEST DOG

A German shepherd named Gunther IV is reportedly the world's richest dog with an estimated personal fortune of $373 million. You can buy a lot of Bonio with that kind of money. He inherited his fortune from his father, Gunther III, who was owned by certifiable German countess and multi-millionaire Karlotta Liebenstein. She was so attached to her favourite pet that when she died in 1991 she left him everything, including her portfolio of properties. Apart from splashing the cash on bitches when the inheritance filtered down to him, Gunther IV (or at least human representatives acting on his behalf) bought Madonna's eight-bedroom Miami villa for $7.5 million in 2000. The pampered pooch now owns several houses and mansions, including a villa in the Bahamas, complete with its own butler, and travels around in a chauffeur-driven limousine. To illustrate that he is one lucky animal, he entered a raffle and won a rare white truffle worth $1,500, which is apparently a favourite delicacy of society dogs when they're not rummaging in bins or digging up bones.

HIGHEST JUMP BY A DOG

In October 2006, Cinderella May, a greyhound owned by Kate Long and Kathleen Conroy, of Miami, Florida, cleared a height of 5 feet 8 inches at the Purina Incredible Dog Challenge National Finals in Missouri. Three years later, Stacy Clark, from Aberdeenshire, Scotland, unofficially measured her collie Blitzen jumping a height of 6 feet while playing in the sea. There was also an unconfirmed report of a dachshund from Dorset jumping higher still – but that was only after his owner accidentally trod on his tail.

MOST DOUBLE-DUTCH ROPE SKIPS
IN ONE MINUTE BY A DOG

A four-year-old Australian kelpie rescue dog named Geronimo completed 128 double-Dutch rope skips in a minute on the US TV show *Today* on 7 April 2014, beating her previous world record of 113. Her owner, Samantha Valle, from Long Island, New York, says it took Geronimo just five weeks to master the two-rope skip.

DOG THAT CAN HOLD MOST TENNIS BALLS IN MOUTH

Augie, a golden retriever owned by the Miller family from Dallas, Texas, set a new Guinness World Record by successfully gathering and holding five regulation-sized tennis balls in her mouth at the same time on 6 July 2003.

DOG THAT FETCHED MOST GOLF BALLS

A mongrel terrier with a talent for fetching lost balls was awarded lifetime membership of his local golf club in 2006. Deuce was rewarded for returning more than 3,000 balls to members of Pontnewydd Golf Club in South Wales over a period of five years, his owner Jim Phillis being at pains to emphasize that Deuce never, ever chased moving balls. In spite of the official recognition, Deuce remained the only member not allowed in the clubhouse, because dogs are banned.

DOG WITH LARGEST VOCABULARY

In 2013, Chaser, a Border collie living in Spartanburg, South Carolina, was recorded as knowing more than 1,200 words – the largest vocabulary of any dog. Chaser was taught by her owner, psychologist John W. Pilley, who bought her as a puppy in 2004 and started training her for up to five hours a day. He would show her an object, say its name forty times, then hide it and ask her to find it, while repeating the name all the time. He aimed to teach her one or two new names every day, along with revision for any words she had forgotten. Having such an intellectual pet is not without its challenges. "She still demands four to five hours every day," said Dr Pilley in 2011. "I'm 82, and I have to go to bed to get away from her!"

FASTEST BALLOON BURSTING DOG

Anastasia, a Jack Russell terrier who lives in Los Angeles with her owner and trainer Doree Sitterly, broke her own world record by popping 100 balloons in 44.49 seconds on TV's *Live with Regis and Kelly* in February 2008. Anastasia has also done acting and modelling (on the dogwalk rather than the catwalk), appearing in various commercials and even gracing the pages of *Vogue* magazine.

MOST SUCCESSFUL DRUG SNIFFING DOG

In her seven years as a sniffer dog between 2007 and 2014, Megan, a springer spaniel based at Gatwick Airport, Sussex, made 100 drugs finds, detecting 485 pounds of cocaine worth in excess of $50 million. In their first year, sniffer dogs are not expected to make even one find; Megan made ten. Her handler, Steven Martin, attributes her success rate to her unusually large nose and long muzzle. "When she is out and about being her normal self, she can be quite sensitive," he says, "but when she's working she is indestructible. When she wants to find the drugs, there's nothing that will get in her way. Once she puts her harness on she has these powers and she goes off and does what she has to do." Yet he admits their relationship did not get off to the most auspicious of starts. "She rolled over and weed on me."

LARGEST DOG WEDDING

The record for the world's largest dog wedding was set at Littleton, Ohio, on 19 May 2007 by 178 canine couples who entered holy muttrimony. After holding paws, they were told: "You may now sniff the bride."

MOST EXPENSIVE DOG WEDDING

Two dogs were "married" in a $250,000 black-tie ceremony in New York on 12 July 2012. Baby Hope, a small Coton de Tulear adopted by Wendy Diamond, took Jake Pasternak's former stray poodle Chilly in holy muttrimony at a charity event to raise awareness for homeless animals. The groom had tie-dyed fur in blue, purple and red and wore a smart tuxedo, while the bride looked enchanting in a $6,000 custom-made dress. Some fifty doggie guests attended the nuptials, many wearing top hats, and they enjoyed a seven-piece orchestra as well as a five-tiered wedding cake topped with a model dog. The ceremony was paid for by Wendy Diamond, who decided against calling herself the mother of the bride because Baby Hope was fifty-six in dog years. Afterwards Diamond said: "I am beyond happy. These dogs are so sweet. It's a perfect match." Alas, there is no prospect of the perfect match producing perfect puppies as the bride and groom had been spayed and neutered, making the wedding night something of a redundant affair.

MOST DOGS WALKED SIMULTANEOUSLY BY ONE PERSON

Guinness World Records states that Joseph Orsino managed to walk thirty-five dogs simultaneously for a distance of just over one kilometre in Pittsburgh, Pennsylvania, on 1 October 2011. They ranged in size from a 170-pound Newfoundland to a 5-pound Yorkshire terrier. He had twenty dogs in front of him and fifteen smaller dogs walking behind him in a straight line. It should be noted that Mr Orsino is a highly experienced dog trainer who knew each dog personally. He has followed more leads than Columbo. In other words, this is not a record to be attempted on a whim after a few drinks.

LONGEST TIME FOR A DOG KISSING A HUMAN

At Planet Dog Store's annual Valentine's Day Dog Kissing Contest in Portland, Maine, owners allow their pets to kiss and lick their faces (including their lips) ad nauseam, and the longest unbroken pooch smooch is declared the winner. The smearing of tasty substances on the owner's face to prolong the canine kiss is frowned upon. Store manager Jim Williams says: "We don't encourage artificial enhancers, like smothering their face with liver or meat, but we also don't frisk people coming in. The fact is, every dog is different. Some are good lickers and kissers, and others aren't." At the 2012 event, Beau, an eleven-year-old Yorkie and dachshund mix, took the prize by planting a 59-second smacker on her owner, Linda Walton. The pair set tongues and tails wagging by retaining their title the following year with a lingering wet embrace of 45.8 seconds. Why didn't the kiss last as long as the previous year's? Perhaps Beau hadn't brushed his teeth beforehand.

HIGHEST JUMP BY A PIG

In August 2004, Kotetsu, a young pot-bellied pig, set a new world record for the highest jump by a porker by clearing a height of 27.5 inches at a farm in Japan. He must have been delighted to learn that his fitness regime meant he would make lovely lean bacon.

LONGEST DIVE BY A PIG

Miss Piggy, a five-month-old sow owned by former Australian pig farmer Tom Vandeleur, dived into the record books in July 2005 by leaping a distance of 10 feet 10 inches into a pool from a 16-foot-high platform at the Royal Darwin Show. "It was a brilliant dive, it really was," said Vandeleur. "She just launched herself off the ramp and it was a beautiful motion. Her front legs were tucked in and her back legs were spread out. Pigs are water animals. They love the water, they've got no fear of it. It's just the height problem they have to overcome, but Miss Piggy does everything herself. She's not pushed or anything. She goes up the 16-foot ramp herself."

FIRST PIG TO FLY

In a light-hearted attempt to prove that pigs could fly, J.T.C. Moore-Brabazon, later Lord Brabazon of Tara, took a pig for a 3.7-mile flight in a Voisin airplane that took off from Shellbeach airfield on the Isle of Sheppey, Kent, on 4 November 1909. The pig was placed in a wicker basket, which in turn was strapped to a wing strut of the aircraft. A hand-written sign attached to the basket read: "I am the first pig to fly."

FIRST LIFE-SAVING PIG

Owned by Victoria Herberta, of Houston, Texas, Priscilla the pig hit the headlines on 29 July 1984 when she rescued an eleven-year-old boy from drowning. Paddling in Lake Somerville, Priscilla spotted that young Anthony Melton was in difficulties in deep water and swam to his aid. The boy had already gone under twice before Priscilla used her snout to keep his head above water until he could grab hold of her harness, and she then dragged him to the safety of the shore. A justifiably proud Ms Herberta revealed that swimming was Priscilla's idea of a grand day out. "It's now her favourite outing but she hated it at first. She squealed and cried about going in the water the first few times. I had to hold her in my arms and walk into the water with her. This despite the fact that her father Ralph was a swimming star. He was a swimming pig at Aquarena Springs in San Marcos." So it ran in the genes. As befitted a star from her snout to her trotters, Priscilla lived a life of luxury. She had the run of the house, her own bed and bedroom (although she sometimes shared Ms Herberta's bed), and feasted on a regular diet of tuna fish sandwiches, avocados, chocolate chip cookies and cheeseburgers, washed down by nine cases of Mountain Dew – a fizzy soft drink – each month. Priscilla's bravery was duly recognized by an award from the American Humane Society, with both owner and pig wearing matching purple outfits to the ceremony. Priscilla declined to give interviews after the presentation but Ms Herberta interpreted a casual oink as meaning: "She really appreciates it."

FIRST ANIMAL TO BE GIVEN AN OBITUARY IN *WISDEN CRICKETERS' ALMANACK*

Only one animal has ever been honoured with an obituary in the bible of cricket, the *Wisden Cricketers' Almanack*. The 1965 edition recorded the death of Peter the Lord's cat who regularly used to attend matches at the London ground. The obituary read: "CAT, Peter, whose ninth life ended on November 5, 1964, was a well-known cricket-watcher at Lord's, where he spent 12 of his 14 years. He preferred a close-up view of the proceedings and his sleek, black form could often be seen prowling on the field of play when the crowds were biggest. He frequently appeared on the television screen. Mr S.C. Griffith, secretary of MCC, said of him: 'He was a cat of great character and loved publicity.'"

CAT THAT CAUGHT MOST MICE IN A LIFETIME

Towser, a long-haired tortoiseshell cat that worked as a mouser at the Glenturret Distillery in Crieff, Scotland, for twenty-four years from 1963 until 1987, is listed as having caught an estimated 28,900 mice in her lifetime – an average of three a day. A stickler for efficiency, she laid her kills out on the floor each morning to be inspected by the stillman. Her hunting skills were such that her paw prints were later used to decorate some of the distillery's bottles, and today a statue stands in her honour at the site. Towser certainly proved a tough act to follow as her successor, Amber, apparently failed to catch a single mouse during her stint in rodent control.

CAT THAT STOLE MOST CUDDLY TOYS

When teddy bears began appearing regularly outside her bedroom door in 2013, Londoner Daisy Ayliffe thought she had a secret admirer. The mystery lasted a month – until she caught her five-year-old cat Zaza creeping in through the cat flap carrying a soft toy. In total the cat burglar snatched seventeen cuddly toys – ranging from a Roman gladiator to Winnie the Pooh – from neighbours' homes and gardens before her crime wave was ended, when she and her owner moved to a flat with a walled garden.

MOST EXPENSIVE CAT WEDDING

The groom arrived in a Rolls-Royce, the bride in a helicopter. Hundreds of VIP guests strained to catch a glimpse of the star-studded couple – a pair of disease-stricken cats named Phet and Ploy who were "married" in a $16,000 ceremony in Thailand's largest disco in September 1996. Their owner, Wichan Jaratarcha, staged the extravagant occasion because his business suddenly took off after he found Phet (the groom) near the Burmese border. The part-Siamese had a "diamond eye" (a type of glaucoma), which left him blind but which is seen as a good luck omen by Thai people – so much so that Jaratarcha later returned to the area and found Ploy, a female with the same eye condition. Deciding that the cats were in love, he planned a wonderfully weird wedding, at which the best man was a parrot and the maid of honour was an iguana. Phet wore a custom-made pink tuxedo with lace cuffs while Ploy wore a matching pink satin gown. Rings were even made to fit their paws. The 500 guests donated $60,000 in cash and gifts, and after exchanging meow vows, the newlyweds went on a honeymoon river cruise followed by a trip to the vet.

MOST ACCOMPLISHED CAT PIANIST

Nora, a grey tabby cat rescued from a New Jersey animal shelter, has demonstrated a remarkable talent for playing the piano in a music style that *The Times* described as "half-way between Philip Glass and free jazz". From the moment she moved into her new Philadelphia lodgings – with owners Betsy Alexander and Burnell Yow – Nora was fascinated by the two grand pianos in the house. At first she would climb on top of the piano lids and chase her reflection, but after a couple of years of studying other people playing, she jumped up onto the seat and began playing the piano herself. The fact that she sat at the piano using only her front paws immediately set her apart from other cats that make a noise simply by walking across the keys. Without waiting to be invited, she would play duets with Alexander – herself a piano teacher – and Alexander's students, showing a particular fondness for Bach, although unkind critics said it sounded more like Bach *de*composing.

Nevertheless, when a YouTube video of Nora's piano playing was uploaded in 2007, she became nothing short of an internet sensation, attracting 17 million hits in two years. She appeared on several TV shows – even playing live (the downfall of many a less furry artist) – and received congratulations from the Piano Man himself, Billy Joel. To the doubters, Alexander said: "This is her own thing; it's not a trick. It's not something we taught her. She plays when we're not in the room; sometimes she plays when we don't want her to play. I can be teaching a child or an adult who is trying to concentrate and then Nora hops on the bench." Elton John, Chopin, Scott Joplin, Liberace, Ray Charles, Lynsey de Paul, Russ Conway, Semprini, Richard Clayderman, Winifred Atwell, Rick Wakeman, Mrs Mills, Bobby Crush, Joe "Mr Piano" Henderson; your boys took a hell of a beating!

MOST PATRIOTIC CAT

Oleg Bouboulin's cat Margo became an internet star in Russia in 2014 by impersonating a soldier and standing to attention every time the Russian national anthem is played. The cat stands on her back legs without moving a muscle when the anthem plays, and even relaxes her body in anticipation as the tune is about to end. Bouboulin says: "I can only assume she has been watching the parades out of the window because we don't have a TV. When I first heard the anthem on the radio and saw her at the same time, I realized she really was standing to attention."

MOST REGULAR FELINE BUS PASSENGER

When Susan Finden adopted a five-year-old male cat from an animal rescue centre in Weymouth, Dorset, in 2002, she originally named him Morse (after the TV inspector) but soon changed it to Casper (after the friendly ghost) because he kept disappearing. It was not until she moved to Plymouth in 2006 that she discovered just how independent he was. For three years, she set off on her daily commute to work assuming that in her absence Casper probably did the things that most cats do during the day – namely sleep, chase birds for a bit, cough up a hairball in a part of the house where no one will find it and then go back to sleep. However, in early 2009, she learned that instead of lazing around the house he had been riding on buses, completing an eleven-mile round trip virtually every day to Plymouth city centre and back.

The First Devon & Cornwall bus company drivers told her that he would politely queue with other passengers at the bus stop outside her house, jump on to his favourite seat and remain there until the bus returned home. As the drivers became accustomed to their unusual passenger, they always ensured that he got off at the right stop. He became so famous that the bus company plastered some of their buses with his picture and said they had no intention of charging him a fare as in cat years he was an OAP anyway and so was entitled to a free bus pass. Sadly Casper's story does not have a happy ending because in 2010 he was run over and killed by a taxi that did not stop. The *Plymouth Herald*'s headline summed up the anger of the nation: "CELEBRITY CAT KILLED IN HIT AND RUN". The *Guardian* – no less – devoted an editorial to Casper's passing, noting that although he had a thing about buses, he had little road sense. "That could have been his undoing," it wrote. "But, all things considered, what a ride it was."

FIRST CAT TO CIRCUMNAVIGATE AUSTRALIA

Between 1801 and 1803, ship's cat Trim accompanied his master, English Captain Matthew Flinders, on his voyages to circumnavigate and map the coastline of Australia. Trim was perfectly suited to the role, having been born at sea onboard Flinders' ship *Roundabout* during her voyage from the Cape of Good Hope to Australia's Botany Bay. The kitten – jet black with a white star on his chest and white paws – came to Flinders' attention after falling overboard while the ship was in harbour. The crew members were impressed to see that the little cat apparently had no fear of water and that it managed to swim back to the vessel before climbing aboard by scaling a rope. Flinders decided to take Trim on all his expeditions, first returning to England and then on HMS *Investigator* for the mapping voyages around the coast of Australia. There, Trim established himself as top cat, presiding over the various dogs onboard. When the ship became unseaworthy, Flinders and Trim boarded the *Porpoise* for the return journey to England, but on 17 August 1803 it struck a coral reef and was wrecked. The survivors, including Flinders and Trim, swam ashore to Wreck Reef Bank in the Coral Sea where they endured two long and difficult months. Eventually a rescue ship arrived, but when this had to stop for repairs on the French island of Mauritius, Flinders was imprisoned as a spy. Trim loyally remained with his master in captivity until a French woman offered to give the cat a proper home as a companion for her young daughter. Flinders reluctantly agreed, but within two weeks Trim had vanished and, despite offering a handsome reward for his return, Flinders never saw him again. He suspected his pet had been eaten by hungry slaves. Flinders was held for seven years by the French and died in 1814, shortly after his return to England. However, neither he nor Trim have been forgotten, and to this day bronze statues of the pair stand in Sydney's Mitchell Library, where the café is also named after Australia's first seafaring cat.

LONGEST-SURVIVING TWO-FACED CAT

Born with two faces, two mouths, two noses and three eyes, Frank and Louie, a cat owned by Marty Stevens, of Worcester, Massachusetts, entered the *2012 Guinness World Records* book for being the world's longest-surviving Janus cat, a rare group named after the Roman god with two faces. Janus cats usually survive for just a few days, but Frank and Louie made feline history by celebrating his twelfth birthday on 8 September 2011. Naturally his life is not without its challenges. Both of his noses work but he can only see out of two of his three eyes. Also, one of his mouths lacks a lower jaw and is not connected to his oesophagus so he is unable to eat with it. But he gets by with the bits that do work. In 1999, Frank and Louie's breeder had taken him to the Cummings School of Veterinary Medicine at Tufts University, Massachusetts – where Stevens was working at the time – to be put down at just one day old, but Stevens asked if she could take the cat home, knowing that there was little chance of him surviving. So to be able to mark his twelfth birthday was a remarkable achievement. She said: "It's funny because people walk up to him thinking it's a nice, fluffy white cat and they're walking up with a big smile on their face to pat him, like 'Oh, what a beautiful cat.' And I see a look of horror when they actually see his face!"

CAT WITH MOST TOES

Bandit, a cat owned by Beth Stuart, of Hoboken, New Jersey, has a record twenty-nine toes, which make it look as if he is wearing mittens. Born in a dumpster in 1997, Bandit is a polydactyl (multi-digit) cat, enabling him to surpass the average cat that has a more modest eighteen toes – five on each front paw and four on each back paw. Author Ernest Hemingway was a lover of polydactyl cats, and was given a white six-toed cat named Snowball by a ship's captain. Hemingway's former home in Key West, Florida, has now become a museum where up to fifty polydactyl cats live, some of them descendants of Snowball.

CAT THAT PREDICTED MOST DEATHS

The Grim Reaper of the cat world is Oscar, who lives at a nursing home in Providence, Rhode Island, and who has displayed an uncanny knack of knowing when patients are about to die. By 2010 he had accurately predicted over fifty deaths simply by curling up and sleeping next to the dying residents. He would stay by the patient until the moment of death, whereupon he would then walk quietly away – no doubt satisfied with a job well done. In fact, he was so reliable that as soon as staff saw him sleeping next to a patient, they would call family members to warn them to expect the worst sooner rather than later. Understandably, in view of his reputation as a harbinger of doom, some relatives requested that Oscar be removed from the room, to which he reacted by pacing up and down outside the door, miaowing loudly in protest and hissing menacingly at the vulnerable. As one doctor summed up: "He is not a cat that's friendly to living people."

MOST FLATULENT CAT

There is bound to be a whiff of controversy surrounding this category, but the honour goes to Lenny, a black-and-white shorthair stray, who was returned to Scottsville Veterinary Hospital and Pet Adoptions in Washington in March 2014 for "farting all the time". Lenny had been rescued from a Rochester, New York park the previous month and nursed back to health at Scottsville before being adopted. However, just two days later his new owner returned him with the suggestion that the cat's frequent, pungent emissions might make him better suited to an outdoor life.

LONGEST-SERVING CAT MAYOR

In 2014, Mayor Stubbs celebrated his seventeenth year as mayor of the small town of Talkeetna, Alaska – an impressive feat for any elected official, but even more so in view of the fact that Stubbs is a cat. Stubbs was voted into office in July 1997 after Lauri Stec, manager of Nagley's General Store, found him in a box full of kittens in her parking lot. She named him "Stubbs" because he did not have a tail.

Although his title is honorary, he has done much to boost tourism in the area with as many as forty people a day dropping into the store, which is his main hangout, in the hope of meeting the mayor. "He's good, probably the best we've had," Stec told CNN. "He doesn't raise our taxes, he doesn't interfere with business, and he's honest." The mayor sleeps on a sumptuous fur-lined mushing sled but his only other demand is his daily drink of water laden with catnip, which he takes from a wine glass at a nearby restaurant. Like all politicians, Mayor Stubbs has been involved in a few scrapes down the years. He once escaped being shot by teenage louts with BB guns and on another occasion fell into a deep-fat fryer, which, thankfully, was switched off and cool at the time. In a separate moment of rashness, perhaps fuelled by too much catnip, he hitched a ride on a garbage truck, but jumped off before coming to any harm.

His most alarming experience, however, occurred in August 2013 when he was attacked by a loose dog and suffered serious wounds, resulting in a nine-day stay at an animal hospital. Donations towards his care and "get well soon" cards flooded in from all over the world – surely a unique experience for any politician. Happily, he was quickly back at his post, performing one of the duties from which he derives the greatest pleasure – keeping a close watch on the goldfish in the store's bowl. Everyone knows that politicians' lives can be hazardous, unpredictable and often brief, but it probably helps if, like Stubbs, you have nine.

CHIMPANZEE WITH LARGEST VOCABULARY

Kanzi, a thirty-three-year-old bonobo chimp who lives at the Great Ape Trust in Des Moines, Iowa, is able to understand 3,000 words and can "say" about 500 of them through a touch screen to order his favourite foods and toys and even to express emotion, thus making him considerably more communicative than many human males. He can also play Pac-Man to the second level and play music. Indeed, Kanzi and his sister Panbanisha once jammed with Peter Gabriel, playing the keyboard while the former Genesis frontman played the synthesizer. Demonstrating that there is seemingly no end to his talents, Kanzi can also cook, having been filmed breaking up kindling to make a fire, sliding open a box of matches and striking a match against the box before lighting his fire. He then carefully threaded marshmallows on to a stick, toasted and ate them. *Celebrity Masterchef* surely awaits.

MOST PROLIFIC CHIMPANZEE ARTIST

Congo, a chimpanzee at London Zoo, painted or drew more than 400 artworks in just two years, between the ages of two and four. He first learned to draw after being offered a pencil by zoologist and author Desmond Morris, and soon turned his talents to painting. Adopting a style described as "lyrical abstract impressionism", Congo began painting regularly with Morris, appearing with him on the TV series *Zoo Time*.

Morris observed that when a picture was taken away before Congo considered it to be finished, the chimp would scream and have an artistic tantrum. On the other hand, if Congo considered one of his works to be complete, no amount of persuasion could get him to continue. Let's be honest, it would have taken more than a few grapes to persuade Leonardo da Vinci to add a few extra gratuitous brush strokes to the "Mona Lisa", so why should Congo have been any different? Sadly Congo's artistic career was cut short in 1964 by his death from tuberculosis at the age of ten, but his fame lived on. Pablo Picasso was said to be a fan of Congo's paintings and hung one of the ape's pictures on his studio wall after receiving it as a gift. In 2005, Congo's paintings were included in an auction alongside works by Renoir and Warhol. While their efforts failed to sell, three of Congo's paintings were snapped up by American art collector Howard Hong for over $26,000.

MOST PROLIFIC HORSE ARTIST

Down the centuries many of the world's greatest artists have chosen to paint the noble horse but very few horses have been tempted to reciprocate the gesture by taking up brush and easel themselves. An exception was Cholla, a semi-wild Mustang mix owned by Nevada ballerina Renee Chambers. In 2004, when Cholla kept following Chambers around while she painted the corral, her husband joked: "You should get that horse to paint the fence." Instead Chambers nailed a piece of paper to a railing, bought some watercolours and handed a brush to Cholla, who gripped it in his teeth and stroked the paper. He then started painting on a regular basis, contemplating his next masterpiece between mouthfuls of hay.

In 2008, Chambers entered one of Cholla's earlier works, "The Big Red Buck", for an art competition in Italy and, overcoming their initial surprise at receiving an entry from a horse, the jury selected it for exhibition. Critics hailed Cholla's paintings, which have sold for up to $2,200, as possessing "the fire of Pollock", and in 2009 thirty of his original water-colours were exhibited in Venice. Chambers believed Cholla's international acclaim was proof of his artistic talents. "Yes, it's a novelty that a horse can paint," she once said, "but it's not about novelty anymore. It's about his validation as an artist. It's an innate ability he has. He wants to paint."

MOST NUMERATE HORSE

Wilhelm von Osten, a nineteenth-century Berlin mathematics teacher, was convinced that animals had hidden depths of intelligence, and to prove his point he set about teaching a cat, a bear and a horse some basic arithmetic. The cat was predictably indifferent to the whole exercise, the bear was downright hostile, but Hans the Arab stallion picked it up quickly and could soon use his hoof to tap out numbers up to ten that were written on a blackboard. Before long he was able to add, subtract, multiply, divide, and come up with the correct answers to square roots and fractions. He could also understand German and calculate calendar days. So if von Osten asked him, "If the first day of the month is a Tuesday, what is the date of the following Friday?'" Hans would correctly tap his hoof four times. He could also tap out the time of day and even learned how to spell words, giving one tap for an "A", two for a "B" and so on, although anything much beyond "H" made his legs ache.

Thrilled by his equine protégé, in 1891 von Osten began taking "Clever Hans" all over Germany but, unlike other sideshow operators of the time, he never charged admission. Hans rarely disappointed. His answers were found to be 89 per cent accurate and his grasp of mathematics was said to be the equivalent of that of a fourteen-year-old human. Naturally there were sceptics, but von Osten, being a man of science, was happy to submit Hans to close scrutiny and an independent commission of thirteen people ruled in 1904 that there was no trickery behind Hans's responses.

The investigative reins were then taken up by psychologist

Oskar Pfungst who, after exhaustive experiments, found that Hans only got the answer right if the questioner knew the correct answer and if the horse had an unobstructed view of that person. Pfungst concluded that Hans, while undeniably intelligent, simply picked up on unconscious communication from his human questioners to know when to stop tapping. Von Osten who, like Hans, was notoriously bad-tempered when things went wrong, dismissed Pfungst's findings and continued to show the horse around Germany to great acclaim. For his part, Hans made his feelings clear by giving Pfungst more than one savage bite during his investigation.

FASTEST PARROT ON A MOTORBIKE

In June 2012 at New Hampshire Motor Speedway, Myles S. Bratter rode his motorcycle at a speed of 78 mph with his seventeen-year-old pet macaw, Rainbow, perched untethered on his shoulder.

PARROT THAT CAN SAY "HELLO" IN THE MOST LANGUAGES

Bibi, a Congo African grey parrot owned by American Greg Moss, can speak greetings in twenty languages – English, Swahili, Japanese, Mandarin Chinese, German, French, Hawaiian, Spanish, Italian, Hebrew, Finnish, Polish, Arabic, Hindi, Russian, Bengali, Greek, Portuguese, Czech and Korean. She can also count to five in English, Chinese, Japanese and German, and to three in Spanish and Korean. This makes her a true polyglot.

MOST PSYCHIC PARROT

As well as understanding over 950 words and being capable of conducting actual conversations, N'Kisi, an African grey parrot owned by Aimee Morgana of New York, demonstrated psychic tendencies. According to scientist Rupert Sheldrake, who closely studied her behaviour in a 2001 experiment, the parrot could read her owner's mind by repeating what she was looking at on a card, even though she was in another room. Of 123 comments made by N'Kisi during the test sessions, 32 directly corresponded to the images Morgana was looking at, convincing Sheldrake that the bird was telepathic.

BIRD WITH LARGEST VOCABULARY

Puck, a budgerigar owned by Camille Jordan, of Petaluma, California, made it into the 1995 *Guinness World Records* for possessing a vocabulary of 1,728 words. Rather than just mimicking, Puck could create his own phrases and sentences. For example, on Christmas morning 1993, he was heard to say: "It's Christmas. That's what's happening. That's what it's all about. I love Pucky. I love everyone." Alas, Puck did not have long to enjoy his fame, for on 25 August 1994, just a few months after being accepted into the Guinness book, he died of a tumour at the age of five.

MOST ACCOMPLISHED DANCING COCKATOO

A male sulphur-crested cockatoo named Snowball has been hailed as the first non-human creature capable of genuinely dancing to music. Whereas other animals and birds might throw the odd shape worthy of a "Dad dance" at a wedding, Snowball has been observed not only spontaneously dancing to human music but also possessing the ability to adjust his movements according to the tempo, a behaviour previously thought only to occur among humans.

His talent first came to light when he was seen bobbing his head to his favourite song, the Backstreet Boys' "Everybody (Backstreet's Back)". When Snowball ended up in an Indiana bird shelter in 2007 after becoming "difficult to manage", the shelter's owner, Irena Schultz, was amazed to see him lifting his legs in time with the music "like a cancan girl". So she uploaded a video of the boogying bird to YouTube, where it received over 200,000 views in a week. The YouTube clip was brought to the attention of California-based neuroscientist Dr Aniruddh Patel who said his "jaw hit the floor" when he first saw it. Unable to believe that a cockatoo could dance so rhythmically to human music, he compared it to that of a dog reading a newspaper out loud.

LONGEST SURVIVING HEADLESS CHICKEN

The day of 10 September 1945 was much like any other for Lloyd Olsen – until his wife Clara sent him out to the yard of their farm in Fruita, Colorado, to kill a chicken for dinner. Armed with his trusty axe, Olsen selected a five-and-a-half-month-old Wyandotte cockerel named Mike as the ideal candidate for the cooking pot. It seemed like a routine chore, but although the implement severed the bird's head, it missed the jugular vein, leaving one ear and most of Mike's brain stem intact. Consequently, although he was somewhat lacking in the head department Mike was able to carry on living for another eighteen months, making him the most crowed about cockerel in the United States.

At first when Mike continued staggering around and trying to preen himself (a futile gesture since he no longer possessed a beak), Olsen put it down to the type of delayed reaction that had frequently been reported among freshly beheaded poultry, but when the bird flatly refused to keel over and die, the farmer sensed that something truly unusual had occurred. Touched by Mike's defiance in the face of overwhelming odds, Olsen decided that he should be spared the pot and instead began caring for him as a pet. He fed him a mix of water and milk via an eyedropper and also gave him small grains of corn. Mike gamely responded by trying to crow (the actual sound being described as more of a gurgle in the throat) and attempting to peck for food with his neck. This was one proud cockerel!

Over the next eighteen months, his weight increased from 2.5 pounds at the time of the failed execution to nearly 8 pounds, Olsen describing him in interviews as "a fine, robust specimen of a chicken except for not having a head". As Mike's fame spread, Olsen realized there was money to be made and began charging visitors 25 cents a head to see the feathered miracle. Mike was insured for $10,000 and began touring in sideshows along with other unusual creatures such as a two-headed calf, but the headless chicken was in a league of his own and was soon gracing magazine covers. At the height of his popularity, he earned $4,500 a month – the equivalent of around $50,000 in today's money. It has been said that his success resulted in a wave of copycat chicken beheading, but no other bird lived for more than a day or two. Mike was one of a kind.

Even so, the Olsens were aware that, with Mike's tenuous grip on life, their gravy train could be derailed at any time. That moment finally came in March 1947 when, travelling back from tour, they stopped over at a motel in Phoenix, Arizona. In the middle of the night Mike started choking, but because the Olsens had accidentally left the eyedropper used to clear his open esophagus at the sideshow, they were unable to save him. Mike the headless chicken was no more. However, his legend lives on, and since 1999 every third weekend in May has been designated "Mike the Headless Chicken Day" in Fruita, with events including the 5k Run Like a Headless Chicken Race and Pin the Head on the Chicken.

MOST NUMERATE CHICKEN

They say don't count your chickens until they're hatched – possibly because J.J. the amazing counting hen could do it for you. Dubbed "the Carol Vorderman of poultry", J.J. has learned to count using playing cards. When her owner, Helen Jones, from Felmingham, Norfolk, presents J.J. with a numbered card, she pecks at it the corresponding number of times. To prove that she is definitely no bird brain, J.J. has also started learning how to play noughts and crosses.

RABBIT WITH LONGEST EARS

Nipper's Geronimo, an English Lop rabbit owned by Waymon and Margaret Nipper, of Bakersfield, California, had ears measured at a record 31.12 inches long at a Kansas rabbit show, in 2003.

LARGEST LITTER OF RABBITS

Breeding is pretty much what rabbits do best, and on 30 December 1997 a New Zealand White/Californian cross belonging to Peter Maur gave birth to a litter of twenty-six kits, twenty-four of which survived. Appropriately the bumper bunny was called Motherload.

MOST RABBITS SNUGGLED WITH IN A HAMMOCK

When actress Cameron Diaz appeared on the US TV show *Late Night With Jimmy Fallon* on 26 June 2009, she gamely set a new world record by cuddling up to forty-eight rabbits in a hammock. If there was any justice in the world that record would have stood forever, but instead, barely a week later – on 3 July – a spoilsport by the name of Australian radio DJ Nathan Morris shared a hammock with fifty rabbits in Perth. If it's any consolation, the bunnies that snuggled up to the lovely Ms Diaz would have had more stories to tell their grandchildren, which, given the enthusiasm of the average rabbit, were probably born about two weeks later.

FIRST BEAR TO CADDIE ON A GOLF COURSE

Hercules, a ten-foot-tall trained grizzly bear weighing half a ton, made history in September 1980 by caddying for comedian Bob Hope at a show business golf tournament at Turnberry, Ayrshire. It should be said at this point that there was no indication that Hercules could tell the difference between a six-iron and a Centurion tank, but it didn't really matter as his on-course duties were somewhat restricted by the fact that Hope was terrified of bears – ever since he and Bing Crosby were nearly killed by one while making the movie *Road to Utopia*. For Hercules, however, his golfing debut was another step towards international stardom in a career that saw him wrestle with Roger Moore in the James Bond movie *Octopussy*, feature on the cover of *Time* magazine, and promote everything from the Miss World contest to vodka.

The young bear was bought for £50 from a wildlife park in 1975 by wrestler Andy Robin and his wife Maggie, and lived with them at their Scottish ranch where he enjoyed the freedom of the place and quickly became their "surrogate son". Robin had wrestled a muzzled black bear called Terrible Ted in Toronto, Canada, in 1968, and by lasting fifteen minutes in the ring with the beast had earned himself a sizeable sum of money. Now he saw Hercules as the ideal opponent in a sport that was never short of publicity gimmicks. Playing the role of a gentle giant, Hercules would go on to draw audiences of fifteen million on ITV's *World of Sport* programme, which in turn led to TV acting roles and commercials. At home, the friendly bear drank coffee and beer (Maggie Robin described him as "a very happy drunk") and let people sit on his back.

When his celebrity status went stratospheric in August 1980 it was not because of lurid tales about a salmon addiction or a secret love cub, but because he went walkabout on a TV commercial for Kleenex tissues. The commercial (with Hercules as The Big Softy) was being filmed on Benbecula, an island in the Outer Hebrides, but the bear managed to escape and, despite a search party involving the army and hundreds of volunteers, he was missing for twenty-four days before a crofter spotted him swimming. He was flown by helicopter back to the Robins but had lost half his body weight. He was promptly given a humanitarian award by Animals in America for "failing to harm any wildlife while starving" and was named Personality of the Year by the Scottish Tourist Board.

As his fame soared, Hercules met Margaret Thatcher, received a letter from the Queen inviting him to appear in a

Royal Variety Performance and a telegram from Ronald Reagan congratulating him on becoming the new mascot for the University of California. He appeared on US TV chat chows and did cabaret in Las Vegas, where he was billed as "stronger than Superman, heavier than The Incredible Hulk". Alas, part of his big scene in *Octopussy*, where he pinned Roger Moore against a circus bus, was cut in the final edit because it showed the actor looking decidedly shaken, if not stirred. Maggie Robin remarked: "Roger was clearly more at ease with women than bears."

His career finally ended when he stumbled and slipped a disc in his back while making a TV wildlife documentary in the late 1990s. He never fully recovered, and died in 2001, to be buried in a homemade coffin next to his swimming pool at the Robins' ranch. In 2013, a statue was erected in his honour on North Uist, the scene of his eventual capture following his great escape. Although he could have killed them at any time, his owners never had any worries that Hercules would keep his huge claws to himself. "He couldn't stand the smell of blood," said Maggie. "He wouldn't eat any meat unless I'd cooked it first and even then he could be very fussy. He was my real-life teddy bear. He never once let us down."

FIRST LLAMA TO CADDIE ON A GOLF COURSE

After a birdie, an eagle and an albatross, a new creature entered golfing vocabulary at the Cherwell Edge Club in Oxfordshire in 1997 – a llama. Club professional Joe Kingston discovered that Henry the llama made an ideal caddie, because not only are llamas used to carrying far heavier loads than a bag of golf clubs, but their soft, padded hooves don't damage the precious greens. Once the round was over, Henry even popped into the clubhouse for a well-earned drink and some sugar. Furthermore, there was no danger of him depositing natural hazards all over the course. "Henry's very well behaved," said his owner Mary Pryse. "We know if he wants to go to the toilet – he starts humming. It's what llamas do if they're uncomfortable."

FASTEST SNAIL OVER DISTANCE
OF THIRTEEN INCHES

The World Snail Racing Championships were first staged at Congham, Norfolk, in the 1960s after founder Tom Elwes witnessed a similar event in France. Now around 200 of the world's fastest snails gather every June for a series of races which take place on top of a table covered with a damp cloth, as snails prefer soft going. Each competitor's shell is marked with a number to help identification. After all, you wouldn't want to be cheering on the wrong snail, would you? On a shout of "Ready, Steady, Slow", the snails race unassisted from the centre of a circle to the outside – a distance of thirteen inches, which is the equivalent of nearly a mile for a mollusc. The standard time is around 3.5 minutes, but the world record was set in 1995 by a speedy snail called Archie who completed the distance in a remarkable 2 minutes 0 seconds at a top speed of 0.0062 mph. Photographers who tried to capture the moment said he was just a blur. The 2008 winner was named Heikki Kovalainen after the Finnish Formula One driver. Snailmaster Neil Riseborough, who starts each race, is proud of the event's credentials. "It's a good clean sport," he says, "and fortunately we've not had any doping scandals yet. No snail has failed a random slime sample." Even so, to be on the safe side, he probably keeps a close eye on any snail named Lance Armstrong.

MOST SNAILS ON FACE

In May 2009, Fin Keleher, from Sandy, Utah, celebrated his eleventh birthday by allowing forty-three live snails to be put on his face. During his birthday party he made four separate attempts at breaking the previous record of thirty-six, sitting back in a reclining chair while slimy molluscs collected from neighbours' gardens were arranged so that they covered virtually every inch of his face. Explaining his technique, he said: "I closed my eyes and sucked my lips in so the snails could crawl on that." It was probably some time before his mother gave him a birthday kiss.

FIRST DEVICE THAT ALLOWS OWNER TO TAKE PET FISH FOR A WALK

Worried that his pet goldfish Malcolm was getting bored with swimming around his bowl for days on end, former sheet metal worker Mike Warren-Madden, from Holmfirth, West Yorkshire, designed and built a device called an Aquatic Perambulator so that he could take the fish for a walk. Consisting of a fish bowl on a stand on wheels, with a long handle, the contraption certainly appeared to bring fulfilment to Malcolm, who lived to the ripe old age of twelve. The inventor said: "If a fish is in a bowl on a shelf swimming in circles, it must get bored. I decided it would be fun to take it down to the pub. We had some right looks around town, we stopped traffic. I suppose it's not every day you see someone taking a fish for a walk."

FIRST BABOON SOLDIER

A baboon named Jackie served in the South African army on the Western Front during the First World War. He was owned by Albert Marr and lived on the family farm in Villieria, Pretoria. When Marr was called up in August 1915, he asked army chiefs if Jackie could come too, and to his surprise they agreed. Initially a mascot for the 3rd Transvaal Regiment, Jackie was later made a private and given messenger and watch duties as well as his own uniform, pay book and rations. He apparently learned to stand to attention and even salute when in the presence of superior officers, all of whom were human – at least in terms of species. He would also light cigarettes for his fellow soldiers and made an excellent sentry on account of his sharp hearing and sense of smell, which enabled him to detect an enemy far earlier than his colleagues.

He spent three years in the trenches, and when Marr was injured in the shoulder during a battle in Egypt, Jackie stayed beside him until the stretcher bearers arrived, licking the wound and generally comforting his friend. In April 1918, Jackie himself was wounded by an exploding shell at Passchendaele in Belgium, as a result of which his right leg was amputated. He was subsequently promoted to the rank of corporal, awarded a medal for bravery and, on his discharge from the army, given a military pension. The world's first baboon soldier returned to the family farm, where he died three years later on 22 May 1921.

FIRST BEAR SOLDIER

When soldiers from the Second Polish Transport Company found a baby brown bear wandering the hills of Iran in 1943, they adopted him and named him Wojtek, meaning "smiling warrior". They raised him on condensed milk from an empty vodka bottle and soon the 6-foot-tall, 250-pound bear became part of the unit, even enjoying beers and cigarettes with his fellow soldiers. In 1944, he was officially enlisted into the Polish Army as a private, and was trained to salute and to carry mortar shells and boxes of ammunition during battle. It is said that he never dropped a single crate. He also distinguished himself by discovering an Arab spy hiding in the unit's bath hut. While the spy was recovering from the shock of coming face to face with a full-grown bear, his captor was rewarded with his favourite bottle of beer. After the war, Wojtek moved to Edinburgh Zoo, where former Polish soldiers would often toss him cigarettes, which he proceeded to eat as there was nobody around to light them for him. The ursine warrior lived out his remaining days at the zoo until his death in 1963.

MOST BEES ON BODY

When American animal trainer Mark Biancaniello wore an 87-pound bee beard made up of 350,000 insects in 1998, he opened up a veritable hornets' nest. For since then, there have been several attempts to wear even bigger mantles of honey bees, not only on the face but over the entire body. The bees are usually lured from their hives by a queen bee placed in a small cage under the wearer's chin. In 2005, wearing little more than underpants and goggles, plucky Irish beekeeper Philip McCabe tried to break the record using heavier native black bees, but after two hours he had only attracted about 200,000 bees weighing a total of 60 pounds and was forced to give up because his feet were numb. Having, suffered no stings during the failed attempt, he finally stepped off the scales and was immediately stung seven times. However, on 9 March 2009, Indian Vipin Seth did set a new world record by wearing a beard composed of an estimated 613,500 bees, weighing a total of 135 pounds.

LONGEST TIME SPENT LIVING IN A
ROOM FULL OF SCORPIONS

Between December 2008 and January 2009, Thailand's self-proclaimed "Scorpion Queen", Kanchana Ketkaew, spent thirty-three days and nights living in a small room with over 5,000 scorpions, during which she was stung thirteen times. It may come as no great surprise to learn that Ketkaew, who has also kept a live scorpion in her closed mouth for over two minutes, is married to Thailand's "Centipede King", Bunthawee Siengwong. They met while performing at a snake farm, he put a live centipede in his mouth during the marriage ceremony, and they spent their wedding night sleeping in a coffin.

MOST RATS DOWN A PAIR OF TIGHTS

As part of his stage act, former rat-catcher Ken Edwards, from Stockport, Greater Manchester, stuffed forty-seven live rats down a pair of tights – while he was wearing them. According to broadcaster Brian Johnston, who visited Edwards for his long-running radio series *Down Your Way*, "as far as Ken was concerned, being able to take home some of the rats was one of the perks of his job. He kept about a hundred of them in cages in his garden, all fully checked by veterinary laboratories and treated with antibiotics." Edwards trained his rats for appearances in horror movies such as *Black Death* and *1984* and, more alarmingly, took them to discos up and down the country in company with his assistant Dave Potts under the stage name "Ratman and Robin".

MOST RATS KILLED IN A YEAR

With up to 10 per cent of Bangladesh's crops destroyed by rats each year, the country's Department of Agriculture organizes annual rat-killing contests. In 2008, the title went to impoverished farmer Binoy Kumar Karmakar who used traps, poison and flooding to slay a record 39,650 rats over the calendar year. After producing the rodents' tails as proof of his killing prowess, he won the first prize of a 14-inch colour TV.

MOST FLIES KILLED IN A DAY

In her capacity as a voluntary pest controller, eighty-year-old Chinese pensioner Ruan Tang kills up to 1,000 flies a day in the city of Hangzhou. She has been feverishly swatting insects since the year 2000, and devotes eight hours a day to the task – acquiring a level of expertise that means no fly is safe from her predatory eye. Explaining how she became the country's leading flycatcher, she says: "I had retired and was looking around for something to do to help the community and I noticed how much flies were troubling people in the summer. I decided that killing flies was the best way for me to be useful." Her neighbours are certainly appreciative of her efforts. One described her as "a fly-killing specialist, our heroine".

MOST PETS BURIED IN A BACK GARDEN

The *Daily Mirror* reported in 2004 that Jean Pyke had created a cemetery for twenty-two dead pets – cats, dogs and budgies – in the back garden of her home in Hayling Island, Hampshire, where they were buried alongside the ashes of her late husband Theo. Each burial place had an inscribed Italian marble tombstone and each pet was laid to rest in a specially made casket with a satin lining, pillow and duvet. She said: "I was not just going to put them in a plastic bag and send them off in a dustbin. They were my best friends and we have shared a lot of love."

MOST JUMPERS KNITTED FOR PENGUINS

Lyn Blom, a member of Knits for Nature, an Australian conservation group run by Phillip Island's Penguin Foundation, has knitted more than 300 woolly jumpers for penguins, including sweaters in the colours of every Australian Rules football team. The jumpers help the birds recover from the effects of oil spills, by keeping them warm and by preventing them cleaning the toxic oil away with their beaks. The volunteers have created some 300 different designs for the penguins to wear, and even staged a competition to find the most creative jumper. The winning entry had an octopus and seaweed crocheted onto it. Another one had little red budgie-smugglers and a six-pack, a nod to Australian Prime Minister Tony Abbott who was photographed so frequently in his Speedos on the beach that his wife reportedly banned him from wearing them again in public.

MOST SNAKES SMUGGLED IN A BRA

A forty-two-year-old woman tried to smuggle seventy-five live snakes into Sweden by hiding them in her bra. Customs officers in Stockholm became suspicious when they noticed that she kept scratching her chest, and on further inspection of her heaving cleavage they found dozens of baby grass snakes writhing around in her bra and six lizards crawling about under her blouse. The woman said she was planning to start a reptile farm.

MOST FISH SMUGGLED UNDER A SKIRT

Customs officials at Melbourne Airport, Australia, had their suspicions aroused by a female passenger in 2005 after they heard strange flipping noises coming from underneath her skirt. When they decided to take a peek, they discovered that she had strapped on an apron of plastic water-filled bags containing fifty-one live tropical fish.

MOST BIRDS SMUGGLED IN A PAIR OF TROUSERS

Sony Dong was arrested at Los Angeles International Airport in April 2009 for attempting to smuggle fourteen live songbirds into the US from Vietnam by strapping them in pouches to his lower legs beneath his trousers. Customs officials were alerted by the large number of bird droppings on his shoes.

MOST MONKEYS STRAPPED TO WAIST

Would-be smuggler Roberto Sol Cabrera flew from Lima, Peru, to Mexico City in July 2010 with eighteen small monkeys hidden about his person. He might have succeeded in his mission had he not panicked when subjected to a random security check at Mexico City's international airport. After his arrest, he revealed that the animals had travelled in his luggage but that he had put them in socks attached to a girdle around his waist as he passed through customs in order "to protect them from X-rays".

MOST RATTLESNAKES HELD IN THE MOUTH

Texan Jackie Bibby has been handling rattlesnakes for over forty years, and is the holder of five world records that few people would want to beat. These include holding 13 rattlesnakes in his mouth at the same time (thankfully by the tail) in July 2012, sitting in a bathtub with 195 rattlesnakes, lying in a sleeping bag with 109 rattlesnakes and, because that obviously wasn't dangerous enough, going head first in a sleeping bag with 24 rattlesnakes. It's clear to see that Bibby has a thing about rattlesnakes. He first became hooked as an eighteen-year-old when he attended a local rattlesnake sacking. "I didn't know a rattlesnake from a cobra," he says, "but I was a thrill seeker. I got 30 dollars, a trophy and my name in the paper."

Perhaps the most remarkable aspect of his subsequent career is that he has only been seriously bitten twelve times. His closest brush with death was when he tried a Medusa act for the one and only time. "I was bitten in the head, but it was what they call a dry bite. That's where the snake does inject venom, but is really just trying to give a warning to get away. I was very lucky. That could have been a death sentence. I have not and will not do that stunt again." Otherwise he is fairly relaxed about working with the deadly reptiles and says it is by no means the most terrifying thing he has done. "Jumping out of airplanes is way scarier than handling snakes," he said in a 2012 interview. "I've done that 59 times and have never gotten used to it. But just like with rattlesnakes, you can never conquer fear, but you can control it."

FASTEST TIME TO CATCH THIRTY CHICKENS IN A CAGE

On the set of a 2011 TV show in Jakarta, Indonesia, Panca Wibowo took 1 minute 51 seconds to catch thirty chickens in a five-metre-square cage. The record for catching thirty free-range chickens is considerably longer.

BIGGEST WHALE EXPLOSION

When a 45-foot-long, 8-ton sperm whale washed up dead on a beach near Florence, Oregon, in November 1970, the local authorities were at a loss to know what to do with it. It was clearly too late to administer the kiss of life, it couldn't be incinerated and nobody wanted to cut it up. So they decided to blow up the whale carcass using half a ton of dynamite. As a precaution, sightseers were moved back a quarter of a mile, but the explosion was so powerful that it sent huge chunks of rotting whale meat flying into the air and raining down on spectators. One lump smashed through the roof of a parked car, which fortunately was unoccupied at the time. Try explaining that to your insurance company.

BIGGEST LUMP OF EARWAX

The largest lump of earwax ever recorded was a ten-inch-long plug extracted from a twelve-year-old male blue whale that beached on the California coast in 2007. Scientists predicted that the candle-like substance, which smelled foul, would tell us a lot about the whale's life – such as the fact that he didn't use cotton buds.

LONGEST FOSSILIZED POOP

An eye-watering forty-inch-long poop, found in Washington State, earns the coveted title of the world's longest fossilized stool. Dating back between five and thirty-four million years, it was put up for auction in 2014 in Beverly Hills where it was so long it had to be presented in four sections. It eventually sold for $8,500 to an anonymous private collector from the Midwest. Describing the cherished coprolite, the auction house said: "It boasts a wonderfully even, pale brown-yellow colouring and terrifically detailed texture to the heavily botryoidal surface across the whole of its immense length." Scientists probing the origin of the faeces say they have no idea what species was responsible for producing the super poop.

FIRST HELICOPTER MADE FROM A DEAD CAT

When his pet cat Orville, named after pioneering aviator Orville Wright, was run over by a car, Dutch artist Bart Jansen wanted to commemorate his passing in a dignified, appropriate manner. So he had him stuffed and turned into a helicopter. Jansen joined forces with radio control helicopter expert Arjen Beltman to build a flying mechanism that was attached to the dead cat's body so that Orville could speed through the air as fast as a bird, which, Jansen suspected, would have been his dearest wish had he still been alive. Describing the Orvillecopter as "half cat, half machine", Jansen added sombrely that "after a period of mourning, Orville received his propellers posthumously". The *Guardian* summed up the project with the headline: "IS IT A BIRD? IS IT A PLANE? NO . . . IT'S A DEAD CAT WITH PROPELLERS".

CHAPTER 7

That's Entertainment?

FIRST ARTIST TO PAINT WITH HIS PENIS

Of the millions of artists in the world, most work with a brush or a knife, but one Australian prefers to paint with a different tool – his penis. Tim Patch was actually born in Sussex, but in 1977 the former builder migrated to Australia where he began exhibiting woodcarvings. Then in 2005 he drew a smiley face on the back of a urinal with his penis and decided to recreate it at home using paint. After he told a friend about painting by members, she encouraged him to make an exhibition of himself at a New Year's Party and his alter ego – Pricasso – was born.

Since normal paint contains lime, which erodes the skin, he always uses water-based paints. He also first daubs his dick in Vaseline so that he can work for hours at a time without causing irritation as he finds that a condom inhibits his strokes. Understandably, perhaps, most celebrities are wary of having him paint their portrait in person, but he has built up quite a following at private parties. "I think I'm just as good as anyone with a brush," he says, "and I'm probably a lot quicker." But not too quick, for although he is very excited about his painting method, fortunately he has yet to produce a seminal work. To date, he has created portraits of such diverse figures as George W. Bush, Tony Blair, the Queen and Hugh Hefner, and while his style may not be to everyone's taste, there is one thing you can be sure of with a genuine Pricasso: it will be well hung.

FIRST ARTIST TO PAINT WITH BREASTS

American artist Kira Ayn Varszegi uses her 38DD breasts as brushes to create unique paintings. She simply applies oil paint directly on to her breasts and presses them against the canvas. Since creating her first breast work in 2001, she has used her ample assets to paint hundreds of pictures, some of which have sold for more than $1,000. She says: "I enjoy finding new ways to get paint on to a canvas, and I like to make people smile. I think my art raises more than a few smiles."

MOST PAINTINGS USING A SINGLE HAIR FROM A BEARD

Mukesh Thapa, from Himachal Pradesh, India, has painted 600 oil pictures by using a single hair of his beard, which he pulled out himself, as an ultra-thin brush. Although he has never had any proper artistic training, he practised his painfully slow technique for six years and now has a gallery dedicated to his works. Each painting can take him up to a year to complete.

LARGEST PAINTING BY MOUTH

To India's R. Rajendran goes the honour of creating the world's largest painting by mouth. Gripping the paint brush between his teeth and using no hands, he daubed different colours onto a huge canvas to make a 30-foot-long, 20-foot-high picture of Mother Teresa in eleven days, from 19 to 30 October 2007, at Chennai. Lest anyone should think him unusual, he is quick to point out that he doesn't always paint with his mouth. Sometimes he uses his tongue . . .

MOST ACCOMPLISHED ARTIST USING
BOTH HANDS SIMULTANEOUSLY

Every YouTube video of a cute kitten, a tap-dancing lizard or a dog that looks like Vladimir Putin is immediately described as being an internet sensation, but in the case of Chinese artist Xiaonan Sun the term is merited. For his video shows him drawing uncannily accurate portraits of Hollywood actors Morgan Freeman and Tim Robbins . . . simultaneously, by using both hands. It comes as no great surprise to learn that his highly unusual method is self-taught, since few art teachers would entertain the concept.

FIRST PORTRAIT PAINTED WITH A BASKETBALL

Shanghai artist Yi Hong likes to make life difficult for herself by painting with a basketball rather than a brush. By dipping the ball in paint and bouncing it on the canvas, she created a large, lifelike portrait of retired Chinese NBA star Yao Ming in 2012.

MOST CANS FILLED BY AN ARTIST
WITH HIS OWN POOP

Always looking to break new ground, Italian artist Piero Manzoni came up with the wizard wheeze of filling ninety tin cans with pieces of his own poop and calling it art. He labelled his 1961 work "Merda d'artista" ("Artist's Shit") and offered the cans of excrement for sale at a price equal to their weight in gold, which at that time was about £25 per can. A label on each can, printed in Italian, French, English and German, duly identified the contents as "'Artist's Shit', 30 grams net freshly preserved, produced and tinned in May 1961". As the value of Manzoni's bowel product soared following his untimely death in 1963, museums and galleries across the world paid extravagant sums for the cans, one selling at Sotheby's in

2008 for $166,618. A couple of the artist's former associates have added insult to injury by claiming that the cans do not contain poop at all but merely plaster, which stirred up something of a storm in a toilet bowl, but an art dealer from the Gallery Blu in Milan claims to have detected a distinctly faecal odour emanating from a can. So that's okay then. After all, you wouldn't want to pay nearly $200,000 for something that wasn't genuine poop.

LARGEST INFLATABLE TURD

American artist Paul McCarthy built a fifty-one-foot-high inflatable turd for use as an art installation under the title "Complex Pile". Exhibited around the world, the huge brown dollop – the size of a house – has had a chequered history. In 2008, a sudden gust of wind cut it loose from its moorings outside a modern art museum in Berne, Switzerland, and sent it soaring through the air before landing 200 yards away in the grounds of a children's home. Nothing that the young residents had been through could have prepared them for the sight of a giant poop hurtling towards them. The unsavoury incident led to newspaper headlines such as "Up in the Sky: Is it a Turd or a Plane?" Then in 2013, a Hong Kong downpour deflated the tower of excrement, reducing it to a mass of burst brown balloons and leaving the once proud poop looking more like a sorry cow pat.

MOST EXTREME PERFORMANCE ART INVOLVING URINE, PUBIC HAIR AND VOMIT

As a protest against media coverage of gay issues, a group of artists named 5th Passage put on a public performance at a Singapore shopping mall on New Year's Day 1994. The show started with Vincent Leow drinking his own urine. Then Thai artist Joseph Ng, dressed in a black robe and swimming trunks, cut off his own pubic hair and presented it on a plate to delighted onlookers. The grand finale saw Shannon Tham vomiting into a bucket, at which point the shopping centre authorities removed the group. Ng was subsequently charged with committing "an obscene act". He pleaded guilty and was fined $1,000. His lawyer said: "He did it for the love of art and in the interest of expanding the general outlook of art in Singapore."

MOST PROLIFIC UNDERWATER ARTIST

After crushing a nerve in his back – an injury that left him incapacitated for eighteen months – experienced Belgian scuba diver Jamy Verheylewegen suddenly had a vision that he should be painting underwater. Getting straight to work, he strapped thirty pounds of lead to his wet suit and, armed with a weighted easel, synthetic canvas and oil-based paint, saw his career plumb new depths. Since 1983, he has produced well over 400 underwater paintings at depths of up to 120 feet, mostly beneath the Mediterranean. Since colours are difficult to distinguish underwater, he numbered each paint jar and memorized the code – his own version of painting by numbers. He often paints coral towers, flora jungles or rock formations, but rarely fish. "They refuse to pose," he once grumbled. His end products are regularly exhibited underwater with lead weights attached, anyone wishing to view them having to be taken beneath the waves by bathyscaphe.

MOST PROLIFIC TOAST ARTIST

New Zealander Maurice Bennett has made about 100 different artworks – including portraits of the Mona Lisa, Barack Obama, Elvis Presley, Dame Edna Everage and New Zealand rugby player Jonah Lomu – from toast. His largest portraits are over forty feet high and require thousands of slices of bread, which he toasted to different tones to create skin highlights and shadow. They are often mounted on billboards, where the toast is pre-soaked in polyurethane to prevent it going soggy when it rains. "One piece of toast is completely different to another," says the former supermarket worker who has also started making toast mosaics inspired by Maori carvings.

THE BIGGEST MONA LISA MADE FROM CUPS OF COFFEE

A team of eight artists used 3,604 cups of coffee and 564 pints of milk to make a 20-foot by 13-foot replica of the "Mona Lisa" at the Rocks Aroma Festival in Sydney, Australia, in 2009. The cups were filled with different amounts of milk to create the variation in shade.

THE LARGEST PORTRAIT OF BARACK OBAMA MADE FROM VEGETABLES

Using eighty-eight pounds of vegetables – including carrots, chilies, bitter gourd, tomatoes and cucumber – Harwinder Singh Gill, from Punjab, India, created a 10-foot by 12-foot portrait of Barack Obama in November 2012.

MOST WINE CORKS USED IN A PORTRAIT OF MARILYN MONROE

In 2012, to mark the fiftieth anniversary of the actress's death, London-based American artist Conrad Engelhardt created a portrait of Marilyn Monroe from around 2,200 wine corks, with over sixty for her mouth alone. His raw materials are generously donated by local restaurants.

MOST TUBES OF TOOTHPASTE USED IN A PORTRAIT OF ROBIN WILLIAMS

Cristiam Ramos, a Mexican artist based in Orlando, Florida, creates portraits of celebrities like Robin Williams and Miley Cyrus using ordinary tubes of toothpaste. Applying the toothpaste to the canvas first with a finger and later with a brush, he has to apply numerous layers since toothpaste can be almost transparent. As a result each portrait can take him 200 hours and use thirty tubes of toothpaste. "It is very difficult to makes these pictures," he says, "as the toothpaste becomes very sticky and dries quickly. The smell can also be overwhelming, which was challenging during the long days of up to 10 hours working." Frankly, Cristiam, that's why in most normal people's minds toothpaste is for cleaning teeth and paint is for making pictures.

MOST PORTRAITS OF MAHATMA GANDHI DRAWN ON AN EGG SHELL

Manjit Kumar Shah, from Assam, India, used a black gel pen to draw 1,615 portraits of Mahatma Gandhi onto a single egg shell, in November 2012.

FIRST ARTIST TO WIN THE TURNER PRIZE WITH A PICTURE CONTAINING ELEPHANT DUNG

Chris Ofili won the 1998 Turner Prize for "No Woman No Cry", which depicts a weeping woman wearing a pendant of elephant dung. Ofili has incorporated elephant dung into dozens of his artworks, including a controversial 1996 portrait of the Virgin Mary. He was first inspired to use it on a 1992 trip to Zimbabwe, when he went on safari looking for elephants but only found a lot of dung. He packed some as a souvenir and brought it back to his studio in London, and when his supply ran out he turned to London Zoo, drying out the fresh excrement in an airing cupboard. He has even used elephant dung in the mounting of his pictures. Instead of hanging them on a wall, he often perches his finished canvases on two lumps of dung.

LONGEST TIME FOR A PERFORMANCE ARTIST TO SIT AND STARE

Serbian Marina Abramovic spent three months sitting in a chair and staring at people – all in the name of art. Her sit-in at the Museum of Modern Art in New York lasted seven hours a day, six days a week, from March until June 2010 – a total of 700 hours. Visitors were invited to sit in a chair facing her and simply return her silent gaze. The offer was taken up by 1,400 people, including Lou Reed, Björk and Isabella Rossellini. Some spent an entire day with Abramovic, while others managed just a few minutes before the excitement became too much for them.

HOTTEST ART EXHIBITION

Australian artist Edward Obrenovic Fraser, who calls himself Edgy, staged a two-day exhibition of ten abstract paintings at the Singing Sand Dunes in the Qatari Desert in August 2011, amid temperatures of 50°C. Although some of his paintings melted in the intense heat, others were blown about by the desert storms and one of the organizers burnt her legs, Edgy pronounced the venture a resounding success.

FIRST ARTIST TO NAIL HIS SCROTUM TO RED SQUARE

On 10 November 2013, as a protest against Russian leader Vladimir Putin's "police state", twenty-nine-year-old Russian artist Pyotr Pavlensky stripped completely naked, sat down and nailed his scrotum to the icy cobbles in Moscow's Red Square. When police officers arrived on the scene and ordered him to get up, Pavlensky pointed out that he was unable to do so. They hastily threw a blanket over him, managed to free him from the stones and took him to hospital. Pavlensky said afterwards: "I was careful not to rupture a vein but it was very bloody and sore. They wanted to give me antibiotics and other medications, but I refused." For previous performance artworks Pavlensky had wrapped himself in barbed wire (until being released by police with garden clippers) and sewn his lips shut with rough thread. On the latter occasion he was sent for psychiatric examination but was pronounced sane.

LARGEST COLLECTION OF BAD ART

Founded in 1994 by antique dealer Scott Wilson and his friend Jerry Reilly, the Museum of Bad Art in Massachusetts houses some 500 pieces of "art too bad to be ignored". The idea was born when Wilson discovered what has become the museum's signature work – *Lucy In The Field With Flowers* – among garbage waiting to be collected in Boston. Wilson was originally interested only in the frame but Reilly was intrigued by the actual picture, and after hanging it at his home he encouraged friends to seek out other pieces of desperately bad art.

As enthusiasm for the concept spread, the collection was turned into a virtual museum in the form of a CD-ROM, but when a group of disappointed senior citizens on a tour bus stopped by hoping to see it, Wilson and Reilly realized that they needed a physical space to display the paintings. Thus the Museum of Bad Art's first home was in the basement of the Dedham Community Theatre – appropriately just outside the toilet. As with all of the world's great art galleries, security is all-important, and after one of its most treasured paintings, *Eileen* by R. Angelo Le, was stolen in 1996 and not returned despite MOBA offering a reward of $6.50, the museum installed a fake video camera along with a sign saying:

"Warning. This gallery is protected by a fake security camera". Then in 2004 Rebecca Harris's iconic *Self-Portrait as a Drainpipe* was removed from the gallery walls but was soon returned by the thief . . . with a $10 donation. To be considered by the Museum of Bad Art, a painting must have serious intent as well as serious flaws. No paintings-by-numbers or works by children are ever accepted. Even so, one MOBA executive revealed: "Nine out of ten pieces don't get in because they're not bad enough. What an artist considers to be bad doesn't always meet our low standards."

MOST LEAVES PAINTED IN TWENTY-FOUR HOURS

Chityala Gnapika painted 227 leaves of various sizes and shapes non-stop over a period of twenty-four hours in Andhra Pradesh, India, on 29 April 2009.

FIRST SELF-PORTRAIT SCULPTURE USING OWN BLOOD

British artist Marc Quinn made a bust of himself from his own frozen blood. The work, titled "Self", was created by extracting 4.5 litres of his own blood over a period of five months. After making a mould of his face, he froze the blood to form the creepy self-portrait, which is kept in a refrigeration unit at a constant temperature of minus 15°C to prevent melting. It was bought in 1991 by collector Charles Saatchi for a reported £13,000 ($20,000) and was so successful that Quinn has since made a new version every five years to demonstrate the ageing process. He told the *Huffington Post* in 2012: "In the years I'm making a blood head I go and visit my doctor every six weeks and he takes a pint out in the same way as if I was giving blood. I do feel a bit tired the day after, but one of the great things about the sculptures to me is that they are about the amazing regenerative power of the human body, in that I exist, and five of these sculptures exist. So there are about 60 pints of my blood in the world and I'm still alive!"

MOST SCULPTURES OF ENGLAND FOOTBALLERS CARVED FROM A 99P BAG OF BRAZIL NUTS

Armed with a scalpel and a magnifying glass, Surrey-based micro-artist Quentin Devine carved the faces of five England footballers, past and present, onto the contents of a 99p bag of Brazil nuts in readiness for the 2014 World Cup. He spent four days on each sculpture and worked his way through more than fifty nuts before perfecting the images of David Beckham, Alan Shearer, Gary Lineker, Paul Gascoigne and Wayne Rooney. Devine said: "My final piece, Gary Lineker, proved to be a tough nut to crack with his large ear span reducing the already tiny surface area I had to work with. After over 20 attempts, many broken ears and all hope lost, I finally perfected it."

MOST NATIONAL FLAGS PAINTED ON A MUSTARD SEED

Bangladeshi artist Mintu Dey has painted the national flags of seventeen countries – including China, Indonesia and Japan – onto a single mustard seed, even leaving gaps between the flags on every side. He has also painted a map of the world on to a mustard seed, a feat which took him several days and actually made him sick because of the intense concentration required. In 2007, Dey laid claim to painting the world's smallest "Mona Lisa" – a microscopic version created on a piece of paper measuring just 0.7mm by 0.5mm. Critics harshly pointed out that her enigmatic smile was rather lost in the downsizing.

LONGEST TIME SPENT LIVING INSIDE A BEAR CARCASS

French performance artist Abraham Poincheval spent thirteen days living inside the carcass of a bear at the start of April 2014. For the piece titled "Dans La Peau de l'Ours" ("Inside the Skin of the Bear"), Poincheval ate, drank, slept and went to the toilet inside the sterilized carcass while being filmed by two cameras at the Musée de la Chasse et de la Nature in Paris. A spokesperson said: "For him this act signifies a rebirth, a rite of passage, to pass from the world of the dead to that of the living." In October 2012, Poincheval had spent a week in an underground hole beneath a Marseille bookshop.

MOST EXPENSIVE ARTISTIC BANANA

A humble banana exhibited on a window sill at an art gallery in Halifax, Nova Scotia, Canada, in June 2008 was priced at $2,500. Artist Michael Fernandes had originally valued it at a staggering $15,000, not least because he promised to change the banana on a daily basis, eating the old ones and putting progressively greener ones on display to illustrate the banana's transitory nature. However, just one day into the exhibition, a guerrilla group calling itself the Patrick Swayze Collective snatched the banana and replaced it with an apple, into which a face had been carved. The group said it removed the banana because it is "the most radioactive fruit on earth" and represented a terrorist threat. Fernandes was not amused to learn that he had to provide a substitute banana. "I completely respect where he is coming from," said gallery co-owner Victoria Page, "because this interrupts the flow of his project."

MOST EXPENSIVE JAR OF AIR

On a 2014 business trip to the South of France, Beijing artist Liang Kegang collected a jar of fresh Provence air. When he got back to China he put it up for auction before a select group of artists and collectors – and it sold for $860. The auction not only highlighted China's appalling air quality but the fact that some people will pay for anything if you vaguely call it art. Liang was seeking to expose the former. "Air should be the most valueless commodity," he said, "free to breathe for any vagrant or beggar. This is my way to question China's foul air and express my dissatisfaction."

MOST PROLIFIC LINT ARTIST

It was in 1999 when Cheryl Capezzuti's grandmother passed away and her family, removing the lint from granny's tumble dryer, turned to Cheryl and said, as you do: "Make a sculpture out of grandma's lint." The art school graduate had already been sculpting dryer fluff into angels, animals, puppets and whimsical creatures for five years, but it was then that her grandly titled National Lint Project really took off. She has since staged exhibitions at laundromats across Pittsburgh featuring more than 100 of her creations, and has no fear of ever running short of raw material because people all over the world generously send her their dryer dregs. In her own small way she hopes to help people understand the true meaning of lint.

LONGEST TIME TIED TOGETHER BY ROPE

Between 4 July 1983 and 4 July 1984, New York City performance artists Linda Montano and Tehching Hsieh spent the whole year tied together at the waist twenty-four hours a day by an eight-foot rope. When indoors, they had to stay in the same room but were not allowed to touch each other until the year was up.

LONGEST TIME SPENT LIVING IN A HUMAN HAMSTER WHEEL

New York performance artists Ward Shelley and Alex Schweder lived in a giant hamster wheel, which was 30 feet tall and had a circumference of 60 feet, for ten days in March 2014. The wheel was suspended from the ceiling at the city's Pierogi gallery and had furniture nailed to it on both the inside and outside. Schweder, who is afraid of heights, lived on the inside of the wheel at the bottom while Shelley stayed at the top of the wheel, on the outside. Each surface had a bed, desk, chair, dresser and kitchen/bathroom, but because every item of furniture was aligned to its counterpart on the other surface, both men had to sleep, eat and go to the toilet at the same time. To change the furniture settings, they had to walk slowly on the wheel in opposite directions, moving it until the next station arrived. Schweder compared life on the big wheel to living in a two-bedroom apartment and said, "it was an exploration of trust between two people. Every time I want to move, he has to move." Shelley wore a safety harness in bed because he was scared of rolling out. "I was also worried that Alex might start sleepwalking, causing the wheel to take off!"

LARGEST SCULPTURE OF MARILYN MONROE

Forever Marilyn, by US sculptor Seward Johnson, stands 26 feet tall, weighs 17 tons and depicts Monroe in her iconic billowing skirt pose from the 1955 movie *The Seven Year Itch*. Unveiled in 2011, the giant steel and aluminium structure was initially displayed in Chicago where it was vandalized three times partly because of its provocative, sexual nature. Visitors were also accused of licking Marilyn's leg, peering up her skirt and trying to sniff her outsize panties.

MOST COW SCULPTURES MADE FROM BUTTER

Every year, from 1959 until she retired in 2006, housewife Norma Lyon sculpted a life-sized cow from 600 pounds of butter for the Iowa State Fair, maintaining a tradition that dates back to 1911. As a break from cows, she also sculpted butter replicas of Elvis Presley, John Wayne, a Harley-Davidson motorcycle and *The Last Supper*. Before her death in 2011, she was the subject of a book, *The Butter Cow Lady*.

LARGEST PLAY-DOH SCULPTURE

A team of eight model makers spent two weeks building a life-size replica of a Chevrolet Orlando MPV car out of 1.5 tons of blue Play-Doh. The permanently stationary vehicle measured some 15 feet long and 5 feet wide but, despite being made entirely from the Plasticine-like substance, it still managed to perplex one or two traffic wardens when it was parked up in a London street in 2011.

LARGEST POPCORN SCULPTURE

In August 2006, fifty members of the Sri Chinmoy Centre in Jamaica, New York, created a 20-foot-10-inch-tall cake from popcorn. The five-tiered cake was 12 feet 9 inches in diameter at its widest point and weighed 11,688 pounds. It therefore comfortably eclipsed a 13-foot-tall popcorn statue of King Kong made by students from London's Camberwell College of Arts in 2003.

MODEL OF NEW YORK CITY SKYLINE MADE FROM GREATEST NUMBER OF PLAYING CARDS

Ace card stacker Bryan Berg, from Spirit Lake, Iowa, recreated the skyline of New York – including the Empire State Building, the Chrysler Building, the Flatiron and the Yankee

Stadium – from 178,000 playing cards. He built the structure in Times Square in 2005, using no glue, just good old fashioned patience to hold everything together. "Most of the time my structures do not collapse," he explains. "They are very strong and stable. First, there are so many cards in large constructions that the combined weight of all the cards actually adds to the stability of the structure. Second, the weight is supported by the strategic arrangement of cards, called grids. The cards actually prohibit each other from bending and also prohibit each other from falling over." And for the record, his hands do shake occasionally, he doesn't get paper cuts, and he never gets bored.

MOST PAPER SHIPS FOLDED

Peter Koppen, a bus driver from Munich, Germany, folds tiny pieces of paper – about a fifth of the size of a postage stamp – into what he calls microships, although they could easily be mistaken for hats. He was taught the art by his father, and since 1968, when he began experimenting with bus tickets, he has folded more than 200,000 paper ships, making them into colourful collages which have sold for up to $4,800 apiece. In his artist's statement he says: "When viewing the assembled microships, people experience a sense of aesthetic enjoyment. Microships are not political, they practise no social criticism, and they are of no use. In short, they embody the quintessence of art."

TALLEST ORIGAMI GIRAFFE

In June 2009, Himanshu Agrawal and a team of nine students from Mumbai, India, spent twelve hours folding a single 35-foot-square sheet of paper to form an origami giraffe that stood 20 feet tall. Working from a design by American origami master John Montroll, the paper giraffe required over 100 moves and 70 creases.

LONGEST ORIGAMI CATERPILLAR

An origami caterpillar measuring 2,128 feet long – nearly half a mile – was folded by sixty young people in Heiligenstadt, Germany, over a period of twenty-five hours, in October 2004. They used 25,000 sheets of paper.

LARGEST ORIGAMI CRANE

Created by the Peace Piece Project at Japan's Hiroshima Shudo University on 29 August 2009, the world's largest origami crane had a wingspan of 268 feet 10 inches, breaking the existing record for the biggest paper bird by over 10 feet.

LONGEST JUMP BY AN ORIGAMI FROG

American Lisa Hodson made a two-inch-long origami jumping frog from a six-inch square of white photocopy paper in April 1994 – and then watched it spring a world record distance of 29.3 inches, exceeding its usual leap by over 15 inches.

LARGEST BALLOON SCULPTURE
MADE BY AN INDIVIDUAL

New York City balloon artist John Reid set a new world record in 2014 by building a 50-foot-tall Transformers robot, "Poptimus Prime", from 4,302 coloured balloons. It took him forty-two hours to inflate and position all the balloons. His robot was said to be invincible except for one weakness – needles.

FASTEST TIME TO MAKE 100 DOGS FROM ALREADY INFLATED BALLOONS

Using balloons that had already been inflated, Ronald van den Berg twisted them into 100 dog shapes in 5 minutes 48 seconds on 24 August 2002 at Sempach, Switzerland. He was nothing if not persistent for this was the twentieth time he had set a new world record for the discipline in two years, during which period he had reduced his personal best by over seven minutes. If you think that anyone can twist a balloon into an odd shape and call it a dog, you should bear in mind that almost as many criteria have to be met relating to the posture of a balloon dog as would be encountered exhibiting a pedigree standard poodle at Cruft's. For example, the rules state that while the proportions of the balloon dog can vary, both ears and all legs should be approximately the same size. Also, the finished dog should have ten distinct bubbles, including a tail. Mr van den Berg's creations were so lifelike you might have been tempted to take one for a walk – but not on a windy day.

FASTEST TIME TO INFLATE BY MOUTH AND MAKE 100 BALLOON DOGS WHILE STANDING ON STILTS

German entertainer and balloon modeller Tip Top Till (probably not his real name) took 19 minutes 12 seconds to inflate and create 100 balloon dogs in 2000 while standing on stilts. And he blew each one up with sheer lung power rather than a pump, which would plainly be cheating.

FASTEST TIME TO CARVE A FACE INTO A PUMPKIN

Pumpkin sculptor Stephen Clarke, from Havertown, Pennsylvania, carved a face – including eyes, eyebrows, a nose, a mouth and ears – into a single pumpkin in 16.47 seconds on 31 October 2013. His time eclipsed that of David Finkle, from Danbury, Essex, who had carved a pumpkin face in 20.03 seconds in October 2010. Finkle has also made pumpkin sculptures of famous celebrities, including Barack Obama, Michael Jackson, Simon Cowell and, probably the one that required the least work, Wayne Rooney.

LONGEST DISTANCE THROWN BY A MEDIEVAL LEGO WAR MACHINE

America's Jeff Viens built a trebuchet – a medieval catapult – out of Lego, and at the Brickworld 2009 contest in Chicago, his contraption, "The Flinger", threw a missile consisting of four Lego bricks a record distance of 38 feet 7 inches. He has also built the world's biggest Lego trebuchet, "Flinger 2.0" – a six-foot-tall monster created from 5,000 bricks. And before you ask, yes, Jeff is a grown man.

TALLEST LEGO CHRISTMAS TREE

In 2011, a team of four, led by Duncan Titmarsh and Ed Diment, took over a month to build a 39-foot-high Christmas tree from 600,000 Lego bricks. It then took a week to install at London's St Pancras International station – hardly surprising as the tree, with its steel structure and base, weighed about three tons. Father-of-two Titmarsh is the only man in Britain who gets paid to play with Lego all day. As Britain's only professional Lego builder, the forty-three-year-old former kitchen fitter keeps a stockpile of six million pieces in a Hampshire warehouse. "Like most children I loved playing with Lego when I was younger," he says, "but I never thought it would be my job later in life. It was hard at first to make the change from fitting kitchens, and my family and close friends thought I was mad. But I'm thrilled that I did it as this is something that I enjoy doing every day. Most days I do think this is a bit different, but you still have to go to meetings, you still have to meet deadlines and deal with clients. It can be hard work like any other job."

LARGEST CHRISTMAS TREE MADE
OF PLASTIC BOTTLES

Searching for a new slant on the traditional Christmas tree, in 2011 Lithuanian artist Jolanta Smidtiene built a 42-foot-tall version made from 32,000 plastic bottles. Illuminated by 40,000 lights, it formed the centrepiece of festive celebrations in the city of Kaunas.

LARGEST BOUQUET OF ROSES
MADE FROM BANKNOTES

Stung by comments from his girlfriend's parents that he had to own a house and car before he could even consider marrying their daughter, twenty-seven-year-old Chinese computer programmer Chen Li decided to prove that he was a financially viable suitor by proposing with a bouquet of 999 roses made from banknotes. He drew out his life savings from the bank – 200,000 yuan – and began patiently folding the notes into flowers. Each flower contained two notes and took about five minutes to create. Armed with his cash roses, he proposed to his girlfriend on her birthday – 12 February 2014 – and mercifully she accepted, which was just as well considering he had been toiling on the bouquet until two o'clock in the morning for the four previous nights. The newly engaged couple then set about unwrapping the paper roses and returning the money to what is probably now a joint bank account.

OIL RIG MODEL MADE FROM MOST MATCHSTICKS

David Reynolds, a retired oil rig worker from Southampton, spent fifteen years building a replica of the North Sea's Brent Bravo oil rig (where he used to work) from 4,075,000 matchsticks. When finally completed in 2009, the structure weighed over a ton and measured 21 feet long and 12 feet high. He spent up to ten hours a day working on the incredibly detailed model, which became so big it had to be split into fourteen sections and housed in different rooms throughout the family home. "I didn't think it would be this big," he admitted. "I think I just got a bit carried away." His wife Julie would have cheerfully carried the whole lot away. "I am absolutely sick to death at the sight of matchsticks," she sighed, "but I think there is still more to come, unfortunately. But at least I know where he is and what he's doing, so I'd rather have him here than down the pub." Mrs Reynolds' forebodings were well founded. The following year, her husband unveiled a fleet of twenty ships made from 250,000 matchsticks.

WORLD GLOBE MADE FROM MOST MATCHSTICKS

Starting in 2012, US artist Andy Yoder spent two years building a 42-foot-diameter world globe from 300,000 painted matchsticks. He made the Earth's core from plywood, cardboard and expanding foam, then covered it in rice paper and marked out where each match should go in respect of land areas, oceans and weather systems. He took five matches at a time, dipped them in paint and laid them on a piece of wood to dry, becoming so proficient at this procedure that he was soon able to get through a box of 300 matches in fifteen minutes. He modestly described it as "a slightly more complicated paint by numbers project."

LONGEST NON-STOP PIANO PLAYING

Bill Hajak played the piano non-stop for two weeks at the Ripley's Believe It or Not! New York Odditorium in 1939. He had intended to play for an entire month but quit after missing the birth of his daughter.

LONGEST PERIOD SPENT LIP-SYNCHING TO A SONG

British teenager Matt Perren lip-synched to Queen's "Don't Stop Me Now" for 1,101 days – every day for three years. He started on 1 January 2011 when he was fifteen and finished on 5 January 2014, by which time he was eighteen. Taking two pictures of himself miming each day, he created a time-lapse video which showed him ageing from a teenager into a young man and changing his hairstyle slightly but still doggedly wearing what appeared to be the same T-shirt.

FASTEST DRUMMER

At the World's Fastest Drummer Extreme Sport Drumming event (who knew such a thing existed?) in Nashville, Tennessee, on 13 July 2013, Canadian-born Tom Grosset set a new world record for speed drumming by hitting 1,208 strokes in one minute. It meant his hands were moving more than twenty times per second. He trained for the record by practising an hour a day, every day, for seven years, quite probably making him the neighbour from hell.

LARGEST DRUM KIT

Amateur musician Mark Temperato, a reverend at the Breath of Worship Church in Lakeville, New York, has a drum kit consisting of more than 900 pieces, and he says he has no intention of stopping until he reaches the magic 1,000. It takes "RevM", as he likes to be known, an hour to hit every one of the cymbals, bells, drums and horns, which he can just about reach from his specially made 28-inch-high chair. The set weighs around 5,000 pounds and when he goes on the road, it takes four people fourteen hours to assemble it and another ten hours to pack it all away again afterwards.

SMALLEST VIOLIN

In 2009, Chen Lianzhi, from Guangzhou, China, made a violin that measured just one centimetre long. He used a 0.1-millimetre drill to shape a piece of maple wood the size of a thumbnail before fixing all the component parts together with glue. However, he lamented that, because the strings were so thin, the micro violin was not very easy to play. This could explain why sensible people – the name Stradivarius springs to mind – make them considerably bigger.

VIOLIN MADE FROM MOST MATCHES

According to *Ripley's Believe It or Not!* James A. Davis, of Caryville, Tennessee, made a violin from 5,327 matches in 1938. He kept it in a special case built from 18,593 matches.

SMALLEST GRAND PIANO

In 2011, Japanese company Sega Toys produced the world's smallest fully functional grand piano, measuring 9.8 inches wide, 7 inches high and 13 inches long. The $600 piano, which comes with a miniature seat, boasts a keyboard featuring a full eighty-eight keys that are each just 4 millimetres wide. Let's just say Jerry Lee Lewis would have struggled to get his leg over, which goes to show there's a first time for everything.

LONGEST TIME PLAYING AN ELECTRIC ORGAN WITH THE TONGUE

Discovering that there was a vacancy in the world record annals for playing the electric organ with either the nose or tongue, Adrian Wigley, from Brownhills, West Midlands, set about rectifying the omission. On 1 March 1984, he succeeded in playing the organ for six hours with his nose and for two hours with his tongue.

LONGEST HYMN SINGING

In July 2005, fifty-four-year-old Terry Coleman, from Denver, Colorado, sang hymns non-stop for 40 hours 17 minutes. During that time he sang 849 tunes, only stopping when his voice eventually gave out.

FASTEST RENDITION OF "LIVIN' ON A PRAYER"

On 27 March 2013, Kerrang! Radio DJ Kate Lawler rattled through the Bon Jovi classic "Livin' On a Prayer" in just 36.1 seconds at the station's studios in the West Midlands. What her version lacked in feeling, it made up for in speed.

MOST CONSECUTIVE RENDITIONS OF "GOD SAVE THE KING"

On the platform of Rathenau train station in Brandenburg on the morning of 9 February 1909, a German military band played "God Save the King" non-stop for sixteen or maybe even seventeen times (people were losing count) while waiting for King Edward VII to emerge. The visiting monarch was delayed inside the train because he was struggling to change into the uniform of a German field-marshal.

MOST CONSECUTIVE RENDITIONS OF THE INDIAN NATIONAL ANTHEM

In July 2013, thirty-two-year-old Rohit Anand, from Haryana, India, sang the Indian national anthem 655 times consecutively – a performance that went on for ten hours. As Jane Austen would surely have said: "Mr Anand, you have delighted us long enough."

FASTEST BACKWARDS RECITAL OF THE ENTIRE LYRICS OF QUEEN'S ALBUM *A NIGHT AT THE OPERA*

In 1990, Welshman Steve Briers, then the world's fastest backwards talker, recited the entire lyrics of the Queen album *A Night at the Opera* backwards in 9 minutes 58 seconds.

LONGEST ROUND OF APPLAUSE

After playing the title role in Verdi's opera *Otello* in Vienna, Austria, on 30 July 1991, celebrated Spanish tenor Placido Domingo received 80 minutes of sustained applause, spanning 101 curtain calls.

THE SAME SONG SUNG IN MOST DIFFERENT LANGUAGES SIMULTANEOUSLY

To celebrate St Andrew's Day on 30 November 2009, staff and students at Glasgow University sang "Auld Lang Syne" in forty-one different languages simultaneously – including Latin, Czech, Gaelic, Thai, Estonian, Arabic, Romanian, Welsh, Ukrainian, Catalan, Maori, Georgian, Malay, Hindi, Urdu, Swahili, Vietnamese, Bangla and Igbo. The resulting sound could only be described as unique.

LONGEST ALBUM TITLE

An album released by UK band Chumbawumba in 2008 had the 156-word, 865-character title: *The Boy Bands Have Won, and All the Copyists and the Tribute Bands and the TV Talent Show Producers Have Won, If We Allow Our Culture to Be Shaped by Mimicry, Whether From Lack of Ideas or From Exaggerated Respect. You Should Never Try to Freeze Culture. What You Can Do Is Recycle That Culture. Take Your Older Brother's Hand-Me-Down Jacket and Re-Style It, Re-Fashion It to the Point Where It Becomes Your Own. But*

Don't Just Regurgitate Creative History, or Hold Art and Music and Literature as Fixed, Untouchable and Kept Under Glass. The People Who Try to 'Guard' Any Particular Form of Music Are, Like the Copyists and Manufactured Bands, Doing It the Worst Disservice, Because the Only Thing That You Can Do to Music That Will Damage It Is Not Change It, Not Make It Your Own. Because Then It Dies, Then It's Over, Then It's Done, and the Boy Bands Have Won. To prevent phone or online ordering going into a second day, the title is generally abbreviated to *The Boy Bands Have Won*.

OLDEST ROCK BAND

Formed in 2007 for a TV documentary, British rock band The Zimmers had a combined age of over 3,000. The forty-strong troupe, led by ninety-year-old Alf Carretta, charted with their version of The Who's "My Generation" before tackling The Prodigy's "Firestarter" and Iggy Pop's "Lust For Life". Although some of the original members – including Carretta – have since died, the band is still going strong, and in April 2012, fifteen members, ranging in age from sixty-six to eighty-eight, appeared on *Britain's Got Talent*. Sexagenarian rocker Dolores Murray enthused: "It's been so exciting, every day has been different. One day in a studio, the next on a plane to Germany, then back for a radio show and on to a photo shoot. I never knew retirement would be so full. It's much more fun than bingo."

LONGEST NON-STOP ELVIS IMPERSONATION

Tamil–Canadian actor and producer Suresh Joachim performed as Elvis for fifty-five hours non-stop at a shopping mall in Toronto, Canada, from 24 to 26 January 2008. He trained for the record attempt by listening to Elvis songs for fourteen days – essential preparation as he didn't really know any beforehand. He sang, danced and wiggled his hips to a total of forty-one numbers – the ones he had learned – over and over again, much to the bemusement of passing shoppers. Joachim, who admitted to being all shook up by the end, was not allowed to remove any part of his costume during the challenge. "It was disgusting wearing the wig all the time," he groaned. "I was sweaty."

LARGEST GATHERING OF ELVIS IMPERSONATORS

On 29 September 2012, 814 people, ranging in age from three to eighty, descended on Porthcawl, Wales, dressed as Elvis Presley to break the Guinness World Record for the largest gathering of Elvises. At the Porthcawl Elvis Festival – the biggest event of its kind in Europe – the impersonators performed the "King"'s 1956 hit "Hound Dog", led by Darren Jones, holder of the coveted title "Best Welsh Elvis". The Elvises, many wearing white jump suits of various sizes, came from as far afield as Germany, Malta and Brazil.

FIRST CONCERT FOR DOGS

The world's first concert for dogs was staged by American composer and musician Laurie Anderson outside the Sydney Opera House on 5 June 2010. Anderson and her band performed a twenty-minute experimental piece to an audience of almost 1,000 dogs and their owners. A section of whale calls drew howls from half of the audience, but as it was the canine half, the howls were seen as a sign of approval. Indeed Anderson was delighted by the response. "It was really fantastic," she said. "They were a great audience. There were no dog fights and the dogs really seemed to enjoy themselves. They were grooving, a lot of them were singing and dancing, they were uninhibited." But everyone knows that dogs can't dance, because they've got two left feet.

MOST PEOPLE HOWLING SIMULTANEOUSLY

Keen to think up a new world record as a way of bringing prestige and publicity to their institution, 296 students and community members from St Cloud State University, Minnesota, took part in a mass Husky Howl on 26 April 2013. The school's teams are known as the Huskies, so the decision to attempt a howling record wasn't entirely random.

MOST MUSICAL INSTRUMENTS PLAYED IN TWO MINUTES

Canadian DJ Mel Sampson played a world record forty musical instruments in two minutes on 18 September 2012. Beginning with the violin, harp and banjo, she raced through the assembled instruments at breakneck speed, only faltering briefly when she struggled at first to get a sound out of the trombone.

MOST VIOLINS PLAYED SIMULTANEOUSLY

Ukrainian violinist Oleksandr Bozhyk played four violins at the same time in Lviv on 8 December 2012 – and he doesn't even have a double chin.

LONGEST CONCERT

The world's longest concert is scheduled to end in the year 2640. Musicians in Halberstadt, Germany, have stretched "As Slow as Possible", a twenty-minute piano piece by experimental American composer John Cage, to last 639 years. Their pipe organ concert started in the medieval St Burchardi Church on 5 September 2001, but because Cage's piece began with a rest, there were seventeen months of silence before the opening three notes were finally played on 5 February 2003. The organ sounds incessantly (it is surrounded by acrylic glass to reduce the volume), so that subsequent notes take the form of chord changes. The thirteenth chord change took place on 5 October 2013 and if you want to make a note in your diary, the fourteenth is due on 5 September 2020.

SHORTEST CONCERT

On 16 July 2007, the White Stripes wrapped up their quirky Canadian tour by playing a single-note concert in St John's, Newfoundland. Having already performed on buses, bridges and school classrooms, Jack and Meg White took to the stage, played a single note (reportedly a C-sharp), announced that they had now officially played in every province and territory in Canada, and walked off. Fans had been told in advance that the free concert would last less than a second.

SHORTEST SONG RECORDED

"You Suffer", a song by British grindcore band Napalm Death from their 1987 debut album *Scum*, is only 1.316 seconds long, making it the shortest recorded song ever. According to Justin Broadrick, who wrote the song with fellow band member Nicholas Bullen: "'You Suffer' was largely a comedy thing, a one-second song. Utterly retarded. We played that song in front of 30 local kids, like, every weekend. We played that song 30 times. It was a laugh." In 1989, the song appeared on one side of a seven-inch single given away free with copies of a compilation album titled *Grindcrusher*. The track on the other side, "Mega-Armageddon Death Part 3" by the Electro Hippies, also lasts around one second, making the disc the shortest single ever released. Each side features one groove at the outer edge of the disc, containing the music, and the remainder of the surface is taken up with etched writing and cartoons.

SHORTEST MUSIC VIDEO

In 1994, another grindcore band, New York-based Brutal Truth, made the world's shortest music video – a four-second epic to accompany their equally brief track "Collateral Damage".

LONGEST SILENT SYMPHONY MOVEMENT

French composer and artist Yves Klein's 1949 work *Monotone-Silence Symphony* consists of two twenty-minute movements, the first an unvarying drone, the second unmitigated silence. It was performed just once in his lifetime (Klein died of a heart attack in 1962), although a 2007 performance in a Paris church was livened up when a pigeon walked in through the open church door and produced its own silent movement. A better-known silent offering is *4'33"*, a three-movement composition by American composer John Cage whose score instructs the performers not to play their instruments at all during the piece. The idea is that the listener will hear the sounds of the environment while *4'33"* is being played, but the more common perception is that it is simply four minutes and thirty-three seconds of silence.

The world premiere of *4'33"* took place at Woodstock, New York, on 29 August 1952, as part of a recital of contemporary piano music. David Tudor sat at the piano and marked the start of the first movement by closing the lid. He only lifted it briefly to signify the end of each movement. Unsurprisingly, the concert did not exactly receive rave reviews, but composer Cage was unrepentant. "They missed the point," he said. "There's no such thing as silence. What they thought was silence, because they didn't know how to listen, was full of accidental sounds. You could hear the wind stirring outside during the first movement. During the second, raindrops began pattering the roof, and during the third the people themselves made all kinds of interesting sounds as they talked or walked out." Or yawned.

In 2010, a Facebook campaign encouraged people to buy a new version of *4'33"* (although in truth it sounded much like the original) in the hope of preventing the winner of Simon Cowell's TV show *The X Factor* from having the Christmas number one in the UK charts. That enough people bought *4'33"* to enable it to reach number 21 on the UK singles chart probably says more about public antipathy towards Cowell than any great love of Cage's piece.

LONGEST FREESTYLE RAP

Rhyming master Austin Antoine, a twenty-two-year-old California arts graduate, rapped continuously for 16 hours 31 minutes 22 seconds on 4 May 2013, even incorporating into his rap suggestions from the audience and those viewing the record attempt live on Twitter.

LISTENING TO THE SAME SONG
MOST TIMES IN 36 HOURS

While on a non-stop 127-mile walking marathon along the entire length of Macedonia in 2009, fifty-year-old Emil Ilic listened on headphones to the song "Si Bastasen Un Par De Canciones" by Italian musician Eros Ramazotti 413 times in thirty-six hours. He played it over and over again while tackling the mountainous terrain, explaining afterwards that he had proposed to his wife at a Ramazotti concert in Italy during that song. "I am a big fan of Ramazotti," he added, somewhat unnecessarily. "I have his complete album collection and I feel an extraordinary energy every time I listen to that song."

MOST "LA"S IN A SONG

The lyrics of Spain's winning 1968 Eurovision Song Contest entry performed by female singer Massiel contained no fewer than 138 "la"s. The lack of imagination stretched to its title, "La, La, La". So whatever else you may say about it, at least it was a song which did exactly what it said on the tin. Bill Martin, writer of the UK runner-up "Congratulations" sung by Cliff Richard, derided the Spanish number as "a piece of rubbish", which in this instance could probably be filed under "fair comment" rather than "sour grapes". Yet remarkably Spain managed to top that in 1979 with their Eurovision runner-up "Su Canción" ("Your Song"), performed by Betty Missiego backed by a children's choir, which managed a record 152 "la"s. The success of both songs proves that when it comes to the Eurovision Song Contest there is little to be gained from writing deep, thoughtful lyrics. Just fill the gaps with plenty of "la, la"s.

MOST COSTUME CHANGES IN A ONE-TAKE MUSIC VIDEO

The four-minute video for Brooklyn-based rock band Eytan and the Embassy's 2012 track "Everything Changes" features eighteen costume changes in a single take. The video, which took a day to rehearse and thirty takes to get right, shows lead singer Eytan Oren being transformed into music legends such as Elvis Presley, Bob Dylan, John Lennon, Elton John, David Bowie, Bruce Springsteen, Sid Vicious, Weird Al Jankovic, Kurt Cobain and Lady Gaga.

MOST BEES ON BODY WHILE PLAYING A MUSICAL INSTRUMENT

As part of his *Thriller Bee Show,* Dr Norman Gary, a retired professor of entomology at the University of California, created a real buzz in the music world by frequently playing the clarinet while more than 75,000 bees swarmed all over him. Perhaps Dr Gary, who was a member of Sacramento jazz band Beez Kneez from 1995 to 2004, should consider doing a duet with Sting.

He covered his body in a special scent to attract worker bees and then performed inside a plexiglass cage to prevent them from escaping. His most alarming moment occurred when he accidentally inhaled a bee while playing the clarinet, although it probably didn't faze a man who is listed in the Guinness World Records for having 109 bees in his closed mouth for ten seconds.

MOST EXPENSIVE AIR GUITAR

In August 2010, an Arizona man sold an air guitar on eBay for $5.50. He claimed it had been used at a Bon Jovi concert.

MOST AIR GUITAR WINDMILLS IN ONE MINUTE

Evoking The Who's Pete Townshend, Jacob Kreeb, from Belleville, Illinois, performed 165 air guitar windmills in one minute on 15 July 2012, at the end of which his arms ached considerably.

LONGEST DISTANCE TRAVELLED TO PLAY MUSICAL FENCES

Most people who look at the fences of Australia see something to keep sheep confined, but imaginative violinists Jon Rose and Hollis Taylor saw them instead as giant stringed instruments spanning a continent. In 2002, the duo travelled 25,000 miles around Australia using violin bows and drumsticks to play hundreds of fences in every state and territory. By placing miniature microphones in the fence posts, they were able to release the results on a CD that perfectly fitted the category Limited Edition. Tracks to cherish include "No. 1 Rabbit-Proof Fence at Starvation Bay", "Electric Fence at Lake Grace", "Dog Fence at Nullarbor", and "Picket Fence in a Quiet Brisbane Suburb". Barbed wire will never seem the same again.

MOST CLASSICAL VINYL RECORDS RECOGNIZED JUST BY LOOKING AT THE GROOVES

In 1981, before a live TV audience, Philadelphia physician Dr Arthur Lintgen correctly identified twenty classical vinyl records simply by studying the shape, construction and length of the grooves for a few seconds. He is the only person in the world to possess this "vinyl vision". He says: "The trick is to examine the physical construction of the recording and look at the relative playing time of each one of the movements or separations on the recording."

He has learned that a Beethoven symphony will have a slightly longer first movement in relation to the second, while Mozart and Schubert tended to compose in such a way that each movement often had the same number of bars. Dr Lintgen has also come to realize that grooves containing soft passages look black or dark grey, but as the music gets louder, the grooves turn silvery. So by correlating what he sees on the record with his vast knowledge of classical music, he is able to match the patterns of the grooves with the composition. Sometimes he can even work out the identity of the conductor and the nationality of the orchestra.

However, his ability is restricted to classical orchestral music by and after Beethoven. He says that pre-Beethoven works are too similar in structure to identify, and when given an Alice Cooper record he said it looked "disorganized". Of course the alternative to attempting to mimic Dr Lintgen's amazing powers is to look at the name on the record.

FIRST VEGETABLE ORCHESTRA

Founded in 1998, the First Vienna Vegetable Orchestra (or Das erste Wiener Gemüseorchester) consists of a sound technician, a cook and ten musicians who play pieces by such diverse artists as Stravinsky and Kraftwerk on instruments made from fresh vegetables. The sounds made from the instruments, which include carrot recorders, clappers made from eggplants, pumpkin drums and zucchini trumpets, are amplified by the use of special microphones. The instruments are made just a few hours before each performance and at the end of the show they are turned into a nice soup, which is the FVVO's version of The Who's Pete Townshend smashing up his guitar.

LONGEST TRACTOR SYMPHONY

A 2014 festival of contemporary music in Valencia, Spain, opened with a half-hour symphony performed by a dozen roaring tractors. Swedish conductor Sven-Ake Johansson stood before the farmyard ensemble with the same reverence as if he were conducting violinists and flautists at Carnegie Hall. His intention was to use the various diesel engines to produce different notes, but to many in the audience the combination of incessant noise and belching exhaust smoke was a far cry from anything even vaguely connected to music. Audience member Mampu Perea Badillo remarked scornfully: "It was a load of old rubbish. It might appeal to those who like to listen to the different strains of engines, but anyone who likes music was left baffled. It sounded like a garage workshop on a bad day." Meanwhile, the driver/musicians described the concert as a new experience. "It certainly was that," agreed Miguel Lopez, another audience member. "And not one I want to repeat."

LARGEST MOTORCYCLE ORCHESTRA

An "orchestra" of 100 bikers revved up their Harley-Davidsons at different intensities at a Stockholm venue in 2000 to perform *WROOM*, a five-minute piece by avant-garde Swedish composer Staffan Mossenmark. They were conducted by Petter Sundkvist, who waved racetrack flags instead of a baton. One critic said the performance had a range from "ominous-and-loud to ominous-and-deafening". Mossenmark has also composed musical pieces designed to be played by snow scooters, boats, cell phones and ice cream vans.

LONGEST DISTANCE MOONWALKED IN TWENTY-FOUR HOURS

On 11 January 2006 at a Canadian nightclub, Suresh Joachim moonwalked a distance of 30.6 miles in twenty-four hours. He embodied the spirit of Michael Jackson again on 15 June 2013 by moonwalking for a record three hours non-stop at the Metro Convention Centre in Toronto.

MOST PRISON INMATES DANCING TO "THRILLER"

As part of their exercise regime, 1,588 prisoners at the Cebu Provincial Detention and Rehabilitation Center in the Philippines took to the prison yard in 2007 and performed a synchronized dance routine to Michael Jackson's "Thriller". Dressed in their orange prison uniforms, the inmates proved an instant hit on YouTube, quickly racking up more than 1.3 million views. An official said that dancing had helped improve the prisoners' behaviour, adding that two former inmates have since become dancers. While serving their sentences, Cebu inmates have also performed mass participation dances to Queen's "Radio Gaga" and several songs from the *Sister Act* movies, but their real ambition is probably to do Foo Fighters' "Breakout".

HIGHEST POLE DANCE

On 21 July 2011, Nottingham Doctor of Psychology and pole dance instructor Kat Humphrey performed a pole dancing routine on the summit of Ben Nevis, the UK's highest mountain, 4,409 feet above sea level. While acknowledging that there is still a certain stigma attached to her favourite pastime, she said: "For me, pole dancing is an addiction and I can't venture outside without wanting to pole dance on every street sign, gate post and lamp post I see. Now with this freestanding, portable pole, I've turned my addiction into something completely new. I can safely say I've been able to boldly pole where no-one has poled before."

LARGEST UNDERWATER DANCE CLASS

On 27 October 2006, 74 students and instructors joyously danced underwater for nearly a quarter of an hour beneath the surface of Australia's Sydney Olympic Park Aquatic Centre. Some judges have harshly commented that any similarity to dancing on this occasion was purely coincidental, perhaps overlooking the fact that the dancers' rhythm was heavily compromised by the cumbersome scuba-diving gear they had to wear. In any case, even John Travolta would have struggled to look cool in a snorkel.

LONGEST BOOK WRITTEN ON A COCONUT

Baby Kanduri Navya Sree, from Andhra Pradesh, India, wrote eighteen chapters of the religious scripture *Bhagavad Gita* onto three coconut shells – a total of nearly 11,000 words equating to around 3,500 words per coconut.

FIRST BOOK WRITTEN WITH NAILS

In July 2013, forty-six-year-old Piyush Goyal, from Uttar Pradesh, India, created the world's first book written with metal nails. He hammered the nails onto A4 aluminium sheets to make a ninety-six-page book expressing Hindi and English thoughts.

MOST LETTERS WRITTEN ON A
SINGLE GRAIN OF RICE

Surendra Apharya, from Jaipur, India, wrote 1,314 characters – the names of 168 countries and regions – on a single grain of rice on 28 February 1991. Before you throw up your hands in disbelief, bear in mind that it was long-grained rice.

MOST LETTERS WRITTEN ON A POSTCARD

Without using a magnifying glass, micro artist Jaffar Siddiq, from Karnataka, India, managed to squeeze 120,000 letters on to a five-and-a-half-inch by three-and-a-half-inch postcard in 2013.

MOST LINES OF POETRY WRITTEN
WITH CHICKEN BONES

While a prisoner in Paris's Bastille for eleven years, French writer René Auguste Constantin de Renneville (1650–1723) was refused the use of either a pen or pencil. Nevertheless the resourceful de Renneville still managed to write 6,000 lines of romantic poetry as well as a ten-volume history book by using split chicken bones dipped in a mixture of soot and wine.

SMALLEST PRINTED BOOK

A Japanese company, Toppan Printing, created a twenty-two-page book in 2013 that is the size of the eye of a needle. Titled *Shiki no Kusabana* ("Flowers of Seasons"), it contains microscopic monochrome illustrations of Japanese flowers such as the cherry and the plum. The pages are 0.75 millimetres in size while the letters are just 0.01 millimetres wide, making the book impossible to read with the naked eye. Instead it has to be viewed through a magnifying glass.

FIRST FULL-LENGTH BOOK WRITTEN
WITHOUT THE LETTER "E"

American author Ernest Vincent Wright's 1939 novel *Gadsby* does not contain a single "e" in its 50,110 words. Wright said his biggest challenge was avoiding all verbs which used "ed" in the past tense but he got round this by writing "did walk" as opposed to "walked". To ensure that no unwanted vowels sneaked in, he tied down the "e" key on his typewriter while composing the final manuscript. Sadly Wright died in the year of publication, his novel was largely ignored, and a warehouse containing the books burned down shortly after printing, destroying virtually every copy. As a result of its scarcity and curiosity value, the few surviving copies of the original printing have subsequently been priced as high as $7,500.

BOOK CHAPTER WITH FEWEST WORDS

Maverick former English soccer player Len Shackleton had little time for authority. To prove his point, in his 1955 autobiography he included a chapter titled "The Average Director's Knowledge of Football" and left the following page blank.

LONGEST STORY WRITTEN IN ALLITERATION

Writer, actor and director Milind Shintre, from Pune, India, wrote a 1,750-word story in the Marathi language in which every word began with the letter "p". "I want to play with words," he enthused. "It's my hobby and passion. I have accomplished loads of records, including the longest mute play." In which, presumably, there were no words at all.

HIGHEST ALTITUDE BOOK SIGNING

On 10 July 2004, American comedian and adventurer Fran Capo performed the world's highest book signing when she signed copies of her books *Adrenaline Adventures* and *Almost a Wise Guy* at an altitude of 19,340 feet on Mount Kilimanjaro. They were signed in 45 mph winds and temperatures of minus 26°C. Exactly a year later, she set a record for the deepest book signing when she signed the same two books plus *Ripley's Believe It or Not! Planet Eccentric!* (in which she featured) in a submersible at the wreck site of the *Titanic* off the coast of Newfoundland, 12,645 feet below sea level.

MOST OVERDUE LIBRARY BOOK

There is a supreme irony to the fact that the record for the most overdue library book belongs to a tome titled *The Book of Fines*. A register of property transactions in Taunton between 1641 and 1648, it was borrowed in 1650 by the Bishop of Winchester from Somerset County Records office. It obviously proved such a riveting read that it remained with the Bishop's office for another 200 years – long after his death – and then with the Church commissioners for another century. When it was finally returned to Somerset County Library in 1985, it was 335 years overdue and had racked up fines of over $4,000.

LONGEST BOOK READING RITUAL

Russian Countess Yekaterina Skavronskaya (1761–1829) listened to – and apparently enjoyed – the same bedtime story 24,090 times. She was lulled to sleep by the same fairy tale read by the same servant every night for sixty-six years, right up until the day she died.

SMALLEST PUBLIC LIBRARY

Operated by John A. MacDonald, the public library in Cardigan on Canada's Prince Edward Island is housed in a building that is just eleven feet square. Even so, it stocks around 1,800 books.

LARGEST MOBILE LIBRARY

Saheb Ibn Abad (938–995), the Grand Vizier of Persia, was such an avid reader that wherever he travelled in the world he was always accompanied by his library of 117,000 books. They were loaded on the backs of 400 camels, which were trained to walk in alphabetical order so that any book could be instantly located.

SHORTEST VALID WILL

The shortest valid will was that of Bimla Rishi, from Delhi, India. Dated 9 February 1995, it consisted of just two words in Hindi, "Serve Ma", meaning "All to Son". Probably the only way the record could be beaten is if someone could be bothered to pay solicitor's fees for a one-word will reading "Broke".

FIRST PERSON TO TYPE EVERY NUMBER FROM ONE TO A MILLION

For six long years, from 1968 to 1974, dedicated mother Marva Drew, from Waterloo, Iowa, used her spare time to type every number from one to a million on a manual typewriter, a feat requiring 2,473 pages. Why? Because her young son's teacher had told the class that it was impossible to count to a million and Mrs Drew was determined to prove otherwise, regardless of the fact that by the time she had finished, the boy was not only in a different class but in a different school.

FIRST PERSON TO WRITE EVERY NUMBER FROM ONE TO A MILLION

Kris Wilson, from Spanish Fork, Utah, spent two hours a day for four years writing by hand on a notepad every number from one to a million. He began his challenge in February 2004 and when he eventually finished he said: "I can't believe that I've actually done it because it's been a dream and everybody thought I was nuts for trying to do it." While accepting that such a repetitive chore was not necessarily to everyone's taste, he pointed out: "It's clean, it's not immoral, it's not illegal and it's not fattening. It was also the only way I was ever going to make a million."

MOST EXPENSIVE MARRIAGE CERTIFICATE

The original marriage certificate from the 26 May 1994 wedding of Michael Jackson to Lisa-Marie Presley sold at auction for $70,800 in January 2010. This comfortably exceeded the $40,000 paid in August 2007 for Elvis and Priscilla Presley's 1967 marriage certificate and the $23,000 paid in December 2007 to secure the 1954 marriage certificate of Marilyn Monroe and Joe DiMaggio.

LONGEST AFTER-DINNER SPEECH

Dr Donald Thomas delivered a speech on Vegetarian Athletic Nutrition at City College in New York which began on Good Friday 1988 and ended on Easter Monday – 32 hours and 25 minutes later. It was a good job the subject matter was so riveting.

MOST LETTERS TO EDITORS

There are people who like to express their views to newspapers on a regular basis . . . and there's Madhu Agrawal. Since 1976, the community activist from Delhi has written over 11,000 letters to the editors of various newspapers in India and abroad. Her most productive year was 2006 when 1,029 of her letters appeared in print. She is married to businessman Subhash Chandra Agrawal who himself has had more than

4,000 letters to editors published in Indian newspapers. It must be a race for the Basildon Bond in their house.

LONGEST WAIT FOR A NEWSPAPER CORRECTION

On 4 March 2014, the *New York Times* printed a correction for misspelling 161 years earlier the name of a man who was sold into slavery and whose memoirs were turned into the Oscar-winning movie *12 Years a Slave*. The correction said that in its edition of 20 January 1853, the *Times* had erroneously spelled Solomon Northup's name as "Northrop" in an article and "Northrup" in the accompanying headline. The mistake was discovered by someone looking through the paper's archives.

FIRST MOVIE DELIBERATELY SHOT
WITH NO FILM IN CAMERA

For reasons best known to himself, Germany-based director Jay Chung went to the trouble of producing, writing and directing a 35mm movie with a crew of twenty over a two-year period but deliberately never put any film in the camera! Wisely he refrained from telling the cast and crew that the nature of his bizarre project meant they were all essentially wasting their time. All that remains of the movie-that-never-was is a snapshot of the crew.

MOST "TAKES" OF A SINGLE MOVIE SHOT

A single close-up shot in the 1980 horror movie *The Shining* directed by Stanley Kubrick where Dick Hallorann (played by Scatman Crothers) explains to Danny (Danny Lloyd) what shining is was shot 148 times, a world record for the most takes. At one point during filming, a despairing Crothers turned to Kubrick and asked: "What do you want, Stanley? What do you want?" It was six-year-old Lloyd's first and only feature-length movie. He later became a science teacher in Missouri.

MOST MOVIES WATCHED IN A MONTH

To obtain better value for money from his Netflix subscription, between 16 April and 15 May 2012, American comedian Mark Malkoff watched 252 films on Netflix Instant at a cost of 3.2 cents per movie. He watched more than 404 hours of video streaming – an average of 8.4 movies every day – starting with *The Graduate* and finishing with *Chasing Ghosts: Beyond the Arcade*. Malkoff's previous stunts included attempting to get thrown out of an Apple store by having pizza delivered there and taking in a live goat. He also raced a bus across Manhattan on a child's tricycle, beating the bus by three minutes, in a protest about the slowness of the city's buses.

LONGEST TIME SPENT RUNNING IN A MOVIE

Surprisingly this was not *Marathon Man* but *Cartoline da Roma* ("Postcards From Rome"), a 2007 Italian documentary film, in which actor Giulio Base, playing himself, ran on screen for 1 hour 14 minutes 10 seconds.

FIRST ACTOR TO WIN AN OSCAR FOR PLAYING AN OSCAR WINNER

Australian actress Cate Blanchett won an Academy Award as Best Supporting Actress for playing Katharine Hepburn in Martin Scorsese's 2004 movie *The Aviator*. Hepburn herself had won four Academy Awards during her distinguished career, thus enabling Blanchett to create her own slice of Hollywood history.

FIRST ZOMBIE MOVIE

The 1919 silent anti-war film *J'Accuse* was partly shot a year earlier towards the end of World War I, with French director Abel Gance demanding extra realism (an ingredient not usually associated with zombie movies) by filming genuine French soldiers at the Front. When one of the main characters is left shell-shocked, he has a vision where dead soldiers dig their way out of their graves and begin marching into his village. As a sad postscript, Gance later learned that many of the soldiers he had filmed playing zombies died for real shortly afterwards. He recalled: "These men had come straight from the Battle of Verdun, and they were due back eight days later. They played the dead, knowing that in all probability they'd be dead themselves before long. Within a few weeks of their return, 80 per cent had been killed."

LONGEST SCREEN KISS

Actors Necar Zadegan and Traci Dinwiddie locked lips for 3 minutes 24 seconds for a scene in the 2010 movie *Elena Undone* directed by Nicole Conn. The lesbian kiss broke the old heterosexual record set back in 1940 when Regis Toomey and Jane Wyman snogged for 3 minutes 5 seconds in the comedy *You're in the Army Now*.

MOST KISSES IN A MOVIE

Playing the title role in the 1926 romantic adventure *Don Juan*, John Barrymore bestowed 127 kisses on Mary Astor and Estelle Taylor.

MOST EXTRAS IN A MOVIE

More than 300,000 extras appeared in the funeral scene of Sir Richard Attenborough's epic *Gandhi*. A total of 94,560 performers were hired under contract (the majority on a fee of about 40p) and these were supplemented by another 200,000 volunteers who responded to newspaper, TV, radio and loud-speaker announcements. The scene, which ultimately occupied just two minutes of screen time, was shot in Delhi on a single morning, 31 January 1981. The dash for the catering truck must have been something to behold.

MOST VEHICLES DESTROYED IN THE MAKING OF A MOVIE

For his third *Transformers* movie – the explosive 2011 offering *Transformers: Dark of the Moon* – director Michael Bay destroyed no fewer than 532 vehicles. All the cars were donated to the production company free of charge as they were flood-damaged and therefore of no value.

MOST VEHICLES WRECKED BY ONE PERSON

Between 1951 and his retirement in 1993, movie stuntman Dick Sheppard, from Gloucester, England, deliberately wrecked a total of 2,003 cars. His roles included helping Michael Caine make a clean getaway with the gold bullion in *The Italian Job* and aiding James Bond to escape his pursuers in *Thunderball* and *Diamonds Are Forever*.

MOST PEOPLE KILLED BY A CHARACTER IN A MOVIE

Wandering assassin and expert swordsman Ogami Itto (played by Tomisaburo Wakayama) killed 150 people in the 1974 Japanese martial arts movie *Lone Wolf and Cub: White Heaven in Hell*, the most slayings by one character in a movie. The action concludes with him single-handedly wiping out an entire legion by slashing, shooting, stabbing, dismembering and beheading everyone in sight. Jane Austen it isn't.

HIGHEST BODYCOUNT IN A MOVIE

Despite being rated PG-13, Peter Jackson's 2003 epic *The Lord of the Rings: The Return of the King* bumped off no fewer than 836 characters. By comparison, harrowing World War II drama *Saving Private Ryan* (1998) managed only 255 on-screen fatalities and *Rambo* (2008) a measly 247. So the message is clear: never pick a fight with a hobbit.

ACTOR WHO HAS DIED MOST TIMES ON SCREEN

Fans of Japanese samurai movies will know that there is always at least one bad guy who meets a particularly gruesome, protracted death on screen, a demise rife with incessant twitching, convulsing, eye-rolling, groaning and spewing of blood. For more than fifty years, that man has often been Seizo Fukumoto, a leading "kirareyaku" actor – i.e. a stuntman who specializes in getting fatally stabbed by the heroic samurai warrior. Fukumoto has died on screen more than 50,000 times and has turned the act of dying into a grotesque art form – or "buzama", as it is known in Japanese cinema.

"Whenever we kirareyakus die," he says, "we have to do it in a way that is unsightly or clumsy, not graceful. In this buzama, we find beauty. To die in an uncool way is the coolest. The way my characters die has a huge impact on the impression the lead character gives in a film. The more cringeworthy the death, the better the hero looks." To this end, Fukumoto has devised a move called the "ebi-zori" or "prawn bend", where, after being run through with the sword, he arches his body back like a king prawn, and then twitches and convulses before finally expiring. He describes it as the perfect way to die in a movie because while the camera remains focused on the hero, he also obtains valuable screen time by turning his face towards the audience before slumping to the ground.

He learned to fall by studying old Charlie Chaplin films. He observed that Chaplin added to the impact by falling down very hard and realized that he, too, needed to fall with sufficient force to make it hurt. Although the weapons used in samurai movies are blunt replicas of real swords, they are still sharp enough to inflict considerable pain, but Fukumoto says it is all part of the job and never holds back. "You can't act pain if you hesitate. You just have to dive in and get cut up with a sword, without fearing injury. I've always given my deaths 100 per cent."

FIRST MOVIE WITH A PUNCTUATION MARK TITLE

Directed by Hash Dave and Allyson Patel, a Hindi horror movie with the title *?* was released in India on 17 February 2012.

LONGEST MOVIE CREDITS

On the closing credits of his 2006 comedy *Clerks II*, director Kevin Smith included all of his friends on MySpace – 163,070 names. Before that, both the original *Superman* and *Once Upon a Time in the West* had closing credits that dragged on for twelve minutes – about 10 per cent of their entire running time.

LONGEST MOVIE TITLE

The title of James Riffel's 1991 horror movie spoof *Night of the Day of the Dawn of the Son of the Bride of the Return of the Revenge of the Terror of the Attack of the Evil, Mutant, Alien, Flesh Eating, Hellbound, Zombified Living Dead Part 2: In Shocking 2-D* runs to 41 words and 168 characters (not including spaces).

FIRST ACTOR TO BE INSURED AGAINST HIS EYES BECOMING UNCROSSED

Silent movie actor Ben Turpin knew that most of his comic appeal was down to his famously crossed eyes – said to be the result of an accident in his youth – and if he ever received a blow to the head on set, he immediately looked in the mirror to check that his eyes had not become uncrossed. He became so fearful at losing his trademark appearance that he eventually bought an insurance policy from Lloyd's of London that would pay him $100,000 if his eyes ever became normal again.

FIRST HOLLYWOOD MOVIE TO SHOW A TOILET FLUSHING

The release of Alfred Hitchcock's 1960 thriller *Psycho* gave nightmares to moviegoers throughout the world – but for some of a particularly sensitive disposition the biggest shock was not the murder, bloodshed, sexual content or dark Freudian undertones, but the fact that it was the first Hollywood movie to show a toilet actually flushing. While toilets had been seen on screen before, it was considered that showing one in action would prove too distasteful for audiences of the time. However, *Psycho*'s screenwriter was apparently so determined to break one of the last taboos that he deliberately wrote a scene where Janet Leigh's character Marion Crane attempts to dispose of some scraps of paper by flushing them down the toilet. Furthermore, the toilet's contents (i.e. the torn-up paper) were clearly visible without any on-screen warning that eyes should be averted. Perhaps because it was upstaged by the shower soon afterwards, the toilet was never credited in the movie, but sources claim its name was John.

MOVIE WITH MOST SWEAR WORDS

Martin Scorsese's 2013 movie, *The Wolf of Wall Street*, starring Leonardo DiCaprio, features the f-word 506 times, an average of 2.81 times per minute, to set a new Guinness World Record for the most swearing in a film drama. The previous record holder was Spike Lee's 1999 serial killer tale *Summer of Sam,* which dropped the f-bomb 435 times. Rarely to be mistaken for a shrinking violet when it comes to matters of profanity, Scorsese's previous personal best was 422 f-words in *Casino* (1995). However, Scorsese could argue that the swearing in *The Wolf of Wall Street* was by no means gratuitous since the book on which the movie is based, by New York stockbroker Jordan Belfort, uses the f-word 737 times. Scorsese's fondness for expletives caused problems with the movie's distribution in the Middle East, the cut version that was screened in cinemas in the United Arab Emirates being a whole forty-five minutes shorter than the original.

FIRST MOVIE TO USE THE WORD "BULLSHIT"

In the 1968 thriller *Bullitt*, Steve McQueen's character, San Francisco cop Lt Frank Bullitt, became the first person in cinema history to use the word "bullshit". He did so while in less-than-polite conversation with ambitious politician Walter Chalmers, played by Robert Vaughn.

FIRST COUNTRY TO BAN MICKEY MOUSE

Mickey Mouse was banned in Germany as early as 1930 for expressing "anti-German feelings". The German Board of Film Censors noted that in a war cartoon the victorious Mickey was clearly French while "his enemies the cats are clearly recognizable as the German army by their German steel helmets". Mickey was subsequently banned in Romania in 1935, on the grounds that the sight of a 10-foot-high rodent might prove frightening to children, and then in Mussolini's Italy where he was simply not considered fascist enough.

FIRST MOVIE WHERE THE ACTORS WERE HYPNOTIZED

German director Werner Herzog's 1976 movie *Heart of Glass* tells the story of an eighteenth-century Bavarian town whose residents become mad after being unable to replicate the red ruby glasswork for which the place is famous. To achieve the desired trance-like state, Herzog ordered every member of the cast bar one (Josef Bierbichler who plays a visionary foresee-ing the town's demise) to be hypnotized before each day's filming. While the actors were in a trance, Herzog gave them their directions and told them how to react when they opened their eyes. There have been suggestions that the technique was later copied on the 1980s US TV soap *Santa Barbara*, but a more likely explanation was bad acting.

LONGEST *STAR WARS* TAPESTRY

London artist and sci-fi fan Aled Lewis spent six months hand stitching the entire *Star Wars* saga onto a 30-foot-long Bayeux-style tapestry. Unveiled in 2014, his Coruscant Tapestry features quotes from each film written in Aurebesh – the fictional system of writing within the *Star Wars* universe – on the surrounding border. After watching and re-watch-ing the films, he mapped out the major plot points and ordered a 10-metre-long piece of continuous fabric from Germany. He said he had always admired the Bayeux Tapestry and wanted to pay his own tribute, but with Darth Vader as William the Conqueror.

MOST CLICHÉD MOVIE LINE

A study of 150 Hollywood movies made between 1938 and 1974 revealed that the line "Let's get out of here" was used at least once in 84 per cent of productions.

LARGEST ANIMAL CAST IN A MOVIE

A record total of 8,552 animals were hired to appear in the 1956 movie version of Jules Verne's *Around the World in Eighty Days*, which starred David Niven as Phileas Fogg. They consisted of 3,800 sheep, 2,448 buffalo, 950 donkeys, 800 horses, 512 monkeys, 17 bulls, 15 elephants, 6 skunks and 4 ostriches, and were cared for by 90 animal handlers.

SMALLEST CINEMA

Pensioner Reginald Harding has converted a spare bedroom in his house in Birmingham, England, into a four-seater cinema. The world's smallest movie theatre boasts a big screen, two classic projectors, red curtains that draw back when a film starts and authentic seats salvaged from a nearby cinema when it closed. He had to knock a hole in a wall of his three-bedroom house to accommodate the main projector, but despite his venture's small scale he insists that it offers the full experience of going to the cinema, although there's not much petting on the back row and it's probably a bit of a struggle for the usher-ette to get down the gangway with her tray of King Cones.

MOST POEMS RECITED

In June 2009, German banker Eckhard Schröder correctly recited 1,959 poems in twenty-four hours. It had taken him just a few months to learn 2,000 works by inspirational author Sri Chinmoy, and if time had not run out he said he could have carried on . . . and on.

LONGEST SOLO NON-STOP SHAKESPEARE RECITAL

Between 16 and 21 July 1987 as part of the International Shakespeare Festival at London's South Bank, British actor Adrian Hilton single-handedly recited the complete works of Shakespeare non-stop for 110 hours 46 minutes. The record had previously been held by a group of ten actors, each playing individual parts, but Hilton, inspired by his friendship with multi-record holder, entertainer and Guinness ambassador Roy Castle, resolved to take on every role himself. So for five days, aided by friends to keep him awake and advice from NASA on nutrition and the effects of sleeplessness, Hilton performed his "Bardathon", playing every single role penned by the Bard, along with all the sonnets and poems.

FASTEST *HAMLET* SOLILOQUY

In 1995, Canadian businessman Sean Shannon recited the 260-word "To be or not to be" soliloquy from Shakespeare's *Hamlet* in just 23.8 seconds. Shannon, who can speak at 655 words a minute, made light of his record-breaking achievement, saying: "I always thought everybody could do it and spoke like that when they were excited. I was very surprised when I realized I speeded up more than most and then – it turned out – more than anyone. I think it is important *not* to think about what you are saying. I gather newscasters do an entire newscast without understanding a word they say. They just say it convincingly and that is probably the best way." He does admit that his mastery of the *Hamlet* speech does rather spoil any production of the play for him. "When the speech comes on, I do tend to get ahead of the actor a little bit in my mind as it is so engrained in my memory." Thankfully he has so far resisted the urge to yell "Get on with it" at Kenneth Branagh.

SMALLEST MOBILE THEATRE

Calling itself "The Smallest Theatre in the World", the Grand Theatre of Lemmings' home is mounted onto the sidecar of a Royal Enfield motorcycle and has seating for an audience of just two. The idea was conceived by British street artist Marcel Steiner, in 1972, after he bought a battered Panther motorbike with a gigantic sidecar, prompting eccentric comedy actor Ken Campbell to joke: "You could build a theatre in that sidecar!" Taking the remark as a challenge, Steiner, who was 6 feet 2 inches tall and weighed 18 stone in his prime, set about building his miniature theatre, resplendent with stage door, box office, Sistine Chapel frescoed ceiling, red plush curtains, a chandelier from Woolworths and a cushioned seat for two. He toured the world with it for thirty years, boasting that it was the only theatre which sold out for every performance. When it burned down at the Edinburgh Festival one year, donations poured in, allowing Steiner to rebuild it in twenty-four hours. He directed and starred in every production, performing dramatizations from *The Raising of the Titanic* to *War and Peace* (complete with cannon). He once performed *The Tempest* in the car park of the Royal Shakespeare Theatre at Stratford-upon-Avon while the RSC was doing the same play inside. Following his death in 1999, the sidecar theatre lay idle for some years but happily it has been restored to its former glory. In 2013 the Lemmings toured the UK with a slightly scaled-down version of *King Kong*.

SMALLEST THEATRE THAT WAS ONCE A PUBLIC TOILET

Transformed from a derelict Victorian gentleman's public lavatory, the Theatre of Small Convenience in Great Malvern, Worcestershire, was founded in 1999 by Dennis Neale, a part-time social worker, keen puppeteer and drama enthusiast. The wedge-shaped stone building measures 16 feet long, and a maximum 10 feet wide. It houses a tiny stage and has an audience capacity of twelve. Mr Neale described it as "a magical building with a wonderfully intimate atmosphere", adding: "Ironically we don't have room for a toilet of our own – the audience have to run across the road to public ones." What a shame W.C. Fields never appeared there.

HIGHEST THEATRICAL PERFORMANCE

There was high drama on board an easyJet flight from Gatwick, West Sussex, to Verona, Italy, on 23 April 2014 when members of the Reduced Shakespeare Company performed a selection of the Bard's plays at an altitude of 37,000 feet, setting a world record for the highest theatrical performance. The hour-long extravaganza – to mark what would have been Shakespeare's 450th birthday in the unlikely event of him still being alive – contained abridged versions of *Romeo and Juliet*, *Macbeth*, *Julius Caesar*, *Othello*, *Hamlet* and *Titus Andronicus*. Although Shakespeare famously declared that "all the world's a stage", the three actors – Simon Cole, Gary Fannin and William Meredith – had to content themselves with the cramped aisle of the plane, making costume changes between the seats at the front.

MOST MUSICAL APPEARANCES IN ONE NIGHT

On 24 February 2004, American model and actress Jerry Hall set a new record by making cameo appearances in six different London musicals on the same evening. Transported through the city by motorbike, she began by appearing onstage at Her Majesty's Theatre at 7.40 p.m. with the cast of Andrew Lloyd Webber's *The Phantom of the Opera*. By 8.04 she was down the road cavorting as a prostitute at the Palace Theatre in *Les Misérables*, and at 8.35 she briefly trod the boards in *Fame* at the Aldwych. The next stop was the Phoenix for *Blood Brothers* before speeding on to the Theatre Royal, Drury Lane, where, at 9.25, she high-kicked with the cast of

Anything Goes. She rounded off her hectic schedule at 10.20 in *Chitty Chitty Bang Bang* at the Palladium. Altogether the forty-seven-year-old Texan spent thirty-three minutes on stage and entertained 9,214 theatregoers. The only problem, she subsequently revealed, was finding time to go to the toilet.

MOST CHARACTERS PORTRAYED BY ONE PERSON IN A TRILOGY OF PLAYS

English writer and actor Joe Bone plays 136 different characters in his one-man shows *Bane, Bane 2* and *Bane 3*, a trilogy of film noir parodies built around comical hitman Bruce Bane. He performed the original play as part of his university exam in 2005 but it subsequently grew into an hour-long solo show that was so successful it has spawned two sequels. He says: "In the first *Bane* I play about 40 characters. I improvise a bit so sometimes the number increases or decreases depending on what I'm doing. The initial idea wasn't focused on trying to perform lots of characters; it was about telling a fun little story. I played the other characters out of necessity to tell the story. As the story grew, the characters increased." While Bone is kept busy on stage, there is little work for the wardrobe department as there are no costume changes.

FASTEST PLAYWRIGHT

Long before Ernie Wise arrived on the scene, Spanish playwright Lope de Vega Carpio (1562–1635) claimed to have written 100 of his plays in less than a day each. In total, he wrote nearly 2,000 plays along with 3,000 poems. In the course of his career, his daily output averaged some twenty pages.

MOST JOKES TOLD IN ONE HOUR

Donald Macleod (stage name Donnie Maroot), from Scotland's Isle of Lewis, set a new world record by telling 580 jokes in an hour at the Park Bar, Glasgow, on 5 March 2014. A sample of his material went: "What would the drummer in the Mexican Beatles be called? – Gringo Starr." If nothing else, he deserved the record for being brave enough to tell jokes like that in a Glasgow bar.

MOST ONE-LINE JOKES WRITTEN

You have probably never heard of him, but George Valentine, a seventy-six-year-old pensioner from Rotherham, South Yorkshire, can lay claim to being the king of the one-liner. Since penning his first joke at the age of twelve, he has written in the region of 110,000 one-line gags, some of which were used by the likes of Tommy Cooper, Bob Monkhouse and Les Dawson. He only ever wrote jokes as a hobby – earning a living by working as a shoe supplier – but now that he has retired he is able to tweet his witticisms on a daily basis to his 215,000 online followers. "I'll only allow myself three minutes to write a joke," he says. "If it doesn't work by then, I'll can the idea. I usually write a one-liner in about two minutes."

YOUNGEST COMEDIAN

Spencer Patterson became the world's youngest comedian when in 1991 at the age of two he appeared in comedy shows alongside his mother, Fran Capo, at the Tropicana in Las Vegas. He had been waiting backstage when he suddenly decided that he wanted to go out front. Invited by his mother, he went on stage with a spur-of-the-moment impression of Richard Nixon, puffing out his chubby toddler cheeks and waving the victory sign. The audience lapped it up. He went on to perform stand-up comedy for the US Marines in Okinawa, Japan, and has appeared in a number of TV and radio shows as both a comedian and ventriloquist. A two-year-old on stage doing comedy; cute or what? Probably what.

YOUNGEST JOKE TELLER IN CLASSICAL GREEK

Hungarian-born John von Neumann (1903–57) was a child prodigy who, at the age of six, could exchange jokes with his father in classical Greek. Eschewing a career doing stand-up in Athens, he became a renowned mathematician.

MOST FAMILY PHOTOS TAKEN IN ONE DAY

To celebrate the release of the late Shammi Kapoor's final Bollywood movie *Rockstar* on 11 Nov 2011 (11/11/11), Ninad Jadhav, from Chhindwara, India, took 11,111 photos of his three-year-old son Anay that day. Unfortunately only 146 were taken when Anay was awake. Lest he should be thought to be favouring one child, Ninad is quick to point out that between 28 July and 28 August 2010 he took no fewer than 28,710 photos of his newborn daughter Aviva. What fun the whole family must have when he gets out the photo albums!

MOST SELFIES TAKEN

Every morning bar one since 23 February 1987, Karl Baden, a photography lecturer from Boston, Massachusetts, has taken a picture of himself in the same position – a total of more than 10,000 selfies. The only day he missed was 15 October 1991, when he was late for a class he was teaching at Rhode Island School of Design. He made a mental note to take the picture when he got home, but forgot. He turned the first twenty-five years' worth of photos into a video illustrating the ageing process. He first came up with the idea when he was a student in 1975, but a friend said the concept was "stupid", a criticism that put him off for twelve years.

Apart from that solitary slip-up, the project has required

iron discipline. "I don't do anything to change my face intentionally," says Baden. "I don't grow beards or moustaches and I keep my hair the same." He uses the same camera and the same lighting, although he has had to change the type of film, simply because the products he used to rely on are no longer made. "I don't use any unusual angles," he adds. "I try to keep all artistic conceits out of the picture. I try to achieve identical images, but I can't always, because I'm human and I make mistakes, and the camera makes mistakes." The sixty-two-year-old has no intention of stopping soon, insisting: "I'll stop when I'm dead."

MOST SELFIES TAKEN IN AN HOUR

Posing on Miami's South Beach on 3 May 2014, Mark E. Miller and Ethan Hethcote took a world record 355 selfies in an hour (demolishing the previous record of 50). They insist that their motivation was not vanity but to encourage positive thinking by way of a smile.

FIRST SUICIDE TO BE CAPTURED ON CAMERA

When twenty-eight-year-old Marion Perloff jumped from the eleventh floor of the Time & Life Building in New York on 23 June 1938, little did she know that her final moments would be captured on film. NBC cameraman Ross Plaisted happened to be testing his video and audio equipment in a nearby building and focused on the young woman's falling body as she plunged past the sixth floor. He then followed her all the way to the ground. Although the dramatic footage he captured was never screened on television, it did not stop rival media outlets (radio and print) warning of the dire threat to civilization posed by the new invention. And that was before anyone had even conceived *Celebrity Big Brother*.

MOST USED WHISTLE ON RADIO

The same whistle was blown for forty-seven years and an estimated 8,000 times on BBC Radio 4's panel show *Just a Minute*. The whistle calls time on guests who must try to speak for a minute on a chosen subject "without repetition, hesitation or deviation". However, the pea in the old whistle, used from the first episode in 1967, had begun to lose its force by 2014, raising the fear that panellists could be left wittering on for vital seconds. So it was finally replaced by a powerful new Acme Thunderer whistle – the type used by soccer referees – although there were concerns that its blast might prove too startling for the show's ninety-one-year-old presenter Nicholas Parsons.

FIRST NEWSREADER TO LOSE A TOOTH ON TELEVISION

Kenneth Kendall was reading the BBC television news on 14 July 1979 when a false crown tooth popped out of his mouth and onto his desk. He gamely continued reading with his mouth almost closed – like a bad ventriloquist – hoping that none of the viewers had noticed.

MOST ENDURING GLOVE PUPPET

Bought for 7s 6d in 1948 by Bradford engineer and part-time magician Harry Corbett to keep his children amused on a wet holiday in Blackpool, Sooty the glove puppet bear made his TV debut in 1952 and is still going strong more than sixty years later. Such is the wear and tear in the mischievous little bear's act that some 6,000 different Sooty puppets have been used on stage shows and television. Harry, who insured the thumb and first two fingers of his right hand for £20,000 (more than $30,000) in the 1950s, treated Sooty like a real person. One year the Corbett family had just set off on holiday and had been driving for nearly half an hour when Harry suddenly stopped the car and turned back – because he had forgotten Sooty. Wherever Sooty travelled, it was always face up and in a neat box with air holes so that he could breathe!

In 1957, Sooty was joined by Sweep the dog and in the 1960s by a panda girlfriend Soo despite the BBC's fears that the move might be seen as introducing sex to children's television. At first the BBC refused to allow Soo to appear, but after a wave of adverse publicity, the Corporation relented – but only on condition that Sooty and Soo must never touch. Sadly the stress of doing Sooty affected Harry's health and he effectively retired in 1976, handing over the reins to his son Matthew. When Matthew, too, retired in 1998, Richard Cadell became Sooty's new co-star. Over the years, Sooty's infamous water-pistol has targeted everyone from Prince Philip to fearsome dog trainer Barbara Woodhouse, but the havoc he created on those occasions was mild compared to the pizza that he threw in 2011 which left magician Paul Daniels with a black eye and made Daniels surely the only person in the history of show business to have been hospitalized by a glove puppet.

LONGEST BROADCAST OF "GOAL!" WITHOUT TAKING A BREATH

During a September 2011 Romanian League match between Voinţa Sibiu and Otelul Galati, Ilie Dobre, soccer commentator at Radio Romania News, broadcast a thirty-one-second-long "Goal!" shout without taking a breath. His effort beat his previous record of twenty-seven seconds set in a Europa League match. In 2013, Dobre also claimed a sixty-eight-second record for the longest "Goal!" shout with just a single respiration. Romanian listeners must be the only football fans in the world who pray for a goalless draw.

WEIRDEST OCCUPATION ON *WHAT'S MY LINE?*

One of the most popular TV quiz shows of the 1950s was *What's My Line?* where a team of celebrity panellists had ten questions in which to guess the jobs of various guests. The show originated in the United States on CBS in 1950 and was launched in the UK by the BBC in 1951 with first the irascible Gilbert Harding and then the genial Eamonn Andrews as chairman. On an early edition of the UK version, the challenger was a saggar maker's bottom knocker, an occupation unknown to the vast majority of the population. Saggars are used to hold and protect pottery during kiln-firing, and making them to the correct specifications is a skilled job, performed by the saggar maker. Making the bases of the saggars is done by placing clay in a metal hoop and simply knocking it into shape. It requires less craftsmanship and is done by the saggar maker's bottom knocker. Sadly, saggar maker's bottom knockers are all but extinct in Britain these days, so if you should be lucky enough to come across one, look after him.

FIRST TV CHANNEL EXCLUSIVELY FOR DOGS

A new daytime TV channel designed solely to be watched by dogs while their owners are out at work was launched in San Diego, California, in 2012. DOGTV's schedule features nearly 800 programmes, each lasting no longer than five minutes to fit a dog's short attention span. The colour is toned down because dogs have a weaker colour spectrum than humans, and the shows' content aims to keep the pets relaxed as well as entertained. So there are no loud noises, no shouty or angry humans, and, most importantly, no other dogs barking. Some owners were worried that the channel would turn their dogs into couch potatoes but it proved so successful that it soon went nationwide where subscribers reported that DOGTV was unexpectedly popular with an audience category not identified in the original research – cats.

HIGHEST NUMBER OF "TAKES"
FOR A TV COMMERCIAL

In 1973, British comedy actress Pat Coombs set a new record
for the most "takes" (twenty-nine) in a TV commercial while
vainly trying to promote a new breakfast cereal. "Every time
we came to the punchline, I just could not remember the name
of the product," she said five years later, still unable to recall
the name. "It was some sort of muesli but the name was prac-
tically unpronounceable."

MOST COMPLAINED ABOUT
COMMERCIAL ON BRITISH TV

A 2005 Kentucky Fried Chicken advert showing call centre
workers singing with their mouths full attracted 1,671 recorded
complaints from UK viewers, many of whom protested that it
would encourage bad manners among children.

MOST GUEST STAR APPEARANCES
ON *THE SIMPSONS*

The late Canadian-born actor and comedian Phil Hartman
(1948–98) made fifty-two guest appearances on *The Simpsons*
over a period of eight years, often voicing the recurring characters Lionel Hutz, an ambulance-chasing lawyer, and
washed-up actor Troy McClure. The show's creator, Matt
Groening, said he took Hartman "for granted because he
nailed the joke every time".

MOST CLAPS ON TV

Long-standing TV hostess Vanna White, who began turning
the letters on the US quiz show *Wheel of Fortune* in 1982,
claps every time a contestant spins the wheel and again when

the puzzle is solved. These claps build up, and by the time the show celebrated its 6,000th episode in 2014 (and Vanna has appeared in all but a handful), it was estimated that she had applauded 4,312,800 times, averaging out at around 720 claps per show. She says she tends to clap with cupped hands, and is proud to point out that she has no calluses.

MOST DIFFERENT OUTFITS WORN ON A TV SHOW

This is another record for Vanna White who has never, ever worn the same outfit twice during her 6,000-plus episodes of *Wheel of Fortune*. Every few weeks she has a fitting where she tries on up to sixty dresses and picks her favourite dozen, although she doesn't get to keep any of them. She prefers to wear elegant gowns on screen but – shock, horror – has been known to slum it in slacks. And if one outfit happens to be a little tight, she says she just holds her breath for thirty minutes.

LONGEST PURSUIT OF AN UNPAID TV LICENCE

A German poet who had been dead for over 200 years was sent two letters by a TV licence-collecting agency threatening to instigate legal proceedings against him unless he quickly settled his monthly $25 bill. Friedrich Schiller had died in 1805 – long before the invention of either television or radio – but that did not prevent agency GEZ sending him two letters in 2008 demanding immediate payment. The letters were sent to a primary school bearing Schiller's name in the Saxony town of Weigsdorf-Köblitz. Headteacher Michael Binder informed the agency that "the addressee is no longer in a position to listen to the radio or watch television" and attached Schiller's CV to his reply. GEZ responded by insisting that Schiller would only be exempt if he could prove that he did not own television or radio sets. After the confusion was finally cleared up, GEZ promised to alter Schiller's status in its computer system.

LONGEST GAP BETWEEN TV APPEARANCES IN THE SAME SHOW

Actor Philip Lowrie first appeared as Dennis Tanner on the long-running UK TV soap *Coronation Street* in 1960 and stayed with the show until 1968. He re-joined the cast in the same role in May 2011, after an absence of forty-three years.

MOST DEATHS IN A TV SOAP

From its debut in 1960 to April 2014, there have been 162 character deaths on the UK soap *Coronation Street*. Methods of dispatch have included being electrocuted by a hair dryer (Valerie Barlow, 1971), hit by a tram (Alan Bradley, 1989) and being frozen to death in a supermarket freezer (Anne Malone, 1998).

SOAP ACTOR WHO "DIED" MOST TIMES IN TWENTY-FOUR HOURS

Veteran Hong Kong actor Law Lok Lam set some sort of record in 2011 when characters played by him died in five different TV soap operas within a period of twenty-four hours. During primetime on 6 April, the sixty-three-year-old actor met a bloody end during a fight in the martial arts drama *Grace Under Fire*, and in *Relic of an Emissary*, his character, Ming emperor Zhu Yuanzhang, expired after an illness. Then on 7 April, he vomited blood before dying in *Fate to Fate*. In two other shows that day, *Police Station No. 7* and *Virtues of Harmony*, Law's death was not actually seen on screen, but it was discussed. Hong Kong broadcaster TVB dismissed Law's unprecedented run of bad luck as "purely a coincidence".

LONGEST TV PROGRAMME SHOWING
A MAN WALKING BACKWARDS

French public TV channel France 4 broadcast a nine-hour programme on 31 March 2014 dedicated entirely to a man walking backwards through the streets of Tokyo. The film, *Tokyo Reverse*, was deliberately screened backwards so that it looked as if its star, Ludovic Zuili, was the only person walking normally. Apparently Zuili had taken dance lessons beforehand to make his movements appear more natural.

LONGEST TV PROGRAMME DEDICATED
SOLELY TO KNITTING

On the evening of Friday 1 November 2013, Norwegian TV channel NRK2 broadcast almost thirteen hours of knitting. The National Knitting Night began with a four-hour discussion about the technique of knitting, and for viewers who found that a little too racy there followed eight-and-a-half hours of live knitting. Network executive Rene Moklebust – surely the world's only TV boss not given to hyperbole – described it as "long, quiet sequences of knitting and spinning". *Cagney and Lacey* it wasn't. Incredibly 1.3 million Norwegians tuned in to watch at least part of the knitting marathon, although many were probably left in stitches. The Slow TV evening followed on the success of NRK2's previous ratings winner – a twelve-hour broadcast of a burning fireplace.

CHAPTER 8

Technology and Games

MOST CONNECTED HUMAN BEING

American software developer Chris Dancy uses more than 700 hi-tech systems to monitor his daily moods and movements, making him even better connected than Kevin Bacon. He employs a range of sensors, apps, devices and services that gather data about his activities and his surrounding environment and creates what he calls his "inner-net", enabling him to know more about himself than any other person on the planet. He nearly always carries two smartphones and wears a smartwatch on one wrist which sends him updates from his phones. On the other wrist, he wears a device that tracks his sleep patterns. He also wears a heart monitor strapped to his chest, a fitness tracker around his upper arm and a posture sensor, which vibrates when he slouches, beneath his waistband. Sometimes he also wears a Google Glass headset, which records everything he sees.

He spent four years connecting the various equipment he wears to the technology in his home, which in turn tells him what he eats, drinks and how he is feeling. Inside his front door he has installed a lighting system that flashes blue if he will need an umbrella because it is going to rain that day, while an app gives him information when he is near something in his home so that he never loses his keys. Leaving nothing to chance, his bed has a special mattress cover that collects additional sleep data. He says: "I now know what to drink, what to eat, when to sleep and when to actually make myself get up. I have lost 100 pounds in weight and have formed better habits thanks to the feedback I'm getting. It's body and mind hacking. When I touch something, I try to make sure it's something I can get information out of. The house knows my behaviours. If I get really stressed out and don't sleep well, when I wake up the light is a certain colour, the room a particular temperature, and certain music plays. My entire life is preconditioned based on all the information that I collect in real time."

With almost his every living moment archived, he regularly uses the data to govern his future actions and responses, which probably sounds spookier than it really is. He explains: "When I was going to a restaurant near my home in Denver, Colorado, I thought, 'What did I eat here last time?' So I went through all the photos from that day and could see exactly what meal it was. There's some other neat stuff, like when I have a meeting with someone on my calendar, all my sensors lock into that, so instead of getting a LinkedIn profile, I'll get how they made me feel the first time I met them. I do take days off with little to no tracking from wearables, but because I have so many systems that automatically track what I'm doing, it's impossible to truly disconnect." Even Dancy's two dogs have been enlisted into his technological revolution. He tracks their daily progress by collecting data via a pet GPS system.

FIRST WEBSITE MADE OUT OF CHOCOLATE

To promote its 2011 cocoa-flavoured beer, Portuguese brewery Sagres hired chocolate master Victor Nunes to reproduce the company's website entirely in chocolate. The finished article was then photographed and turned back into a functional website, with the first online visitors receiving pieces of the chocolate version together with a six-pack of the chocolate beer.

FIRST PERSON TO ATTEMPT TO MARRY A LAPTOP

In 2014, former US lawyer Chris Sevier sought the legal right to marry his laptop computer, or his "machine-spouse" as he preferred to call it. He claimed that he had fallen in love with his Apple MacBook and that he "preferred having sex with it over all other persons or things". He added in his fifty-page court motion that if gay couples "have the right to marry their object of sexual desire, even if they lack corresponding sexual parts, then I should have the right to marry my preferred sexual object. If anything, my marriage to a machine possesses less of a risk, since a possible acrimonious divorce proceeding could be avoided, if the marriage fails." However, a judge rejected Sevier's plea, suggesting that it was "removed from reality". Sevier had previously attempted to sue Apple after he said the mistyping of Facebook on the Safari browser had led him to pornographic images, which "poisoned his life" and caused the breakdown of his marriage. He was suspended from practising law in 2011 partly on mental health grounds.

LONGEST PERIOD OF INSTANT MESSAGING ON A COMPUTER

Twenty-four-year-old Norman Perez, from Burbank, California, typed on a computer keyboard for ninety-six hours in June 2007 to set the first world record for instant messaging. The aspiring actor was challenged to attempt the feat after being spotted week after week in a local coffee shop typing on his laptop to his manager looking for work. During his four days at the keyboard, he received numerous messages from around the world and a wealthy New York socialite fell in love with him, possibly causing a pop-up. She told Perez the only thing that stopped her dating him was her husband: her rich husband.

LONGEST EMAIL

Pranesh Sharma, from Indore, India, sent a 737,106-word email in 2012 about a 19th-century Hindu monk. It was titled "Swami Vivekananda: An Inspirational Personality" and ran to 1,396 pages.

FASTEST REVERSE TYPING ON A COMPUTER KEYBOARD

On 12 January 2012, fast-fingered Asam Vinay Kumar, from Andhrapradesh, India, typed from Z to A on a computer keyboard in only 2.5 seconds – to spell a word that doesn't exist, but apparently that wasn't the point.

FASTEST TYPING WITH NOSE

Mohammed Khurshid Hussain, from Hyderabad, India, set a new world record in 2014 for speed typing with his nose. Pressing his nose to the keyboard, the twenty-three-year-old, who already held a record for fast typing with fingers, took just 48.62 seconds to type the words "Guinness World Records have challenged me to type this sentence using my nose in the fastest time". He says the secret is to type with one eye closed because otherwise it can be awkward to locate the keys.

MOST TEXT MESSAGES SENT IN A MONTH

In the course of one month in 2009, Fred Lindgren, from San Antonio, Texas, sent 566,607 texts from his handset, which works out at 18,887 texts sent a day, 787 an hour or 13 a minute. Whichever way you look at it, that's a lot of texts. So it's no surprise that his monthly phone bill arrived not in an envelope but in a large box. The bill totalled over $120,000 but T-Mobile waived the domestic charges because Lindgren had wisely signed up for free text messaging.

However, he still had to pay for all the international text messages that he sent and received. He subsequently lamented: "It was a lot of hard work, much tougher than I had thought. I couldn't take calls, my phone kept crashing but I'd still do it again if I was sponsored."

MOST TEXT MESSAGES SENT TO ONE PERSON IN FIVE MINUTES

On 19 December 2009, Jack Webster, from Falls Church, Virginia, sent 230 text messages to a friend in five minutes. It is not known whether the recipient of all those texts is still his friend.

MOST SHAKESPEAREAN TEXTS SENT

Furious at being ripped off by a Gumtree seller, twenty-four-year-old Edd Joseph, a graphic designer from Bristol, England, exacted a triumphant revenge in March 2014 by texting him the complete works of Shakespeare so that they arrived in the form of nearly 30,000 individual texts. Joseph felt helpless when he bought a PS3 games console for £80 ($120) but the vendor failed to send the goods or provide a refund. So after discovering that he could copy words from the internet and paste them into a text message without costing him a penny on his unlimited mobile phone package, Joseph decided to send the Derby-based fraudster all thirty-seven of Shakespeare's plays. He sent each play as one text but because they could only be received in 160-character chunks, they buzzed through in a total of 29,305 individual texts, keeping the recipient's phone busy for an entire week. *Hamlet* alone took an epic 1,143 texts while *All's Well That Ends Well* racked up a satisfying 861. To make sure the seller really was getting the message, Joseph sent many of them at night. Predictably he soon started to receive abusive calls from the previously reclusive vendor. "I tried to ask him if he was enjoying the plays," said Joseph, "but he was very confused. I'm not a literary student, and I'm not an avid fan of Shakespeare, but you could say I've got a new appreciation – especially for the long ones."

FASTEST TEXT MESSAGING WHILE BLINDFOLDED

In November 2007, seventeen-year-old Elliot Nicholls from Dunedin, New Zealand, sent a 160-character text message without any mistakes and while blindfolded in 45.09 seconds. In case you're wondering, the message was: "The razor-toothed piranhas of the genera Serrasalmus and Pygocentrus are the most ferocious freshwater fish in the world. In reality, they seldom attack a human."

FASTEST TIME FOR TWO PEOPLE TO TEXT THE WORDS "O ROMEO, ROMEO, WHEREFORE ART THOU ROMEO?" BACK AND FORTH TO ONE ANOTHER

Recordsetter.com reveals that on 22 September 2013, Christine MaKayla, from Fort St John, British Columbia, Canada, and her friend Emily, sent and received seven text messages in 47.3 seconds, each quoting William Shakespeare's speech "O Romeo, Romeo, wherefore art thou Romeo?" This apparently established a new world record, but most remarkable of all is that there was an existing record to break.

MOST FIVE-LETTER PLACE NAMES STARTING WITH "E" DERIVED FROM THE UNDUPLICATED LETTERS OF "LIVESTRONG" SENT IN A SINGLE TWEET

On 7 September 2012, Dinesh Upadhyaya, from Mumbai, India, a man best known for cramming drinking straws and pool balls into his mouth, demonstrated another side to his talents by sending in a single tweet 23 five-letter place names, all beginning with "E" and all derived from unduplicated letters of the word "Livestrong". Unrestricted by length, duplication or the need to tweet, he also managed to make a staggering 2,139 place names using only the letters in "Livestrong" – an anagrammatic feat that must have involved many hours poring over an atlas.

MOST ADAM SANDLER MOVIE TITLES MENTIONED IN A SINGLE TWEET

On 20 January 2014, Bryton Swan, from Barrie, Ontario, Canada, mentioned fourteen Adam Sandler movies in a single tweet. It read: "Grown Ups Jack & Jill Funny People Mr. Deeds Click Spanglish Coneheads Mixed Nuts Couch Airheads The Animal Blended Little Nicky Joe Dirt 2."

MOST RETWEETED SELFIE

A celebrity-packed selfie posted by 2014 Academy Awards host Ellen DeGeneres became the most retweeted image ever on Twitter. The picture, which also included Brad Pitt, Julia Roberts, Meryl Streep, Kevin Spacey, Jennifer Lawrence and Bradley Cooper, had been retweeted more than two million times by the end of the ceremony, briefly causing Twitter to crash. So it wasn't all bad.

FASTEST UPDATE OF RELATIONSHIP STATUS ON FACEBOOK

Moments after Dana Hanna had married Tracy Page at the Mountain Christian Church in Joppa, Maryland, on 21 November 2009, he interrupted the ceremony and pulled out his cell phone so that he could instantly update his status on Facebook. As the congregation – and his bride – looked on in a state of surprise, the software developer calmly changed his status to "married" and tweeted: "Standing at the altar with @TracyPage where just a second ago, she became my wife! Gotta go, time to kiss my bride." Meanwhile the minister, who had been advised of the groom's intentions beforehand, announced: "Dana is updating his relationship status on Facebook," before adding: "It's official on Facebook, it's official in my book." Hanna also handed a phone to Tracy so that she could change her Facebook page. It was not the first time the couple had resorted to technology to break important news. Hanna explained: "When we got engaged, we changed our Facebook statuses and didn't even call anyone since the word would spread on Facebook far faster than it would have over the phone. After doing that, we received a lot of laughs, and some minor criticism from family who were insulted that we couldn't even pick up the phone to call them!"

LONGEST PHONE CONVERSATION

If you thought your wife spent a long time on the phone to her sister, that's nothing compared to Switzerland's Sandra Kobel and Stephan Hafner who, in November 2005, spent 39 hours 18 minutes 24 seconds on a single internet phone call. Stationed in Berne and Zurich respectively, they talked and talked, supplied via the website's chat facility with ideas to keep the conversation flowing. There is no truth in the rumour that the marathon call only ended when Ms Kobel realized she had got the wrong number.

MOBILE PHONE THAT SURVIVED HIGHEST DROP

When Jarrod McKinney jumped from a plane at 13,500 feet over Winsted, Minnesota, on 8 July 2011, he was in such a hurry to get out of the door that he forget to zip the pocket of his baggy skydiving pants, as a result of which his iPhone 4 slipped out and plummeted to the ground at around 120 mph. Given that the same phone had cracked when his two-year-old had accidentally knocked it off a bathroom shelf,

McKinney was not exactly optimistic about its chances of survival. He eventually found it – by using a GPS tracking app – on the roof of a two-storey factory about half a mile away from his landing point. The phone's glass surfaces were shattered but, just for fun, one of his colleagues on the ground decided to call him on it – and to everyone's amazement the phone started vibrating. "It works! It works!" they shrieked. McKinney continued to be able to make and receive calls on the device even though, with its touchscreen shattered, he had to use the BlueTooth connection in his truck to do so.

LONGEST BURNING LIGHT BULB

A five-watt carbon filament electric light bulb has been burning in the Livermore Fire Department House, California, ever since it was installed in 1901. Known as the Centennial Light, it was manufactured by the Shelby Electric Company of Ohio but has comfortably outlived its maker, which closed in 1914. The average light bulb lasts for no more than a thousand hours but Livermore's has burned for close to a million, helped perhaps by the fact that it has hardly ever been switched off. When it moved home in 1976, it was deprived of electricity for only twenty-two minutes during the tense transfer, which was made in a specially designed box and with full firetruck escort. Tourists regularly come to gawp at it, and its 100th birthday in 2001 was celebrated with a community barbecue and live music. Its fan base had a nasty scare on the evening of 20 May 2013 when its dedicated webcam appeared to show that the bulb had finally, tragically burned out. The following morning, an electrician was called in but, far from confirming time of death, he found that the bulb had not burned out at all – it was the power supply that had been faulty. So after nine-and-a-half hours of darkness, there was light once again and the world's most durable bulb was burning brighter than ever.

OLDEST WORKING HAIRDRYER

A Siemens electric hairdryer owned by retired insurance company director John Wilcox and his wife Kay, from Paignton, Devon, was still blowing strong when it celebrated what was believed to be its eightieth birthday in 2010, having never once broke, down or needed a service. Weighing a hefty two pounds, the brown Bakelite model's only controls are on/off and hot/cold, and its sole concession to technological advances was the fitting of a new plug – and that was only because its original round-pin type had become obsolete. Mr Wilcox remembered his mother Florrie using the hairdryer back in the late 1930s but was unable to establish its precise age because she died in 1988 and there was no receipt for it. It was probably a bit late to be asking for a refund anyway.

BIGGEST FART MACHINE

At 7 p.m. on the evening of 24 July 2014, people in the Calais region of Northern France heard a "faint rumble" in the distance. They might have dismissed it as a large truck rolling off the Channel ferry or an airplane high in the skies, but it is pretty safe to say that none would have attributed the sound to a giant fart machine aimed at them from across the water in England. The 16-foot-high contraption, tastefully designed in the shape of a pair of buttocks, was the brainchild of Colin Furze – by day a humble plumber from Stamford, Lincolnshire, but by night a demon inventor of weird mechanical devices. Having already created a 50 mph baby pram and a fire-spurting mobility scooter, he turned his attention to something even noisier – a fart machine in the form of a giant pulse valveless jet engine. He then transported it down to Kent, fired it up on the White Cliffs of Dover and pointed it in the general direction of France. "My neighbours are always telling me I make a lot of noise," he said, "so I thought what about England's neighbours, the French? Let's see if we can make a noise that they can hear. I'm delighted to say we did."

MOST EXPENSIVE GHOST FOR SALE ON EBAY

In 2012, an optimistic vendor by the name of rklassman tried to sell the ghost of former US golfing great Bobby Jones (which he claimed to have trapped in a jar) for $1,000 on eBay. The seller's online description explained: "Earlier this year I began to hear strange voices coming from my garage and specifically my golf clubs. The voice would repeat 'Syringomyelia, Syringomyelia.' At first I had no idea what the ghost was saying, so I googled the word. Syringomyelia is the disease that paralyzed and killed hall of fame golfer Bobby Jones. I asked the apparition, 'Are you Bobby Jones?' The ghost then became visible dressed in 1950s' golfing gear. The ghost said: 'Yes, I am Bobby Jones.' I didn't know what to do, so in panic I took the jar next to me and forced the ghost of Bobby Jones into the container. Thankfully this ghostly version of Bobby Jones was the paralyzed version of him and not the pristine athlete from the 1920s." (Editor's note: It is obviously easier to cram a paralyzed ghost into a jar). The seller went on: "As much as I like having Mr Jones in my house, my wife is petrified of ghosts and is now forcing me to sell him. I have decided to sell Mr Jones on eBay and donate half of the proceeds to the cure Syringomyelia fund. Unfortunately Mr Jones' ghost can only be seen by true believers. If you are not a true believer bid with caution, for you may be unable to see him. I will not be giving refunds." For some unaccountable reason, no one took up rklassman's generous offer.

MOST EXPENSIVE USED TISSUE SOLD ON EBAY

A paper tissue on which Hollywood actress Scarlett Johansson blew her nose while appearing on a 2008 edition of the US TV show *Tonight* sold on eBay for $5,300. To be fair, she knew it was going to be auctioned (for charity), and so, after clearing her sinuses, she put the tissue in a sealed bag and handed it to host Jay Leno. It then sparked a frenzied bidding war before selling for a sum which would buy over 3,500 packs of unused tissues.

MOST EXPENSIVE RUBBER DUCK SOLD ON EBAY

A toy rubber duck sold for $107.50 on eBay in 2004, largely because its owner claimed it was haunted. The owner said his toddler became "possessed" when near the duck and kept throwing it across the room, although in truth that sounds like pretty standard behaviour for a two-year-old.

MOST EXPENSIVE BURIAL PLOT SOLD ON EBAY

An unnamed bidder paid $4.6 million in 2009 for the right to sleep with – or, to be more accurate, be buried immediately above – Marilyn Monroe. The crypt in the exclusive Pierce Brothers Westwood Village Memorial Park in Los Angeles was put up for sale on eBay at a starting price of $500,000, but the final price rose to a staggering $4,602,100. The lucky bidder will certainly rest in peace in exalted company as the park also houses a number of celebrity crypts, including those of Roy Orbison, Natalie Wood, Burt Lancaster, Farrah Fawcett, Walter Matthau and Dean Martin.

FIRST TOWN SOLD ONLINE

The Northern California hamlet of Bridgeville (population twenty-nine) became the first town to be sold online when it was bought on eBay in December 2002. A mystery bidder had agreed to pay $1.77 million, but when he backed out, businessman Bruce Krall snapped up Bridgeville for a bargain $700,000. Krall put the town up for sale again on eBay in 2006 at a starting price of $1.75 million, which included eight houses, a post office and three cows. Entertainment manager Daniel LaPaille bought it for $1.25 million but committed suicide three months later.

MOST GAMES OF SOLITAIRE PLAYED
USING WINDOWS VISTA

In August 2010, Tiffany Smith, of Wodonga, Victoria, Australia, set a new world record by playing 74,150 games of solitaire using Windows Vista.

FIRST VIDEO GAME IN SPACE

When it came to putting the first video game in space, the Russians beat the Americans again, just as they had with Yuri Gagarin in 1961. In 1993, cosmonaut Aleksander Serebov packed the Game Boy version of Tetris for his trip to the Mir Space Station where it spent 196 days and orbited the Earth 3,000 times. His copy sold for $1,220 in 2011.

LONGEST MARATHON WITH A DANCE VIDEO GAME

In June 2013, Carrie Swidecki, a teacher from Bakersfield, California, played Just Dance 4 for 49 hours 3 minutes 22 seconds. So basically she danced to a game for two whole days straight. But it's all in a good cause. Since she started "exergaming", as she calls it, she has lost seventy-five pounds and gone down ten dress sizes.

MOST FISH IN A VIDEO GAME

Guinness World Records states that more than eight billion fish were caught by RuneScape players in 2012. If laid head to tail, these virtual fish would apparently encircle the real world twenty times.

LARGEST VIDEO GAME DISPLAY ON SIDE OF BUILDING

With the assistance of two colleagues, Drexel University professor Frank Lee created a computer programme to play a giant game of Tetris on two sides of a twenty-nine-storey skyscraper in Philadelphia, Pennsylvania, on 4 April 2014. They used hundreds of lights embedded in the glass facades of the Cira Centre to form screens totalling nearly 120,000 square feet. Dozens of people then played this supersized version of Tetris using a joystick from about a mile away.

LONGEST GAME OF TAG

Ten old schoolfriends from Spokane, Washington, have been locked in a playground game of Tag since 1990 – even though they are now all in their forties. As the friends have moved to different parts of the United States there are no geographic restrictions to their game, which is played every year throughout the month of February. The last guy to be tagged in that month has to live with the stigma of being "It" for the rest of the year and so for those twenty-eight days (twenty-nine in a leap year) they become absurdly suspicious, checking all callers to work and home, and even looking under their car before getting into it. "You're like a deer in hunting season," explains one of the ten, schoolteacher Joe Tombari. He speaks from bitter experience. Living in California in the mid-1990s, he was asked by a friend to look at his new car, unaware that another of the players, Sean Raftis, who was "It"' at the time, had flown in from Seattle and was hiding in the boot. When the boot was opened, Raftis jumped out and tagged Tombari whose wife was so shocked she fell backwards and tore a ligament in her knee. "I still feel bad about it," says Father Raftis, now a priest in Montana. "But I got Joe."

FASTEST ROBOT TO SOLVE A RUBIK'S CUBE

Cubestormer III, a robot developed by Mike Dobson and David Gilday over a period of eighteen months, solved a Rubik's Cube in just 3.25 seconds in Birmingham, UK, in March 2014, smashing the previous world record of 5.27 seconds set by the same team's Cubestormer II robot in 2011. The best human time is nearly as fast, but they get to study the cube beforehand whereas the robot included examination time in its solving record. Gilday said afterwards: "We knew Cubestormer III had the potential to beat the existing record, but with the robot performing physical operations quicker than the human eye can see, there is always an element of risk."

FASTEST RUBIK'S CUBE SOLUTION WITH FEET ONLY

Using only his feet, an Indonesian boy named Fakhri Raihaan solved a Rubik's Cube in 27.93 seconds at the Celebes Cube Competition in July 2012.

FASTEST RUBIK'S CUBE SOLUTION WHILE RIDING A BIKE

Andi Malik Burhanudin solved a Rubik's Cube in 1 minute 12.6 seconds while riding a bike in Jakarta, Indonesia. We're hoping it was not on a public highway in rush hour.

FASTEST RUBIK'S CUBE SOLUTION WHILE FREEFALLING IN A WIND TUNNEL

In October 2013, father-of-two James Wilson, from Redhill, Surrey, became the first – and therefore the fastest – person to solve a Rubik's Cube while floating in an indoor skydiving tunnel. Battling artificial 125 mph gusts at the Basingstoke Lesiure Park, which threatened to blow the cube out of his hands, he nevertheless solved the puzzle in 3 minutes 16 seconds.

FASTEST RUBIK'S CUBE SOLUTION WITH ONE HAND

Using only one hand, eighteen-year-old Feliks Zemdegs solved a Rubik's Cube in 9.03 seconds (only just over three seconds outside the record for both hands) at a January 2014 tournament in his home city of Melbourne, Australia. He honed his talent by studying a YouTube video when he was twelve. "In a week I got down to about two minutes, then in a month I was at about one minute and then gradually I got faster." By the age of thirteen, he could solve the cube in eight seconds using both hands (a time only a blink shy of the then world record) and by the following year he was world champion. While undeniably proud, his father Davids admitted his son has an obsession: "It can be annoying while he's trying to solve a cube at the dinner table or while we're watching TV," he said. "He seems to have it glued to his hands. Still, it's harmless." Famous last words because, according to Australian newspaper reports, Feliks's cube-solving prowess has already won him a legion of young female fans who have latched onto the concept of geek chic.

FASTEST RUBIK'S CUBE SOLUTION
WHILE PLAYING THE DRUMS

On 28 December 2011, keen drummer Christopher Ghazel, from Eastsound, Washington, solved a Rubik's Cube in 2 minutes 20.1 seconds with his right hand while playing the drums with his left. On the same day, he also set a world record for the fastest time to solve a Rubik's Cube while balancing on a basketball, but his time of 28.03 seconds was subsequently beaten by Jacob Friedman, of Highland Mills, New York, who performed the feat in 22.26 seconds on 29 September 2013.

FASTEST RUBIK'S CUBE SOLUTION
WHILE BLINDFOLDED

At the 2013 Polish National Championships, Marcin Zalewski solved a Rubik's Cube while blindfolded in 23.8 seconds. He was allowed to study the cube for a few seconds before being blindfolded, and then managed to solve it by memorizing the positions of the colours.

FASTEST TIME TO SOLVE FIVE
RUBIK'S CUBES UNDERWATER

Submerged in a 500-gallon water tank at the 2014 US National Rubik's Cube Championship in New Jersey, Anthony Brooks, a twenty-year-old speed cuber from Brownsville, Texas, solved five Rubik's Cubes underwater in 1 minute 18 seconds to slash 12 seconds off the previous world record. Impressively he only started training for the event the day before.

LONGEST TIME TO SOLVE *THE*
TIMES CROSSWORD PUZZLE

In May 1966, *The Times* of London heard from a Fijian woman that she had just completed its crossword from the issue dated 4 April 1932. The woman was stationed in Fiji as the wife of a civil servant, and the crossword had been in an edition of the newspaper which had been used for wrapping. As a result it had lain uncompleted for thirty-four years before being rediscovered.

LONGEST GAME OF MONOPOLY
PLAYED UNDERGROUND

In 1974, eight boys dug a cave in Greenlay, Colorado, and played an underground game of Monopoly that lasted 100 hours. They were rewarded for their efforts with a cake in the form of a Monopoly board.

LONGEST UNDERWATER MONOPOLY TOURNAMENT

Using a specially created board that was weighted and waterproof, 350 divers played a Monopoly tournament underwater for 1,080 hours (forty-five days) at Buffalo, New York, in 1983.

LONGEST GAME OF MONOPOLY PLAYED IN A MOVING ELEVATOR

In 1970, a group of students at Kansas University played Monopoly in a moving dormitory elevator for fifty hours, during which time it traversed 7,212 floors. They must have thought their record was safe for eternity but they had reckoned without another group of people with too much time on their hands. For just four years later, in 1974, a dozen enthusiasts in Torrance, California, played Monopoly in a moving elevator for 148 hours.

FIRST GAME OF MONOPOLY PLAYED ON A CEILING

In February 1974, two University of Michigan students, David Kemper and David Lichterman, used felt-tip pens to draw a detailed 64-square-foot Monopoly board on the ceiling of their dormitory. To defy the laws of gravity, the pair planned to use helium-filled balloons as tokens but faced two months of frustration when helium proved harder to acquire than they had anticipated. Eventually they made a formal request to Monopoly's manufacturer, Parker Brothers, who immediately sent them a few barrels of the precious gas so that the anti-gravitational game could take place in April.

LARGEST GAME OF MONOPOLY

The largest Monopoly game in history took place at Juniata College in Huntingdon, Pennsylvania, in April 1967, when students took over 258,500 square feet of the campus and used the streets and pavements as the board. Dice, in the form of huge foam-rubber cubes, were thrown from a three-storey fire escape, and messengers equipped with walkie-talkies cycled among the players telling them where to move.

MOST PARTICIPANTS IN A GAME OF TWISTER

On 2 May 1987, 4,160 students from the University of Massachusetts at Amherst played one very large, very confusing game of Twister, in the course of which many of the participants must have made a lot of new friends.

LONGEST GAME OF CONCENTRATION

The longest game of Concentration (the card-matching game also known as Memory) took place on 17 June 1986, when four mathematics students at the University of Saarbrucken in Germany – Julie Glowka, Christiane Dein, Erik Scheid and Georg Lay – played for 18 hours 56 minutes. That was how long it took them to find the 1,200 matching pairs among 2,400 cards.

FASTEST GAME OF OPERATION

Taking part in the Impossibility Challenger Games at Dachau on 30 March 2008, Ralf Laue, from Leipzig, Germany, completed a game of Operation in a world record time of 48.6 seconds. Laue started out as a collector of newspaper cuttings about world records. He then moved on to collecting world record books (he has over 300 from twenty-eight countries) and from there it was a natural progression to setting his own obscure world records. To that end, he set another new standard by opening 1,000 letters in 29 minutes 3 seconds.

LONGEST DISTANCE TIDDLYWINKING

Another of Ralf Laue's life goals was to tiddlywink further than Man had ever tiddlywinked before, and on 30 September 2005, at a fair in Leipzig, he kept going for two-and-a-half miles. He first got into tiddlywinks in 2003 when, after studying his collection of record books, he decided that the solo one-mile speed tiddlywinks record was eminently beatable. Following a period of intensive practice at home, he was ready to demonstrate his newfound skills at that year's Impossibility Challenger Games at Starnberg. Tackling an indoor course in a sports hall, he soon realized that tiddlywinks expertise was less important than physical condition. "Kneeling, running, kneeling again, it was much harder than it looked to the audience," he recalled. "Luckily I am a well-trained long-distance runner, but even after 20 finished marathon races, I've never had an experience like one mile of tiddlywinks. The muscles in my right leg were so stiff because of all the kneeling." The pain and suffering proved worthwhile as he broke the world mile record with a time of 1 hour 6 minutes 1 second, and having hit his stride with some first-rate squidging, he intended to continue for a second mile until, alas, at 2,016 metres, the wink got lost under a moveable wall that partitioned off different areas of the hall. "There was no way to get it back," he lamented, "and I felt that it would not be in the spirit of this record category to replace the wink." Inevitably Laue's one-mile tiddlywinks record was subsequently smashed to pieces by Ashrita Furman who, squidging as if his life depended on it, set a time of 23 minutes 22 seconds on 17 December 2007 in the Dominican Republic.

LARGEST GAME OF SCRABBLE

A giant game of Scrabble covered most of the football pitch at London's Wembley Stadium in 1998 to mark Scrabble's fiftieth anniversary. Pairs of soldiers were on hand to lift the six-foot-square letters into position.

HIGHEST ALTITUDE GAME OF SCRABBLE

To celebrate Scrabble's sixtieth anniversary in November 2008, skydivers Nicole Angelides and Ramsey Kent played the game at an altitude of 13,000 feet after jumping from a plane above Florida. They used a specially reinforced wooden board and adhesive tiles. This was a wise precaution since it has been estimated that there are more than a million missing Scrabble tiles scattered at various locations (but mainly down sofas) around the world.

LONGEST TIME SPENT PLAYING SCRABBLE WHILE TRAPPED IN A CREVASSE

In 1985, Lieutenant Commander Waghorn and Lance Corporal Gill played Scrabble continuously for five days while trapped in a crevasse in Antarctica. Funnily enough, the word they kept coming back to was "Help".

HIGHEST WORD SCORES IN SCRABBLE

Writer and broadcaster Janet Street-Porter once described Scrabble as more addictive than cocaine, champagne and group sex. Certainly the game has become hugely competitive down the decades, even though the first world championships – in London in 1991 – had to be delayed because someone had forgotten to bring the tiles. A five-year-old boy once phoned Leicester police to complain that his sister was cheating at Scrabble, and a resident in a UK old people's home was reportedly thrown out when she admitted that she didn't play Scrabble. Meanwhile at Hagerstown, Maryland, in 1996, a woman was charged with assault after whacking her husband over the head with a Scrabble board. There are a number of wordy records, although worryingly the US Scrabble dictionary has banned all swear words. The highest number of points that can be scored on the first go at Scrabble is 128 with "muzjiks" (Russian peasants). The longest word playable with only vowels is "euouae" (a Gregorian cadence), while the longest word with consonants only is "crwths" (the plural for an old Welsh stringed instrument). The record for the highest word score achieved in competition is held by Dr Karl Khoshnaw from Manchester who, in 1982, scored 392 points with "caziques", the plural for a West Indian chief.

HIGHEST JENGA TOWER

American Robert Grebler was introduced to Jenga in 1984 and became so captivated by it that he bought the worldwide rights. He demonstrated the game all over North America, acquiring such expertise that in 1985 he set a world Jenga record by building forty complete storeys with two blocks into the forty-first. The record, but not the tower, stands to this day.

BIGGEST GAME OF MUSICAL CHAIRS

According to Guinness World Records, the biggest-ever game of musical chairs involved 8,238 participants at the Anglo-Chinese School in Singapore on 5 August 1989. After three-and-a-half hours of frantic running around, fifteen-year-old Xu Chong Wei emerged the winner by sitting on the coveted last chair.

LONGEST HOPSCOTCH COURSE

In September 2012, a team of volunteers built a hopscotch course through the streets of Detroit, Michigan, that extended for 3.75 miles, beating the old record of 3.4 miles set in Eden Mills, Canada. The first person to hop the complete Detroit course was twenty-seven-year-old Beth Rutkowski, closely followed by Eric Lacy who puffed: "This is no joke. It really tests your endurance."

LONGEST GAME OF CHINESE WHISPERS

A group of 1,330 children, aged between seven and eleven, set a new world record for the longest game of Chinese whispers at Arsenal Football Club's Emirates Stadium on 11 July 2008. It took 2 hours 4 minutes for the message to be passed on from the first participant to the last, by which time it had, of course, changed considerably.

LONGEST UNDERWATER GAME OF LUDO

Four divers from Hartberg, Austria, played the board game Ludo underwater for 41 hours 40 minutes between 23 and 24 July 1997.

LONGEST UNDERWATER CARD GAME

In March 2011, a team of sixteen divers, working in shifts so that they could change oxygen tanks, played a traditional Bavarian card game called sheepshead for thirty-six hours at the bottom of a pool in Geiselhöring, Germany. Organizer Eric Schlegelmilch said: "We gave up counting who owed what after an hour. We didn't want anyone going belly up."

LONGEST CONTINUOUS GAME OF POKER

The 1880s was the era of lengthy poker games in America, and a contest in Thurmond, West Virginia, went on for fourteen years – but was played only at weekends. So the record for the longest continuous poker game goes to one run by gambler Dick Clark in Tombstone, Arizona, that lasted non-stop for eight years, five months and three days. It took place from 1881 to 1889 in the town's Bird Cage Theater, an establishment that offered gambling, liquor, risqué entertainment and "women of the night", and was rated the wickedest night club in America by the *New York Times*. Emotions could run high from time to time, as can be seen by the 140 bullet holes that pepper the walls and ceiling.

MOST SIMULTANEOUS GAMES OF CHESS

In February 2011, Iranian chess grandmaster Ehsan Ghaem-Maghami played 604 opponents simultaneously over a period of twenty-five hours. He won 580 of the games, drew 16 and lost 8.

OLDEST MOVIE WITH A CHESS SCENE

In 1903, English filmmaker Robert W. Paul made a silent comedy titled *A Chess Dispute*, which featured two men playing chess and then getting into a fight over a disputed move.

MOST SIMULTANEOUS GAMES OF
CHESS PLAYED BLINDFOLD

In November 2011, Marc Lang, a little-known German chess player, broke a sixty-four-year-old record for playing the greatest number of games simultaneously while blindfolded when he took on forty-six opponents over twenty-one hours. The forty-one-year-old sat in the same room as his opponents at Sontheim in southern Germany but a barrier prevented him seeing their boards. He typed his moves onto a computer screen, which showed only the latest move played. He achieved a success rate of 75 per cent, and although it was pointed out that most of his opponents were barely club standard, at least they could see what they were doing.

CHAPTER 9

Feats of Strength

MOST MOUSETRAPS SNAPPED ON THE TONGUE IN ONE MINUTE

Canadian punk rocker Joshuah Hoover (aka Sweet Pepper Klopek) released forty-seven mousetraps onto his tongue in one minute on the set of *Guinness World Records Gone Wild* in Los Angeles on 7 July 2012. He performs with his brother Burnaby Q. Orbax, who likes to drive five-inch nails up his nose, as the Monsters of Schlock, a sort of latter-day Dangerous Brothers. They have been deliberately hurting themselves and each other for over a decade, although in 2008 they were banned from performing in licensed venues in Alberta on the grounds that they had "the potential to be considered bizarre, grotesque or offensive." Presumably therefore Katie Price has never done a book signing in Alberta either.

MOST CIGARETTES EXTINGUISHED ON THE TONGUE IN SIXTY SECONDS

New York magician Richie Magic is known as "The Human Ashtray" for his ability to put out lit cigarettes on his tongue. On 19 May 2011, the fifty-five-year-old, who himself had been a smoker for forty years, extinguished seventy cigarettes on his tongue in one minute, cramming the burning cigarettes into his mouth five at a time before chewing on them and spitting them out. By the end he was gasping for air and the proud owner of a black tongue. "It takes a while for the tongue to heal after a record like that," he said. "I couldn't eat spicy food for a while." He became a full-time illusionist and sideshow stuntman after retiring from a twenty-six-year career as a Westchester County correction officer, legally changing his surname to suit his new job.

MOST BOTTLE CAPS REMOVED WITH TEETH IN ONE MINUTE

Gonzalo Plaza Sierrio of Spain opened fifty-four bottles of beer with his teeth in Madrid on 15 November 2001.

MOST BOTTLE CAPS REMOVED WITH THE HEAD IN ONE MINUTE

In November 2011, Ahmed Tafzi removed twenty-four bottle caps with his head in one minute in Hamburg, Germany. His newfound fame has led to him being invited to numerous parties to be on standby for when the more conventional bottle opener goes missing.

MOST CLOTHES PEGS PINNED TO FACE

Puerto Rican Kelvin Mercado pinned 163 clothes pegs to his face at a *Ripley's Believe It or Not!* book launch in London on 20 November 2013, leaving only his eyes visible. He avoids practising much because it hurts . . . a lot.

MOST MILK CRATES BALANCED ON HEAD

When it comes to balancing things, John Evans is the head man. For over twenty years, the strongman from Ilkeston, Derbyshire, has stacked all manner of heavyweight objects on his head, including, on 5 July 2008, an incredible 98 milk crates weighing a total of 347 pounds. He has done the same thing with 1,710 eggs, 548 footballs, 429 cans of drink, 300 loaves of bread, 237 pints of beer, 101 bricks, 62 books, 13 water kegs, 12 tables, 11 tyres, 10 fire drums, 6 oil drums, 3 wooden barrels, 2 bunk beds, 2 cement mixers, 2 washing machines, a fridge freezer, a speed boat and a Mini car. Evans, who has diabetes and sight in only one eye, has raised over £200,000 ($300,000) for charity, mostly for the Derbyshire Association for the Blind. He says he doesn't visit the gym but focuses on the psychological side of weightlifting. "I'm usually very calm and I suppose I have to be because of the consequences of what happens if it goes wrong. When you're balancing things with that amount of weight, I do think, I could die here if I have a change of balance. I get a massive adrenaline rush from it though, and because I release air in my body, the weight feels as light as a feather. It's very strange but I love it."

MOST HOT WATER BOTTLES BURST
WITH THE NOSE IN ONE MINUTE

Jemal Tkeshelashvili, from Georgia, can use his nose to blow up hot water bottles to the point where they burst. In 2009, the twenty-three-year-old burst three hot water bottles with his nose in one minute to set a new world record. To prove that he has more puff than anyone else on Earth, his party trick is to burst a hot water bottle while a man is sitting on it.

MOST BALLOONS INFLATED WITH
THE NOSE IN AN HOUR

Sitting on a chair in the local public library, thirteen-year-old Andrew Dahl, from Blaine, Washington, inflated and tied 213 balloons in an hour in April 2008 – with his nose. While Andrew blew through one nostril at a time, his father Doug was put in charge of measuring the inflated balloons to ensure that they met the required minimum diameter of eight inches. Ironically Andrew, who first discovered his rare talent at the age of seven, found that tying the balloons during the record-breaking blow was harder than inflating them, and at one point he had to pause to have a bleeding finger repaired. However, he did caution against popping the balloons after-wards because many contained what had inhabited his sinuses before an hour's worth of prolonged nose blowing.

FASTEST TIME TO INFLATE FOUR
TRUCK TYRES WITH THE NOSE

Holding a 130-foot-long rubber hose to his right nostril and blowing through his nose as hard as he could, sixty-three-year-old Nie Yongbing inflated four truck tyres, with two adults standing on each, in just twenty minutes at Chengdu, China, in January 2014. Throughout the lung-bursting exercise he kept his left nostril and left ear covered to prevent pressure leaks. It took him eight long years to master the art of nostril tyre infla-tion. The idea came about when his doctor advised him to blow up balloons with his nose to improve his health. That's the sort of advice you just don't get on the NHS.

MOST BALLOONS BURST BY A BOTTOM

A lesser-known feat on the CV of former England cricketer Andrew Flintoff is that as part of Sport Relief 2012 he set a new world record by bursting twenty-five balloons with his bottom in thirty seconds. If nothing else it must serve as a good hangover cure.

MOST PLAYING CARDS STAPLED
TO BODY IN ONE MINUTE

Canadian human dartboard Luke LeBlanc (alias Kyle Buckett) stapled forty-seven playing cards to his body in one minute – over his arms, chest, back and head. On another occasion, he put eighty-seven staples into his head. Well, it's a living.

FIRST PERSON TO LIFT A SIX-FOOT-LONG
SOLID OAK TABLE WITH HIS TEETH

Eighteenth-century English strongman Thomas Topham could lift a six-foot-long solid oak table, bearing a 100-pound weight, with just his teeth, and keep it in the horizontal position for an impressively long time while two of the table legs rested against his knees. Known as "Goodpork" to his friends, Topham could also lift a 200-pound weight with just his little fingers, a 27-stone vicar with one hand, and was even said to be able to carry a horse. This last feat may have been apocryphal but few people would have wanted to argue with him. For although essentially a mild-mannered man, he was not averse to throwing his weight around. Offended by an individual at the inn where he was staying, Topham took one of the iron kitchen spits from off the mantelpiece and, according to a contemporary report, "bent it round the fellow's neck like a handkerchief". Topham's end was untimely. He became so enraged on learning of his wife Sarah's infidelities that he stabbed her in the breast and then wounded himself in a manner that quickly proved fatal. He died on 10 August 1749 at the inn he owned, the Bell and Dragon in Shoreditch, London. His wife survived.

MOST ONE-ARM PUSH-UPS ON A RAW EGG

On 21 September 2011, Darryl Learie, from Edmonton, Alberta, Canada, performed sixteen one-arm push-ups on a single raw egg without cracking or breaking the aforementioned egg.

HEAVIEST WEIGHT LIFTED WITH A PIERCED SEPTUM

By attaching a hook to the piercing in his nasal septum (the bit of skin between his nostrils), Canadian professional entertainer Ryan Stock was able to lift a 20-pound rubber-band ball on 3 April 2012. His signature routine is the "Human Meathead", where he forces a large meat hook into his nasal cavity and out of his mouth and then hangs a 15-pound ham from the hook. Not content with that, on 21 March 2012 he used a hook inserted through his nose and out of his mouth to pull a car . . . weighing 1,598 pounds. If only he'd joined the AA.

LONGEST DRILL BIT DRILLED INTO THE NOSE

Ryan Stock's nasal passages took another battering on 16 May 2012 when he drilled a 4.5-inch drill bit into his nose. He drilled to the very edge of safety as another three-sixteenths of an inch would have hit his brain stem. On stage Stock is usually partnered by AmberLynn Walker, who first won his heart by demonstrating her ability to wriggle her body through the head of a tennis racket. She is always on hand in case the emergency services have to be called when Stock is practising a new trick, such as the time he decided to juggle knives with his feet in their back garden and a knife handle caught in the turf, driving the blade deep into his foot. "That wasn't a good scene," he admits. When he is not abusing his nose, he can often be found extinguishing blowtorch flames with his tongue. "I used to do the same thing with cigarettes," he explains, "but they're bad for you."

FARTHEST WASHING MACHINE THROW

In November 2008, thirty-year-old Dariusz Slowik lobbed a 105-pound washing machine a distance of 11 feet 6 inches in Bialogard, Poland, to break the existing world record – held by Australian washing machine throwing champion Bill Lindon – by just nine inches. A discus thrower by trade, Slowik apparently throws kitchen furniture, heavy metal objects and white goods just for fun.

FIRST MAN TO CATCH A CANNONBALL

Danish strongman John Holtum (1845–1919) is the first and only man known to have caught a 50-pound cannonball fired by an assistant from the opposite side of the stage. The first time he tried it he lost three fingers, but after two years of intense training he eventually managed to perfect his technique, catching the speeding cannonball with his gloved hands and lightly padded chest. As soon as he caught it, he threw it to the ground, having learned from painful experience that the ball would burn his flesh if not released immediately. A number of sceptics claimed that chicanery was involved, but their doubts were apparently dispelled after Holtum brought them on stage for a demonstration. He once offered 3,000 francs to anyone who could copy his act. There were no takers. He performed all over the world – even to royalty – drawing huge crowds. With his muscular physique, the ex-sailor became something of a sex symbol in Paris where his adoring female fans went so far as to petition for his act to be banned for fear that he would either be killed or that his beautiful body might be maimed for life. In the end he survived relatively unscathed, married a pretty horsewoman and lived in peaceful retirement in England until his death from natural causes.

MOST PANES OF SAFETY GLASS RUN THROUGH IN ONE MINUTE

Safety glass is designed to be difficult to break, but that failed to stop New Zealand kickboxer and wrestler Reuben De Jong from deliberately crashing through fifteen panes in a minute in 2009 to set a new world record. His 2011 attempt to break through seventeen panes on a Chinese TV stunt show ended in abject failure when he struggled to smash through even one pane, leading to suspicions that either the glass was too strong or the temperature was too cold.

MOST BANANAS BROKEN IN ONE MINUTE

At a world records contest in Jakarta, Indonesia, Irpan Maulana broke fifty-nine bananas in one minute – with his bare hands. The man knows no fear.

MOST DRINKS CANS CRUSHED WITH SHOULDER BLADES IN ONE MINUTE

Fabrizio Milito, a chemistry student from Long Island, New York, is blessed with highly distinctive shoulder blades. "They're not really attached to my back like everybody else's," he says. "Mine jut right out, like angel wings." With his father Giuseppe acting as his assistant, Fabrizio used his bony blades to crush twenty-three empty cans in one minute in February 2013. Giuseppe was philosophical about his son's newfound fame. "I was hoping he was going to become a famous chemist, but this was like number two."

MOST DRINK CANS CRUSHED WITH
BREAST IN ONE MINUTE

Susan Sykes (aka Busty Heart), a former stripper, paralegal and investment firm worker from Boston, Massachusetts, crushed thirty-four empty drinks cans with one breast in one minute in Milan, Italy, on 1 April 2011. She has also used her size 46H breasts to smash planks of wood and reduce melons to pulp, and was cast in Sacha Baron Cohen's movie *The Dictator* where she smashed bricks with her breasts, only for her stand-out scene to be cut for being too raunchy. The daughter of an IBM executive and a schoolteacher, Sykes demonstrated her sizeable talents from the age of eight, coming down the stairs at the family home and removing her clothes to the tune of Shirley Bassey's "Hey, Big Spender". By the time she was thirteen, her father sensed that her expanding chest was attracting unwanted attention from boys and so he sent her to a prestigious all-girls' school, where classmates nicknamed her "Busty".

She first hit the headlines at a 1986 Boston Celtics basket-ball game when, sitting prominently in the crowd and wearing a tight white shirt, she stared into the TV camera and gleefully shook her breasts. "I parlayed 15 seconds of fame into a 30-year career," she said recently. She then enhanced her reputation by playfully placing an outsize bra on Jack Nicholson's head at another basketball game. Turning her assets to her advantage, she embarked on a career as an enter-tainer, wowing audiences with her ability to pick up bowling balls, beer bottles and beer kegs with her breasts. After she appeared on a TV talent show in 2010, one viewer remarked: "She is awesome, but you wouldn't want to be behind her when she's running for a bus."

However, on a few occasions, her bosom has got her into trouble. She was arrested at a baseball game in St Louis, Missouri, for causing a disturbance when fans saw the players sneak out of their dugouts to catch a glimpse of her in the stands, and in 1996 Illinois nightclub customer Bennie Casson sued her for $200,000 after alleging that he was assaulted by her breasts during a performance, causing severe neck injuries.

She was also reportedly branded a national threat in the US after a male audience member died of a heart attack while watching her perform on stage.

MOST DRINKS CANS CRUSHED BY HAND IN ONE MINUTE

After Busty Heart, this seems positively tame. Muhamed Kahrimanovic from Bosnia and Herzegovina crushed seventy-four drinks cans with his hand in one minute on the set of *Guinness World Records* –CCTV in Beijing, China, on 7 December 2011.

MOST COCONUTS BROKEN WITH ONE HAND IN ONE MINUTE

Muhamed Kahrimanovic had earlier set another record by breaking 118 coconuts in sixty seconds with one hand on 4 June 2011. "Hammerhand", as he is known, has also smashed 66 bottles, 55 baseball bats and 80 watermelons in one minute. It is a brave person who shakes his hand to congratulate him.

MOST GREEN COCONUTS BROKEN WITH ELBOW IN ONE MINUTE

Using only his elbow, martial arts expert Keshab Swain, from Bhubaneswar, India, smashed eighty-five green coconuts in a minute in 2012. In the same year, he set another record by smashing eighteen green coconuts with his head in one minute. Then in 2013, this time using his elbow, knee, fist and head, he broke 250 green coconuts in the fastest-ever time of 8 minutes 56 seconds. He first developed his talent for opening a coconut as readily as others open an envelope when, after running away from home at the age of sixteen, he ended up in Goa. Hungry and penniless, he plucked some green coconuts from beachside trees but was unable to break into them with hands, legs or teeth until he finally used his elbow to crack one open. From then on, he practised rigorously to the point where he can now open green coconuts with virtually every part of his body.

FASTEST TIME TO BREAK FOUR COCONUTS USING ONE FINGER

On 21 April 2011 in Milan, Italy, fifty-six-year-old Malaysian Kung Fu expert Ho Eng Hui broke his own world record for piercing coconut shells using only his finger when he breached four (right down to the water) in just 12.15 seconds – 18 seconds faster than his previous best. He first started trying to pierce coconuts with his finger when he was seventeen, but it took him two years and a lot of pain to succeed. He was advised to practise on banana tree trunks. "I did it every time I passed a banana tree," he remembers. "People said I was mad." He then practised on cardboard boxes before finally trying his luck with young coconuts. Although he has broken his finger three times, his digital prowess has earned him fame and fortune with twice-weekly street performances in Malacca. He observes: "This finger of mine actually helps to raise my family!"

MOST TOILET LIDS BROKEN WITH HEAD IN ONE MINUTE

American Kevin Shelley smashed forty-six pine toilet seat lids with his head in one minute on the set of the TV show *The Guinness World Records* in Cologne, Germany, on 1 September 2007. Should anyone be tempted to try this, it is worth pointing out that he broke the forty-six lids one at a time rather than simultaneously. Otherwise he would have set another record either for the world's longest headache or as the first person to die while attempting to break forty-six toilet seat lids with his head.

MOST CONCRETE BLOCKS BROKEN ON THE HEAD WITH A BOWLING BALL

John Ferraro first discovered that his skull was tougher than most people's when, as a boy, he head-butted his way through a solid oak door while chasing his brother. "We were having an argument," he recalls, "and my brother shut a door behind him to avoid me. I ran headfirst through this heavy oak door, cracking it and actually dislodging the hinge screws from the brackets and the frame." Whereas normal people would take care to avoid any similar accidents in the future, Ferraro, from Boston, Massachusetts, chose the opposite tack and has gone on to enjoy a career as an entertainer where he does unspeakable things with his head. These include using his skull to hammer nine-inch nails through sheet metal, to bend nails, coins and layers of sheet metal with his head, and to shatter a baseball bat in half with a single headbutt. His crowning glory came in Milan on 14 April 2011 when he set a world record by having a stack of forty-five concrete blocks broken on his head by a 16-pound bowling ball dropped from above. Tests have revealed that at sixteen millimetres, Ferraro's skull is almost two-and-a-half times thicker than that of the average human, which could explain why, in spite of the battering his head receives on a daily basis, his brain is in perfect condition. "I have never suffered a concussion or an injury from the blunt force trauma," he says proudly. "The doctors are amazed I remain unfazed or unharmed by my performances. Pain isn't a factor anymore, it's about mental strength. You have to believe you are stronger than what is put in front of you and that the object will be bent, broken or smashed. But if I have to bleed for my art, then I bleed."

MOST WALNUTS SMASHED WITH THE HEAD IN ONE MINUTE

Pakistani martial arts expert Mohammad Rashid set a new world record by headbutting his way through 155 walnuts in one minute at the 2014 Punjab Youth Festival in Lahore, literally smashing the previous record of 44 walnuts. However, some of the walnuts, which were lined up on a long table, did not give up without a fight, and at the end Rashid had to wipe away a few spots of blood from his forehead.

MOST IRON BARS BROKEN BY THE HEAD IN ONE MINUTE

In Beijing in 2007, China's Wang Xianfa broke twenty-six iron bars in one minute by smashing them over his skull. If he had a headache afterwards, he wasn't letting on.

FARTHEST PLAYING CARD THROW

American magician Rick Smith, Jr, threw a single playing card a distance of 216 feet 4 inches in Cleveland, Ohio, on 21 March 2002 at a speed of 92 mph, beating the previous world record by 40 feet. He had started performing magic tricks as a seven-year-old but the inspiration for his world record came years later while he was playing baseball for Cleveland State University. One day, a playful sock fight broke out among the CSU team-mates in the locker room. Unable to find a sock to throw, Smith pulled out a playing card from a deck that he always kept in his locker and threw it across the room with such speed and accuracy that it cut his team-mate's arm. With the possible exception of the wounded individual, his team-mates were greatly impressed, as indeed was Smith, who had never attempted such a feat before. Putting his newfound skill to maximum use, he not only broke the world card throwing record but incorporated it into his act, hurling playing cards to slice bananas, carrots, celery stalks and other foodstuffs in half.

TIGHTEST FRYING PAN ROLL

Scott Murphy used his bare hands to curl an aluminium frying pan with a circumference of 12 inches into a tight roll with a circumference of just 6.87 inches in thirty seconds on 30 July 2007 in Myrtle Beach, South Carolina. Apparently he builds up his finger strength and pain threshold by punching walls at least three times a day.

HIGHEST ONE-ARMED HANDSTAND

Norway's Eskil Ronningsbakken has a penchant for performing gymnastic feats in extreme locations, and in October 2013 he set a new world record by balancing on one hand on a rock 2,000 feet above a sheer drop to a fjord. Ronningsbakken began performing at the age of five and always practises his stunts first at low level before ascending in altitude. He said: "When I started to balance at height, people didn't believe in me, they didn't believe this would ever become a job. They used to tell me I was crazy and that one day I would fall down and die. Today the situation is different. I am travelling all around the world to perform. It is a great feeling. When you only have five fingers touching the rock, you feel like you are flying."

MOST NAILS HAMMERED IN BY HAND

On 2 October 1999, German hardman Chu Tan Cuong used his hand to drive 116 nails into a wooden board in eleven minutes.

HEAVIEST SLEIGH PULLED BY SANTA

On 18 November 2013, Canadian strongman Revd Kevin Fast pulled a loaded sleigh weighing 43,982 pounds a distance of 100 feet along a street in Cobourg, Ontario. The sleigh took the form of a trailer-and-truck cab laden with donated food sacks and fake reindeer. It should also be pointed out that Revd Fast was only dressed as Santa; he is not really Santa.

MOST PUSH-UPS IN ONE YEAR

Paddy Doyle, from Coventry, England, did 1.5 million push-ups in one year (1988–89), averaging over 4,000 a day and 170 an hour. He has held more than 140 fitness world records, including the most miles walked carrying a 76-pound back-pack (30 in 2010), the most back-of-the hand push-ups in one hour while carrying a 40-pound backpack (663 in 2008), the most one-armed push-ups in five hours (8,794 in 1996) and the most sit-ups in thirty minutes holding a 50-pound steel plate on chest (932 in 2006).

FASTEST ONE-HAND HOP

Spain's Rodolfo Reyes, who comes from a family of foot jugglers (that's people who juggle objects with their feet as opposed to juggling their own severed limbs), hopped on one hand over a distance of ten metres in 13.6 seconds at the Centro Festival in Oberhausen, Germany, on 9 September 2006.

FIRST PERSON TO GO OVER
NIAGARA FALLS IN A BARREL

Remarkably, the first person in history to risk their life by going over Niagara Falls in a barrel was not some Victorian macho man but a sixty-three-year-old widow. Annie Taylor made the historic jump – on 24 October 1901 – with the sole intention of raising enough money so that she could avoid the poorhouse in her declining years. She used a custom-made oak and iron barrel, which was padded with a mattress in the hope of cushioning her on the 174-foot vertical drop. Nevertheless few people were optimistic about her chances of survival and the launch was repeatedly delayed because no one wanted to be part of what amounted to a potential suicide leap. Her manager, Frank Russell, was warned that he could be charged with manslaughter if she died during the attempt.

To allay fears, a cat was sent over the Horseshoe Falls in Taylor's barrel on 22 October, and when the animal suffered nothing worse than a cut head it was decided that the barrel was strong enough to take a human. So on her sixty-third birthday, the retired schoolteacher from Bay City, Michigan, climbed in to the barrel along with her lucky heart-shaped pillow, the lid was screwed down and a bicycle pump was used to compress the air inside. That hole was then plugged with a cork and Taylor was set adrift above the Falls on the American side. Some twenty minutes later, the barrel was retrieved from the foot of the Horseshoe Falls, and, to the relief of most of the watching thousands, Taylor was pulled out alive, relatively unharmed apart from a small gash on her head. She famously told reporters: "I would caution anyone against attempting the feat. I would sooner walk up to the mouth of a cannon, knowing it was going to blow me to pieces, than make another trip over the Fall."

Alas, she was never able to make much money from her death-defying plunge, partly because Russell ran off with her barrel and she spent what savings she had on hiring private detectives to track it down. She spent her final years posing for photographs with tourists at her souvenir stand and made a small income as a clairvoyant, before dying in 1921 at the age of eighty-two.

On 25 July 1911, Englishman Bobby Leach emulated Annie Taylor's feat by plunging over the Falls in a steel barrel. He survived, but spent six months in hospital after breaking his jaw and both kneecaps in the jump. Fifteen years later, while on a publicity tour of New Zealand, the daredevil Leach slipped on an orange peel and died from complications due to the onset of gangrene. Another Englishman, Bristol barber Charles Stephens, went over the Falls on 11 July 1920 in a barrel with an anvil tied to his feet to act as ballast. He had refused pleas to test the apparatus beforehand and perished when the anvil broke the bottom of the barrel. Only his severed arm was ever recovered and that was subsequently buried in the Drummond Hills Cemetery at Niagara Falls.

MOST CHERRY STEMS KNOTTED WITH A TONGUE IN ONE HOUR

Using only his tongue, Florida firefighter and part-time body-guard Al Gliniecki tied 911 cherry stems into knots in one hour on a 4 September 1997 edition of *The Ricki Lake Show*. Employing a technique taught to him by his ex-wife back in 1982, it takes him just two seconds to knot a stem. Before attempting a tongue-tying challenge, he prefers to keep the stems in lukewarm cherry juice, but on this occasion the TV show producers had stored them in a fridge beforehand. "If they're cold, they poke your tongue," said Gliniecki. "After a hundred or so they feel like needles, and so after breaking the record my tongue was real sore." Cherry stem-tying was Gliniecki's second attempt to get into the record books. He almost broke a record for ice-cream eating in 1976 but froze his vocal cords while practising and was told by the doctor that he couldn't eat anything cold for several days. So the record attempt was cancelled. He has also been struck twice by lightning, but that wasn't deliberate.

HEAVIEST VEHICLE PULLED WITH BEARD WHILE WEARING ROLLER SKATES

Inline skating champion Kapil Gehlot, from Jodhpur, India, used his beard to pull a Hyundai Accent car weighing 2,306 pounds a distance of 226 feet 3 inches while wearing roller skates on 3 July 2011.

MOST TELEPHONE DIRECTORIES
TORN IN THREE MINUTES

Christian pastor Ed Charon certainly liked to put on a bit of a show for his congregation. So while preaching the gospel from the pulpit of his church in Branson, Missouri, he would work himself and the worshippers into a frenzy by ripping telephone books in half. Beginning with relatively small phone books for minor sins, he would build up in size as he warned against increasingly dangerous addictions until he reached the grand finale (maybe adultery or armed robbery), at which he would claw apart a 1,000-page phone directory and declare: "God can break those habits!" This was no overnight whim. It had taken him seven years and an estimated 65,000 phone books to get to that level. Blessed with abnormally large hands, he trained with a vengeance, tearing over 100 phone books a day to stay in shape. He scoured motels and recycling plants for fresh supplies, picking up any directory that would otherwise be thrown out or incinerated. Portland, Oregon phone books were his favourite because they had slightly thinner pages. "Of all the phone books I've torn," he said, "I've found that the Portland ones tear better." He also insisted that the only proper way to tear a phone book was from top to bottom. Anything else, he said, was "the girl's way". He set his sights on the world record for phone-book tearing and first achieved that goal in 2002 with a total of nineteen books in three minutes. After a rival had snatched it from him, Charon regained his title in 2004 with thirty-nine, before, on 14 September 2006 at the age of seventy-one, he ripped through fifty-six of his beloved Portland directories (each containing 1,006 pages) in three minutes at the Branson Mall. After that, his crowning glory, he decided to retire, only to die the following year from a heart attack.

MOST VEHICLE LICENCE PLATES TORN IN ONE MINUTE

At the 2013 Coney Island Strongman Spectacular, Chris Rider tore fifteen State of Pennsylvania vehicle licence plates apart with his bare hands in one minute. Rider, who goes by the stage name of Haircules on account of his ability to bend three forged steel horseshoes with his hair, has even torn a pair of licence plates simultaneously. However, he emphasizes that ripping them is not for the faint-hearted. "The potential for serious injury surrounds this feat," he explains. "I speak from first-hand experience. The most severe injury I have sustained thus far from tearing a plate was a cut which ran from just below my pinky finger all the way to my elbow."

MOST BENCHES BALANCED ON TEETH

Li Hongxiao has been balancing objects in his mouth since he was a child. Nobody probably worried too much when it was just the odd pencil or toothbrush, but as with all obsessions these things can escalate alarmingly and before too long he had moved on to the hard stuff with bamboo poles, ladders and wooden benches. The first time he tried balancing twelve benches on his teeth, he needed eighteen stitches in his lower lip. It was a painful lesson. However, he pressed on until, in Chongqing, China, in February 2012, before a crowd of bemused shoppers, the thirty-year-old set a new world record by balancing twenty-three wooden benches weighing a total of 152 pounds – almost as much as his body weight. Each bench was over 3 feet long, 18 inches high and weighed 3 kilos (6.6 pounds), and he held the position for eleven seconds to smash the previous record of fourteen benches. Although they had no idea why he was doing it, the spectators applauded warmly and then carried on with their shopping.

HEAVIEST WEIGHT LIFTED WITH TONGUE

British strongman Thomas Blackthorne lifted a 27 pound 8.9 ounces weight hooked through his tongue in Mexico City on 1 August 2008. According to Guinness World Records, this is the heaviest weight that anyone has ever lifted by tongue.

MOST COCA-COLA BOTTLES LIFTED WITH EYELASHES

Ashok Verma, from Agra, India, made it into the 2001 edition of the *Limca Book of Records* by lifting three 50-ounce bottles of Coca-Cola with a string that was attached to his eyelashes. He announced that his ultimate ambition was to pull a car with his eyelashes.

HEAVIEST AIRPLANE PULLED WITH TEETH

In June 2013, Zsolt Sinka, a Hungarian strongman, pulled a fifty-ton Airbus A320 airplane a distance of 128.5 feet along the tarmac at Budapest Ferenc Liszt Airport in fifty-two seconds – with his teeth. One end of a rope was attached to his mouth, the other to the front wheel of the plane. After his record-breaking tooth tug he was presented with a model plane, which he promptly bit. Sinka is known in his homeland as "Popeye", presumably for his impressive strength rather than for having an extremely thin girlfriend.

HEAVIEST HELICOPTER PULLED WITH LEFT EAR

With one end of a rope tied to his left ear and the other end tied to the front wheel of a 1,215-stone military helicopter, Lasha Pataraia, a twenty-seven-year-old former wrestling champion from Georgia, pulled the chopper a distance of 86 feet along tarmac in Tbilisi in November 2007. It took him twenty seconds and three tries. Then in November 2012, using only that same trusty left ear, he pulled an eighty-ton truck a distance of 70.5 feet. Afterwards he said he was waiting to hear (if he still could) from Guinness as to whether he had set an official world record.

HEAVIEST BUS PULLED WITH HAIR

Manjit Singh, a fifty-nine-year-old from Leicester, attached a clamp to his ponytail and pulled an 8.5-ton, London double-decker bus a distance of seventy feet through Battersea Park on Guinness World Records Day in 2009. He said he had no special regime for creating his seemingly unbreakable hair. "I just use shampoo, like the kind you can get in any pound shop up and down the country." The father of four built his hair up to Samson-like strength after failing to pull a similar bus with his ears in 2007. If at first you don't succeed, find another body part.

LONGEST DISTANCE PULLING A HEARSE WITH HAIR IN UNDER TWO MINUTES

On 18 November 2013, Polish performance artist Anastasia IV pulled a 2.5-ton hearse for a distance of sixty-five feet along London's Shaftesbury Avenue with her hair in just over a minute. Anastasia, who has her golden locks insured for £1 million ($1.7 million), first realized she had strong hair when she used to challenge boys at school back home in Poland to a tug-of-war contest, pulling the rope with just her hair. After her latest feat, she admitted: "It's as painful as it looks."

HEAVIEST WEIGHT BENCH PRESSED BY A NONAGENARIAN

Sy Perlis, a ninety-one-year-old strongman from Arizona, set a world record for the bench press in his exclusive age group by lifting 187.2 pounds in June 2013, beating the previous record by some 50 pounds. As the sole participant in the ninety-year-old-and-over division, victory was something of a formality, but Perlis did it in style, prompting Gus Rethwisch, President of the World Association of Benchers and Deadlifters, to enthuse: "He's in great shape. He looks like he could be in his seventies." Perlis did not start weightlifting until he was sixty and only entered his first competition in 2008. At ninety-one, he was still training five days a week and said of his new hobby: "It gave me the opportunity to do something to test myself for one thing, and I didn't have to run around to do it."

MOST ROPE SKIPS ON A BED OF NAILS ON TOP OF ANOTHER PERSON

In January 2014, in Fremont, Indiana, pastor and strongman Jon Bruney and his wife Amy broke an obscure world record involving skipping and a bed of nails. He took a 125-pound board with 3,000 nails driven through it and placed it on top of his chest, whereupon his wife climbed onto the board and began skipping rope. To break the existing record (yes, someone had actually tried it before), Amy had to complete 70 skips, but in the end she blew it away with a total of 117. Her husband said afterwards: "I told her, 'Don't stop, no matter what you hear below.' I actually got the wind knocked out of me. The rest of the week my ribs were sore." Well, they wouldn't have been if he had stuck to breaking sensible world records, like something to do with crocheting.

MOST ARROWS BROKEN WITH THE THROAT IN ONE MINUTE

A former bodyguard for Sylvester Stallone, Mike Gillette snapped eleven arrows against his throat in one minute at the 2013 Coney Island Strongman Spectacular in New York.

MOST MEN BACK LIFTED

Born near Montreal, Louis Cyr (1863–1912) hailed from a robust French Canadian family. His father was of modest proportions but his mother was positively Amazonian, standing 6 feet 1 inch tall and weighing nearly nineteen stone. She was not a woman to get on the wrong side of, especially as it was quite a long journey.

Louis clearly inherited her strength, weighing close to eighteen pounds at birth and later flexing his youthful muscles by lifting a farmer's heavily laden wagon out of a muddy mire in which it had become stuck. Following stints as a lumberjack and a police officer, the stocky Cyr became a professional strongman and on 1 December 1891, before a crowd of 10,000 at Sohmer Park in Montreal, he won a tug-of-war against four horses. Cyr successfully resisted the pull of four huge draught horses, two each side, even though the grooms were cracking their whips to encourage the horses to pull even harder.

The following year, he perfected the spectacular back lift, where he would set a number of men on a heavy platform resting across two trestles. Cyr would then duck beneath the platform, position his back below the centre and raise both the platform and its human passengers clear of the trestles. In London, he lifted an estimated 3,635 pounds by this method, but returning to North America, he surpassed that mark in Boston, Massachusetts, on 27 May 1892 by back lifting eighteen "bulky" men, who, combined with the platform on which they were standing, amounted to a total weight of over 4,000 pounds. A century after his death, he is commemorated in Montreal by the Parc Louis-Cyr, where, since 1970, a statue has stood of "The Strongest Man in History".

HEAVIEST HULA HOOP TYRE

In 2013, Paul "Dizzy Hips" Blair, from Las Vegas, Nevada, used a ninety-eight-pound tractor tyre as a hula hoop, prompting one blogger to declare excitedly: "Hula hooping doesn't get any manlier than this!" Blair discovered the joys of the hula hoop as a freshman in college and has also held records for the largest hula hoop (43 feet 4 inches), the most revolutions of a hula hoop in one minute (205) and for the most hoops twirling at once from a standing start (136).

MOST WATERMELONS CHOPPED ON THE STOMACH IN ONE MINUTE

Using Celia Curtis's stomach as a chopping board, Australia's Jim Hunter chopped twenty-five watermelons with a machete in one minute in Sydney on 16 August 2005.

FASTEST TIME TO PEEL THREE COCONUTS WITH TEETH

After six years practising husking coconuts with his teeth, Gautam Varma, from Bangalore, India, set a new world record on 3 August 2010 by peeling three coconuts with his teeth in forty-two seconds. Proving that he is blessed with stamina as well as speed (and obviously mighty molars), Varma has also husked fifty-one coconuts in thirty-eight minutes with his teeth. Oh, and in case you're interested, he can also climb a forty-foot coconut tree holding a bicycle in his mouth.

FARTHEST DISTANCE TO PROPEL A DIME BY EARLOBE

When he was a child, Monte Pierce, from Bowling Green, Kentucky, used to tug on his earlobes to the extent that they grew longer and longer and increased their elasticity until they were eventually able to snap back like a slingshot. They permanently hang down an inch, but when required he can stretch them to an alarming five inches. Nicknamed "Slingshot

Ears", he puts his giant lobes to work by using them to launch coins, and on 16 February 2008 he set a new world record by propelling a US dime a distance of 11 feet 8 inches. "Many people's ears are longer than mine," he says, "but they can't do what I can do." He can also pull his earlobes up over his eyes, wrap his neck with them or put the left one into his mouth, which is handy if he ever wants to eat his own ear.

LONGEST FULL BODY CONTACT WITH ICE

Dutchman Wim Hof, known as "The Iceman", sat in a tank filled with ice cubes up to his neck for a world record time of 1 hour 52 minutes 42 seconds in New York on 17 November 2011. He has also swum under ice for 120 metres on a single breath wearing just shorts and goggles; run a full Arctic marathon in temperatures of -20°C wearing shorts; and reached the summit of Mount Kilimanjaro in shorts. He can withstand extreme cold because he has learned to regulate his body temperature. Whereas an ordinary person's body temperature drops dangerously low after exposure to ice (certainly with exposure of nearly two hours), Hof is able to retain his core temperature at around 37°C, apparently just by concentrating hard. To prove that he is equally at home with extreme heat as extreme cold, in October 2011 he ran a full marathon through Africa's Namib Desert without drinking any water.

MOST POWERFUL KICK RECEIVED TO THE GROIN

You might wonder why any man would actively choose to be kicked in the groin harder than anyone in history, but that would be to ignore the extremes that some people will go to in order to set a world record. So step forward – gingerly perhaps – Kirby Roy, a black belt in the karate discipline of combat ki. Roy has endured thousands of full-force groin kicks over the years, as a result of which the nerves of his testicles have suffered so much damage that they no longer register pain to his brain. On 26 April 2009, the US TV show *Sports Science* decided to put his pain threshold to the test by getting American Gladiator Jesse "Justice" Smith, a 6 foot 8 inches martial arts expert, to shin-kick Roy in the groin at 22 mph with 1,000 pounds of force, powerful enough to lift him completely off the floor. Roy took the kick without any hint of pain and was subsequently given a clean bill of health at hospital. For the record, he is married with children and claims to lead an active sex life.

FIRST PERSON TO LIFT A BABY ELEPHANT WHILE CLIMBING A LADDER

Polish-born circus performer Siegmund "Zishe" Breitbart (1883–1925) was billed as the "Strongest Man in the World" in his heyday for feats of strength that included bending iron bars around his arm in floral patterns, biting through iron chains and pulling a wagon-load of people with his teeth. But arguably the former blacksmith's greatest claim to fame was a routine where he picked up a baby elephant and then climbed a ladder while carrying the animal. Breitbart's career was curtailed prematurely following an accident during a strong-man demonstration in Germany. He was hammering a railroad spike with his bare hands through five one-inch-thick oak boards that were resting on his knee when he got so carried away that the nail pierced his leg. He contracted blood poisoning and, despite undergoing ten operations during which both legs were amputated, he died from the infection eight weeks later.

CHAPTER 10

Collections and Hobbies

LARGEST COLLECTION OF LOVE DOLLS

Bob Gibbins, from Madley, Herefordshire, has spent £100,000 ($160,000) on his collection of 240 life-sized, anatomically correct, love dolls, ranging from cheap $600 blow-up dolls to top-of-the-range models like $11,000 Jessica. Known as "The Hugh Hefner of the Love Doll World", the sixty-three-year-old mechanic and father of two is so fond of his dolls that he has adapted one to become his ballroom dancing partner. Remarkably, his wife Lizzie happily supports his unusual hobby, joining him on shopping trips to buy new clothes for the dolls before spending hours dressing them up. Bob loves having afternoon tea with his silicone harem and taking them for walks or drives in the country, but even though some wear extremely provocative outfits, he insists that he never uses them for sex. "I do find most of them attractive," he says, "especially since they were created with perfect physical assets, but that's as far as it goes. After all, they're part of the family."

LARGEST COLLECTION OF DOLLS DRESSED AS NUNS

You've probably heard the one about the two nuns in a bath; well how about the 525 nuns in a basement? The Woods Nun

Doll Museum, which can be found below stairs at the Cross in the Wood Shrine in Indian River, Michigan, displays 525 dolls and 20 mannequins, all dressed as nuns and modelling the habits of 217 different religious orders. The record-breaking collection is the work of Sally Rogalski who began collecting dolls and dressing them in nuns' habits as a young girl in 1945 to "preserve a bit of the history of the Catholic Church". Her efforts impressed those in high places – in 1988 she and her husband Wally received a special blessing from Pope John Paul II for "helping to promote vocations to the priesthood and religious life through their doll collection".

LARGEST COLLECTION OF PULL TABS FROM ALUMINIUM CANS

By 2014, after several years of dedicated acquisition, former Scout leader Todd Mannebach, from Des Moines, Iowa, had built up a collection of nearly twenty-four million pull tabs from aluminium cans.

LARGEST COLLECTION OF BELLY BUTTON FLUFF

"Some people gaze into their navel for inspiration: I look into mine and see navel fluff." So says Graham Barker, a librarian from Perth, Western Australia, who has been collecting his own belly button lint in glass jars since 1984, during which time he has rarely missed a day's harvest. He devotes a mere ten seconds a day to collecting the fluff, right before he steps into the shower, but his dedication is such that he has now filled over three large jars even though the total amount of loose lint weighs barely twenty-three grams. It was on studying his navel one night that he became curious as to how much fluff one person can produce in a lifetime, and like all of the world's great thinkers he has pulled out all the stops – and indeed the lint – to discover the answer. He points out that his collection is unique and in excellent condition. "Like uncirculated banknotes or stamps, my navel fluff is in mint condition. When harvested, I remove any body hair from the fluff, then store it immediately in a jar, where it remains uncontaminated." It never goes mouldy and does not smell, meaning that lint from twenty-five years ago is indistinguishable from the new stuff. Perhaps realizing that he would never have enough to stuff a cushion, he recently sold his first three jars' worth to a museum for an undisclosed sum, but is already well on his way to filling a fourth. He hopes in time to fill another five jars, vowing to stop only when he is no longer physically capable of collecting his fluff. He acknowledges that there are a few other navel lint collectors out there. "When I ran a navel lint survey many years ago a handful of respondents, who were all men, confessed to having saved up some of their lint at some point, but none had continued with it. One guy might have persisted, but he got married and his wife ordered him to stop."

LARGEST COLLECTION OF AIRLINE SICK BAGS

Over forty years ago, Dutchman Niek Vermeulen had a bet with a friend as to who could accumulate the most of any one item. One day, Vermeulen was using a sick bag on which to scribble expenses during a flight and kept the bag in his briefcase. The idea for his record-breaking collection was born and by 2010 he had amassed a total of 6,016 sick bags from 1,142 different airlines in 160 countries. His favourite sick bag is one from the NASA space shuttle *Columbia* that spent sixteen days in space.

LARGEST COLLECTION OF BANANA-RELATED ITEMS

Fred Garbutt is curator of the International Banana Museum in Mecca, California, home to over 19,000 banana-related items. They range from telephones and lamps, knives and slippers to an eight-foot-long banana couch. Garbutt bought the museum and its contents in 2010 from Ken Bannister who, as founder of the International Banana Club and therefore very much Top Banana, had built up the collection from scratch. Naturally Garbutt wears all yellow and drives a banana-coloured Volkswagen Beetle. The museum will not change under his watch. "It's going to stay family friendly," he says. "It's a banana museum, there's no reason to put anything in there that you wouldn't want your children to see. I'm sure there are a lot of battery-operated objects that would not be appropriate."

LARGEST COLLECTION OF BANANA LABELS

Since 1991, Becky Martz, from Houston, Texas, has collected more than 14,600 banana labels from all over the world. She knows no embarrassment when it comes to acquiring new labels. She admits to removing the sticker from a banana in a friend's hospital ward and to snatching the label off a rotten peel lying in the street. "I couldn't help myself," she explains. "I didn't have those stickers." Worryingly, she has recently started on broccoli and asparagus bands, too.

LARGEST COLLECTION OF NAIL CLIPPINGS

Richard Gibson, of Lafayette, Louisiana, has been religiously hoarding his fingernail and toenail clippings since February 1978, and although he has refrained from actually counting them he calculates that they run into the thousands. He says he cuts them sparingly, but even if he only trimmed them once a month and managed an intact clipping for each digit, he would have well over 4,000. Allowing for occasional break-ages and those awkward corners, the true total is probably much higher, but whatever the numbers it's safe to say that it is the largest collection of its kind.

It started as a result of his own curiosity. He was clipping his nails one day when, instead of throwing them out, he decided to put them in a manicure box to see how long it would take to fill. In the end it took him two years but by then he was well and truly hooked on his new hobby and transferred the clippings to a large glass jar, which he kept on the mantelpiece, taking care to hide it from visitors. The jar is now full, forcing him to switch them to an even bigger container. That's the great thing about nail clipping collecting; it is a gift that keeps on giving. His achievement has won its way into *Ripley's Believe It Or Not!*, although his ex-wife is apparently not impressed. "She's always been annoyed by the clippings jar," he laments. There's just no pleasing some people.

LARGEST COLLECTION OF TONY BLAIR'S TOENAIL CLIPPINGS

Surprisingly these were not to be found in a waste paper bin in the Blair bedroom but preserved in alcohol in a jar at the Surrey clinic of market gardener-turned-alternative healer Jack Temple. Blair's wife Cherie apparently sent the clippings to Temple who claimed that he could detect any future health problems that might befall the then Prime Minister simply by swinging a crystal pendulum over the severed nails. Temple died in 2004 at the age of 86, which must have been something of a disappointment since he confidently expected to live until at least 140. However, death to him was little more than a blip as he claimed to have had 120 previous lives and said he could trace his origins back 97,000 years.

LARGEST GUM COLLECTION

Sarah Maughan started collecting gum as a fifteen-year-old in 1948, when she bought a packet of Popeye bubble gum – and by 2011 the seventy-seven-year-old was able to display 1,445 different types of gum in her home at Idaho Falls, Utah. Pride of place in her collection went to a 1984 pack of Michael Jackson bubble gum.

LARGEST COLLECTION OF ALREADY CHEWED NICORETTE GUM

Unable to smoke on a long-haul flight to Europe in 2006, Los Angeles resident Barry Chappell started chewing Nicorette gum, and since there was nowhere to put the gum when he had finished chewing it, he played with it and twirled it into a little ball with his fingers. That was Barry Chappell's Eureka moment. After that, each piece of gum he chewed was added to the ball until, six years and 95,200 pieces of gum later, he had created a gigantic gum ball weighing 175 pounds. As a bonus, he had also stopped smoking.

LARGEST COLLECTION OF TOILET SEATS

Retired plumber Barney Smith, from San Antonio, Texas, built up a collection of 1,100 wooden toilet seats. He picked them up in the course of his work over a period of more than forty years and decorated each one individually with photos, paint and even car registration plates. Bizarrely his collection began when he was looking for a base on which to mount a set of deer antlers and found that a toilet seat provided the ideal dimensions. At first he kept his hobby to himself, but in 1992 he decided to allow the public to be privy to the largest collection from the smallest room.

LARGEST COLLECTION OF SOCK MONKEYS

Randy Walker has a collection of more than 600 sock monkeys at his home in Lawrence, Kansas. He started collecting them in 1982, picking them up at flea markets, garage sales, antique malls and auctions. Some of his monkeys talk, others have eyes made out of seashells while one strange specimen actually has three eyes. "Sock monkeys are iconic," he explains. "For the baby boomers, almost everybody had one. They're like people. Even though they're made from the same basic things (socks), every one is a little bit different. Each one has its own personality. I've never made one myself, but one day I'll give it a try."

LARGEST COLLECTION OF COW HAIRBALLS

Randy Walker's sock monkeys are just part of his Museum of the Odd, which contains such eclectic items as a toothbrush used by singer Ray Charles and a glove worn by Tom Thumb, once the smallest man in the world. He also boasts a collection of seven cow hairballs, ranging from the size of a baseball to more than eight inches in diameter. Since, unlike cats, cows are unable to cough up hair, the hairball collects in one of the animal's stomachs before being removed during slaughter. Smooth and round (except one which is a bit furry), they are immaculately displayed under glass in what may quite possibly be the world's only collection of cow hairballs. At the very least, it is a niche market.

LARGEST COLLECTION OF SUGAR PACKETS

Germany's Marianne Dumjahn began collecting sugar packets in 1982, and when counted in 2012, her collection totalled 398,572 different ones. Such is her standing that she is the leader of a sugar club in Mainz. Sweet! If you want to know a word to describe Marianne, it's sucrologist.

LARGEST COLLECTION OF BUTTONS

To a surprisingly large number of people, buttons are seriously creepy (the phobia of them is called koumpounophobia), but to Franco Jacassi they are a thing of beauty. He keeps more than ten million buttons in his vintage clothing showroom in Milan, Italy, having first become fascinated with them as a child when his godmother gave him boxes of buttons to play with to keep him quiet while she sewed. "I liked red buttons," he says. "I don't know why, but I imagined them as Napoleon's soldiers. I used to play button war, with different colours playing the role of different armies. I like their colours, I liked how they reflected light and I liked the snapping sound they made against wood surfaces." As he got into serious collecting, his more extravagant purchases have included $1,500 for a single ivory French Revolution button that depicts a peasant tugging on a nobleman.

LARGEST COLLECTION OF MARBLES

There's no danger of Sam McCarthy-Fox losing his marbles – for he has more than 50,000 of them tucked away in the loft of his home in Worthing, West Sussex. He has been collecting marbles since the 1960s and keeps them in boxes, giant wine bottles and even a glass head. Explaining his passion, he once said: "It's a lovely feeling when you place your hands in a huge jar of marbles and just let them run through your fingers."

LARGEST COLLECTION OF CEMENT MIXER PHOTOGRAPHS

Retired trucker Ronnie Crossland, from Sharlston, West Yorkshire, gave up trainspotting because it was too boring and turned his attention to cement mixers instead. He became fascinated by them after watching a new one being delivered to a building site in 1987 and eventually built up a collection of more than 1,000 photos of cement mixers. He travelled over 200,000 miles in pursuit of his passion, carrying with him at all times two cameras plus a pair of binoculars for that essential close-up. "People think I'm crazy," he said, "but mixers are things of incredible beauty to me." However, not everyone appreciated his enthusiasm. "One builder threatened to bash me with a spade when I asked to photograph his mixer. He thought I was making fun of him."

LARGEST COLLECTION OF RABBIT-RELATED ITEMS

When Candace Frazee gave her then-boyfriend Steve Lubanski the affectionate nickname "Hunny Bunny", little did she know that it would lead to a record-breaking obsession that resulted in the couple filling their Pasadena, California, home with 29,000 items of rabbit-related memorabilia. And as you would expect with rabbits – even stuffed ones – that number is still growing. Their house has been turned into a rabbit museum, displaying not only toy bunnies but also a handful of live specimens. When their real rabbits die, Frazee and Lubanski keep the corpses in the freezer next to tubs of ice cream and their wedding cake until they can afford to freeze-dry and exhibit them. Touchingly, Frazee has never forgotten how Lubanski bought her a pet rabbit as a token of their love on their first Valentine's Day together. So to celebrate their nineteenth wedding anniversary she secretly took one of the dead rabbits from the freezer and had it freeze-dried for $500 before presenting it to him over a candlelit dinner. Who says romance is dead? The rabbit, yes; but romance, definitely not.

LARGEST COLLECTION OF CABBAGE PATCH DOLLS

Pat and Joe Prosey are so obsessed with their collection of 5,000 Cabbage Patch dolls that they treat them like children – even though they have a real grown-up daughter of their own. They had to build a separate 6,000-square-foot extension to their house in Baltimore, Maryland, to accommodate their collection and it costs over $1,000 a month to keep the dolls in their pampered, climate-controlled world. Joe, a retired shipyard worker, also spent $2,000 on building a luxury playground where their dolls play with other collectors' dolls. "Looking after them is a 24-hour job, seven days a week," says Joe. So what first attracted the couple to the toy dolls which, without wishing to sound too unkind, are downright ugly? The Proseys' lives changed forever in 1985 when Pat got her first Cabbage Patch doll, Meg, for $50. Soon she picked up a boy doll, Kevin, and husband Joe began to take an interest, too. One day he was at a water-skiing event when he spotted a miniature wet suit hanging on a shop wall. Worryingly his first thought was: "That'll fit a Cabbage Patch kid." He always calls them "kids". "We don't use the word D-O-L-L," says Joe. "They might hear." The next weekend, he dressed Kevin in the wet suit and took him water-skiing, seemingly unconcerned about the strange looks he received. He then began writing a column in a collectors' newsletter using Kevin's voice. Now he carries Kevin with him wherever he goes, even addressing shop staff through the doll. Pat concedes that the men in white coats might soon come knocking. "I can see where a lot of people think we're not quite right," she says. "You could even say our daughter thinks we're out there." That certainly appears to be the case, because long-suffering daughter Vicki – very much the Marilyn Munster of the family – steadfastly refuses to acknowledge Cabbage Patch doll Kevin as her brother.

LARGEST COLLECTION OF TOOTHPASTE TUBES

US dentist Val Kolpakov has a collection of 2,200 tubes and tins of toothpaste, including such diverse flavours as chocolate, whiskey, champagne, bamboo, pumpkin pudding, green tea and curry. He also has a German brand dating back to World War II that was made with radioactive compounds in the belief that it would restore unhealthy gums. His obsession began in 2002 when, surfing the internet, he stumbled across a reference to a German man, Carsten Gutzeit, who had collected 500 tubes of toothpaste. "If there was a record I had to beat it," says Kolpakov, who is known as "Dr Val" to his patients in Marietta, Georgia. "I didn't realize how much fun it can be; how many different toothpastes exist. I thought that collecting toothpaste was a nice hobby for a dental professional. It allows you to learn more about your profession. I had friends all over the world, so I asked them to mail me toothpaste from the countries where they lived." But the trouble with being a high-profile record holder is that it can set you up as a target and, according to goldenbookofrecords.com, New Yorker Ronan Jordan has recently laid claim to Dr Val's crown with a collection of 3,750 empty tubes of toothpaste.

LARGEST COLLECTION OF TOOTHBRUSHES

After undergoing years of dental work, artist Maryly Snow, from Oakland, California, started collecting toothbrushes in 1981 as a joke. Through word of mouth, others began to hear about her grandly titled International Toothbrush Collection and started sending her unusual toothbrushes from around the world. The collection, which includes musical children's toothbrushes, ones whose bristles are coloured to match a national flag, and even brushes in the shapes of dolphins and guns, now totals more than 2,100. When it comes to records, she is, therefore, the toothbrush holder.

LARGEST RUBBER DUCK COLLECTION

Charlotte Lee, from Seattle, Washington, is listed as having the world's biggest collection of rubber ducks, her total standing at 5,631 when last counted. She started her collection in 1996 and has rubber ducks in every shape, style and size, including ones that glow in the dark, ones whose eyes can be popped out, ones that smell like fruit and ones that are big enough to ride on. Ironically her husband is an avid duck hunter. "I like the ducks, he likes the hunt," she said. "It's a good partnership."

LARGEST VACUUM CLEANER COLLECTION

Known to his fellow vacuum cleaner enthusiasts quite simply as "Mr Vacuum Cleaner", James Brown, from Heanor, Derbyshire, has been collecting the household machines since he was eight, and by 2013 he had acquired 322 different models of vacuum, putting him well ahead of the competition. Brown, who describes himself as "the ultimate clean freak", is so proud of his collection that in 2010 he opened Britain's first ever vacuum cleaner museum, to which, wisely, admission is free. His unusual passion first manifested itself when he started repairing cleaners after school and in the summer holidays, but instead of fizzling out it developed even further in his teens, as his collection grew to over fifty. Of his newfound status as a world record holder, he says: "I've set a tough target to beat, but there are more collectors out there than you might think. All I've ever wanted is to work with vacuum cleaners."

YOUNGEST VACUUM CLEANER COLLECTOR

Every mother's worst nightmare is that her son will grow up addicted to alcohol, drugs or cheap women. MaryLynn Krichbaum knew almost as soon as her son Kyle was born that he would develop a different kind of addiction – one for which, as yet, there is no known cure – hoovering. Speaking in hushed tones, she recalled the moment she first realized her son might have a hoovering problem: "When Kyle was a baby in his little baby seat and I'd be vacuuming, he would just be mesmerized by the vacuum and would follow it everywhere." He acquired his first vacuum at the age of one, dressed up as a Dirt Devil for Halloween when he was two, and by the time he was six he was vacuuming religiously during school recess. One of his teachers, who wished to remain anonymous, sighed: "It's not that he didn't like recess. He just preferred to stay inside vacuuming. One day he would vacuum one side of the room and the next day he would do the other side. He'd also vacuum the principal's office – anywhere he could vacuum." By the age of fifteen, Kyle had amassed a collection of around 200 vintage vacuum cleaners, including a functioning 1908 Hoover 0 that was worth about $10,000, and his addiction was so bad that he was vacuuming his own house in

Adrian, Michigan, up to five times a day. He also made extra pocket money by repairing neighbours' cleaners and hoovering their carpets. And what did he spend his earnings on? More vacuum cleaners, of course. "Some people like baseball better than football," he explains. "Well, I like vacuums better than everything."

LARGEST COLLECTION OF KEY CHAINS

Since he began collecting them in 2001, Brent Dixon, from Valdosta, Georgia, USA, has collected 41,418 non-duplicate key chains at the last count. As Brent has to get around in a wheelchair because of muscular dystrophy, his mother encouraged him to start a collection because she thought it would have a positive effect. "It started out as something for me to do," he said. "I thought maybe I'd get a couple hundred of them. I had that many in the first few weeks and it just grew from there." He was presented with his Guinness World Record award in 2007 by the town's mayor John Fretti, who told the proud nineteen-year-old: "Brent, your record has put Valdosta on the map."

LARGEST PRIVATE COLLECTION OF MENUS

Jacques Rouet, the former business partner of designer Christian Dior, kept 15,000 menus in his Paris apartment, acquired over a twenty-year period and including one from the Elysée Palace in 1905, honouring the King and Queen of Spain and listing twenty-nine courses. His weirdest menu dated back to the siege of Paris in 1870, when the Prussian Army had the city surrounded, leaving the French unable to obtain food. "So they slaughtered the animals in the zoo and then ate rats," said Rouet. "That's why you have dishes such as haunch of dromedary and leg of antelope on the menu."

LARGEST PRIVATE COLLECTION OF CHINESE RESTAURANT MENUS

Harley Spiller began collecting Chinese restaurant menus after moving to New York in 1981 and now has more than 5,000 from around 80 different countries – his earliest menu dating back to 1879. He specializes in takeaway menus, the oldest of which is from 1916. "It's one of the nice things you can ask a friend to do," he says, "to bring you a Chinese takeout menu from their trip, because it's so lightweight and it's free!"

LARGEST COLLECTION OF MOBILE PHONE HANDSETS

The website goldenbookofrecords.com states that Michelle Kipling, from Milford Sound, New Zealand, has collected 1,850 cell phone handsets.

LARGEST COLLECTION OF DICE

Since he started gathering dice in 1977, Kevin Cook, from Colorado Springs, has built up a collection of around 50,000, thereby knocking spots off all his rivals. Once he realized that he possessed more dice than anyone he knew, he started thinking about the world record and spent two years trawling libraries and later the internet in the hope that he wouldn't be able to find anyone with a larger number of dice. As fate would have it, the one person who did have more lost the lot in the 1989 San Francisco earthquake. Sometimes the dice just roll your way.

LARGEST COLLECTION OF BACK SCRATCHERS

Dr Manny Rothstein, a dermatologist from Fayetteville, North Carolina, has built up a collection of 675 back scratchers from seventy-one countries. His obsession began in the mid-1970s when he received a plastic two-handed back scratcher in the post as a promotional giveaway from a drug company. At first he just put it to one side, but then he began to notice that back scratchers come in all shapes and sizes and soon he was itching to collect them. "It occurred to me, how many different ways can you make a long stick with a hand on the end? I was just amazed." Starting from scratch, he has acquired an impressive array of implements, which line the walls of his office as his wife won't let him bring them home. The collection includes back scratchers made of ceramic, glass, jade, brass, silver, wood, plastic, leather and corn cobs. Sadly one of his largest specimens – a four-foot-long scratcher made from a plaster mould of a bear's footprint with a caribou horn handle – was stolen from his office in 2007. Dr Rothstein is at a loss to explain why anyone would steal such a thing, particularly because he appears to be the only back scratcher collector in the world. Indeed, the lack of competition has stifled his growth. "Every two weeks or so, I receive a new back scratcher as a gift from patients who have been on vacation, and about once a month I'll buy one on eBay, but since there's nobody else who collects them, I can't trade with anybody, which is what I'd really like to do."

LARGEST PERSONAL COLLECTION OF BEDS

King Louis XIV of France, who reigned from 1643 to 1715, hated washing and took only three baths in the whole of his adult life. However, he loved beds and owned 413 of them in his various palaces. His favourite bed was at Versailles, the royal château southwest of Paris.

LARGEST COLLECTION OF CRAB MEMORABILIA

When people hear that Dr Darren Martin used to study crabs, they tend to jump to the wrong conclusion. It is only when they learn that he studied marine biology, not gynaecology, at university that they understand the basis for his record-breaking collection of more than 450 items of crab memorabilia that fill his house in High Wycombe, Buckinghamshire. His crustacean collection began in the mid-1990s. "It started with someone giving me a crab-shaped pencil sharpener and then things snowballed from there. Crab memorabilia started coming from all directions (a kind of pincer movement, you might say) – clocks, toys, stamps, glasses, books, mugs, etc. If it had a crab on it, I was given it. But the greatest crab in my collection is my daughter Hannah. She was born between 22 June and 22 July, therefore making her Zodiac sign Cancer, the crab. It was pure coincidence, though. I'm not that well organized."

LARGEST COLLECTION OF EMPTY PIZZA BOXES

Scott Wiener's Brooklyn apartment is home to 597 different empty pizza boxes from forty-two countries, some dating back forty years. He is equally keen on the boxes' contents and reckons he gets through fifteen slices of pizza in an average week. Then again, it is all part of his job, which is taking visitors on tours of New York City pizzerias. "I don't think there are any other collections of pizza boxes," he admits. "Most boxes end up in the trash. They're not collectors' items – it's like saving used tissues. But because my life revolves around pizza, to me it's a priceless collection." Yet while he admires the designs, surprisingly he does not approve of pizza boxes as a concept. "I actually dislike eating pizza out of boxes. I love the boxes for what they represent, but for transporting pizza, they're terrible. The box traps the pizza in steam, which breaks down the cardboard, which you then end up tasting."

LARGEST COLLECTION OF BARS OF SOAP

For more than forty years, Gail Santos, from Tijuana, Mexico, has been collecting bars of soap. She currently has about

15,000 soaps from fifty-four different countries and in over 200 fragrances.

LARGEST COLLECTION OF MILK BOTTLES

Paul Luke, a former milkman from Stanford-Le-Hope, Essex, has a collection of over 11,000 different milk bottles stored away in a mini-museum, along with milkmen's uniforms, caps, badges, milk churns and three old milk floats. Not only has he collected the bottles but he has gone to the trouble of filling each one with polystyrene balls to give the impression of milk. Luke, who also runs the Milk Bottle News Collectors Club, which boasts over 120 members across the UK, collected his first bottle in 1987 when he was nine. "I thought it would be interesting to start collecting the different ones but it got a bit out of hand."

LARGEST COLLECTION OF SQUEEZY KETCHUP BOTTLES

Liu Xiaoping, from Shanghai, China, has a collection of 750 squeezy ketchup bottles of various designs. The fact that he refuses to recognize glass ketchup bottles suggests he may have had that all-too-familiar experience with apparently reluctant contents and a pale carpet.

LARGEST COLLECTION OF CHRISTMAS LIGHTS

The Richards family, from Canberra, Australia, put up 502,165 Christmas lights around their home for the 2013 festive season. They first held the record in 2011 with 331,038 lights, only to lose it to a family in New York who put up 346,283, but this time they left no bulb unturned. David Richards started work on the display in the October and carried on every weekend until he had used more than thirty-one miles of wire to create a dazzling light show that was to his taste if not necessarily his neighbours'. "Most of them love the display," he said, before adding ominously, "although some haven't spoken to me since the 2011 record."

LARGEST COLLECTION OF WITCHCRAFT-RELATED OBJECTS

After his attempts to open The Museum of Witchcraft in Stratford-upon-Avon foundered in 1947 due to local opposition, the late Cecil Williamson had better luck on the Isle of Man four years later, setting up his collection in an old mill with Gerald Gardner as its resident witch. After the two men fell out (imagine the curses they could have put on each other), Williamson moved the museum around the country, eventually settling in 1961 on the Cornish village of Boscastle where it remains to this day, attracting more than 35,000 visitors annually. Exhibits include human skulls, torture devices, satanic artefacts, a witch's phallic tusk and a particularly fetching poppet – a doll that was used as a curse to resolve an unwanted pregnancy. The doll has real pubic hair sewn between its legs and a dagger embedded in its abdomen. Nice. Nobody seems to know exactly how many items of witch memorabilia the museum currently holds – perhaps counting them would be bad luck and bring about a plague of locusts or a hail of serpents – but there are definitely over 2,000 and it is widely accepted as the biggest of its kind.

LARGEST COLLECTION OF BALLPOINT PENS

Since childhood, Angelika Unverhau, from Dinslaken, Germany, has been avidly collecting ballpoint pens and now has more than 220,000 different types from 146 countries. In order to share the love, she founded a club for like-minded souls who meet twice a year to trade ballpoint pens.

LARGEST COLLECTION OF PENCILS

Kandy Pedington is to pencils what Angelika Unverhau is to ballpoint pens. Pedington, from Houston, Texas, has been collecting pencils for nearly twenty years and now has over 32,000 from 100 countries and which have been manufactured by 500 companies from around the world. However, there is a new kid on the block in the shape of schoolboy Tushar Lakhanpal, from Delhi, India, who has been collecting pencils since the age of four and already has in the region of 15,000, including two believed to have been used by Queen Elizabeth II.

LARGEST COLLECTION OF PENCIL SHARPENERS

The world's only museum dedicated to the pencil sharpener can be found in Hocking Hills, Ohio, where Revd Paul A. Johnson built up his collection of some 3,500 different models until his death in 2010. He started collecting them in 1988 as a hobby to occupy his retirement and went on to acquire sharpeners that pay homage to everything from Barbie dolls and the space race to the fallen World Trade Center in New York City. Yet his is not the biggest collection in the world. According to Guinness, that honour goes to Greece's Demetra Koutsouridou who has a collection of 8,514 different pencil sharpeners that she has amassed since 1997. At least with collecting pencil sharpeners you can see the point.

LARGEST COLLECTION OF RULERS

A collection of rulers would indeed be a vision to behold. "The one doing his expenses in front of the fire, that's Nero, the one in the glass case with his head missing is Charles I, and the empty display case is Ethelred the Unready." However, possibly because they are markedly easier to acquire than former heads of state, schoolboy Ameya Gupta, from Delhi, India, prefers to collect measuring rulers, and since he started in 2010 he has amassed 1,854 rules from twelve different countries. Collecting tends to run in the family as his aunt Anuradha has over 30,000 matchboxes and cousin Kanika has a stockpile of 5,100 erasers. Meanwhile, Anuradha's sister-in-law, Priyanka, has also entered the record books by collecting 13,096 name slips.

LARGEST COLLECTION OF MATCHBOXES

Prateep Tankanchanrverukul, from Thailand, collected more than 100,000 matchboxes in the 1990s and even made some of them into a tasteful jacket.

LARGEST COLLECTION OF MATCHBOX LABELS

Steven Smith, from Great Yarmouth, Norfolk, had collected 1,054,221 different matchbox labels from 130 countries as of May 2011, some dating back to the nineteenth century. His interest started when he was a seven-year-old and used to walk along the seafront and pick up matchboxes that had been discarded by visiting holidaymakers and sailors. The latter proved particularly rewarding as they brought with them matchboxes – and therefore the labels – from exotic foreign climes. He also has over 20,000 actual matchboxes and needs a fire extinguisher in every room of his house as many still contain live matches.

LARGEST COLLECTION OF CLOTHING TAGS

Tao Chun Lin from China has a collection of more than 102,000 clothing tags that he has built up since the 1970s. There must be a very good reason why someone would go to the trouble of cutting off and collecting clothing tags but for the moment it eludes us.

LARGEST COLLECTION OF WALMART RECEIPTS

Between 1996 and 2002, Derek Dahlsad, of Fargo, North Dakota, posted online a receipt of every purchase he made at Walmart. Derek's Big Website of Walmart Purchase Receipts displayed more than 150 receipts and encouraged visitors to comment on his purchases. Blogger Anne D. Bernstein says that it became part soap opera, part sociological study. "It was strangely emotional following Derek's life via his shopping habits. When he stopped buying Ultra Maxi Pads, it was a clue that something was up with his marriage. Bingo. He got divorced."

LARGEST COLLECTION OF SCRATCHCARDS

Dave Mannix from Cheshire spent twenty years and £80,000 (about $120,000) building up his collection of 100,000 National Lottery scratchcards. It includes every National Lottery scratchcard released since their introduction in 1994 except for one – the 1994 Christmas special edition card which he has been unable to lay his hands on. Most of the cards he bought were already used and therefore had no value, but, much to the annoyance of his partner Sue, 10,000 remain unscratched and have now expired. He could have been sitting on a $7.5 million fortune but the pristine collector in him chose not to tarnish the cards by removing the telltale silver films. Instead he put them up for sale, hoping that the next owner would scratch the cards and tell him how much he could have won over the years.

LARGEST COLLECTION OF TEAPOTS

China's Tang Yu has a collection of over 30,000 different teapots, some dating back to the Song dynasty (960–1279). He has been collecting them since 1955.

LARGEST COLLECTION OF HUSBANDS

American grandmother Linda Wolfe made Elizabeth Taylor look positively monogamous. Wolfe (born Linda Lou Taylor) has been married twenty-three times, stating that she is "addicted to the romance" of getting wed. Either that or she has a serious addiction to confetti. Linda, from Indiana, first got married in 1957 when she was just sixteen to a thirty-one-year-old man named George Scott. The union lasted for seven years – the longest and happiest of all her marriages – but since then it has been downhill all the way. Over the subsequent decades, she married a one-eyed convict, a Mormon preacher, assorted plumbers, barmen and musicians, and one man, Jack Gourlay, three times. Two of her conquests turned out to be homosexual, two were homeless and at least one hit her. Another put a padlock on her fridge. She has had seven children by her different husbands and been a stepmother to many more.

Her last marriage, in 1996, was a publicity stunt as it made the groom, Glynn Wolfe, the world's most married man with a total of twenty-nine weddings. He died a year later aged eighty-eight. In 2009, sixty-eight-year-old Linda revealed that she was on the lookout for husband number twenty-four. "I would get married again," she said, "because, you know, it gets lonely." She shrugs off her record-breaking achievement. "When I was younger I was just a snot-nosed kid, but the neighbourhood boys were all in love with me. They all wanted to marry me." And most of them did.

LARGEST COLLECTION OF WINDMILLS

Known as "The King of the Windmills", the late Frank Medina, of Stockton, California, began collecting old American Aeromotor windmills in 1976 and at one point had more than 2,000, including a wooden one made in 1874. He began collecting windmills when he became dismayed that many old ones were being cut up for scrap. "I've loved

windmills since I was a little boy," he said in a 1991 interview. "There was a windmill at my grandmother's house
where we'd visit when I was a kid. At night, it would clang
and clink and squeak and put me to sleep. So my collection
is the fulfilment of a lifelong dream." However, by 2004 he
only had sixty windmills, having sold the others to pay for a
costly divorce.

He might have lost most of his windmills, but even at the
age of ninety-six he still had all his teeth and was listed by
Ripley's Believe It or Not! as being the oldest man in the
world with all his teeth who has never had a cavity.

LARGEST COLLECTION OF TRAFFIC CONES

David Morgan, from Burford, Oxfordshire, has a collection
of more than 550 different traffic cones, a haul that would put
any drunken student to shame. As a sales director of a plastics
factory which is the world's largest producer of the cones, he
proudly boasts that he owns a specimen from at least three-
quarters of every type of cone ever made. Some people can
love their job just a little too much. He keeps them in a garage
where the subdued lighting prevents the plastic from melting
and confesses to being fascinated by the finer points of their
design. "It's really interesting," he told the Oxford Mail.
"There are so many shapes, sizes and colours. And the models
are always changing." His "journey" (to quote every reality
TV show on earth) began in 1986 when his company was
involved in a legal dispute with a competitor over the design
of a cone. To prove the design had previously existed, Morgan
travelled the UK in search of cones and hasn't been able to
stop. "I'll find out where the roadworks are and go and look
for them," he says. "But the best ones are from more unusual
places, like village halls and from undertakers, who always
have different ones and look after them. Everywhere I go, I
collect them, but I always take new ones with me and swap
them. I would never pinch one, as they're a safety product. I
usually ask the foreman, but people aren't really bothered,

and most of the cones I get have been stuck on their own for years – sometimes 15 years after the roadworks have finished." He is particularly proud of a Malaysian cone (found washed up on the Isles of Scilly) and a 1956 rubber cone from Scotland – the oldest in his collection. "I am still looking for a rare five-sided cone from Manchester," he added. "I hear about sightings, but by the time I get there, they've gone. It's like looking for Elvis."

LARGEST COLLECTION OF BELT BUCKLES

From 1974 to 2004, Canadian Chester Lindgren collected 1,642 different belt buckles, at which point, as a world record holder, he decided to retire gracefully.

LARGEST COLLECTION OF KITCHEN TIMERS

If presented with a kitchen timer by their daughter, a lot of people might be mildly insulted by such an affront to their cooking prowess, but Edeltraud Dreier, from Berlin, Germany, saw it as the springboard for building up the world's largest collection of kitchen timers. She has now collected more than 1,300 different models from as far afield as Singapore, Japan and Canada – surely a guarantee that there is never again a burnt offering in the Dreier household.

LARGEST COLLECTION OF NAPKINS

A Slovakian woman, Antonia Kozakova, has a collection of more than 63,000 napkins that has taken her sixteen years to compile. She says she will not rest until she reaches 100,000, adding that her ultimate goal in life is to have a napkin with her face and name on it. Surely that is every woman's dream.

LARGEST COLLECTION OF SALT AND PEPPER SHAKERS

Little did Belgian-born Andrea Ludden know, when she bought a pepper mill at a garage sale in the mid-1980s, that it would be the start of a lifetime's collection. As it didn't work properly, she bought a couple more. "I used to stand them on the window ledge of my kitchen," she said in 2012, "and neighbours thought I was building a collection. Nothing could have been further from my mind!" Soon she had around 14,000 shakers on shelves all over the house, prompting her husband Rolf to issue her with an ultimatum: "You either find somewhere to put these things or it's a divorce." So she created the Museum of Salt and Pepper Shakers in Gatlinburg, Tennessee, and later, as the collection continued to grow, a second museum in Guadalest, Spain. She currently has over 40,000 pairs of shakers, which are divided between the two museums and include salt and pepper pots in such inventive shapes as headstones, skulls, toilets and human feet.

LARGEST COLLECTION OF US PRESIDENTIAL PET MEMORABILIA

Founded in 1999 by Claire McLean, the Presidential Pet Museum in Glen Valley, Virginia, is home to over 1,500 items related to the pets of US presidents past and present, ranging from an alligator presented to John Quincy Adams to Calvin Coolidge's raccoons and Woodrow Wilson's tobacco-chewing ram. Items on display include the cowbell worn by Pauline Wayne Taft, the last cow to graze on the White House lawn, and a portrait of the Reagans' dog Lucky made from her own fur.

LARGEST COLLECTION OF MODEL ELEPHANTS

From the moment he received an ornamental elephant as a gift from his sister-in-law on his wedding day in 1967, Ed

Gotwalt developed a fascination for pachyderms. He began collecting elephants in all sizes – eventually reaching over 10,000 – and eight years later, at the suggestion of his wife, opened Mister Ed's Elephant Museum in Orrtanna, Pennsylvania. Sadly, the museum and 2,000 of its exhibits were destroyed by fire on 5 July 2010, but thousands of elephant donations poured in from all over the world and the business was able to reopen fully in February 2011.

LARGEST COLLECTION OF TIEPINS

Kevin Godden, from Folkestone, Kent, began collecting tiepins in 1977 when he started work and received the first pin from his father, and now owns more than 1,300. His personal favourite is one bought for him by his sons for his fortieth birthday and which spells the word "DAD".

LARGEST COLLECTION OF UMBRELLA COVERS

One can understand the interest in collecting umbrellas, with their sometimes ornate handles, but umbrella covers? Yet not only is there a woman in the world who dedicates her life to acquiring umbrella sleeves, she has also opened a museum to display them. The Umbrella Cover Museum in Peaks Island, Maine – unsurprisingly the only one of its kind in the world – was founded in 1996 by Nancy 3. Hoffman (yes, that is her name) and is now home to over 700 umbrella covers from fifty different countries. Her path to enlightenment began when she was clearing out a closet and came across seven umbrella covers looking sad and unloved.

Some of the sleeves in her definitive collection even have their own *X Factor*-type back story. When not singing "Let a Smile Be Your Umbrella" to her own accordion accompaniment, Hoffman regales visitors with the tale of an American contractor in Iraq who was caught in a violent hailstorm in Baghdad. His green umbrella was destroyed beyond repair but the cover made its way back to the United States where it now stands proudly as part of the museum's collection. You couldn't make up a compelling story like that.

"The museum is about covers from ordinary people," says Hoffman, "but it's not only about collecting. It's about finding a way to slow down and see the beauty in what may on first glance appear to be a mundane or silly item." There is also a serious conservation message here because the current trend is for traditional fabric covers to be replaced by plastic. Hoffman can identify with how candle makers must have felt when electricity first arrived on the scene and sees her museum as a way of preserving these style icons in captivity before they become extinct in the wild. So forget giant pandas and tigers: think umbrella covers.

LARGEST COLLECTION OF COMPASS BOXES

After collecting assiduously for fourteen years, Peter Schoeman, from Baltimore, Maryland, boasted 700 geometry compass boxes by the summer of 2013.

LARGEST COLLECTION OF FISH POSTERS

Bob Toelle, from British Columbia, Canada, collects only posters that feature fish and has amassed more than 750 from around the world – saltwater and freshwater. His hugely impressive list of poster titles includes "Pacific Northwest Spawning Salmon", "Lake Tanganyika Cichlids", "Native Fish of the Upper Mississippi River", "Threatened Freshwater Fish of Croatia", "Oil-Rich and Cartilaginous Fish from Ireland" and "Wrasses".

LARGEST COLLECTION OF NAIL POLISH

Samantha Henderson, from Philadelphia, Pennsylvania, has a collection of more than 1,300 bottles of nail polish.

LARGEST COLLECTION OF TEA BAG LABELS

It takes an unusual mind to decide that the most rewarding part of a tea bag is its label, but at the last count, Germany's Felix Rotter had collected 8,661 tea bag labels from eighty-eight countries.

LARGEST COLLECTION OF BAGPIPES

Some people believe that the best sound bagpipes make is when they crackle on the fire. Danny Fleming, a Scottish police officer from Grimsby, would certainly beg to differ as he has spent £130,000 ($200,000) over the last forty years building up a record-breaking collection of 105 bagpipes. He started his collection at the age of ten in 1973 and now has models which date back to 1918 as well as a set of pipes in gold, silver and ivory worth more than £12,000 (nearly $20,000). He says that each bagpipe in his collection is playable, which sounds less of a boast and more of a threat.

LARGEST COLLECTION OF AUTOGRAPHED DRUMSTICKS

After catching a drumstick hurled into the audience by Joe Franco at a Good Rats concert in 1980, New York student Peter Lavinger set about collecting them. He now has more than 1,300, all of which have been played, signed and presented to him by such famous drummers as Ringo Starr, Phil Collins, Dave Grohl, Stewart Copeland, Mick Fleetwood, Charlie Watts, Don Henley and Nick Mason. At the height of his acquisition period, Lavinger devoted up to sixty hours a week to his obsession, often waiting patiently backstage or in the crowd to accost an unsuspecting percussionist. His collection is now valued at over $1 million. "No one can duplicate what I've done," he says. "I created a niche and filled it."

LARGEST COLLECTION OF COMBS

For years Betty and Ralph Miller displayed their collection of 3,000 ornamental hair combs, dating from 100 BC to the 1940s, at their home in Homer, Alaska, as the Miller Comb Museum. According to Antique Comb Collectors Club International – and they should know – it is the largest collection of combs in the world. When it comes to more modern, plastic combs, New Yorker Helen Roberts has collected over 900, to ensure that she will never have a bad hair day.

LARGEST COLLECTION OF BRAS

Chen Qingzu, a forty-five-year-old health worker from Sanya, Hainan Province, China, has collected more than 5,000 bras over the past two decades and hopes to put them all in a dedicated bra museum. Whenever he travels to another city, he contacts local college students and asks them to give him their ill-fitting bras. He says his interest in bras is purely based on his concerns for women's breast health but concedes that "some of my friends think my hobby is a bit strange and many of the girls I asked thought I was a bra fetishist."

LARGEST COLLECTION OF CHAMBER POTS

From humble beginnings in 1990, lawyer Manfred Klauda, from Munich, Germany, has collected more than 9,400 chamber pots, the earliest being a 2,000-year-old Syrian model. His collection also includes an early "porto-potty", which Austrian Emperor Franz Josef kept at the home of his mistress, and the grand toilet of mad King Ludwig II of Bavaria who was, frankly, potty. For some years, Klauda kept his prize exhibits in a museum of the unusual, alongside collections of pedal cars, perfume bottles, padlocks, corkscrews and the world's first Easter Bunny museum. Alas, in 2006, the museum closed, meaning that visitors to Munich would have to find somewhere else to sober up after the Oktoberfest.

LARGEST COLLECTION OF HANDKERCHIEFS

Mrs Shubhangi Apte, from Raipur, India, has a collection of 3,472 handkerchiefs – a record that is definitely not to be sneezed at.

LARGEST COLLECTION OF HOTEL MENU CARDS

Shubhangi Apte also has a taste for hotel menu cards and over a period of five years has collected 3,814 from various establishments in India, Malaysia, Singapore and Dubai.

LARGEST COLLECTION OF LIGHT BULBS

Dr Hugh Hicks, a dentist from Baltimore, Maryland, owned a collection of over 75,000 light bulbs from around the world which he displayed at his Mount Vernon Museum of Incandescent Lighting from 1964 up to his death in 2002. His fascination apparently started when, as a baby, he showed no interest in playing with toys so his grandmother put a light bulb in his crib to amuse him. Among his cherished exhibits were the original torch of the Statue of Liberty and the headlamps from Hitler's Mercedes Benz. Friends said that whenever Dr Hicks switched on a new bulb, his face would light up.

LARGEST COLLECTION OF PHONE CARDS

Sunil Joseph, from Kerala, India, has been collecting phone cards since 1997, and by 2013 had amassed more than 12,000, including recharge coupons, chip cards and SIM cards, from 245 different countries.

LARGEST COLLECTION OF CLOCKS

Every wall of Jack Schoff's small studio apartment in North Berwick, Maine, is lined with clocks – over 1,500 in total. He began collecting them around 2003 when health problems left the former naval shipyard pipefitter literally with time on his hands. "I was going stir crazy, so I started taking clocks apart and putting them back together, just for something to keep busy." He began buying old clocks from yard sales and as word of his new hobby spread, people started leaving broken or unwanted clocks on his doorstep. When he learned that the existing world record was held by a German with 921, he set about beating that mark, a feat he had achieved by the summer of 2008. His apartment became a tourist attraction for visitors from all over the United States, particularly at noon to hear the cacophony of different sounds. Most of his income is now spent on batteries, while he estimates that it takes him up to a month to adjust every clock in his collection for daylight saving time.

However, in 2011, Schoff's world record was usurped by Bill Williams, from Colyton, New Zealand, who revealed that he owned no fewer than 3,021 clocks, worth anything from 50 cents to thousands of US dollars. He started collecting in 1988 and has since accumulated timepieces at an average rate of ten per month, to the occasional bemusement of those around him. "My friends and family look at each other with a knowing smile," he says. "I don't think I'm eccentric, but then again most eccentric people don't." The former teacher takes his responsibilities seriously and winds up 150 of his clocks every Saturday to varying times so that the chimes sound at irregular intervals to entertain visitors. He keeps all bar about thirty of the clocks at a museum he set up in 2005, in Colyton's former church, after his wife Kathy got fed up with his ticking obsession. Not that she has room for complaint, given that she has her own collection of more than 1,000 mermaid ornaments.

LARGEST COLLECTION OF WALKING STICKS

After twenty-five years of dedicated collecting, Billy Sutton, from Cartersville, Virginia, is able to boast a collection of 932 walking sticks – the largest in the world. He has sticks made of wood, silver and ivory, and even has one that can be unscrewed and doubles as a flask. Another contains a sword. According to Sutton, it doesn't matter what it looks like, it's whether or not it feels good in your hand. And yes, he was talking about walking sticks.

LARGEST COLLECTION OF ICE LOLLY STICKS

Denmark's Poul Lykke Jepsen has 449 different ice lolly sticks that he has collected since 1988.

LARGEST COLLECTION OF "DO NOT DISTURB" SIGNS

While staying at a hotel in Sheffield, England, in 1985, Jean-François Vernetti, with a Swiss accountant's eye for detail, spotted a spelling mistake on a "Do Not Disturb" sign, which, let's be honest, takes some doing even in a British hotel. It inspired him to the sort of eccentric behaviour not usually associated with accountants, and has led to him collecting 11,111 different kinds of "Do Not Disturb" signs from hotels in 189 countries across the world. When travelling to a particular destination, he often goes to the trouble of changing hotels mid-trip in the hope of acquiring a new "Do Not Disturb" sign.

LARGEST COLLECTION OF FOUR-LEAF CLOVERS

Edward Martin, Sr, from Cooper Landing, Alaska, began searching for four-leaf clovers in 1999, and by 2008 the seventy-seven-year-old had already collected more than 160,000. He once found more than 100 in a single day, even though the odds of finding just one four-leaf specimen are about 10,000 to 1. Martin snatched the record from George Kaminski, a Pennsylvania prisoner who had taken the title in 1995 by plucking 72,927 four-leaf clovers from prison yards. However, the good luck associated with four-leaf clovers then deserted Kaminski, who had spent much of his life in prison for various crimes, when the authorities transferred him to a low-security prison that did not have much clover in its grounds. As Martin crept ever closer to the record, the incarcerated Kaminski grumbled in a 2005 interview: "This guy's got the whole world. I have two or three acres."

LARGEST COLLECTION OF SANTA CLAUS MEMORABILIA

What do old geography teachers do when they retire? Do they go off in search of oxbow lakes, glacial tills or a nice escarpment? Well, if Jean-Guy Laquerre, from Boucherville, Quebec, Canada, is anything to go by, they also collect Santa Claus memorabilia. He started collecting in 1988 after discovering a papier-mâché Santa in the home of an aunt who had died, and has since acquired more than 25,000 items, ranging from figurines to blankets and tablecloths to toilet seat covers. "It awakened the child in me," he says, "and now I just can't get enough Santas."

LARGEST COLLECTION OF PALINDROMES

Ninad Jadhav, from Madhya Pradesh, India, has a collection of 1,111 palindrome items. His collection includes stamps, coins, currency notes, soaps, wrist watches and travel tickets. Jadhav, who was married on a palindrome date, named his daughter Aviva, which is also a palindrome. The oldest item in his collection is the year 1881.

LARGEST COLLECTION OF CHOCOLATE WRAPPERS

Martin Mihál, from the Czech Republic, began collecting empty chocolate wrappers from around the world in 1989 at the age of nine, and by 2014 his collection had grown to 120,000, the oldest dating back to the 1890s. "I used to collect stamps," he says, "but I wanted to collect something really different. Then I received some wonderful Swiss Lindt and Nestlé chocolates whose wrappers were much more beautiful than any Czech wrapper at that time." He reached the milestone of 1,000 wrappers in 1997 but the real game-changer came the following year when he gained access to the internet and was able to trade with like-minded souls. He reckons he has wrappers from 110 different countries but is still lacking examples from around 30 of the smaller chocolate-producing countries, including Cape Verde, Bangladesh, Fiji, Panama and Tajikistan.

LARGEST COLLECTION OF COFFEE MUGS

Melisa Arthur, from Des Moines, Iowa, has been collecting coffee mugs since she was twelve, and forty years later her total stands at 20,000 from eighty-eight different countries.

LARGEST COLLECTION OF BUS TICKETS

According to Guinness, Ladislav Sejnoha of the Czech Republic has built up a collection of 200,000 different bus tickets from thirty-six countries. Another keen collector of bus tickets is Glasgow's Ray McCormick who at the last count had acquired a more modest 43,356, the majority used by himself or requested from other passengers after use. Ray's love of bus tickets began when he was nine and has continued ever since, even though he is now well into his forties. Some childhood cravings are just too good to give up, and unlike sweets, bus tickets don't rot your teeth.

LARGEST COLLECTION OF SOVIET BUS STOP PHOTOS

At one time or another we have all been forced to sit through someone else's seemingly endless collection of holiday photos, but New Yorker Christopher Herwig's travel snaps require greater stamina than most. For he is obsessed with bus stops in the former Soviet Union and can proudly boast the biggest collection of photos of them in the world. His twelve-year quest began in 2002 and took him more than 18,000 miles by car, bus, bicycle and taxi through thirteen countries and produced more than 1,000 pictures, the best of which he put into a book, fittingly titled *Soviet Bus Stops*.

He says he was attracted to them because, unlike most things in the region where everything was standard, the bus stops were often different and appeared to represent one of the few opportunities for artistic licence. As a result the bus stops regularly feature murals, statues and inventive roof structures. In Kyrgyzstan, he even found some that were shaped like a Kyrgyz hat. However, the locals did not necessarily share Herwig's view that their bus stops were cool rather than hideous and, thinking that he was seeking to portray their country in an unflattering light, sometimes reacted angrily when he started taking pictures of the shelters. In Abkhazia, his driver accused him of being a Georgian agent and of photographing sensitive material. "He demanded a bribe," says Herwig, "otherwise it would be 'straight to the militizia and a firing squad'. Needless to say, he was not convinced by my story that 'I have only come to your country to see your pretty bus stops'. In the end, I had to use two camera cards. I'd shoot one photo on one card which I could show the cops, and then put in the real card to take the rest. I'd keep the real card in my underpants and no-one wanted to search there."

LARGEST COLLECTION OF VEHICLE HUBCAPS

San Francisco may be "The Golden Gate City", New Orleans "The Queen of the Mississippi" and Amsterdam "The Venice of the North" but the town of Pearsonville, California (population seventeen at the last head count), has its own unique, if somewhat less romantic, title – "The Hubcap Capital of the World". It owes its status to the exploits of its founder, "Hubcap Queen" Lucy Pearson, who once boasted a collection of more than 200,000 vehicle hubcaps, all of which were available for sale. She and her mechanic husband Andrew founded Pearsonville in 1961, and when his business attracted all manner of old cars, Lucy took a shine to their hubcaps, prompting Andrew to tell their daughter: "The old lady's lost her mind." Lucy remained unbowed. "They're just all so pretty," she said. "Somebody loses a hubcap, they're sick till they find it. I've usually got them. It makes me feel good that I've got them. My hubcaps is my hobby. I talk to people and show them my hubcaps."

LARGEST COLLECTION OF PENISES

Opened in 1997, the Icelandic Phallological Museum in Reykjavik showcases retired teacher Sigurdur Hjartarson's lovingly assembled collection of over 280 penises from ninety-three different kinds of mammal, ranging from the sixty-seven-inch front tip of a blue whale's penis to a tiny hamster member which can only be seen under a magnifying glass. His interest was first aroused in childhood when he was given a cattle whip made from a bull's penis. Now his collection attracts 11,000 visitors a year – 60 per cent of them women – although staff at the local tourist office are said to blush with embarrassment if asked for directions and information. Inevitably the museum guest book includes comments such as: "I've never seen so many penises – and I went to boarding school!" In 2011, the museum, which also displays lampshades made from bull scrotums, obtained its first human penis (generously donated by a ninety-five-year-old Icelander on his death), but its detachment did not go according to plan and it was reduced to a small, shrivelled heap barely worthy of exhibition. So Hjartarson says he is still searching for "a younger and a bigger and better one".

LARGEST COLLECTION OF SHRUNKEN HEADS

Maryland cleaning supplies salesman Robert L. White, who died in 2003, had a penchant for shrunken human heads and his private collection of thirty-six was billed as the largest in the world. Head shrinking was a popular pastime among the Jivaroan tribes of Ecuador, and the trade in shrunken heads – or tsantsas – was so profitable (selling for $250 each in the 1950s) that unscrupulous businessmen started making counterfeit versions. White also collected around 50,000 items of memorabilia relating to John F. Kennedy, including his passport, credit card, a brick from the Dallas School Book Depository (the building from which he was fatally shot) and a paper cup he sipped from in 1960.

LARGEST COLLECTION OF VHS COPIES OF THE MOVIE *SPEED*

To Ryan Beitz, of Moscow, Idaho, the 1994 action movie *Speed*, starring Keanu Reeves, is way ahead of the rest. So much so that he has made it his life's mission to collect every VHS cassette of the movie that exists. At the last count, he had reached 550 plus 26 laser discs, but he only uses the discs to trade off for more tapes. His weird obsession began when he was penniless in Seattle and had to buy Christmas presents for his family. At a pawn shop, he found six copies of *Speed*, so he thought it would be a neat joke to give everyone the same gift if only to show that he loved them all equally. He says: "It was then I realized it was really fascinating to have that many copies of a thing. What really cemented it was when I went down to another pawn shop, and they had 30 copies. I said, 'I'll take them all.' They sold them to me for 11 cents a copy." He hasn't stopped collecting *Speed* tapes since, even though he acknowledges that his quest is utterly meaningless. "That's why I don't bother counting them often, because, like, who really cares?" *We* do, Ryan. We do.

LARGEST COLLECTION OF *STAR WARS* MEMORABILIA

Steve Sansweet has collected over 300,000 items of *Star Wars* memorabilia – the largest in the galaxy – including toys, models, posters, life-size exhibits and pinball and arcade machines. He houses this vast collection in the barns of a former chicken ranch at Petaluma, California, which he has converted into a non-profit museum called Rancho Obi-Wan. It goes without saying that Sansweet, who has written sixteen books on the *Star Wars* franchise, is something of a fan.

LARGEST COLLECTION OF VIDEO GAMES

Michael Thomasson's love affair with video games started inauspiciously. He was twelve when his grandparents bought him his first game, Cosmic Avenger, for Christmas, but he had to wait another year before he could actually play it because his parents had not been able to track down the sought-after console. More than thirty years later, he has amassed over 11,000 games in the basement of his Buffalo, New York, home – despite selling off his collection in 1998 to pay for his wedding. He never pays full price for the games, restricting himself to a budget of $3,000 a year, but estimates that his collection is worth around $800,000. He freely admits that he is so busy buying that there are some games in his collection that he hasn't even played yet.

LARGEST COLLECTION OF SUPER MARIO MEMORABILIA

Mitsugu Kikai, from Tokyo, Japan, was born in 1985 – the same year that Nintendo released its first Super Mario video game. One of the first things his parents bought him was a Super Mario cereal bowl, and when he got older he started collecting everything related to the moustachioed Italian plumber. He currently has a collection of over 5,440 Super Mario items.

LARGEST COLLECTION OF SMURF MEMORABILIA

There are certain character traits that it's probably best to keep secret from your neighbours. Arsonist is one that readily springs to mind. Smurf collector is another. That hasn't deterred Karen Bell, from Ayrshire, Scotland, who over the past thirty years has built up a collection of 4,482 items of Smurf memorabilia at the last count. It takes up an entire room of her house, at which husband Brian has drawn the line. He says: "I don't always understand Karen's love of Smurfs but as long as her addiction doesn't spread to the other rooms in the house then I can live with it. The only Smurf memorabilia outside of the spare room I've agreed to is a Smurf feeding mat for the cats – and even that's pushing it!"

LARGEST COLLECTION OF TROLLS

The home of Ray Dyson, a fifty-two-year-old cement finisher from Edmonton, Alberta, Canada, is filled with 1,754 troll dolls – the fruits of a collection he started in 2002 after his co-workers told him he looked like a troll. He has caveman trolls, elephant trolls and even biker trolls and is so taken with the little people that he sports a troll tattoo on his right bicep.

LARGEST COLLECTION OF MARTHA STEWARTS

On the New York set of her TV show *Martha* on 20 September 2005, American domestic goddess Martha Stewart gathered 163 of her namesakes. They included Martha Stewarts who were married to men with equally famous names – a Rod and a Jimmy – plus a bulldog named Martha Stewart.

LARGEST CELEBRITY AUTOGRAPH
COLLECTION . . . SIGNED WITH HIS OWN NAME

When Paul Schmelzer contacts the rich and famous, he asks them: "Can I have my autograph?" For Schmelzer, from Minneapolis, Minnesota, is not the usual kind of autograph hunter: he wants celebrities to sign *his* name rather than theirs. The idea came to him while watching an eight-year-old boy with Asperger's Syndrome ask jazz musician Ben Sidran for his autograph. When Sidran obliged, the boy snapped: "Not your name. Mine!" Schmelzer has so far found over seventy famous people willing to play the game, including Yoko Ono, architect Frank Gehry and Dan Castellaneta, the voice of Homer Simpson. He has also had his share of disappointments, mainly from celebrities who, on receiving a written request, fail to understand the twist and sign their own name instead. He recalls: "When I had the chance to meet artist Chuck Close, I asked him to sign my name on a poster featuring his 1968 'Big Self-Portrait'. He gamely agreed but later in the day, during a signing session, he forgot and signed his own name. Funny to be disappointed to get a famous artist's autograph!"

LARGEST COLLECTION OF ITEMS
BEARING THE NUMBER 786

At the last reckoning, N. Krishnamoorthy, a railway employee from Maharashtra, India, had collected more than 600 items bearing the three-digit number 786, including Indian currency, rail and bus tickets, lottery tickets, a hotel receipt, SIM card number, a lock and key, a cheque number, a cell phone number, courier slips, rail pass and a loan application form number. He was inspired to start his collection in 1994 when he noticed that the banknote he had pulled from his wallet began with 786, which is considered a lucky number in Islam. He is so diligent that, rather than use a banknote containing 786 for his bus fare home from work, he elected to walk the three miles instead.

LARGEST COLLECTION OF CELEBRITY HAIR

John Reznikoff, from Westport, Connecticut, has collected the hair of more than 120 dead celebrities, including John F. Kennedy, Albert Einstein, Napoleon Bonaparte, Marilyn Monroe, Beethoven, Charles I, Eva Braun and Elvis Presley – and his collection has an estimated total value of $10 million. His most cherished possession is a $500,000 lock of Abraham Lincoln's hair, taken from the president on his deathbed after he had been shot in the head. But it's not just any old lock of hair – it's the very strand that covered the bullet wound on the night of the assassination. When a *New York Times* reporter asked Reznikoff about the pieces of detritus stuck to the hair, he was told simply that it was dried brain matter. Reznikoff decided to concentrate solely on dead people after his 2005 payment of $3,000 to Neil Armstrong's barber for some of the astronaut's hair prompted Armstrong to threaten legal action. "So I don't do living celebrities anymore," says Reznikoff. "That has the connotations of a rabid fan running around with scissors, and that's a dangerous brew."

MOST VALUABLE COLLECTION OF POTATO CRISPS THAT LOOK LIKE FAMOUS PEOPLE

In her line of work, Myrtle Young, a former quality inspector for Seyfert Foods in Fort Wayne, Indiana, started collecting potato crisps (chips) that looked like someone or something. She soon had a range of salty snacks in shapes that resembled, among others, a duck, Moby Dick, Mickey Mouse, a dog, a candle, Yogi Bear, a sleeping bird and George Bush – and when she took her prize collection to Oklahoma City for a TV show it was insured for $1 million. "My most famous chip," said the eighty-six-year-old in a 2010 interview, "is my Bob Hope chip. He sits on cotton in a special case with a lid on it to protect him from any kind of damage. This is my favourite chip and I don't think I could ever find another one like it. I used to have a chip that resembled Alfred Hitchcock, but it had a little accident. It broke into a million pieces."

BIGGEST BRA BALL

In January 2001, San Francisco artist Emily Duffy asked friends and family to send her their old bras. As contributions dropped in from such far-flung places as Australia, Israel and Japan, she patiently hooked the bras together, end to end. The work was finished on 9 November 2003, by which time her cups did well and truly runneth over as the resulting BraBall stood five feet tall, weighed 1,800 pounds and contained an incredible 18,805 bras. What is particularly impressive about Duffy's record-busting bra ball is that she has kept a detailed note of the contributions on her website www.braball.com. Thus she is able to tell us that the project received the support of 1,255 donors, the most generous city was Oakland, California (with 117 bras), and more bras were donated by women called Susan than any other name. Bizarrely there was a veritable cleavage of bra balls doing the rounds at the time, as rival San Francisco artist Ron Nicolino created his own Big Giant BraBall of 14,000 bras which he towed around California behind a 1963 pink Cadillac dubbed the BraMobile. Bra Wars broke out when the two artists argued so fiercely about who had the original idea that insults were traded and lawyers consulted. In truth, it was all a bit of a storm in a D-cup.

BIGGEST BALL OF FOIL

According to the record books, Richard Roman, of Alliance, Ohio, built a foil ball that weighed 1,615 pounds in 1987. Most of the foil he used was donated by a local company. Unusually no rival foil ball has yet bettered that mark. Since 2004, the Flying Pie restaurant in Boise, Idaho, has been striving to break the record with a ball named Flora, using foil donated by customers, but as of 2012 she weighed a mere 475 pounds – at this rate she will not be ready to claim the title until 2031.

LARGEST BALL OF STAMPS

Weighing in at 600 pounds and measuring 32 inches in diameter, the world's largest ball of stamps resides in a philatelic museum in Boys Town, Nebraska. It contains 4,655,000 stamps stuck together, layer upon layer, by the tongues and fingers of the Boys Town Stamp Collecting Club over a six-month period from 1953. As the museum's director speculated: "It must have been an exceptionally cold winter."

LARGEST RUBBER BAND BALL

Clothing store worker Joel Waul spent five years collecting 730,000 rubber bands and making them into a giant ball weighing 9,432 pounds and standing seven feet tall. The ball was so big – the size of a small estate car – that it had to sit on the driveway of his home in Lauderhill, Florida, until it was bought for an undisclosed sum in 2009 by Ripley's Believe It or Not! Neighbours were sad to see the local landmark go. One said: "I'll miss it. When I give directions I can't say anymore that I live next to the big blue ball." Waul said he planned to use the money from the sale to enrol in a Seattle stunt school where students are set on fire when they graduate.

LONGEST RUBBER BAND CHAIN

Parents are forever complaining that all children want to do these days is spend hours in their room surfing the internet. What happened, they cry, to the simple pleasures of their own childhood, like making nuisance phone calls and underage drinking? Well, for those parents who bemoan a lack of creativity and imagination among kids of today, what could be more creative than making a chain from 22,140 rubber bands?

That's what eleven-year-old Allison Coach, from Chesterfield Township, Michigan, did in 2010 – and when the chain was unwound from its stand it stretched a record-breaking 1.3 miles long.

LONGEST GUM WRAPPER CHAIN

This is dedication: Gary Duschl, from Virginia Beach, Virginia, has devoted half a century of his life to making a chain from chewing gum wrappers. He started it in 1965 and, as of March 2014, it consisted of 1,871,538 wrappers, measured 78,550 feet (nearly 15 miles) long and weighed 1,101 pounds. He has added an average ninety-one wrappers a day to his chain and the estimated value of the gum used is $131,007. If stretched out from end to end, it would take a person six hours to walk the entire length, or fifteen minutes to drive in a car at 60 mph. He says: "I started the gum wrapper chain at school. As some of the kids were making them, I asked them to show me how to do it. My competitive nature took over and I had to have the longest chain in the class, then the school, then the town and I just kept going from there. The chain is made up of Wrigley's wrappers only, but unfortunately Wrigley's has stopped putting wrappers on their gum in North America, which makes finding suitable wrappers more challenging." Even so, Duschl, who has recently retired from his job as a plant manager, has no intention of resting on his laurels and says his ultimate goal is for his chain to reach the full marathon distance of 26.2 miles.

LONGEST PAPERCLIP CHAIN BY AN INDIVIDUAL

Although teams of students have managed to construct paperclip chains measuring over twenty miles in length, the longest known chain built by an individual was the 8,202-foot effort of Germany's Thomas Paul in 1992. He made it during the school holidays from 111,000 paperclips.

LONGEST PAPERCLIP CHAIN BY AN INDIVIDUAL IN TWENTY-FOUR HOURS

Working around the clock on 13 February 2004, twenty-two-year-old maths teacher Dan Meyer, from Sacramento, California, assembled a 5,340-foot-long chain from 54,030 paperclips, thereby smashing the previous world twenty-four-hour record of 22,025 paperclips set by Belgium's Jeanine Van der Meiren in 2000. Following a failed attempt in 2003, Meyer took the whole thing very seriously and calculated that to break the record he had to work faster than 3.9 seconds per clip. "I went through boxes of paperclips before the actual attempt, looking for the best way to chain two clips, looking for the best way to position the clips in front of me, looking to shave off any fraction of a second." Fuelled by coffee, pizza, bagels and grapes, and helped by a volunteer who kept pushing fresh paperclips his way, Meyer succeeded in his quest to create a mile-long chain with thirty minutes to spare. However, the effort took its toll. "The last four hours, I was not a happy camper," he told the *Sacramento Bee*. "My fore-finger and thumb would not work at all." It was probably a chain reaction.

LARGEST BALL OF CLINGFILM

Seven-year-old Jake Lonsway, from Bangor Township, Michigan, took eight months to build a giant ball of clingfilm that weighed 281.5 pounds and had a circumference of 138 inches. At the 2007 weigh-in, he learned that he had beaten the previous record-breaking clingfilm ball by 31.5 pounds and 10 inches. The idea came about after he had begged his mother to let him take part in an attempt to break the record for the most people wearing Groucho Marx glasses simulta-neously. When that bid failed, to make amends she searched through the books for a record that was breakable, brought home a small ball and encourage family and friends to donate yards of plastic wrap. The end result was so enormous that it took up most of the garage. A pair of Groucho glasses would have been a lot less hassle.

HEAVIEST TWINE BALL

Starting in March 1950, Francis A. Johnson worked four hours a day for twenty-nine years to roll what was then the world's biggest ball of twine. As the ball grew, he could no longer wrap it by hand and had to use large railroad jacks just to move it. The ball stopped growing when Johnson died in 1979 from emphysema, which sadly may have been caused by nearly thirty years of inhaling twine dust. Measuring 40 feet in circumference and weighing 17,400 pounds, it is currently housed in a specially made gazebo opposite the town park in Darwin, Minnesota, where locals are so proud of the giant ball that every year they celebrate Twine Ball Day on the second Saturday in August.

Johnson's efforts inspired Frank Stoeber, a farmer from Cawker City, Kansas, to create a rival twine ball in 1953, and eventually he had over 1,600,000 feet of twine rolled into a ball 39 feet in circumference. Stoeber's untimely death in 1974 might have been expected to bring a halt to the ball's broadening girth, but the townsfolk of Cawker City have continued to add to it, expanding it to 19,973 pounds, although it is no longer the work of a single person. Not to be outdone by Darwin, Cawker hosts an annual Twine-a-thon in the third week of August, when visitors come from far and wide to make the ball bigger still.

Whatever their respective merits, both balls have been dwarfed by the exploits of dump attendant James Frank Kotera (also known as JFK) who started rolling his twine ball in Lake Nebagamon, Wisconsin, in 1979. At the most recent weigh-in, it tipped the scales at 20,545 pounds, making it indisputably the world's heaviest twine ball. He keeps it in an open enclosure on his lawn alongside a smaller 47-pound companion ball, "Junior", made of string.

LARGEST BALL OF BARBED WIRE

To add to the confusion over who in America has the biggest twine ball, from 1987 to 1991 retired brick mason J.C. Payne, of Valley View, Texas, gathered all the plastic twine he could from neighbouring farms and dairies to create a 41.5-foot-circumference ball, which he named "Clonia Crew". At around 12,000 pounds, it is, however, considerably lighter than the other contenders, prompting his rivals to claim that he deliberately wound the ball loose just to make it big and seize the record.

Having achieved his goal, Payne needed a new hobby to occupy his time and became hooked on barbed wire. So he set about rolling the world's largest ball of barbed wire and would happily travel 180 miles just to get his hands on some fencing that he had heard was being ripped out. His wife Elsie Ruth helped him add to the ball by pulling him around it with a tractor. By the time he died in 2004, it had reached a height of nearly 12 feet, weighed around 24,000 pounds (12 tons) and consisted of an estimated seventy miles of wire. At the last reported sighting, it was still sitting in his old back yard, having also become the world's largest ball of rust.

LARGEST PENNY PYRAMID

Over a two-month period from November 2011 to January 2012, Tom Haffey, from Denver, Colorado, collected 626,780 pennies which he then built into a pyramid weighing about 4,000 pounds. He said defiantly: "In my life, people have always told me I can't do something and I wanted to prove them wrong. I wanted to join the book of world records, so I found something I could do and I went ahead and did it."

FIRST PERSON TO TYPE FROM ONE TO ONE MILLION IN WORDS

On 25 November 1998, after sixteen years and seven months at the typewriter, Les Stewart, from Mudjimba, Queensland, Australia, finally achieved his goal of typing every number from one to one million in words. His last lines were: "Nine hundred and ninety-nine thousand, nine hundred and ninety-nine; one million." Knocking the socks of Marva Drew, who typed the same numbers in figures using 2,473 pages, Stewart's finished list filled 18,890 pages and used up seven manual typewriters and about 1,000 ink ribbons. Using just the one finger, he typed an average of three pages a day, maintaining the discipline needed for such a marathon venture by making sure he typed for twenty minutes on the hour, every hour. Asked why he chose to undertake such a time-consuming and frankly pointless task, he said that he didn't really have much else to do and besides he quite liked typing.

MOST MARRIED COUPLE

David and Lauren Blair, from Hendersonville, Tennessee, have a hobby that is unusual even by the standards of this book – they can't stop getting married. By the summer of 2013 they had tied the knot a staggering 106 times in such diverse locations as a *Romeo and Juliet* theatre set, the observation deck at Niagara Falls, various Hard Rock cafés, on the set of a production of *Mamma Mia* and at a Kentucky funeral home. The couple met in 1982, but the first time David proposed, Lauren said no, only to change her mind three months later when she caught the bouquet at her cousin's wedding. Their first wedding was in Los Angeles on 6 May 1984, and their second was the following day in a church in her home city of Chicago. Five days later, while on honeymoon, they decided to renew their vows and have continued to do so at regular intervals ever since. Lauren says: "It started because we were both in long-term relationships in the past that didn't work out. We knew we were meant for each other and wanted to continually share that vow experience. We've already been married on every numbered day of the month so every day is our anniversary, even on leap year. We've been married on 01/01/01, 02/02/02, 03/03/03 and so on, finishing that goal on 12/12/12. We're hopelessly in love."

CHAPTER 11

Mind Games

MOST NAMES AND FACES MEMORIZED IN FIFTEEN MINUTES

Boris Nikolai Konrad would make an excellent eyewitness. At the 2010 Germany Memory Championships, the Munich neuroscientist matched 201 names to faces after being given just fifteen minutes to study them. This is how it works. A series of unknown faces is presented to each competitor with corresponding names underneath. The faces are then re-presented in a different order without names, and the competitor must identify them correctly. Konrad says his technique is to transform each name into an image (e.g. Tom = tomato), and he adds that his memory is so good he can give long conference presentations without any notes. However, even he is occasionally fallible. "When I was invited to go on Japanese television, I went to the airport but forgot my passport. You see, it is a different type of memory."

MOST DAYS OF THE WEEK BETWEEN THE YEARS 1600 AND 2100 CORRECTLY IDENTIFIED IN ONE MINUTE

In 2010, Cuban American genius Yusnier Viera – "the Human Calculator" – worked out the correct day of the week for ninety-three randomly chosen calendar dates between 1600 and 2100 in just sixty seconds. He assigns code numbers to the year and month and then applies a multi-staged mathematical formula, or algorithm, to come up with the answer. It also helps that he possesses a brain so sharp it has been calculated at one in seven billion.

FASTEST RECITAL OF THE PERIODIC TABLE

Ten-year-old Poorvie Choudhary, from Jodhpur, India, recited all 118 chemical elements from the periodic table in 10.24 seconds on 25 January 2012. She has also recited it five times in one minute.

YOUNGEST PERSON TO RECITE THE PERIODIC TABLE WHILE STANDING ON HIS HEAD

Not to be outdone, in July 2012, Poorvie's eight-year-old brother, Daksh Choudhary, recited all 118 chemical elements in the periodic table in just 49.31 seconds while performing a headstand. Sibling rivalry at its finest.

YOUNGEST PERSON TO CALCULATE INSTANTLY THE NUMBER OF SECONDS IN FORTY-EIGHT YEARS

Like his father and great grandmother, Zerah Colburn had an extra digit on each hand and foot, but while this may have given him a slight advantage over his contemporaries when working out small sums, it could not explain his remarkable ability to solve the most complex mathematical problems. Born in Cabot, Vermont, in 1804, Zerah first demonstrated his skills as a human calculator shortly before his sixth birthday. After just six weeks' schooling, his father Abia overheard the boy repeating his multiplication tables and became aware that he had a child prodigy on his hands when Zerah correctly multiplied 13 and 97. Soon he was able to solve the square root of 1,449 and the number of hours in 38 years, 2 months and 7 days.

Zerah became such a sensation that his father exhibited him for money throughout the United States, where he was advertized as "The Calculating Child", a term that was probably intended as a compliment. In 1812, the pair sailed to England and Zerah was bombarded with questions from disbelieving experts. He was asked how many revolutions a 12-foot coach wheel would make in 256 miles and within two seconds had given the correct answer of 112,640. Another interrogator asked him how many minutes there are in 48 years, and before the question could be written down, master Colburn replied, "25,228,800", instantly adding that the number of seconds in the same period was 1,513,728,000.

The free-spending Abia lapped up the adulation, but eventually funds began to run low and he urged Zerah to seek more profitable employment as an actor. This venture, which took the duo to Ireland and Scotland, proved an abject failure, and to make matters worse, by the time he reached adulthood, Zerah's powers of computation had deserted him. After his father's death, he worked as a preacher before dying of consumption in 1839.

YOUNGEST PERSON TO IDENTIFY 200 DIFFERENT MODELS OF CAR

In 1984, two-year-old Anthony McQuone, from Weybridge, Surrey, could speak Latin, quote Shakespeare and identify and repeat the trademark symbols of 200 different models of car. He told bemused reporters that all the information was relayed to him by an invisible grown-up named Adam.

YOUNGEST PERSON TO NAME
ALL US STATE CAPITALS

Shruthi Vairavan, from Redmond, Washington, was able to name every US state capital and count up to thirty when she was just twenty-five months old, which was more than George W. Bush could do when he was fifty-five.

FASTEST RECITAL OF US STATES AND CAPITALS

Nikesh Thapaliya, from Nepal, can recite all fifty US states in 16.46 seconds without looking and can list all the US states with their respective capitals in random order in 49.79 seconds. He can also name the capitals of 215 countries of the world – and used to hold the world record for the most snorts in ten seconds (39), which, in light of his other efforts, does seem a bit like dumbing down.

MOST NATIONS AND THEIR CAPITALS
RECALLED IN ONE MINUTE

On 8 November 2013, Monu Kumar Shukla, from Bhopal, India, set a new world record by recalling fifty-three nations and the names of their capitals in one minute.

MOST CITY SKYLINES MEMORIZED AND
DRAWN AFTER ONE HELICOPTER RIDE

London-born autistic savant Stephen Wiltshire can draw from memory a detailed city skyline after seeing it just once from the air. For example, in 2009, the man known as the "Human

Camera" produced an accurate 19-foot-long drawing of 305 square miles of New York City following a single twenty-minute helicopter ride. He has repeated the feat with London, Tokyo, Hong Kong, Frankfurt, Madrid, Dubai, Jerusalem, Sydney, Hamilton City (Bermuda), Shanghai and Rome. When he took his short helicopter ride over the Italian capital, he was able to remember it in such detail that he drew the exact number of columns in the Pantheon.

MOST BOOKS MEMORIZED

The inspiration for Dustin Hoffman's character in the movie *Rain Man*, American mega-savant Kim Peek (1951–2009) memorized around 12,000 books during his lifetime by reading two pages at a time – one with his left eye and the other with his right. It took him just eight seconds to scan and remember a page. He could therefore race through an entire book in about an hour and remember almost everything he had read, regardless of the subject matter – whether it was history, literature, sport, geography or music. After reading and memorizing a book, he would always place it upside down on the shelf to show that he had finished it. He could also ask a stranger their date of birth, tell them what day of the week they were born on, and what story was on the front page of the major newspapers. However, although he was classed as a genius in fifteen subjects, he consistently scored below average in IQ tests. His talent did have its occasional drawbacks. He memorized so many Shakespearean plays and musical compositions and was such a stickler for accuracy that he had to stop attending performances because he would stand up and correct the actors or the musicians. His father said: "He'd stand up and say: 'Wait a minute! The trombone is two notes off!'"

MOST PI PLACES MEMORIZED

In November 2005, twenty-four-year-old Chinese graduate Chao Lu recited pi from memory to 67,890 places without making a single error. The attempt took him just over twenty-four hours and was the result of twelve months of practice. Yet even though he had broken the existing record by 25,695 digits he was disappointed because he had planned to recite 91,300 digits, only to trip up on the 67,891st by saying it was a 5 instead of a 0. No doubt he is a sensation at dinner parties – long ones.

MOST DICTIONARY ENTRIES MEMORIZED

Mahaveer Jain, from Lucknow, India, entered the record books in 2003 by memorizing verbatim all 80,000 individual entries in the *Oxford Advanced Learner's Dictionary*, right down to their page numbers. The engineering graduate, who earned the nickname "Dictionary Man", said he memorized the entire contents of the book's 1,500 pages in just ten months.

FASTEST TIME TO MEMORIZE A DECK OF PLAYING CARDS

At the 2011 German Open Memory Championship, the host country's Simon Reinhard took just 21.19 seconds to memorize a shuffled deck of 52 playing cards with no errors. This beat his own world record of 21.90 seconds set the previous year. He began competing in memory competitions in 2005 and has since gone from strength to strength. He uses a technique called the "Method of Loci", a device which, according to Roman legend, was developed some 2,500 years ago by the poet Simonides of Ceos who was the sole survivor of a building collapse during a dinner he attended. Simonides was subsequently able to identify the dead, who were crushed beyond recognition, by remembering where they had been sitting. Basically it works by associating things that you need to remember with places that you know well. By then mentally walking through those places, you are able to remember the order of the items – in Reinhard's case, playing cards. The Method of Loci has also been used by Hannibal Lecter – as fine a recommendation as you could wish for.

MOST LANGUAGES SPOKEN BY ONE PERSON

Sir John Bowring, the English-born Governor of Hong Kong from 1854 to 1859, could speak 100 different languages, making him a hyperpolyglot. He was also familiar with, but not fluent in, another 100 languages and specialized in translating traditional European folk songs into English. It's a tough job but somebody has to do it.

FASTEST TIME FOR ADDING TOGETHER 100 SINGLE-DIGIT NUMBERS

In 1999, twenty-nine-year-old Spanish accountant Alberto Coto took just 19.23 seconds to add correctly 100 randomly selected, single-digit (0–9) numbers in his head. He has held Guinness World Records in fourteen different categories of mental arithmetic, and between 2008 and 2010 he was officially the fastest human calculator in the world.

MOST WORDS SPELT BACKWARDS IN ONE MINUTE

In January 2014, Shishir Hathwar, a twenty-seven-year-old Indian government employee from Bangalore, spelt forty words backwards in a minute to break the existing world record by five words. He says the secret of his success lies in rapidly visualizing words, breaking them down into smaller words and then spelling them backwards. He regularly spells eight-letter words backwards and can happily rattle off "hippopotomon-strosesquipedaliophobia" (a fear of long words) in reverse.

FASTEST TIME TO READ FIFTY WORDS BACKWARDS

Rio Riono Jatmiko read fifty words backwards in a time of thirty-seven seconds during a 2013 episode of *World Record* on the Indonesia TV station Trans7.

HIGHEST NUMBER REACHED
WHILE COUNTING ALOUD

To raise money for charity, Jeremy Harper, a thirty-one-year-old software developer from Birmingham, Alabama, counted aloud from one to a million, averaging approximately sixteen hours of counting a day. It took him eighty-nine days – from 18 June to 14 September 2007 – during which time he did not leave his apartment or shave. The grand count could be watched live on the internet, and cameras were placed throughout his apartment to make sure he never missed a number. "I just love to have a good time," he said, perhaps ironically.

LONGEST COLOUR SEQUENCE MEMORIZED

During a challenge in April 2012, Sancy Suraj Singh, from Singapore, memorized a sequence of 160 randomly generated colours on a computer screen at the rate of two seconds per colour. He then wrote the sequence on a piece of paper without making a single error.

MOST ACCOMPLISHED LIAR

The World's Biggest Liar competition is held every November in Santon Bridge, Cumbria, in honour of Will Ritson

(1808–90), landlord of the Bridge Inn, who was renowned for his fanciful tales. One of his yarns was that turnips grew so large in the Lake District that locals used to carve into them to make cow sheds. Perhaps people were just more gullible in those days. Without using props or scripts, today's competitors have five minutes to tell the biggest and most convincing lie. Politicians and lawyers are not allowed to take part because they are considered to be professional liars. Local farmer John Graham (aka Johnny Liar) is the most accomplished liar in the history of the event, having won on seven occasions between 1994 and 2008. Or so he claims.

GREATEST NUMBER OF END OF THE WORLD PREDICTIONS

Based on his interpretations of the prophecies in the Book of Daniel, from 1831 to 1841, American Baptist minister William Miller told anyone who would listen that the world was going to end sometime between 21 March 1843 and 21 March 1844. As many as 100,000 of his followers sold their possessions and took to the mountains in readiness for the climactic event. The period passed without incident, but the Millerites kept their faith and, following further consultation, the date was changed to 18 April. Again the day came and went, so Miller switched it to 22 October 1844, but when nothing untoward happened then either, the date became known by Millerites as The Great Disappointment. In the wake of the failed prediction, Millerite churches came under attack, presumably from people who were angry at still finding themselves alive. In desperation, the group plucked other possible dates out of the air, including April, July and October 1845. Miller continued to wait for the world to end right up until his death in 1849.

CHAPTER 12

Intrepid Travellers

FASTEST TIME TO LICK EVERY ANGLICAN CATHEDRAL IN UK

Over a period of twenty-three months, between January 2011 and December 2012, Lawrence Edmonds licked all sixty-four Anglican cathedrals in the UK – forty-two in England, eight in Scotland, eight in Northern Ireland and six in Wales. Beginning at Norwich Cathedral and finishing in St Asaph, Wales, Edmonds travelled nearly 10,000 miles tonguing the stone-work of some of the nation's most historic buildings in order to win a bet with his friend Adam Drury and thus avoid having to run naked around his home city cathedral of York. Since he had to provide photographic evidence of each cathedral lick, he sometimes had to ask complete strangers to capture the moment on camera. "It wasn't the licking I found embarrass-ing," he said, "it was being caught doing it, particularly if a crowd gathered." Regarding the actual taste of the buildings, he described Worcester as "exceedingly gritty and salty", Durham as "disappointingly bland" but Lincoln as having "a very refreshing and mossy taste". The stone at Ripon was "tongue-piercingly cold and would soon give me a splitting headache" but even worse was Wakefield, which tasted "foul, sickly and sweet". However, he was full of praise for Lichfield, writing: "The reddened sandstone was beautifully warm on the tongue without any hint of saltiness or other foul taste to ruin the experience."

FASTEST CROSSING OF AUSTRALIA WHILE PUSHING A WHEELBARROW

In 2009, sixty-five-year-old David Baird, from Weston-super-Mare, Somerset, took 112 days to complete an epic 2,557-mile run across Australia from Perth to Sydney while pushing a wheelbarrow. He didn't suffer a single puncture but had to dive into bushes on four separate occasions when passing trucks nearly blew him off the road. His feet bore the brunt of the pain in 46°C heat. He said afterwards: "All my adult life my feet have been a size 10 but within three weeks they had spread out and I had to change to an 11. Two weeks later I needed a 12. My feet feel huge. I'm convinced my arms have got longer too."

LONGEST DISTANCE PUSHING AN INVISIBLE FRIEND

Irishman Frank Muldowney pushed an empty wheelchair – supposedly containing his invisible friend Harvey – on a 4,000-mile, eighteen-month journey across Australia in a bid to achieve world peace. In an adventure inspired by the imaginary character in the 1950 James Stewart movie *Harvey* (where Harvey was in fact an invisible giant rabbit), Muldowney set off from Perth on 2 April 2006, and arrived in Byron Bay, New South Wales, on 29 September 2007. On the way, his friend, who was thought not to have been a giant rabbit, was kissed, hugged, arrested and, sadly, run over. Being invisible, however, he came to no harm.

FASTEST SAILING WHEELBARROW PUSH ACROSS THE SAHARA DESERT

Revd Geoffrey Howard, a twenty-nine-year-old Anglican clergyman from Manchester, England, pushed a specially made Chinese sailing wheelbarrow across the Sahara Desert from Béni Abbès in Algeria to Kano in Nigeria – a distance of 1,946 miles. He set off on 20 December 1974 and reached his destination on 23 March 1975, completing the marathon push in ninety-three days. His barrow with its large sail profited from the prevailing trade winds and had also been fitted with unusually large wheels to reduce resistance. He was inspired to undertake the journey after occupying the position of a missionary in Nigeria. "I saw how farmers there walked miles to market with their produce on their heads. They could not go a few miles further to a town where they could get a better price because they were not strong enough. Nor could they take a bag of fertilizer on their return journey because it was too heavy for them to carry. They were so poor they had no mechanical means to carry anything. A wheelbarrow like mine could be homemade and I wanted to show how it could make a world of difference to people's lives in developing countries. Besides, I'd always wanted to cross the Sahara."

LONGEST DISTANCE TRAVELLED TO MAKE DAUGHTER A PRINCESS

Some dads will do anything for their daughters, so when six-year-old Emily Heaton asked her dad Jeremiah whether she would ever be a real princess, he set out to make her wish come true by travelling 7,000 miles from the family home in Abingdon, Virginia, to Africa. After conducting some intense online research, the father of three found an uninhabited, 800-square-mile patch of mountainous land called Bir Tawil – situated between Egypt and Sudan – which has been unclaimed for over 100 years because of a discrepancy in borders drawn up at the start of the twentieth century. So

Heaton set off on the long journey, which ended with fourteen hours across the open desert, to plant a flag (designed by his children) there on 16 June 2014 in the hope that it would eventually be formally recognized as the Kingdom of North Sudan, ruled by King Heaton and Princess Emily. "I wanted to show my kids I will literally go to the ends of the earth to make their wishes and dreams come true," he told the *Washington Post*. Although there was no official confirmation that his trip had been successful (his claim would have to be legally approved by neighbouring countries and the United Nations), on his return home he and his wife made a crown for Emily and insisted that she be addressed in future as "Princess Emily". Just in case.

FIRST MAN TO CROSS THE ENGLISH CHANNEL USING A CLUSTER OF HELIUM BALLOONS

American adventurer Jonathan Trappe crossed the English Channel in May 2010 in a chair tied to dozens of helium-filled balloons. He spent about an hour-and-three-quarters drifting silently over the water from Kent to Dunkirk. After cutting off some of the balloons to help his descent, he narrowly avoided a power line and made a textbook landing in a French cabbage field. Asked why he undertook the crossing, he answered: "As children, didn't we all dream of holding a bunch of balloons close and taking to the skies?" Not those of us who were latex intolerant, Jonathan.

FIRST OCEAN CROSSING BY A BOAT MADE FROM BEER CANS

In September 1977, three men completed the 2,400-mile voyage from Darwin, Australia, to Singapore on a boat made from 15,000 beer cans. The Chairman of the Darwin Reconstruction Commission, Clem Jones, and two local businessmen, Lutz Frankenfeld and Paul Harding, set sail on the

Can-Tiki, a 27-foot-long, 12-foot-wide motor-powered vessel consisting of beer cans stuck together with resin and asbestos powder. The voyage through 60-foot-high waves took the crew thirteen days and they were greeted by hundreds of well-wishers on their arrival in Singapore. The only downside, as Frankenfeld testifies, was that ironically there was no beer to drink on the boat. Three years earlier, Frankenfeld had founded the annual Darwin Beer Can Regatta, an event where all manner of beer-can craft take to the water. The idea was born simply because empty beer cans are just about the most plentiful commodity in Australia.

LONGEST VOYAGE BY BATHTUB

On 9 October 1983, twenty-two-year-old Bill Neal, from Salcombe, Devon, completed an 1,800-mile voyage from London to Kotka, Finland, in a five-foot-long, fibre-glass, Jacuzzi-type bathtub. He was accompanied by three friends in a support boat and his journey took him almost four months. He had hoped to sail on to Leningrad but the mean-spirited Soviet authorities prevented him from doing so. Instead he had to settle for dropping a bottle into Soviet waters with a cryptic message for President Andropov.

FIRST CROSSING OF THE ENGLISH CHANNEL BY BATHTUB

In June 2005, comedian Tim FitzHigham became the first man to row across the English Channel in a bathtub when he completed the voyage in 9 hours 6 minutes for Comic Relief. Having made it across the Channel, he proceeded to perform a 110-mile celebratory lap of honour all the way round Kent and up the Thames before finishing at Tower Bridge. He rowed the last 120 miles in the tub (named *Lilibet II* after the childhood nickname of Queen Elizabeth II) with a broken shoulder. With some admirers suggesting that FitzHigham was the greatest British sailor since Nelson, the bathtub's manufacturers, the legendary Thomas Crapper and Co. Ltd, were so impressed that they made a special limited edition lavatory to mark the occasion and called it the FitzHigham. It was only the second commemorative lavatory in history, the other having been made for Queen Victoria's Diamond Jubilee in 1897.

FARTHEST VOYAGE DOWN THE RIVER THAMES IN A PAPER BOAT

This was the voyage that first put Tim FitzHigham on the map. For eight days in March 2003, he paddled a paper boat 160 miles down the River Thames, overcoming eight capsizes, a nasty cold and a homicidal swan. In doing so, he broke a record that had stood for 383 years, having been set in 1619 by John Taylor, an eccentric Jacobean poet, who managed just 40 miles before his paper vessel sank. Explaining his mission, FitzHigham revealed: "It was the world's oldest surviving maritime record and what seems more surprising is not that people had tried to break it and failed but that people had actually tried to break it! I had never been in a boat before and had no idea how hard it would be. I'd made paper boats before and they hadn't sunk, albeit when I was five and the Lego men that skippered them may have been a bit lighter than me, but I thought, it's got to be much the same thing."

LONGEST DISTANCE ROWED IN BOAT TO PROPOSE MARRIAGE

Some people do go to great lengths to pop the question, but few can match the sheer determination of twenty-seven-year-old Harry Martin-Dreyer who rowed 3,000 miles across the Atlantic Ocean to propose to his girlfriend. The Londoner had met Lucy Plant when they were students at Bristol University, and some six years later, on 1 December 2013, he and his friend Alex Bland set off from Gran Canaria in a small rowing boat bound for Barbados ostensibly to raise money for leukaemia and diabetes charities. It was only when they were partway through their fifty-day voyage that Martin-Dreyer revealed to his crewmate that there was another purpose to the Atlantic crossing. He kept the diamond engagement ring in a waterproof bag while, rowing in two-hour shifts, they battled extreme heat, fifty-foot-high waves, seasickness, blisters, inquisitive sharks and being hit in the face by a flying fish before finally arriving in Port St Charles, Barbados. "We could barely walk when we got out of the boat," said Martin-Dreyer. "We were wobbling on our feet like Bambi and walking into pillars. So when I dropped down on one knee, Lucy thought I had fallen over. It took her a while to work out what I was doing. It was a risky strategy – you should never assume it is a given – but happily she said yes." Miss Plant added: "It was a complete surprise. I kept saying, 'no, no, no' – and Harry said: 'Can I take that as a yes?'"

FASTEST CROSSING OF THE UNITED STATES ON ROLLER SKATES

Averaging thirty-eight miles a day, Russell "Rusty" Moncrief made the 2,595-mile crossing of the USA from Florida to California on roller skates in 69 days 8 hours 45 minutes, from 5 January to 15 March 2002.

FASTEST DRIVE ACROSS THE UNITED STATES AND BACK IN REVERSE GEAR

Between 26 July and 13 August 1930, James B. Hargis, of Maplewood, Missouri, and his mechanic, Charles Creighton, drove their Model A Ford 1929 roadster in reverse from New York to Los Angeles without once stopping the engine. While they rested in Los Angeles for two days, the engine was left running. They then made the return leg of their "Seeing

America Backward" tour and reversed into New York on 8 September, having driven a total of 7,180 miles in forty-two days. They travelled at an average speed of just over 10 mph and slept in a specially constructed seat in the car. The forward gears were removed from the vehicle's transmission before they set off, and, crucially, the car was fitted with an extra-wide rear-view mirror to stop them crashing into things.

LONGEST DISTANCE DRIVEN IN REVERSE

For thirty-seven days, between 1 August and 6 September 1984, Brian "Cub" Keene and James "Wilbur" Wright drove their Chevrolet 9,031 miles in reverse through fifteen American states and parts of Canada. Although the car bore a prominent sign "Stuck in Reverse", it did not impress law enforcement officers in Oklahoma who insisted that the pair drive forwards out of the state.

LONGEST TIME DRIVING A TAXI IN REVERSE

Since 2003, Harpreet Devi has been driving his taxi around the streets of Bhatinda, India, in reverse. He began driving backwards when his car became stuck in reverse gear and he had to drive thirty-five miles home. Deciding that he was a safer driver going backwards than forwards, he redesigned the gearbox of his Fiat to have four reverse gears and only one forward and was granted special permission by the Punjabi state government to drive his unique car on the open road. Using an ambulance siren and adding headlights to the back of his car so that other motorists can see which direction he is travelling, he reaches speeds of up to 50 mph. "I don't have a video screen or radar on my dashboard," he said, "so I have to turn around and drive. It does mean that I experience frequent pains in the neck and I have had severe vomiting in the past. I also got a severe backbone problem from driving so fast in reverse, because my whole body gets contorted. But sometimes you have to suffer to achieve something. So it's right that I should be experiencing pain."

LONGEST DISTANCE DRIVING A CAR ON TWO SIDE WHEELS

Italian stuntman Michele Pilia drove a modified 1983 BMW 316 on its side on two wheels for a distance of 230.5 miles, around a stadium in Cagliari, Sardinia, on 26 February 2009.

LONGEST DISTANCE DRIVEN IN A TAXI

Three friends from university drove 43,319.5 miles around the world in their twenty-year-old black London cab, Hannah, to complete the longest-ever journey by taxi. Paul Archer, Johno Ellison and Leigh Purnell drove across four continents, fifty countries and ten time zones on a marathon drive that took fifteen months and clocked up £79,006.80 (about $120,000) on the meter. Their route, which took in Australia, was deliberately designed to be circuitous because, as everyone knows, taxi drivers always take the longest way round. The trio arrived back in London in May 2012 with tales of how they were arrested in Moscow, narrowly avoided being kidnapped by the Taliban in Pakistan and how Archer was deported from Iran as a suspected spy. They also became stuck on the border of Moldova with the wrong visas but eventually managed to gain admission to the country because a friend's mother knew the president!

LONGEST DISTANCE DRIVEN IN A TUK-TUK

Teachers Richard Sears and Nick Gough, both from Guildford, Surrey, spent sixteen months driving 26,325 miles around the world in a 395cc tuk-tuk – those open-side, three-wheeled machines which add much to the chaos of urban Asian streets, and which boast the style and durability of the average milk float. The pair set off from London in August 2012 and reached their destination of Buenos Aires, thirty-nine countries later, in December 2013. They actually broke the existing tuk-tuk record a month earlier when they arrived in the Peruvian capital of Lima – after dragging their ailing vehicle the last forty-three miles. It was only when a mechanic looked at it that they learned that a hole which had been covered to stop a diesel leak earlier in the trip was in fact designed to relieve pressure on the engine. Previously their tuk-tuk, which boasted a top speed of 30 mph (downhill), had been hit by a truck in Malaysia, become stuck on several treacherous mountain crossings and been harassed by elephants in Botswana. And there is only ever going to be one outcome in an encounter between an elephant and a tuk-tuk. They chose their mode of transport so that "they would stick out like a sore thumb". In that respect, too, they succeeded. Police officers in Africa were particularly bemused by the sight of the rickety little three-wheeler. Gough said: "We were stopped by a police officer on the Kenya/Uganda border who said, 'Your bottoms must hurt a lot. I can't believe you'll ever have children, and if you do, they're only going to be girls!'"

LONGEST DISTANCE BOUNCED ON A SPACE HOPPER

Phoebe Asquith, a twenty-four-year-old teaching assistant from Scarborough, Yorkshire, bounced 4.1 miles around the town on a space hopper in 4.5 hours in May 2013, at an average speed of a little under 1 mph.

LONGEST DISTANCE WALKED ON HANDS

An Austrian by the name of Johann Hurlinger walked 870 miles on his hands from Vienna to Paris in 1900. It took him fifty-five days, hand-walking ten hours each day, at an average speed of 1.58 mph.

LONGEST DISTANCE WALKED IN TWENTY-FOUR HOURS WITH SOMEONE ELSE STANDING ON YOUR FEET

In 1989, Michael Stobart, from Loughborough, Leicestershire, walked six miles in twenty-four hours with Dorothy Bowers standing on his feet.

FASTEST CROSSING OF THE SOLENT IN A PUMPKIN

In October 2013, Dmitri Galitzine, an artist who works with oversized vegetables, took 1 hour 56 minutes to complete the three-mile crossing of the Solent from Gosport to the Isle of Wight in a hollowed-out pumpkin powered by an outboard motor. He sourced the 800-pound squash at the Mere Brow Giant Pumpkin Show in Lancashire and said he chose a pumpkin as his vessel because they are naturally buoyant (you certainly never see an unhappy one) and have a waterproof exterior. The previous day in Portsmouth, this time in a non-motorized, 600-pound pumpkin, he had set a new world record for the fastest 100-metre pumpkin paddle, finishing the sprint in exactly two minutes. Grower Mark O'Hanlon could hardly contain his pride that Galitzine had crossed the Solent in one of his pumpkins. "He saw it growing, he came to see it being loaded," said O'Hanlon with tears welling up in his eyes. "He was so determined this was going to happen despite everybody telling him it was a bonkers idea – because, to be honest, going in the sea in large vegetables is not a good idea."

FASTEST TIME TO PUSH A BATH TEN MILES

Members of Hampshire's Yateley Hockey Club pushed a bath on wheels a distance of ten miles in 1 hour 41 minutes 44 seconds on 11 July 1987. For the record, Giles Hancock sat in the bath while Rowan Atkins and Alan Hancock pushed.

FIRST PERSON TO VISIT EVERY COUNTRY
IN THE WORLD WITHOUT FLYING

In a mission that gives hope to everyone who has a fear either of flying or of airport baggage handlers, Liverpudlian globetrotter Graham Hughes visited 201 "countries" in the world over a period of nearly four years without once setting foot on a plane. Instead, on a budget of just $100 a week, he travelled by cargo ship, bus, taxi or train to cover 160,000 miles in 1,426 days, and to prove it he took a selfie in every country. He set off from Uruguay on 1 January 2009 and finished on 26 November 2012 in South Sudan, a country that did not exist when his journey began. Surprisingly, he found it easier to enter North Korea, Afghanistan and Iraq than the Seychelles, where he needed seven attempts because of the threat from Somali pirates. He spent four days in a leaky boat to reach Cape Verde, was jailed for a week in Congo on suspicion of being a spy and was saved from Filipino Muslim fundamentalists by a lady-boy called Jenn! At the end of his trip, Hughes said: "I wanted to show that the world is not some big, scary place, but in fact is full of people who want to help you even if you are a stranger."

MOST JOURNEYS ON SAME SEAT IN SAME TRAIN

Since 2001, Dandu Krishnam Raju, of Palakol, India, has been making the round trip to his company's head office in Hyderabad on the second and third day of each month – and he always sits in the same seat on the same train, adding up to a total of more than 300 identical journeys. At first it was purely by chance that he was allotted berth number 35 in S-7 coach of the Narasapur–Hyderabad Express (train number 17255), but when he realized he had been given the same seat on the return journey, too, he became attached to it, although not literally as the train was a gum-free zone. So when booking his tickets in future, he started asking for the same berth, and since he regularly booked up to three months in advance, his favourite seat was always available.

FIRST RUBBER CHICKEN IN SPACE

Boldly going where no rubber chicken has gone before, Camilla was launched into space attached to a helium balloon in March 2012 by NASA scientists in California. Wearing a knitted spacesuit and helmet, and with a modified lunchbox as a spacecraft, she rose to an altitude of 120,000 feet in order to test radiation levels during a solar storm. She also carried four cameras, a cryogenic thermometer and two GPS trackers, and spent ninety minutes in the stratosphere before the balloon burst and she parachuted safely back to Earth. Camilla was first adopted as the mascot of NASA's Solar Dynamics Observatory in 2009 and quickly proved a hit on social media sites, building up 6,500 Twitter followers. "We didn't know how the public would react to a rubber chicken," said SDO's Romeo Durscher. "It caught me completely by surprise." Soon children, adults and astronauts alike were queuing up to have their picture taken with Camilla at NASA events as she made a meteoric rise up the pecking order.

She went on to make four more journeys into space in 2012, wearing a new spacesuit knitted from plastic bags by Sue Drage from Rugby, Warwickshire, who specializes in making accessories from recycled items. "I'd never had a client like Camilla before," she admitted. "I thought it was a live chicken the first time I heard about it. It took me three attempts – I'm not one for giving up – and I had to get a rubber chicken to check the sizes, but I managed it in the end."

FIRST REPLICA PASTRY IN SPACE

A team of Sicilian amateur scientists successfully launched a replica pastry into space on 2 February 2014. The clay model cannolo – a cream-stuffed roll symbolic of the island – soared nearly 100,000 feet into the stratosphere. It was attached to a large helium-filled balloon and a homemade rocket (made from an insulated ice cream box) which was equipped with two cameras and a GPS tracker to record its historic journey. As the Cannolo Transporter rose, atmospheric pressure decreased, causing the balloon to expand until it eventually burst, allowing the pastry to return to Earth by parachute. The brains behind the $500 space mission, Fabio Leone and Antonella Barbera, said the aim was to improve the image of Sicily, which has long been associated with organized crime, although it is unclear how launching a fake pastry into the sky was going to achieve that.

FIRST POTATO ASTRONAUT

In November 2010, children at a school in Devon launched a potato 90,000 feet into space aboard a homemade spaceship *Spudnik2*. Pupils at Landscove Church of England Primary School dressed the potato as Santa Claus before placing it in the special shuttle, which was made from a plastic drink bottle, tying it to a helium weather balloon and launching it from the village car park. After spending 2 hours 20 minutes in space, the pioneering potato floated back to Earth 140 miles away in Hampshire with the aid of a parachute. As the children could not rely on the potato's eyes to record the adventure, they fitted it with a camera. In case you're wondering what happened to *Spudnik1*, just think mash.

FIRST LEGO SHUTTLE IN SPACE

Most people who build a toy Lego space shuttle are quite happy to allow their imagination to do the rest, but teenage Romanian physicist Raul Oaida decided he actually wanted to send his model into space. So in central Germany on 31 December 2011, after gluing the Lego bricks together, he attached the miniature shuttle to a helium balloon and watched it soar twenty-two miles towards the edge of space. The toy craft spent three hours in the skies in temperatures so cold that ice particles started to form on the bricks, before it landed safely with the aid of a parachute in a field 155 miles away. No doubt inspired by the success of his space mission, two years later Oaida built a life-size, functional car entirely out of Lego. Powered by air, the car was made from 500,000 pieces of Lego and boasted a top speed of 18 mph.

FIRST LEGO MAN IN SPACE

On 16 May 2011, the NASA space shuttle *Endeavour* carried a Lego set to the International Space Station where it was assembled by astronaut Cady Coleman, who, incidentally, also holds the record for playing the first flute in space. Three months later, three Lego figures – depicting seventeenth-century Italian astronomer Galileo and Roman gods Jupiter and Juno – hitched a ride aboard the NASA solar-powered spacecraft *Juno* on its mission to reach the planet Jupiter by 2016.

On a somewhat smaller scale, on 7 January 2012, two teenagers from Toronto, Canada, Mathew Ho and Asad Muhammad, launched a two-inch-tall Lego man clutching a Canadian flag sixteen miles into space attached to a twenty-two-foot-diameter helium balloon. He floated safely back to Earth ninety-seven minutes later.

MOST TRAVELLED LEGO MAN ON TERRA FIRMA

From 2013, a Legoman photographer accompanied real-life photographer Andrew Whyte on a year-long trip around the UK. Whyte, from Portsmouth, carried the little figure in his pocket wherever he went and then proceeded to photograph him in the foreground of 365 interesting locations.

MOST TRAVELLED GARDEN GNOME

Murphy, an ornamental gnome, travelled 25,000 miles around the world in a seven-month period in 2008 after being snatched from Eve Stuart-Kelso's front garden in Gloucester, England. With echoes of the 2001 French film *Amélie*, Murphy was eventually returned along with a carrier bag containing an album of forty-eight photos showing him in exotic locations – abseiling down a mountain, standing in a shark's mouth, swimming in the sea and riding a motorbike. Also enclosed were stamped immigration permits to prove that the eight-pound gnome had visited twelve countries on three continents – South Africa, Swaziland, Mozambique, New Zealand, Australia, Singapore, Thailand, Cambodia, Vietnam, China, Hong Kong and Laos. Murphy's adventure was the work of Simon Randles, a twenty-two-year-old law graduate from Reading University, who chose the gnome as his travelling companion after spotting him from a passing bus. He crept back to take Murphy one night, leaving behind a note explaining the gnome's prolonged absence. It read: "A gnome's life is full of time for reflection, and while surveying your garden one summer morning, I began to get itchy feet. There's more to life than watching daily commuter traffic and allowing passing cats to urinate on you." "I felt a degree of guilt," Randles admitted afterwards, "as it could have been a treasured heirloom, but the gnome was a great icebreaker on the trip. It made friends with a lot of people. It was difficult getting it through customs though and every time it appeared on the scanner they demanded to see it." When Murphy did finally return home at the end of his world tour, he was a bit battered and bruised and missing his feet, but as Mrs Stuart-Kelso remarked philosophically: "That's no real surprise given that he was sent abseiling down a mountain!"

MOST TRAVELLED PLASTIC SKELETON

Susan Weese, from Albuquerque, New Mexico, travelled more than 15,000 miles around the world with a life-size, anatomically correct, plastic human skeleton named Sam (short for Samantha). Sam also set a record for the most photographed plastic skeleton as Weese took pictures of her every day for a year in diverse locations – such as posing with Roman legionnaires at the Colosseum, riding a gondola in Venice, enjoying a beer in Germany and attending a Chicago Cubs baseball game. Weese, fifty-seven, who has previously worked on medical illustrations, had the idea for the adventure after driving around with a skeleton (not Sam) in the passenger seat of her car one Halloween. When other drivers honked their horns in appreciation, she realized she could be onto something. Their worldwide jaunt began on 1 November 2012, but it was not without its problems. "Sam weighs 42 pounds," explained Weese, "and if I carry her in my arms I get bruises everywhere. She also flies over-sized, which made it hard getting through airports. She got held up by the Department of Agriculture in Newark, New Jersey, because they had to make sure she was not real bone."

MOST TRAVELLED PUPPET

Kermit the Frog's holiday photos are enough to make anyone green with envy. He has trekked along the Great Wall of China, gazed in awe at Icelandic geysers and the Grand Canyon, sat next to the Sydney Harbour Bridge and admired his own star on Hollywood's Walk of Fame. He has even visited the Texas city named in his honour. At this point, it should be explained that this is not the real Kermit but a puppet lookalike owned by Markus and Conny Morgenroth, from Frankfurt, Germany. The couple have been taking the toy on foreign holidays and business trips since 2006, during which time he has visited more than thirty-five countries and clocked up over 360,000 air miles. Kermit's global itinerary has included Florida, Helsinki, Melbourne, Dublin, Hawaii, Bratislava, Beijing, Vienna, Stockholm, Dubai and Tokyo. Mr Morgenroth, a computer software manager, says: "I love the idea of taking Kermit to real-life places and putting him next to real-life things we all recognize. Whenever possible, my wife and I take him with us on our travels. There was only one time that we forgot him, and we were not happy about it at all. We often meet people who are big fans of Kermit. When we were at Kermit's star on the Hollywood Walk of Fame, we couldn't leave for ages because so many people wanted to take pictures with him as well."

MOST TRAVELLED CARDBOARD CUTOUT

Two years after the death of her father, Jay, in 2012, New York photographer Jinna Yang took a six-foot-tall, life-sized cardboard cutout of him on a month-long, 10,000-mile journey around the world for the trip of his dreams, visiting iconic landmarks including Iceland's Skógafoss waterfall, the Eiffel Tower and the Colosseum. A friend scored the cutout so that it folded easily and became portable, but her unusual, strangely rigid, travelling companion still attracted plenty of puzzled looks. "Many people stopped me in the street," she said, "asking me if it was a famous person. Most of the time when you see a life-sized cutout, it's of Justin Bieber or One Direction, and it's usually in a nine-year-old's room. My father never had the chance to travel the world, but now he has, albeit in cardboard form."

MOST TRAVELLED MANNEQUINS

Two mannequins owned by artist Suzanne Heintz, from Englewood, Colorado, have travelled more than 10,000 miles around the world in the past fifteen years for a series of weird family portraits. Her plastic loved ones – ever-serious husband Chauncey and never-growing teenage daughter Mary Margaret – have been photographed with Heintz in various international locations as part of an art project titled "Life Once Removed". She came up with the idea after her mother kept badgering her about when she was going to get married.

Seeing the mannequins for sale, Heintz decided to create her own perfect – if silent – family. "Yes, I'm a grown woman playing dress-up and house," she says, "but it's all for a darn good reason. And it's not because I need medication. It's because I have the right to decide how my life looks. But if you think it's hard travelling with your family, try travelling with a family of nude quadriplegics. It's just short of torture."

FARTHEST DISTANCE TRAVELLED WITHOUT ANY MONEY

German broadcaster Michael Wigge travelled 25,000 miles around the world in 2010 – without spending a penny. To clarify, he never spent any money; he must have gone to the toilet on a number of occasions. He set off from Berlin in June, and, by working his passage (maybe that requires clarification, too), he journeyed through eleven countries, finally arriving in Antarctica 150 days later in November. Although he had planned the trip for a year, building up a network of useful contacts, he also relied greatly on the kindness of strangers who agreed to offer him a lift in their car or give him a bed for the night. At first, he scrounged for food in garbage bins but soon abandoned the dumpster diving when he found that he could offer to clean a restaurant's floor, wash the dishes or even tell a joke in return for a sandwich. He crossed the Atlantic from Europe to Canada on a container ship, paying for the voyage by doing menial onboard jobs like changing the oil in the engine room. In Las Vegas, he took part in street pillow fights for $1 a time, and in San Francisco he earned tips by "pushing heavy tourists up the hills". His toughest assignment was carrying tourists' luggage in Peru for five days along a fifty-mile mountain route. "I was the worst porter the Andes had ever seen," he admitted frankly. "I did not have the stamina to keep up. After just two days, the tour operators put the luggage I was supposed to be carrying on horseback and let me walk at my own pace."

FIRST PERSON TO VISIT ALL NINETY-FOUR AUSTRALIAN PLACE NAMES MENTIONED IN THE SONG "I'VE BEEN EVERYWHERE"

In 1959, Australian country singer Geoff Mack wrote the song "I've Been Everywhere", which mentioned ninety-four Australian place names whose only connection was their ability to rhyme with each other. Fifty years later – in December 2009 – Peter Harris, an Englishman living in Australia, set off on an adventure to visit every place mentioned in the song's lyrics. He completed his 18,750-mile mission on 4 September 2011 by visiting Birdsville in Queensland. There are also versions of the song for North America, New Zealand, Britain and Ireland, Germany, Finland, Belgium, and even the Faroe Islands, although the last-named's lyrics run to little more than a couple of lines.

FASTEST FULLYFUNCTIONING TOILET

By fitting a powerful 140cc motorbike engine to a toilet bowl, Lincolnshire plumber Colin Furze (he of the giant fart machine) created a superloo that can travel at 55 mph – the perfect machine for a man constantly on the go. He added four gears to the handlebars and installed a towel rail and toilet roll holder for authenticity. He also incorporated a button on the handlebars so that the toilet can be flushed on the move. Speaking at the machine's 2013 unveiling, Furze admitted: "It is quite scary to drive, as the water in the toilet makes it very top heavy and I get wet when I go over any bumps. The toilet seat is also quite slippery, so it's hard to stay on and stop myself from sliding off when I go fast."

FASTEST SOFA

The simple sofa has come a long way since the days when it just used to sit in the lounge watching the television and acting as a magnet for lost keys, coins and sweet wrappers. In September 2011, Australian Glenn Suter drove a motorized sofa at a top speed of 101 mph at Camden Airport, near Sydney. Powered by a 1.4-litre Suzuki superbike engine, the sofa smashed the world speed record for living-room furniture, previously set at 92 mph by Englishman Marek Turowski in 2007. Suter's sofa, which was attached to a large table, complete with bowl of fruit and a cup of coffee, was designed by Paul Kinnon, who admitted: "It's the oddest vehicle I've ever built. With race cars, you can use the aerodynamic body kit, but with the couch it was just a matter of doing what we could. We tried to break the airflow with the coffee table."

FASTEST BED

In November 2008, Englishman Edd China achieved the dubious title of the fastest man in bed when he drove a motorized bed on wheels at a top speed of 69 mph on a private road in London. The Maidenhead mechanic also holds world records for the fastest garden shed (58 mph in 2011), the fastest office (87 mph in 2006) and the fastest milk float (77.5 mph in 2013).

FASTEST BANANA

Back in 2009, Steve Braithwaite had a eureka moment. Braithwaite, who is originally from Woodstock, Oxfordshire, but now lives in Kalamazoo, Michigan, spotted a banana in a fruit bowl on the counter of a gas station. We're guessing that this was not the first time in his fifty-plus years that he had set eyes on a banana, but on this occasion, instead of simply thinking it looked nice to eat, he was suddenly struck by the thought that the fruit's aerodynamic shape would be ideal for a car. So over the next two years, he spent $25,000 on building an 85 mph banana. He equipped his banana-shaped car with a Ford V8 engine, which, he quite rightly observes, makes it the only fruit to have a V8 engine. "The best thing about the banana car," he adds, "is when kids see it. You just see them yank on their mothers' arms and shout 'banana, banana!'" Naturally the bright yellow vehicle attracts a good deal of attention, which he says can be frustrating if he's trying to get anywhere in a hurry. Here's a thought, Steve: drive a sensible car.

FASTEST MOTORCYCLE HEARSE

Self-styled Heaven's Angel, the Revd Ray Biddiss, from Bradford, West Yorkshire, reached speeds of more than 114 mph on his specially built trike hearse at Elvington Airfield, in May 2011, to set a world record for the fastest motorcycle hearse. The fifty-seven-year-old spent $30,000 converting a Triumph motorcycle into the 2.3-litre Rocket Hearse, a super-powered three-wheeler that incorporates a glass coffin carrier and ensures that the deceased will always get to the crematorium on time. He uses it for personalized funerals that can feature rock music, videos and webcam link-ups. An avid biker, he came up with the idea after a brush with death on the road. He said: "I nearly got wiped out on a ride and realized if I had been I would have had to be carried to my funeral in a car, and I didn't want that. So I had the idea of an all-in-one hearse. I wanted to create the most powerful of all coffin carriers – a vehicle that maintains the integrity of a motorcycle and appeals to the most passionate of bikers. I know some people get taken in a motorbike sidecar but a true biker wouldn't be seen dead in one of those."

FASTEST MOBILITY SCOOTER

David Anderson and Matthew Hine created the dream machine for old boy racers everywhere – a mobility scooter that can do over 100 mph. On 30 August 2014, Hine sped around Jurby Motordrome on the Isle of Man at a top speed of 107.6 mph to break the record for the world's fastest mobility scooter by over 25 mph. The pair custom-built the machine from scratch using a kart chassis and incorporating split exhausts and a few other modifications while still retaining that essential look of a mobility scooter, including, of course, the shopping basket. Before any pensioners think of buying one to slash their journey time to the Post Office, it is unable to be registered for road use because it has no front brakes.

FASTEST SHOPPING TROLLEY

In August 2013, Matt McKeown, from Plymouth, Devon, rode a jet-propelled shopping trolley at 70.4 mph along the strip at a North Yorkshire airfield – the fastest that any human has ever travelled in a shopping trolley. He built his record-breaking trolley (which, in case you are wondering, is not aisle-legal in any of the major UK supermarkets) after finding it in a ditch and fitting it with a jet engine, a 250cc Honda engine, and kart wheels as stabilizers. "It was the first time I've actually been scared driving that thing," he said afterwards, before confirming that he had no desire to go any faster on it but was turning his attention instead to a motorized wheelbarrow. It is tempting to say he's off his trolley.

LONGEST JOURNEY PUSHING A SHOPPING TROLLEY

The South African pair of Frans Pretorius and Shaun Jan Johan Meintjies pushed a shopping trolley a distance of 88.3 miles around the Klerksdorp City Mall in twenty-four hours on 3–4 September 2004. Unconfirmed reports stated that a subsequent attempt to break the record was wrecked because the participants were unable to resist stopping to buy a packet of chocolate biscuits that were on special offer.

LONGEST JOURNEY IN THE INNER TUBE OF A TYRE

Forty-one-year-old Cheng Yanhua paddled 1,500 miles down China's Yangtze River – from his home town of Jizhou to Shanghai – on the inner tube of a tyre. He said: "I put a basin in the tyre for my feet, while sitting on a board on top of the tyre. And I had two small bamboo paddles. That was all." He drifted on the current for forty-three days before finally arriving in Shanghai in August 2007. He had to complete the last hour of his voyage on a coastguard cutter as Shanghai authorities were worried that he might be a hazard to the city's busy river traffic – a valid concern as most boat captains would not exactly be expecting to encounter a guy on a tyre.

LONGEST VOYAGE BY A BOAT MADE
OF PLASTIC BOTTLES

In July 2010, the *Plastiki*, a sixty-foot catamaran constructed from 12,500 recycled plastic bottles, reached Sydney Harbour at the end of an 8,000-mile voyage across the Pacific from San Francisco. Throughout the four-month voyage the crew of six relied on renewable energy, including solar panels, wind turbines and bicycle-powered electricity generators, and used water recycled from urine.

LONGEST DISTANCE TRAVELLED BY
A MESSAGE IN A BOTTLE

An English schoolboy's message in a bottle washed ashore sixteen months later in Australia at the end of a record-breaking voyage of over 9,000 miles. Following an unsuccessful first launch where it travelled just a few metres, nine-year-old Cade Scott tossed the bottle into the North Sea at his local beach in Sunderland in August 2011. Sealed inside the wine bottle was a *Doctor Who* postcard on the back of which Cade had written: "I love *Doctor Who*. If found, please send back with your name and address and how old you are. Cade." In January 2013, he received a reply from twenty-five-year-old Matthew Elam who wrote: "Hi Cade, thanks for your postcard. I found it while celebrating Christmas on the beach in Perth, Western Australia! Happy New Year." Cade's father, Terry, described the bottle's voyage as "phenomenal", adding: "You wonder where it has been and what it has seen." Yes, if only wine bottles could talk . . .

OLDEST MESSAGE IN A BOTTLE TO BE FOUND

Scottish fisherman Andrew Leaper made the catch of a lifetime by discovering a ninety-eight-year-old message in a bottle when it got caught up in his net while he was trawling the waters off the Shetland Isles in 2012. The message was part of a 1914 research project to map Scottish sea currents and offered a reward of sixpence to the finder. "It was like winning the lottery," he beamed, which illustrates how much a Scotsman values sixpence. Coincidentally the previous world record was set onboard the same Shetland-based fishing boat, *Copius*, by Mark Anderson, a friend of Leaper, and who was also onboard this time around. Leaper joked: "I can tell you that my friend Mark Anderson is very unhappy that I have topped his record. He never stopped talking about it!"

BIGGEST AIRPLANE TO BE SUBMERGED AS A TOURIST ATTRACTION

In 2011, a forty-year-old, 157-foot-long Tupolev 154 airplane – once owned by former Bulgarian dictator Todor Zhivkov – was lowered to a depth of seventy feet into the water off the Black Sea coast about two miles from Varna to become the country's latest tourist attraction. Stripped of its engines and cables to avoid polluting the sea, the plane's final destination was to act as an artificial reef. It was hoped that sea vegetation would grow around it and lure shoals of fish, which in turn would make the location popular with scuba divers, particularly those nostalgic for the trappings of the old Communist regime.

SHORTEST SCHEDULED FLIGHT

The world's shortest scheduled flight is Loganair's twice-daily shuttle between the neighbouring islands of Westray and Papa Westray off the north coast of Scotland, the only instance where the safety demonstration takes longer than the flight. The 1.7-mile hop aboard the eight-seater plane takes just two minutes, but pilot Stuart Linklater, who completed the journey more than 13,000 times before retiring in 2013, says that with a favourable wind he has flown the route in only forty-seven seconds. The in-flight movie is probably a photograph of Al Pacino.

FIRST NAKED FLIGHT

The world's maiden naked flight carried eighty-seven nude passengers from Miami, Florida, to Cancun, Mexico, on 3 May 2003. The flight, which was arranged by a Houston, Texas, travel agency specializing in naturism, saw all the passengers except for the captain and crew cast aside their clothes as well as their seat belts when the plane reached its cruising altitude. No hot tea or coffee was served for fear of spills.

LONGEST INVERTED FLIGHT

On 24 July 1991, US airshow pilot Joann Osterud flew her biplane upside down for 4 hours 38 minutes 10 seconds on the 658-mile trip from Vancouver to Vanderhoof, British Columbia, to break the world inverted flight record of 4 hours 5 minutes 22 seconds that had been set by American aviator Milo Burcham back in December 1933. Osterud trained for her stunt by hanging upside down from a special rig in her living room for up to an hour at a time. Describing the experience of inverted flight, the forty-three-year-old said: "After an hour you feel like you have a really bad head cold. Your ears plug up. Then your face swells up." Asked moments before take-off why she was doing it, she replied with commendable honesty: "Because I'm not too smart."

HIGHEST ALTITUDE WEDDING

On 7 August 2013, five couples exchanged vows at an altitude of 41,000 feet on board a Fiji Airways flight from Auckland, New Zealand, to Nadi. Over 440 couples from New Zealand had entered a competition in the hope of being selected for the business class wedding, with the pilot flying south before doubling back in order to ensure that the plane was above New Zealand throughout the ceremony so that the marriages could be legally recognized under the country's law. The newlyweds' health was then toasted with champagne, which thankfully was not accompanied by some sort of chicken mush in a tinfoil dish.

HIGHEST ALTITUDE JOB INTERVIEW

ImageNet Co., described as one of Japan's leading internet apparel retailers, held job interviews in August 2005 at an altitude of 12,388 feet on the summit of the country's highest mountain, Mount Fuji. The company said it wanted to make sure that new employees would have what it takes to scale the heights of business.

LONGEST DURATION FLIGHT BY A PAPER PLANE

Once the preserve of the school classroom, the paper airplane has now developed into a serious aeronautical device in its own right with attendant competitiveness. American Ken Blackburn held the record for nearly thirty years, but in 2009 his time of 27.6 seconds was pipped by Japanese engineer

Takuo Toda, who managed to keep his paper plane airborne for 27.9 seconds. Made from a single sheet of paper with no cuts, Toda's design measured four inches from tip to tail. In December of the following year, Toda broke his own record with an indoor flight of 29.2 seconds at a high-ceilinged building in Hokkaido. Afterwards Toda, chairman of that respected body the Japanese Origami Airplane Association, said his achievement was merely the next step in his ambition of launching a paper plane into space.

FARTHEST DISTANCE FLOWN BY A PAPER PLANE AT A SOCCER MATCH

At a friendly soccer international between England and Peru at London's Wembley Stadium on 30 May 2014, a laminated paper plane launched from the upper tier by England fan Blair Valentine sailed 100 yards through the air before striking Peruvian defender Hansell Riojas on the pitch below. Despite England's 3–0 win, it was Valentine's guided missile which drew the loudest cheer of the night from the crowd as it hit Riojas gently in the side of the head. Within three days, the incident had clocked up almost three million views on YouTube. The twenty-two-year-old from Horsham, Sussex, who constructed the plane from a "noisemaker" given out to fans to clap against their hands during the game, said afterwards: "I'm not a paper plane enthusiast or anything like that. I just used to do them at school like everybody else. I saw that other people were throwing them, so I made one. It took about a minute to make and I remember seeing it sailing through the air. It took a kick just as it got down towards the pitch to help it go that bit further and then it almost took a right-hand turn before hitting the guy square in the side of the head. It was perfect."

FARTHEST DISTANCE FLOWN BY A BIRDMAN

First held in 1971, the International Birdman contest celebrates the pre-Wright Brothers days when men believed that they could fly by strapping a large pair of wings to their bodies and taking a giant leap into the unknown. The only difference is that at the International Birdman it is not a leap into the unknown but a leap into the English Channel . . . off Worthing Pier. Competitors run off an elevated ramp at the end of the pier and there is a £10,000 (about $17,000) prize for anyone who "flies" forwards a distance of 100 metres. When legendary ski jumper Eddie "The Eagle" Edwards had a go in 1989, he managed just eleven metres before splashdown. With many of the less serious aviators looking upon the event as an opportunity to dress up, entrants have included a pantomime horse, Donald Duck, a flying squirrel, Doctor Who, a skateboarding cow and the Pope.

In 2009, forty-seven-year-old Steve Elkins, from Hope, Derbyshire, set a new world record of 99.86 metres, thus tantalizingly missing out on the big money prize even though he claimed that video footage showed he had exceeded the distance. Elkins said he felt cheated. There was further controversy in 2013 after experienced Northumberland birdman Ron Freeman spent an unprecedented seventeen seconds in the air and flew 141.5 metres, only to be denied the prize because he had taken advantage of strong winds to fly sideways off the pier rather than forwards. However, there were no arguments at the 2014 event when Freeman flew a mightily impressive 159.4 metres (522 feet) in his adapted hang-glider the Geordie Flyer, although he had to share the prize money with Wiltshire's Tony Hughes who also broke the 100-metre barrier, reaching 117.1 metres (384 feet).

FARTHEST DISTANCE FLOWN BY A HUMAN CANNONBALL

The official world record for the farthest human cannonball flight is 193 feet 8.8 inches by American David "The Bullet"

Smith, Jr, in Milan, Italy, on 10 March 2011. Smith, who followed in the footsteps of his father and two older sisters as a professional projectile, was launched from a twenty-six-foot-long cannon and travelled at over 74 mph, reaching a maximum altitude of 75 feet. Describing what it's like to be a human cannonball, he says: "You climb down inside the cannon and prepare yourself for a blast that sends you from zero to about 50 mph in one-fifth of a second. You've got four seconds between when that cannon fires and when you're going to land, and a lot has to happen in that four seconds. You've got to recognize the way you came out of the cannon and correct your flight a little bit and do a somersault before you come crashing into the net. The whole thing's pretty wild and thrilling. When you tell them what you do for a living, people either think it's the coolest thing or they say, 'What, are you crazy?' My wife thought it was a unique pickup line when I first met her."

FIRST HUMAN CANNONBALL TO BE FIRED ACROSS AN INTERNATIONAL BORDER

In August 2005, Smith's father, David "Cannonball" Smith, Sr, was fired head first from a cannon across the US–Mexico border, taking off in Tijuana and landing south of San Diego. He took the precaution of waving his passport in the air before being propelled high over the border fence and into the United States. His other spectacular stunts have included being fired over a forty-three-foot-high Ferris wheel and also a baseball scoreboard. A former maths teacher, Smith, Sr, joined the circus as a trapeze artist before building his first cannon at the age of thirty-two and starting up a high-calibre family dynasty. So far, his wife, six of his children, his niece and her husband have all gone ballistic for a living. He didn't necessarily want his children to follow him into cannon-balling. "I didn't have a choice," he said. "I mean, kids, they grow up watching their dad do that stuff and then they want a cannon of their own. What am I going to say?"

LONGEST PUB CRAWL

Six friends from the West Midlands have been on one long pub crawl for over thirty years, visiting a different hostelry every Saturday night and drinking in more than 18,000 pubs, hotels and wine bars. Originally a team of twenty when they set off in 1984, the Black Country Ale Tairsters had slimmed down to six members by 2012 – father and son John and Peter Hill, John Drew, Kelvin Price, Richard Hill and Gary Mountain. They have visited inns in every county and region of England, Wales, Scotland and Northern Ireland. They keep a detailed written and photographic record of each pub they go to and even have their own score ratings cards, which they give to each landlord. Among the souvenirs they have collected on their travels are over 130 box files full of beer mats. Luckily partners are generally understanding. Crystal Tromans, girl-friend of Kelvin Price, said: "When I started going out with Kelvin, it was clear from the start that beer was part of the package. They have done it for so long, you know what you're getting into. You can't complain." In 2013, they reached a notable milestone by completing their pub crawl of Wales, having visited all 3,905 watering holes in a seven-year quest which saw them travel 76,000 miles. Peter Hill sums up: "I'll be doing this for as long as I can. It's hard to think of a hobby which is so much fun."

MOST VISITS TO PUBS NAMED THE RED LION

While staying in a pub in England's Lake District on 9 April 2011, Cathy Price, a personal trainer from Preston, Lancashire, read a sign stating that the Red Lion was the most popular pub name in the UK. On the spot she resolved to visit every Red Lion in the country, and long after the effects of that first drink have worn off she has continued with her selfless mission. In September 2014, she called in at her 500th Red Lion – near Whipsnade Zoo in Bedfordshire – leaving her with just over 100 more to visit. Her personal best is eleven

Red Lions in one day, although sometimes she arrives to find that the pub has closed down and become a "Dead Lion".

LONGEST DISTANCE MORRIS DANCED

Sixteenth-century English comic actor William Kempe appeared in a number of Shakespeare's early plays and was regarded as the leading physical clown of his day. He specialized in improvised jigs (usually performed after the play), which, according to *Encyclopedia Britannica*, "ranged from the wildly ridiculous to the overtly sexual". Alas, this tendency for improvisation did not go down well with Shakespeare himself who, not unreasonably, preferred his actors to stick to the script. He alluded to it when *Hamlet* warns: "Let those that play your clowns speak no more than is set down for them." It has been suggested that this was a barb directed at the ad-libbing Kempe. Whatever, the two men fell out and Kempe left Shakespeare's troupe in 1599. Seeking another way of entertaining the good folk of London and anxious to show the Bard what he had lost, Kempe then undertook what he would later call his "Nine Days Wonder". In February and March 1600, he morris danced all the way from London to Norwich – a distance of over 100 miles – in nine days, cheered on every prancing step of the way by enthusiastic onlookers. Clearly there wasn't much else to do back then. The positive publicity he received from the stunt enabled him to return to acting the following year, but his joy was short-lived as he died in 1603 when the plague hit London.

LONGEST DISTANCE DRIVEN IN A CAR WHILE HEADING A FOOTBALL

Agim Agushi, from Kosovo, travelled 4.4 miles in a car through Antalya, Turkey, on 17 August 2004 while heading a football. There are two points to be made here: firstly, Agushi wasn't driving and secondly, it was an open-topped car. If you're thinking of trying to break this record, it is important to take both factors into consideration.

LOWEST ROADWORTHY CAR

The Mirai, a battery-powered car created in 2012 by students and teachers from Okayama Sanyo High School in Asakuchi, Japan, measures just 17.79 inches from the ground to the top of the vehicle. Harada Kazunari, the school principal, conceded that it could be scary to drive the "Squashmobile" along a busy street, where the biggest danger was being run over by other cars. So for that reason whenever it ventures out onto the streets, it is guarded back and front by normal-sized cars. The Japanese mini auto snatched the record from British designer Perry Watkins, whose Flatmobile (converted from a 1963 Hillman Imp) stands 19 inches high and sold at auction for $15,000 in 2012.

CAR COVERED WITH MOST POSTAGE STAMPS

In 1936, Ed Hadley, from Casper, Wyoming, owned a car that was covered in 10,000 postage stamps. To advertise his ice cream and florist shop, he and five members of his family worked steadily for six weeks sticking the stamps, which came from sixty different countries, to the car's exterior. He then coated the stamps with a layer of varnish to protect them from the weather. He drove the car around for a year, and once it had served its publicity purpose, he invited local children to prise the stamps off with their pocket knives.

CAR COVERED WITH MOST STICKY NOTES

To play a prank on their co-worker Walt, Scott Ableman and a dozen of his colleagues from a company in Washington, DC, spent two hours in December 2006 covering virtually every inch of Walt's Jaguar car with 14,000 coloured sticky

Post-It notes. Only the licence plates and bonnet ornament were left exposed. Luckily Walt saw the funny side and, after removing the notes from the windscreen so that he could see, he drove it home to show his family.

CAR COVERED WITH MOST TOY CARS

Young British artist James A. Ford bought a 1984 Ford Capri on eBay for $150 with the sole purpose of turning the car into an art project by covering its exterior with 4,342 Matchbox toy cars. He spent three years, from 2003 to 2006, on the project, and called the finished vehicle General Carbuncle, a tribute to General Lee, the car from *The Dukes of Hazzard*.

OLDEST DRIVING INSTRUCTOR

Ninety-four-year-old Laura Thomas, from Pembroke Dock, Wales, celebrated seventy-five years as a driving instructor in 2014 – and in that time she has never been in an accident (even though she never uses dual controls) and none of her pupils has taken more than two attempts to pass their test. She started driving in 1938 when her brother bought her a car for Christmas, and passed her test two months later, becoming the first person in her area to do so. She soon started giving lessons to friends and, despite never advertising, estimates that she has taught more than 1,000 people to drive. The great-grandmother reckons her hairiest moment was probably when a pupil pulled the car's steering wheel off when she asked him to perform an emergency stop. Her daughter, Joan Stace, told the *Mirror*: "She taught me to drive when I was 17, and she's still telling me how to drive when I'm 74. When we're out and about she says, 'Do you realize you have failed your test there?' I sometimes throw my hands up in horror and say, 'Maybe you should take some time to relax, Mum!'"

LONGEST DISTANCE RIDING TWO HORSES
AT ONCE IN A STANDING POSITION

On 4 April 2008 at the Jaipur polo ground in Delhi, India, Mahesh Sharma rode two horses at the same time in a standing position for a distance of 9.3 miles. He completed the ride in twenty-three minutes at an average speed of just under 30 mph.

LONGEST MODERN-DAY HORSE RIDE
IN A FULL SUIT OF ARMOUR

In 1989, Scottish modern-day knight Dick Brown rode a horse for the 208 miles between Edinburgh and Dumfries while wearing a full suit of armour. It took him – and the horse – four days.

LONGEST DISTANCE RUN WITH A FRIDGE ON BACK

Tony Phoenix-Morrison, from Hebburn, Tyneside, ran 1,009 miles from John O'Groats, Scotland, to Land's End, Cornwall – forty marathons in forty days – with an eighty-eight-pound fridge on his back. The forty-nine-year-old grandfather, known as "Tony the Fridge", completed his epic journey with a kitchen appliance in September 2013, having run about seven hours per day. Despite suffering repeated hip pain from carrying his unusual load, the seasoned marathon runner insisted it was definitely not a case of a fridge too far.

LONGEST DISTANCE WALKED WITH A DOOR ON BACK

For five weeks in 2003, thirty-year-old carpenter Brian Walker, from Newcastle upon Tyne, walked all the way from Land's End to John O'Groats while carrying a solid, forty-pound pinewood door on his back. He said he was inspired by his father, Harry, having once carried a door home from a builder's yard four miles away.

FASTEST RUN ACROSS CANADA
DRESSED AS A SUPERHERO

Dressed as comic book superhero The Flash, twenty-seven-year-old adventurer Jamie McDonald, from Tredworth, Gloucestershire, ran 5,000 miles coast to coast across Canada in 331 days. He left St John's, Newfoundland, on 9 March 2013 and arrived in Vancouver, British Columbia, on 3 February 2014, having run the equivalent of 200 marathons. In the course of his eleven-month solo run, he was beaten up and robbed while celebrating New Year in Banff, Alberta, forced to sleep rough, battled temperatures of minus 40°C and wore through ten pairs of trainers. He began the feat just two weeks after cycling 14,000 miles from Bangkok to Gloucester, during which he was shot at and arrested. Whoever said record breaking was glamorous?

FIRST PERSON TO WALK THE
LENGTH OF BRITAIN NAKED

Former truck driver and Royal Marine Stephen Gough walked the length of Britain from Land's End to John O'Groats in 2003–4 wearing only boots, socks, a rucksack and occasionally a hat. The reason that The Naked Rambler, as he became known, took so long to complete the walk was because he was frequently arrested and imprisoned en route for offending public decency. He repeated the feat two years later and was again arrested more than twenty times – especially in Scotland – including once for contempt of court after appearing naked before a judge.

OLDEST POTATO FARMER TO RUN
FROM SYDNEY TO MELBOURNE

The 544-mile Sydney to Melbourne Ultramarathon – run between what were then Australia's two largest Westfield shopping centres, Westfield Parramatta in Sydney and Westfield Doncaster in Melbourne – took place annually from 1983 to 1991. The record time of 5 days 5 hours 7 minutes was set by Greek runner Yiannis Kouros in 1985 (the first of his five wins in the event), but the true hero came in that inaugural year when Victoria potato farmer and part-time athlete Cliff Young won at the ripe old age of sixty-one.

Young trained for the event by spending three days rounding up sheep on the family farm while wearing gumboots, and said afterwards that during the race he imagined he was chasing sheep. Luckily he didn't try counting them. Yet it was a different animal that provided his tactical inspiration – the tortoise from the fable about the hare and the tortoise. For while the other runners hared off, Young jogged along at his own pace and, by going to bed later than his rivals and getting up earlier, he managed to keep running while they slept. He took the lead during the first night and was never headed again, eventually winning by 10 hours, with only six athletes finishing. His time of 5 days 15 hours 4 minutes was almost two days faster than the record for any previous run between the two cities. His winning smile was all the more engaging for being toothless, as he always removed his false teeth before he ran because they clattered about in his head.

FIRST PERSON TO WALK BACKWARDS ACROSS THE GRAND CANYON

On 24 September 2008, fifty-six-year-old fitness fanatic Bill Kathan, from Brattleboro, Vermont, became the first person to walk backwards across the Grand Canyon from rim to rim. Starting from one side, he walked in reverse down to the basin and back up the other side in 15 hours 23 minutes – a hike that covered a distance of twenty-four miles and included a 6,000-foot total elevation change.

FASTEST BACKWARDS RUN ACROSS THE UNITED STATES

Arvind Pandya of India ran 3,187 miles backwards across the United States from Los Angeles to New York in 107 days, between 18 August and 3 December 1984. Six years later, he ran the length of Britain backwards, completing the 874-mile trek from John O'Groats, Scotland, to Land's End, Cornwall, in 26 days.

LONGEST TIME SPENT WALKING BACKWARDS

Mani Manithan, a mobile phone salesman from India's Tamil Nadu state, has walked everywhere backwards since 14 June 1989 in a worthy, if naive, attempt to achieve world peace. He even climbs stairs backwards and once walked 300 miles backwards and naked from his home village to the city of Chennai. Yet still the world's warmongers were not sufficiently impressed to lay down their arms. He says he has been walking backwards for so long that "walking normally is more of a challenge – my mind has forgotten how to do it." We're sure it will soon come back to him.

MOST BUILDINGS CLIMBED WITH NO SAFETY GEAR

Known as "The Human Fly", George Polley was an early version of Spiderman, climbing 2,000 buildings using just his bare hands and no safety ropes. His unusual career began in 1910 when, admiring an unaffordable suit in a Chicago store window, young Polley told the owner: "I'd stand on my head on top of this building for a suit like that!" The owner accepted the challenge, and George got his suit along with a wealth of publicity. As his fame spread, he was regularly hired for store openings. He was sponsored by the Essex Motor Car Company, which paid him a reported $200 for each building he climbed. In Boston, Massachusetts, he climbed 406 feet up the thirty-two-storey Custom House Tower; in Hartford, Connecticut, he scaled three buildings in one day; and in Providence, Rhode Island, he shinned up a flagpole blindfold. In 1920, he set off to climb the fifty-seven-storey Woolworth Building in New York, then the tallest in the world, but on the thirtieth floor a police officer stuck his head out of a window and arrested him for climbing a building without an official permit. Polley loved to play to the crowds by faking a slip while hundreds of feet above ground, but his luck ran out in 1927 when he died during an operation to remove a brain tumour at the age of twenty-nine.

HIGHEST MOUNTAIN CLIMBED ON STILTS

In August 2011, Ashrita Furman, a man seemingly unable to refuse any challenge, climbed California's 9,407-foot-high (2,867 metres) Mount Baden-Powell on a pair of three-foot-tall metal stilts. He may well have surpassed that altitude a month earlier when he travelled to Peru with the intention of climbing the 10,009-foot-high (3,050 metres) Cerro Machu Picchu on stilts. Sadly he was refused entry to the mountain as the only person with authority to grant him permission was not around. It was his day off.

LONGEST DISTANCE WALKED ON STILTS

Setting off from New York in July 1957 and finishing in Los Angeles in November of that year, American Pete McDonald crossed the United States on a pair of 26-inch-high metal stilts, walking 3,200 miles in 124 days for a fee of $1,500.

TALLEST STILTS EVER WALKED ON

On 1 November 2008, at the eleventh time of asking, Australian stuntman Roy Maloy managed to walk five steps on a pair of stilts that were 56 feet 6 inches tall and weighed nearly 66 pounds. He had to be lowered onto the stilts through an open sixth-floor window of a tower block.

LONGEST DISTANCE WALKED IN
A PAIR OF IRON SHOES

Since 2006, fifty-three-year-old Chinese factory worker Zhang Fuxing has walked nearly thirty miles in a pair of iron shoes, each of which weighs more than 440 pounds, to cure his back pain and haemorrhoids. He walks fifteen metres a day in the weights, which are strapped on to his everyday shoes, even though it takes him over a minute to manage ten paces. He claims that his crippling back pain vanished just months after donning the heavy metal shoes. He is so confident in their powers that he has started manu-facturing them, and has already sold at least ten pairs to health-conscious neighbours. The solid blocks may not look terribly fashionable (they do little to enhance a pair of Guccis), but they can be left outdoors safe in the knowledge that few people would be able to steal them.

LONGEST DISTANCE WALKING BACKWARDS
WITH A TURKEY ON HEAD

To highlight Britain's obesity epidemic, eccentric performance artist Mark McGowan walked backwards for eleven miles through the streets of London in 2003 with a twenty-seven-pound dead turkey on top of his head. Along the way he shouted at overweight people through a homemade loud hailer.

LONGEST DISTANCE ROLLED ALONG THE GROUND

To promote peace, holy man Lotan Baba has, over the years, rolled his body more than 19,000 miles along the ground to various Indian cities, often smoking a cigarette while in motion. In 1993, the Rolling Saint, as he is known, completed an epic 2,500-mile roll across India, covering up to ten miles a day. A team of a dozen assistants swept the ground in front of him with brooms, but he still had to negotiate puddles, city traffic and herds of elephants. Children sometimes lobbed him sweets and other items of food, which he would try to catch in his mouth at each rotation. Earlier in his life, he undertook penance by standing under a banyan tree for seven years and eating grass, thereby setting a world record for the longest time spent standing under a banyan tree and eating grass.

LONGEST DISTANCE CRAWLED

Over a period of fifteen months, ending on 9 March 1985, thirty-two-year-old Jagdish Chander crawled 870 miles from Aligarh to Jamma, India, to appease the Hindu goddess Mata.

LONGEST ESCALATOR RIDE

Multiple record holder Suresh Joachim travelled 140 miles up and down the escalators at the Westfield Shopping Centre in Burwood, New South Wales, Australia, over a period of six days between 25 and 31 May 1998.

LONGEST ROCKING CHAIR MARATHON

Between 24 and 27 August 2005, Suresh Joachim rocked continuously on a rocking chair for seventy-five hours at the Hilton Garden Inn, Toronto, Canada. An hour-and-a-half into the challenge, he warned that comfort – not fatigue – was the biggest barrier he had to overcome. "It's very comfortable, but maybe too comfortable. I'm rocking back and forth, so I'm going to get sleepy. That could be a very difficult problem." Happily the record books show that he managed to ward off any feelings of drowsiness and kept on rocking, but it was a still a lot of time to spend going nowhere.

LONGEST BACKWARDS MOTORCYCLE RIDE

For some people, simply riding a long distance isn't enough; they have to do it backwards. Hou Xiaobin did just that on his motorcycle in Binzhou City, China, in October 2006, sitting with his back to the handlebars for 93.21 miles. It is surely an oversight that no record exists for the most people run over by a motorcycle on the same day.

FARTHEST DISTANCE FOR RIDING A MOTORCYCLE ON WATER

"Say the words motocross bike and I smell the word hospital," confessed British TT rider and all-round daredevil Guy Martin. But the possibility of ending up in traction was never going to be enough to deter him from attempting a challenge, and in 2013 he set a new world record when he rode his motorbike a distance of 208.5 feet on water at Bala Lake in North Wales. To encourage the bike to hydroplane across the surface of the 100-foot-deep lake like a skipping stone, he entered the water down a shallow ramp at a steady 45 mph while sitting as far back on the machine as possible. A light-weight aluminium ski was also attached to the rear wheel to help keep the bike afloat. The only certainty about riding a bike on deep water is that it will end in a crash when the hydroplaning stops, and so before the record attempt Martin underwent a series of practice crashes to perfect his dismount and escape in order to ensure that he didn't wake up to find himself surrounded by men in white coats.

FASTEST MOTORCYCLE WHEELIE ON ICE

Using special studs on his tyres, fearless stunt rider Ryan Suchanek clocked a speed of 109.5 mph while performing a motorbike wheelie across a frozen Lake Koshkonong, Wisconsin, on 1 February 2014. He managed to stay upright for more than 200 metres to break his previous world record of 108.5 mph set the previous year. Making his achievement all the more startling is the fact that in 2007 he was hit by a car while riding home from work and when he finally woke up six weeks later he found that his left leg had been amputated below the knee.

LONGEST WAIT TO BE REUNITED WITH A STOLEN MOTORCYCLE

Donald DeVault was reunited with his 1953 Triumph Tiger 100 motorcycle in November 2013 – forty-six years after it was stolen. The bike, which had acquired vintage status over the missing decades, was about to be shipped from Los Angeles to Japan when customs agents checking the vehicle identification number discovered that it had been reported stolen in February 1967. So instead it was returned to seventy-three-year-old DeVault at his home in Omaha, Nebraska. When the bike was stolen, it was worth $300; today it's worth around $9,000. "I bet there's a lot of stories she could tell me," said a delighted DeVault, straddling the machine, "because a lot's happened in 46 years. I wish she could talk." Ah, but that's the drawback with motorbikes, Donald. They may be exhilarating to ride, but they're not renowned for being great conversationalists.

LARGEST MOTORCYCLE WEDDING PROCESSION

Avid bikers Peter Schmidl and Anna Turceková had a wedding procession of 597 motorcycles when they got married in Bratislava, Slovakia, on 6 May 2000, helped in part because their nuptials clashed with a major local bike event, Chopper Show 2000.

MOST PEOPLE ON ONE MOTORCYCLE

The sight of dozens of people hanging precariously to the sides of Indian trains is simply part of the daily commute, but, even by the eccentric transport customs of the subcontinent, motorcycles generally cater for a maximum of two persons. However, on 28 November 2010, no fewer than fifty-four members of the Indian Army Service Corps Motorcycle Display Team managed to squeeze onto a single Royal Enfield Classic 500 motorbike. Admittedly the machine did have a narrow platform around the edge to accommodate all the standing passengers but it still had to be ridden 1,000 metres down a runway in Bangalore to set a new Guinness World Record.

LONGEST MOTORCYCLE

When he was not busy designing the world's fastest toilet or the world's biggest fart machine, Lincolnshire plumber Colin Furze built the world's longest motorcycle – a seventy-two-foot-long monster that could carry twenty-five people. It took him a month in 2011 to convert the 125cc scooter into a vehicle the length of a tennis court by use of an extended aluminium frame. He constructed it in three parts in his mum's back garden and then bolted them together. He even managed to ride it for over a mile at a nearby airfield runway, reaching a top speed of 35 mph. He said afterwards: "When I first got on it I thought it would never work, and at a slow speed it's almost impossible to keep upright. But once you get going it becomes a bit easier, although it is a real strain on your arms as it has such heavy steering. It wobbled a huge amount as I drove along and apparently the back of the bike was weaving around all over the place. The motorbike was so heavy and difficult to drive that I think it would be impossible to make a longer one. I think this record will stand for a very long time."

BIGGEST MOTORCYCLE

At Motor Bike Expo 2012 in Verona, Italy, Fabio Reggiani unveiled a 5,000cc monster machine that stood 16 feet 8 inches high, 33 feet long and weighed over 5.5 tons, making it six times larger than a regular motorcycle. It may sound like a dream to ride until you realize that for a bike of that size to stay upright it needs a pair of stabilizers, which somewhat reduces its cool factor.

FASTEST MOTORCYCLE HANDLEBAR WHEELIE

On 11 July 2006 at Elvington Air Field, York, Irishman Enda Wright revved his 97 Honda Fireblade up to a speed of 108 mph before throwing his legs over the handlebars and performing a wheelie.

LONGEST DISTANCE JUMPED ON A HARLEY-DAVIDSON

American stuntman Seth Enslow flew a distance of 183.7 feet between ramps near Australia's Sydney Harbour on 2 March 2010 to set a new world record for the longest distance jumped on a Harley-Davidson. The previous record of 157 feet, set by Bubba Blackwell in Las Vegas, had stood since 1999. Enslow even had to smash the record twice on the day – after the assembled media cameramen were not ready for his first jump of 175 feet.

MOST BUSES JUMPED OVER BY A MOTORCYCLE

On 29 August 1983, Welsh stuntman Chris Bromham took off on his motorbike at just under 100 mph, soared thirty feet into the air and cleared a world record eighteen double-decker buses at Norman Park, Bromley, Kent. He had been married just three weeks at the time and his jump beat

American daredevil Evel Knievel's old record of fourteen buses.

MOST MOTORCYCLES JUMPED OVER BY A BUS

In a novel twist to the Evel Knievel spectaculars that were popular in the 1970s, a double-decker bus driven by Hans Tholstrup drove up a seven-foot ramp and jumped over thirteen motorcycles at Sydney Showground, Australia, in 1980. The vehicle was called Dick Smith's Flying Bus, and Smith, who at the time was editor of *Australian Geographic* magazine, was also on board, gamely clinging to a pole at the rear of the bus performing conductor duties. Smith had no safety harness as the bus flew through the air, his only protection being a couple of bed mattresses on the stairs. The bus had no engine but was pushed to a speed of 65 mph by a Land Rover which then peeled off. As the bus landed steeply with an almighty thud, it crushed the fourteenth and end bike in the line (luckily they were all scrap machines) and buckled alarmingly in the middle. The bus's tyres also blew on impact. Although driver Tholstrup's safety equipment amounted to little more than standard straps plus a boat lifebelt positioned between his body and the steering wheel, he emerged unharmed, as did Smith, to wild cheers from the crowd. This was not Smith's first venture into the absurd. In 1978, he had attempted to tow an iceberg from Antarctica to Australia in order to obtain extra supplies of fresh water.

LONGEST MOTORCYCLE VOYAGE

A Harley-Davidson that was swept out to sea by the 2011 Japanese tsunami washed ashore the following year on the coast of Canada, some 3,125 miles away. The rusted bike was found half-buried in the sand on Graham Island, off the coast of British Columbia, and was identified as belonging to Ikuo Yokoyama who immediately asked for it to be sent back.

LONGEST DISTANCE CYCLED BACKWARDS WHILE PLAYING THE VIOLIN

Christian Adam, of Lübeck, Germany, learned to ride a bicycle at the age of four and began playing the violin three years later. Then in 2007 he had the brainwave of combining his two talents with the added twist of sitting backwards on his bike and wearing a tuxedo. His world record for cycling backwards while playing the violin is 37.56 miles in 5 hours 9 minutes. He would have gone on for longer had he not crashed into another cyclist who was out for an afternoon ride, oblivious to the fact that history was in the making. Unfortunately for Adam, the other cyclist happened to be the local police inspector, meaning that his joy at setting a world record was tempered by having to pay for the cost of repairs.

FASTEST BACKWARDS BICYCLE RIDE

Sitting backwards on the handlebars of his bicycle, Norwegian Eskil Ronningsbakken pedalled down a wet and winding three-mile mountain road at Trollstigen at speeds of up to 50 mph in November 2013. It may sound foolhardy, but when you're someone who has previously hung upside down from a hot-air balloon, done a handstand on the edge of a hotel roof and cycled on a tightrope between two mountains, it's really just another day at the office.

LONGEST DISTANCE CYCLED STANDING ON HANDS

The Czech Republic's Martina Štepánková, who was the individual artistic cycling world champion in 1998, 1999 and 2002, set a new world record by riding a distance of 3,125 metres – that's about two miles – by standing on her hands the whole way. One hand was on the handlebar and the other was on the saddle.

MOST STAIRS CLIMBED BY BICYCLE

It must be tough enough trying to walk up 2,000 stairs of a skyscraper, so imagine what it would be like trying to ride a bicycle up them – especially one with no saddle and doing it in such a way that your hands and feet never touch the ground. Well, on 17 March 2013, thirty-one-year-old Polish extreme cyclist Krystian Herba hopped on his bike up 2,754 steps to reach the 100th floor of the Shanghai World Financial Centre. It took him 1 hour 21 minutes 53 seconds to go 700 steps further than any cyclist had gone before. It was the eighth skyscraper bike climb for the PE teacher from Rzeszow. Next time, take the lift.

LONGEST DISTANCE CYCLED ON HONEYMOON

American–Belgian newlyweds Amy and Wim Meeussen cycled all the way to China for their 2007 honeymoon – a distance of 6,780 miles across Europe, North Africa and Asia. "We had never done any biking before," recalls Amy. "We didn't even know about butt pain before we started." Although they encountered numerous potholes and patches of broken glass, they only suffered three punctures throughout the entire trip. The 305 days they spent away from home must also constitute one of the world's longest honeymoons.

FASTEST BICYCLE RIDE DOWN AN ACTIVE VOLCANO

Since the mid-1800s Nicaragua's Cerro Negro volcano has erupted twenty-three times, but the menacing mountain is now a tourist attraction thanks to the extreme sport of volcano boarding. After scaling the 2,400-foot-high peak in 2006, Australian Darryn Webb was looking for a faster way to come down. He tried surfboards, fridge doors, mattresses, anything he could find, until he finally settled on a wooden sled, which has gone on to form the basis for the sport. The current speed record on a sled is 54 mph, but back on 12 May

2002, Frenchman Eric Barone made an even faster descent of Cerro Negro – on a bicycle. A former stunt double for Sylvester Stallone and Jean-Claude Van Damme, Barone reached the incredible speed of 107 mph before crashing. He thus broke the world record and five ribs.

FIRST PERSON TO CYCLE AROUND SOUTH AMERICA DRESSED AS A CLOWN

In 2001, Alvaro Neil gave up his job as a lawyer in Oviedo, Spain, and sold his car so that he could cycle around South America dressed as a clown. Nineteen months later, the man who calls himself The Biciclown had ridden 19,200 miles through ten countries. Finding the experience considerably more rewarding emotionally (but certainly not financially) than being a lawyer, in 2004 he set off on a new cycling challenge – to clown his way around 100 countries in 10 years, performing to people who had never seen a clown before. Some might say they should count themselves lucky.

LONGEST DISTANCE CYCLED UNDERWATER

Two former British Royal Marines, fifty-four-year-old Chris Sirett and forty-year-old Brian Stokes, cycled underwater for a world record distance of 100.13 miles at the 2012 Southampton Boat Show. Wearing full diving equipment, they jumped into the water-filled tank and cycled on exercise bikes for fifteen hours, at which point the adventure was brought to an end because both men were feeling light-headed and nauseous.

MOST CONCRETE STEPS ROLLED DOWN AND UP

Every morning, fifty-two-year-old Li Chia deliberately rolls down thirty concrete steps at Changle Park in Xi'an, China, and once he reaches the bottom he slowly rolls back up to the top again. This may appear a particularly pointless exercise, but Li does it to massage his body by making sure that every pressure point comes into contact with the hard concrete. "I got the idea from rolling on pebbles at a health club," he says, "and when I couldn't find any pebbles at my local park, I decided to try the steps and was surprised to find it really works. I don't believe that any masseuse would be able to give me the sort of massage I get from the impact of the steps." He has been undertaking this strange daily ritual for more than three years, during which time he has descended and ascended in excess of 66,000 steps without suffering a single bruise.

OLDEST PAPER GIRL

When her grandson elected to give up his newspaper round in 1979, Beryl Walker offered to take it over – and in 2014 the eighty-eight-year-old former Post Office worker from Gloucester, England, was officially acknowledged as the oldest paper girl in the world. In those thirty-five years, she has clocked up over 40,000 miles on her bicycle and delivered half a million newspapers, working six days a week and cycling over eight miles a day. "We're all very proud of her," said her son David. "Mum goes out in all weathers and nothing seems to bother her. She is on her third bike. The first was a 1940s model and the second one was stolen. This latest model – she calls it Hercules – has served her well." Beryl confirmed that she had no intention of stopping any time soon. "I'll give it up when it gives me up," she said. Remarkably at the time of her award Beryl was not even the town's oldest newspaper deliverer. That title belonged to ninety-two-year-old World War II veteran Jack Mews, the UK's oldest paper boy.

LONGEST TANDEM RIDE WITH A FULL-SIZED ARTIFICIAL SKELETON ON THE BACK SEAT

Inspired by the recordsetter website, Kadhim Shubber, a final-year physics student at Imperial College, London, cycled 891 miles from John O'Groats to Land's End in July 2012 with a full-sized fake skeleton on the back of his tandem. Now you're probably thinking that the record for the longest tandem ride with a full-sized artificial skeleton on the back seat is so specialized, to put it politely, that nobody has even set one before, but you'd be wrong. There was an existing record to break – 437 miles, set back in 1987 by Art Hoffman (and skeleton), from Louisville, Kentucky.

FASTEST TANDEM RIDE THE LENGTH OF BRITAIN

In 1966, Pete Swindon and John Withers rode a tandem bicycle the length of Britain – Land's End to John O'Groats – in 2 days 2 hours 14 minutes 25 seconds.

FASTEST QUADRICYCLE RIDE THE LENGTH OF BRITAIN

Hugh Catchpole, George Unwin, Tom Bethell and Richard Nicholls rode a four-man recumbent cycle weighing 250 pounds the length of Britain in 10 days 15 hours in 2012.

FASTEST UNICYCLE RIDE THE LENGTH OF BRITAIN

In September 2009, Sam Wakeling and Roger Davies rode unicycles from Land's End to John O'Groats in 6 days 8 hours 43 minutes.

LONGEST UNICYCLE RIDE

Lutheran pastor Revd Lars J. Clausen rode a unicycle a distance of 9,136 miles on a 205-day journey around the United States, from the west coast to the Statue of Liberty and back again, in order to raise money for Eskimos in Alaska. He started in Washington State on 22 April 2002 and finished on Los Angeles on 12 November, having visited all fifty states. He rode about fifty miles a day on his thirty-six-inch unicycle, travelling at a steady 10 mph. This was definitely not a speed test. Asked about his unusual mode of transport, he replied: "I started unicycling when I was 10 years old, and although it took me a couple of weeks to learn, I have been unicycling ever since. Fifteen years ago, I bicycled across the country, and it was one of the greatest experiences of my life. My wife and I honeymooned on a bicycle. So the unicycle seemed like a natural thing to do this time." He reckoned he fell off the unicycle every couple of weeks, but the falls bothered him less than the effort of pedalling up and down hills. "The unicycle had no gears, so I couldn't coast down hills. Although it had a special brake that set the wheel at a certain rotation rate while descending a hill to relieve the pressure on my ankles, I had to pedal constantly just to stay balanced. I estimated that I completed around 3.5 million pedals in total."

LONGEST DISTANCE RIDING A
UNICYCLE ON BEER BOTTLES

Germany's Lutz Eichholz is the undisputed king of riding a unicycle along the mouths of a row of vertically standing beer bottles. In September 2011, he achieved a distance of 8.93 metres, which is just over 29 feet, and beat his previous world record by a metre.

MOST ROPE SKIPS ON A UNICYCLE IN ONE MINUTE

Peter Nestler performed 237 rope skips on a unicycle in one minute at a school in Conroe, Texas, on 20 February 2013, beating the previous world record by 17. He achieved his goal even though the excitement and anticipation meant that he had only got thirty minutes of sleep the previous night.

MOST BUNNY HOPS ON A UNICYCLE

In February 2013, a young American, Nick Maranville, performed 800 consecutive bunny hops on a unicycle, breaking the previous world record by thirty-two. His YouTube post makes for incredible viewing – if your idea of a good video is seeing someone bounce up and down for five minutes.

MOST STAIRS CLIMBED ON A UNICYCLE

Sweden's Peter Rosendahl is billed as the fastest man on one wheel by virtue of having ridden 100 metres on a unicycle in 12.11 seconds from a standing start in Las Vegas, on 25 March 1994. He began riding a unicycle at the age of seven and five years later predicted that he would be the unicycle world champion and a world record holder. He has gone on to hold over thirty unicycling world records, including one for hopping up 525 stairs on a unicycle in 9 minutes 27 seconds and another for ascending 56 stairs in 30 seconds on a unicycle.

FASTEST SKATEBOARD RIDE THE LENGTH OF BRITAIN

In 2010, teenagers Matt Elver, Charlie Mason and Lee Renshaw, all from Plymouth, Devon, skateboarded from John O'Groats to Land's End in twenty-one days, averaging just under fifty miles a day and beating the previous record by five days. Renshaw gamely skated on for 300 miles despite suffering a blister that infected his leg to below the knee, while

Elver admitted that it had been a tough challenge. "I didn't know what to expect when we started out," he said, "but going up some of the hills in Scotland and the Lake District, I thought I might die." But he didn't.

LONGEST TRACTOR WHEELIE

Long-haul trucker Mike Hagan, from Whitehall, Montana, drove a farm tractor a distance of 7.6 miles on just its two rear wheels in 2009. The successful run broke his own world record of 5.3 miles set the previous year, and was the culmination of five years of intense preparation. Hagan said his record was a tribute to the late Evel Knievel, curiously a man not overly associated with tractors.

LONGEST WHEELCHAIR WHEELIE

Xie Junwu travelled sixteen miles on the rear wheels of his wheelchair around a school athletics track in Jiangsu, China, on 12 May 2012.

LONGEST TRACTOR JOURNEY

In 2005, Vasilii Hazkevich drove a tractor a distance of 13,172 miles on a three-month round trip, starting and finishing in Vladimir, Russia. However, this admirable feat might not have been appreciated if you were unfortunate enough to have been stuck behind him the whole way.

FASTEST TIME TO DRIVE A MECHANICAL DIGGER THE LENGTH OF BRITAIN

In May 1997, Hugh Edeleanu drove a mechanical digger from John O'Groats to Land's End in 22 hours 10 minutes 30 seconds, cutting nearly 11 hours off the old record. He powered his customized, turbo-charged excavator at an aver-age speed of 40 mph, compared to a normal JCB's maximum of 18 mph.

FASTEST TIME TO RIDE A MOTORIZED TOILET THE LENGTH OF BRITAIN

Tank Regiment Sergeant Hank Harp, from Crewkerne, Somerset, drove a three-wheeled motorized toilet from Land's End to John O'Groats in thirty days, from 21 August to 20 September 1999. It was all cisterns go for Sgt Harp as he sat on the seat of the chemical toilet, which was powered by a twenty-four-volt electric motor, giving it a modest top speed of 4 mph. He was able to store all the supplies he needed for his 874-mile journey in the bowl. Sgt Harp only made his way into the record books by a twist of fate, being a late replace-ment in the hot seat after the original driver pulled out. Perhaps his predecessor got cold feet if the idea was first sold to him as spending a month on the toilet while being watched by hundreds of strangers.

FASTEST TIME TO RIDE A LAWN MOWER THE LENGTH OF BRITAIN

Darren Whitehead, forty, from Stoke-on-Trent, and Tony Dwight, thirty-nine, from Wigan, travelled 1,071 miles from John O'Groats to Land's End (including a detour across the Welsh border) in five days in August 2011 aboard two ride-on lawn mowers. They drove for up to twelve hours a day and waved at children to relieve the monotony. Acknowledging that the two men made a strange sight, Whitehead said: "A lot of people were open-jawed as we went past and some shook their heads in bemusement."

LONGEST LAWN MOWER RIDE

Setting off from Portland, Maine, in May 2000, Gary Hatter rode on a lawn mower for 14,594.5 miles, arriving in Daytona Beach, Florida, in February 2001. Riding on average for ten hours a day, his 260-day ride took him through all forty-eight contiguous US states as well as Canada and Mexico. His diesel-powered mower hit a top speed of 9 mph and was fitted with lights and mirrors to make it roadworthy. As one man went to mow, he took it to places where few lawn mowers have been before, climbing the auto road up Mount Washington in New Hampshire, where temperatures plunged from 27°C at the start to below freezing at the summit, and receiving a police escort through the Lincoln Tunnel in New York City.

LONGEST RICKSHAW PULL

Sitdek Ahmad Ali from Malaysia pulled a rickshaw a distance of 1,351.5 miles in fifty days between October and November 2000, averaging just under thirty miles a day.

LONGEST SEGWAY JOURNEY

Tired of their corporate jobs in Phoenix, Arizona, aspiring filmmakers Josh Caldwell and Hunter Weeks handed in their resignations to pursue a friend's crazy idea of riding a two-wheel motorized Segway with a top speed of 10 mph across the United States from coast to coast. With Weeks filming the adventure for the subsequent documentary, aptly titled *10 MPH*, Caldwell set off from Seattle, Washington, on 8 August 2004 and rode the two-wheeled electronic scooter for 4,064 miles along the back roads of America, finally reaching Boston, Massachusetts, more than 100 days and 400 battery charges later on 18 November. In the course of their seven-teen-state journey, they introduced the Segway to Native Americans and toured Chicago escorted by Segway-riding police officers, although Caldwell also fell foul of an Illinois police officer who admonished him for travelling at 10 mph on a road with a 45 mph speed limit. He might have explained in his defence that he was going as fast as he could.

LONGEST DISTANCE HITCHHIKED BY A ROBOT

HitchBOT, a two-foot-tall robot created by Ontario university researchers David Harris Smith and Frauke Zeller, hitchhiked 3,728 miles across Canada from coast to coast. Immobile apart from one motorized arm that it used to hitch rides, HitchBOT set off from Halifax, Nova Scotia, on 27 July 2014 and arrived on the Pacific coast at Victoria, British Columbia, three weeks later on 18 August. Although it was built from an old beer cooler bucket, solar panels and a computer, and had foam pool noodles for its arms and legs, the gumboot-wearing robot had no problem getting lifts from passing motorists. In fact, at the very start of its journey HitchBOT was picked up just two minutes after being left on a roadside near Halifax airport. At the outset, its creators had feared that the robot might be kidnapped or destroyed either by latter-day Canadian Luddites, or simply those with a thirst for publicity, but except for a small crack on the plastic part of its head, no medical attention was required. En route, it enjoyed tea at a luxury hotel, attended a tribal powwow in Wikwemikong, Ontario, and gate-crashed a wedding in Golden, British Columbia, where it even took to the floor, no doubt showing fellow revellers exactly how to do the robot dance.

MOST NAKED RIDERS ON A ROLLERCOASTER

On 9 August 2010, 102 naked thrill-seekers rode the Green Scream roller-coaster at Southend-on-Sea, Essex, breaking the existing world record of thirty-two naked riders set in Staffordshire back in 2004.

LONGEST DISTANCE LEAPFROGGING

On 19 July 1974, Mike Barwell and Wally Adams from East Yorkshire leapfrogged a distance of 17 miles 342 yards (27,670.6 metres) in eight hours. They averaged one leap every five yards along the disused railway line between Sutton and Hornsea, Humberside.

MOST HOUSE MOVES

Since marrying in Yorkshire in 1955, Orina Wyness, from Blackpool, has lived in sixty different houses – on average living in a different house every year and some for just a few weeks. She had to move home whenever her husband Ray, a naval petty officer, received a new posting. As a result she has lived all over the UK, from the Lake District to Cornwall and many points in between, as well as in France, Gibraltar, and at least half a dozen different locations in Australia. Their daughter attended sixteen schools in eight years. Although moving house is supposed to be one of life's more stressful experiences, she has taken it all in her stride. "It's exciting. I just like moving. I like waking up in a different setting. If we fancied going on holiday, we just got up, took all our possessions and moved house instead. It's like a disease. We just can't settle wherever we are. It is constantly in your subconscious, thinking, 'Right, where are we going to move next?' We're thinking about just drawing a triangle between the places we've been and going wherever is in the middle." That would work out somewhere around the Seychelles. It certainly beats Blackpool.

FIRST PERSON TO RACE – AND BEAT – A LONDON UNDERGROUND TRAIN

Commuter James Heptonstall jumped off a London Underground train at one station, sprinted along to the next station and managed to catch the same train with two seconds to spare. The thirty-year-old environmental consultant from Hampstead undertook the 2014 challenge on the Circle Line, dashing off the train at Mansion House and running 415 yards (380 metres) overground to rejoin it at Cannon Street to the acclaim of his fellow passengers. He completed the stunt in just eighty seconds, having chosen a section of the network where the stations are close together and where there are not too many steps to negotiate. Even so, he still had to tackle seventy-five steps and two ticket barriers. He said he did it to show that travelling on foot can be just as fast as taking the Tube – at least over a short distance.

FASTEST TIME TO VISIT ALL 270 LONDON UNDERGROUND STATIONS

On 16 August 2013, Geoff Marshall and Anthony Smith visited all 270 London Underground stations in 16 hours 20 minutes 27 seconds, knocking eight minutes off the previous record. Although the pair refused to divulge their exact route, they finished at Heathrow Terminal 5 and revealed that they started from the outside of the map before working their way into Central London. "It takes more skill than people think," said Marshall, a forty-one-year-old freelance video producer for whom it was the second time he had held the record in twenty-five attempts. "You have to get off one line and run to the other. We ran from Cockfosters to High Barnet, so it's a combination of athleticism and the ability to decode a Tube timetable. People tar you with a trainspotter brush, but I've never written down a train number in my life."

FASTEST TIME TO VISIT ALL 468 NEW YORK CITY SUBWAY STATIONS

A team of six English invaders broke the world record for the fastest time to travel the entire New York City Subway system when they completed the challenge in 22 hours 26 minutes 2 seconds on 18 November 2013. Andy James, Steve Wilson and Martin Hazel had also once held the London Tube challenge, and for their Big Apple mission they were joined by Glen Bryant, Peter Smythe and Adam Fisher. "Winning the challenge is all about the navigation," said James, "but you also have to sprint through some stations to keep on track. You don't get any sleep in 24 hours."

FASTEST TIME TO TRAVEL ON EVERY BUS ROUTE IN BUENOS AIRES

Between September 2011 and April 2012, writer Daniel Tunnard, a Yorkshireman living in Argentina, travelled on all 141 bus routes in the city of Buenos Aires, documenting his journeys in a blog and book titled *Colectivaizeishon*. On a typical day, he would take three routes, sitting on buses for up to fourteen hours. The whole adventure cost him a mere 380 pesos (about $80). He said: "The 39 from Barracas to Chacarita is my favourite because there's a sign on the window wishing you a happy birthday, even if it isn't your birthday. You don't get that kind of random salutation on other buses."

FIRST PERSON TO TRAVEL THE LENGTH OF BRITAIN BY BUS FOR FREE

Armed with a selection of bus timetables, a toothbrush and clothes, sixty-one-year-old Richard Elloway, from Wellington, Somerset, made the journey from Land's End to John O'Groats and back free of charge by using a national concessionary pass, which, in 2008, allowed free travel on local buses in off-peak hours for passengers over the age of sixty. He completed the first leg in 7 days 6 hours and the return journey in 7 days 2 hours 30 minutes, having got on and off nearly eighty buses. "I treated it as a race," he said afterwards, "but I appeared to be the only one taking part."

FASTEST TIME TO TRAVEL THE LENGTH
OF BRITAIN ON PUBLIC BUSES

Following months of poring over timetables and planning his route, Adam Mugliston, a sixteen-year-old Suffolk schoolboy, broke the record for the fastest journey from Land's End to John O'Groats by public bus, completing the journey in 4 days 10 hours 44 minutes. He set off from Land's End on the number 1 bus at 7.21 a.m. on 23 June 2014 bound for Penzance and, after overnight stops at Bridgwater, Crewe, Newcastle and Dundee, he finally stepped off the X97 bus at John O'Groats. He had travelled 1,167 miles on thirty-six different buses, spending £170 ($290) on tickets.

FASTEST TIME TO VISIT ALL EIGHTY-
EIGHT COUNTIES IN OHIO

In 2006, Dan Miller succeeded in his quest to visit all eighty-eight counties in Ohio in less than a day by making the trip in a time of 23 hours 34 minutes 50 seconds. Spurred on by this triumph, three years later he set foot in all sixty-seven counties in Alabama in 22 hours 8 minutes 40 seconds. In 2010 he called in at all sixty-seven counties in the New England states in 26 hours, and in 2012 he jumped in all five Great Lakes in 8 hours 51 minutes 44 seconds, every road trip setting a new world record. He says his long-term goal is to visit all 3,142 counties in the United States.

FASTEST TIME TO VISIT EVERY PLACE
IN BRITAIN BEGINNING WITH "Z"

Between September 2004 and April 2005, journalist Dixe Wills visited all forty-one places in Britain that begin with the letter "Z", from Zantman's Rock off the Isles of Scilly to Zoar, a farm in Shetland, via Zion Place in Somerset and the hamlet of Zabulon in Carmarthenshire, Wales. In the accompanying book, *The Z to Z of Great Britain*, he wrote: "The best find was Zennor, a tiny village in Cornwall. It only has a population of 100, but it is a magnet for history: from its megalithic burial chamber to the ill-fated commune set up by D.H. Lawrence [and] to Ethiopian emperor Haile Selassie seeing out some of World War II there."

FIRST PERSON TO SLEEP ON EVERY SCOTTISH ISLAND

Yorkshireman Andy Strangeway became the first person not only to land on but also to sleep on all of Scotland's 162 islands that cover an area of forty hectares or more. It took him nearly four years, from 6 September 2003 to 29 August 2007, and ended with him being the first person for five years to land on Soay in the St Kilda archipelago, the westernmost point in the UK. His thirst for adventure unquenched, in September 2012 he completed another challenge by becoming the first person to sleep on the summit of all fifty-two counties of England and Wales, ranging in altitude from Caernarvonshire (Mt Snowdon, 3,560 feet, 1,085 metres) to Huntingdonshire (Bush Ground, 262 feet, 80 metres).

MOST DIFFERENT TYPES OF TRANSPORT USED IN ONE YEAR

Although not related to the great explorer, eighty-two-year-old Edwin Shackleton, from Bristol, England, proved himself to be an intrepid adventurer in 2009 by travelling on 136 different modes of transport in the course of the year, including garbage truck, glider, rickshaw, fire engine, hovercraft, electric milk float, tractor, husky dog sled, hot-air balloon and steam roller. His original goal was 100, but he became so addicted to finding new ways of getting around that he continued his travels into 2011, by which time he had racked up 200 different methods of transportation, adding to his impressive list the likes of Segway, coracle and camel. He was even able to turn adversity into opportunity. "Once I was driving home and a deer crossed in front of me and I hit it," he recalled. "The deer was killed and my car was damaged, but at least there was the unexpected bonus of being able to add a break-down truck to my list."

MOST STARBUCKS VISITED

Since 1997, Rafael Antonio Lozano, Jr (or "Winter", as he prefers to be known) has been a man on a mission – a mission to have a coffee in every Starbucks in the world. When he conceived the idea, it must have seemed eminently achievable as there were only about 1,400 shops globally, but the chain's rapid expansion was such that by the middle of 2014 the soft-ware programmer from Houston, Texas, had visited over 11,700 Starbucks as far afield as Japan, Lebanon and Turkey, and still had at least 200 to go. With new stores opening all the time in far-flung locations, the complete coffee set may always remain tantalizingly out of reach. To complicate matters further, the global recession forced the sudden closure of a number of branches, including sixty-one in Australia in 2008 which shut down before he could get there, thus leading to the discontent of our Winter. Starbucks often gives only a few days' notice of closure, leaving him with a mad race against time. He once spent $1,400 on a plane ticket just to purchase a cup of coffee from a Starbucks in British Columbia, Canada, before it closed. Better latte than never. Devoting three months a year to "Starbucking", he has so far spent in excess of $120,000. He admits to having a "mild addiction" to coffee, but the occasion when he drank twenty-nine cups in a single day in southern California was too much even for him and left him feeling "awful". Despite his setbacks, it seems he has no intention of quitting. "Pointless though it might be," he says, "a goal is a goal."

CHAPTER 13

Unwanted Records

MOST ARRESTED PERSON

A sixty-five-year-old Lexington, Kentucky, man, Henry Earl (alias James Brown) has been arrested more than 1,500 times and has become such a celebrity that his police mugshots have been turned into an online video. He has spent a total of over 6,000 days in custody during his lifetime, almost entirely on charges of public intoxication and disorderly conduct. Basically since his first arrest in 1970, he has spent every third day in jail. He was first imprisoned when he was twenty for carrying a concealed weapon, but after that slow start he steadily got into his stride and was imprisoned 230 times in the course of the 1980s. He clocked up his 1,000th arrest in 2002, romping ahead of his nearest rival, Edward Rooks, who had amassed 652 arrests by 2004 until his untimely death made it unlikely that he would add to that total. Indeed Earl, too, would undoubtedly have been arrested many more times, had judges not become less lenient with him in recent years by sentencing him to three months per conviction. He was once offered the chance to relocate to Pittsburgh so that he could get away from the elements that keep drawing him back to drinking, but he declined to move because he loves Lexington. As his latest attorney, Stephen Gray McFadden, put it: "The good thing [about Lexington] is, he knows where stuff is. The bad thing is, he knows where stuff is."

MOST FAKED KIDNAPPINGS

Between 2001 and 2006, a Spanish woman, Josefa Sanchez Vargas, conned her estranged husband into paying ransoms totalling over $700,000 to secure the release of their children after faking their kidnapping on no fewer than seven separate occasions. Her web of deceit began when she told husband Pedro that strangers had snatched their daughter Sara and were demanding $40,000 for her safe return. Pedro duly paid up, but a year later Josefa claimed that Sara had been taken again, this time to settle a drug debt. Pedro paid $57,000 for the girl's release. In 2003, Josefa told Pedro that their son Emilio had been snatched after she failed to pay $42,000 she owed to a clothing wholesaler. Once again, Pedro paid up and the boy was "returned" unharmed. In 2004, Josefa faked another kidnapping, again of her teenage son Emilio, claiming that drug dealers were demanding $70,000 for a package of cocaine that the boy had lost. Pedro obligingly paid the ransom. In December 2005 and January 2006, Josefa claimed yet again that Emilio had got himself into trouble and was being held to ransom because he had taken the virginity of a thirteen-year-old gypsy girl whose family was demanding $200,000 in blood money. Finally in September 2006, Josefa concocted a story that the unlucky Emilio had again been abducted from outside their Madrid home. On this occasion, the boy himself called his father, claiming his attackers were torturing him and were threatening to kill him unless a ransom of $300,000 was paid. However, by now even the gullible Pedro had begun to suspect that he was being taken for a mug, and had hired a private detective to investigate. When, minutes after making the call, Emilio was spotted by the detective having a drink with friends, the game was up. In 2008, Josefa was jailed for three-and-a-half years yet Pedro insisted that he still had feelings for his wife of seventeen years, to the extent that he renounced his right to claim back the money.

FASTEST ARREST AFTER POSTING OWN MUGSHOT ON FACEBOOK

Sought by police in Freeland, Pennsylvania, in connection with an assault six months earlier, Anthony James Lescowitch, Jr, was arrested just forty-five minutes after making the mistake of sharing a wanted picture of himself on his own Facebook page. Freeland Police posted the wanted bulletin on their Facebook page in January 2014 but three minutes later the thirty-five-year-old suspect reposted the picture of himself on his page and wrote underneath "lol I f****** love it, A**HOLE". Almost immediately an investigating officer, posing as an attractive woman, began chatting online with Lescowitch about the post, and within half an hour he had agreed to meet her. When he turned up at the arranged location, police officers were waiting to arrest him.

LONGEST PERIOD ON THE RUN AFTER ESCAPING FROM PRISON

From unwanted records to a most wanted – Irishman John Patrick Hannan who, as of 2014, was still at large after escaping from Verne prison in Dorset fifty-nine years earlier. Hannan was just thirty days into a twenty-one-month sentence for car theft and assaulting two police officers when, one night in December 1955, he and fellow prisoner Gwynant Thomas made their bid for freedom by scaling the prison wall with knotted bedsheets. The men, both twenty-two, were wearing grey prison overalls but broke into a nearby petrol station and stole overcoats. Thomas was quickly arrested after the two fugitives were spotted by a truck driver, but Hannan remained elusive despite an intense manhunt involving tracker dogs and roadblocks. In 2001, long after Dorset police had stopped actively searching for him, it emerged that Hannan had broken the world record for the longest prison escape, previously held by an American, Leonard Frisco, who, after being on the run for forty-five years and eleven months, was turned in by his son following an argument. In recognition of Hannan's achievement *in absentia*, Guinness went so far as to promise him a place in their book – provided he gave himself up. Nobody was exactly holding their breath.

LONGEST TIME FOR BURGLAR TO BE STUCK UP CHIMNEY

The fully-clothed skeletal remains of bungling burglar Calvin Wilson were discovered in the chimney of a former gift shop in Natchez, Mississippi, in January 2001. He was identified by his wallet, having last been seen alive in 1985. Speculating as to how Wilson had come to spend over fifteen years in a chimney, Adams County Sheriff Tommy Ferrell said: "His criminal record shows he was a burglar, so the suspicion is that he was crawling down the chimney to burglarize the business, became lodged and died." He added that breezes from a nearby river probably prevented neighbours from detecting that a body was decomposing in the chimney.

LONGEST TIME LIVING WITH A CORPSE

When Elaine Bernstorff died in 1972, instead of being given a proper burial, her surviving siblings, Anita, Frank and Margaret, decided to keep her body in the two-storey house in Evanston, Illinois, which they all shared. They guarded their privacy fiercely and no outsiders were permitted to enter the house. Neighbours merely assumed the family was embarrassed by the shabby state of the place, little realizing that a dead body was hidden inside. Then, in 2003, Frank died at the age of eighty-three. The remaining sisters covered his corpse with blankets and put him in a separate room from

Elaine. Life continued as before until Anita died in May 2008, aged ninety-eight. Left alone, Margaret became more outgoing with neighbours, offering them flowers from the garden and on one occasion even allowing an odd-jobman inside the house, but when asked about her siblings, she said Anita was upstairs sleeping and that Frank had moved to live with relatives in Indiana. The family's grisly secret was finally uncovered in November 2008, at which point Margaret was moved out of the house – after thirty-six years of living with corpses. She spent her final three years in a retirement home where, according to her obituary in the local paper, "she discovered a fresh new enthusiasm for life".

MOST MARRIAGE REJECTIONS

Britain's Keith Redman first asked his girlfriend Beverley to marry him in 1976 on her sixteenth birthday. She said no. Over the ensuing years, he proposed another 8,500 times – and was turned down 8,500 times. He tried leaving romantic notes around the house, candlelit dinners for two, romantic trips abroad, and sometimes just asking her out of the blue while they were watching TV. Finally, when she was thirty-nine, she figured that he must be serious and so she agreed to marry him. The reluctant bride said: "I'd given Keith many excuses but they could all be summed up in one word – fear."

MOST DELAYED POSTCARD

A postcard from nineteen-year-old English soldier Alfred Arthur, sent to his sister Ellen as he was about to leave for World War I, was finally delivered in 2010 – ninety-four years late. To compound the blunder, it was delivered to the wrong address. Alfred wrote the postcard in January 1916 from his camp in Newhaven, East Sussex, the day before he was shipped over to France. It said: "Dear Nell, Just a postcard to let you know I have not forgotten you. On the other side you will see our orders for next week. Poor me, I shall need your pity. Drop me a line, from brother Alfred." However, the postcard only reached its destination decades after both the vendor and the intended recipient had died. Alfred was killed in battle in 1918 and Ellen died in 1964. When the card was finally delivered, it was put through the door of the house opposite the address in Norwich. Lauren Bleach, who lives there, said: "It came with the rest of the post. We couldn't believe our eyes. At first we found it amusing that it had taken 94 years for Royal Mail to deliver it, and even then they delivered it to the wrong door. But then as we started to read what the postcard said, we were so emotionally taken by it."

LONGEST TIME TO FORGET COMPUTER PASSWORD

Remembering a gaggle of online passwords represents one of the major challenges of modern life. Birthplaces, pets' names, first schools, favourite root vegetables – we use them all as online memory tools. Inevitably most of us forget or lose them from time to time, but police officers in Delhi, India, took absent-mindedness to a new level when they managed to lose a computer password for eight years. The lapse occurred at India's anti-corruption agency, the Central Vigilance Commission, where, from 2006 to 2014, officers were unable to access a portal holding 667 complaints. One police officer blamed the oversight on a "technical problem" and insisted that the complaints were now finally being dealt with. And you thought your company's IT department was slow!

MOST GOLF SHOTS ON A SINGLE HOLE

Playing in a qualifying round of the 1912 Shawnee Invitational for Ladies tournament at Shawnee on Delaware, Pennsylvania, American golfer Maud McInnes took 166 strokes for the 130-yard, par-3, sixteenth hole. Her problems began when she drove her tee shot into the fast-flowing Binniekill River and the ball sailed off downstream. Instead of taking a penalty and hitting another tee shot, the resourceful Maud clambered into a rowing boat with her husband at the oars and set off in pursuit of her ball. A mile-and-a-half farther down the river, while her faithful spouse kept score, she finally succeeded on beaching the ball on terra firma. She then had to hack her way through woodland and dense undergrowth to make it back to the sixteenth green, but remained undeterred – and so it was that 165 shots and nearly two hours after teeing off, she holed out. It is not known whether she qualified for the later stages of the tournament.

HIGHEST GOLF SCORE IN A ROUND AT A MAJOR TOURNAMENT

All golfers have bad days but Maurice Flitcroft made a career out of it. At Formby in the qualifying competition for the 1976 British Open, the forty-six-year-old chain-smoking crane driver from Barrow-in-Furness shot a record-breaking round of 121 – 49 over par. This was perhaps not surprising as he had only been playing for eighteen months and had never previously set foot on a golf course. Instead his practice had been confined to the beach, which at least should have stood him in good stead for the numerous bunkers that he would encounter on his fateful round. Even then his score was only a rough estimate as his marker lost count on a couple of holes. Flitcroft went out in 61 and came back in a marginally better 60 despite a traumatic 11 at the tenth hole. Afterwards he was far from downcast, telling reporters who had latched on to his calamity: "I've made a lot of progress in the last few months and I'm sorry I did not do better. I was trying too hard at the beginning but began to put things together at the end of the round." The championship committee did not share his optimism and invited him to withdraw from round two, a request with which he reluctantly complied. They were so appalled that he had been allowed to slip through the net that they refunded the £30 ($48) entry fee to the two unfortunates drawn to play with him. One enterprising journalist drove to Flitcroft's mother's house. "I've just come from the Open, and I'd like a word with you about your son Maurice," he said. "Oh," replied his mother. "Did he win?"

The indomitable Flitcroft tried again in 1983, this time masquerading as a Swiss professional by the name of Gerald Hoppy. Playing in the qualifying round for the Open at Pleasington, he got as far as the ninth hole, by which time he had already taken 63 strokes. At that point, Royal and Ancient officials, smelling a rat, caught up with him and suggested that Herr Hoppy might care to retire. Flitcroft lamented: "Everything was going well and according to plan until I five-putted the second."

MOST FAILED ATTEMPTS TO HIT A HOLE-IN-ONE ON A SINGLE DAY

When William Voltz, a self-confessed "duffer" golfer, scored an ace on the 136-yard tenth hole at the Beverly Shores Country Club course in Michigan City, Indiana, he bet Harry Gonder, a twenty-five-year-old golf professional, $25 that he could not do the same. Reckoning that if Voltz could get a hole-in-one anybody could, Gonder eagerly accepted the wager. So a few weeks later, at 10 a.m. on 20 June 1939, watched by 150 interested spectators, two official witnesses and with the assistance of half a dozen caddies to tee up and retrieve balls, he set out to prove his point. Ball after ball he hit towards the flag. His eighty-sixth attempt finished just fifteen inches short but, for the most part, he was struggling to find his range. As the hours ticked by, he started to feel hungry and after 941 shots he stopped for refreshment in the hope that it would improve his fortunes. The ploy nearly worked, because his 996th effort hit the pin and bounced three inches away. At 8.10 p.m., his 1,162nd stopped six inches short and, beginning at last to get into his stride, his 1,184th missed by just three inches. Alas, it was to prove a false dawn. As the church bells struck midnight, Gonder struck his 1,600th tee shot. Like most of its predecessors, it failed to worry the flag. By now fatigue had set in. His hands were blistered and sore, his arms leaden and his back weary. Still he battled on and was nearly rewarded twice in the space of a few minutes. His 1,750th shot hit the pin, as did his 1,756th, the latter ending up no more than an inch from the hole. That cruel blow seemed to persuade him that perhaps he should call it a day (and a half). So at 2.40 a.m., 16 hours 40 minutes after first teeing off, Gonder's 1,817th shot finished ten long feet from the flag – and he gave up. Bloodied but unbowed, he told reporters: "I sure am disappointed. I was certain I could make it, but now I'm convinced that a hole-in-one is just a matter of luck."

LONGEST FOOTBALL RUN IN WRONG DIRECTION

Roy Riegels earned his place in American Football folklore following a highly individual move in the 1929 Rose Bowl when he ran sixty-nine yards in the wrong direction. Midway through the second quarter, Riegels, playing as centre for California Golden Bears, collected a fumble from Georgia Tech's Jack "Stumpy" Thomason thirty yards from the Georgia end zone and set off on an electrifying run. The 71,000 crowd rose in unison. They had never seen anything like it – because Riegels was running the wrong way, towards his own team's end zone. Radio commentator Graham McNamee yelled into his microphone: "What am I seeing? What's wrong with me? Am I crazy? Am I crazy? Am I crazy?" Riegels explained afterwards: "I was running toward the side-lines when I picked up the ball. I started to turn to my left toward Tech's goal. Somebody shoved me and I bounded right off into a tackler. In pivoting to get away from him, I completely lost my bearings." Team-mate Benny Lom chased Riegels all the way, screaming at him to stop, and finally brought him to earth at California's three-yard line. But the seeds of defeat had already been sown. As a result of "Wrong Way" Riegels' aberration, Georgia picked up two points which were to prove crucial as they eventually edged home

8–7. A distraught Riegels, who said he thought the shouts from the crowd were screams of encouragement, became an unlikely American hero. He received a mountain of fan mail including a marriage proposal in which he and his bride would walk the wrong way in church.

SHORTEST INTERNATIONAL RUGBY CAREER

On his way to Paris to make his international debut for the French rugby union team against Scotland in 1911, Gaston Vareilles jumped off his train to buy a sandwich at a country station. Alas, the buffet service was so slow that by the time he returned to the platform his train had disappeared into the distance, and even though he was a winger he had little hope of catching it. Although he did eventually reach the ground, he only made it as far as the dressing-room door, at which point he was told in no uncertain terms where he could stick his baguette. He was never selected to play for his country again.

FIRST SOCCER PLAYER TO LOSE A FINGER
WHILE CELEBRATING A GOAL

After setting up Servette's third goal in a 4–1 away win over Schaffhausen in the Swiss Super League in December 2004, midfielder Paulo Diogo jumped up onto the metal perimeter fence to celebrate. Having only recently got married, he failed to spot that his newly acquired wedding ring was caught in the barrier until he jumped back down, leaving both the ring and most of his finger behind on the fence. While stewards searched frantically for the severed finger, referee Florian Etter added insult to injury by booking Diogo for his prolonged celebration. His misery was complete when surgeons at Zurich hospital declared that they were unable to reattach the severed portion of finger and advised amputation of the stump.

LONGEST BAN RECEIVED BY SOCCER REFEREE FOR HITTING ANOTHER REFEREE

In September 1995, referee Dave Lucas was banned from football for five years for knocking fellow referee Pete Wall unconscious in front of two West Midlands schoolboy teams. Owing to a mix-up, both men had turned up to referee an under-11s match between Birmingham teams Springfield Lions "A" and Oldwinsford. In a row over which of the two should take charge of the game, Mr Wall was laid out, although he was eventually able to referee the game following treatment. A spokesman for the Birmingham County Football Association said: "There are regular cases of players or managers assaulting referees, but as far as I'm aware it is unprecedented for a ref to hit another ref."

LOWEST POINTS TOTAL BY A SOCCER TEAM IN A SEASON

Playing their home games in Bulgaria's Vasil Levski National Stadium, PSFC Chernomorets Burgas Sofia (not to be confused with a more successful rival club, PSFC Chernomorets Burgas) finished the 2006–7 season with a points total of minus two. They drew 1 and lost 29 of their 30 games, scoring just 8 goals and conceding 131, but finished in the red because they were given a three-point penalty for not registering enough youth players. Heavily in debt, the club withdrew from the Bulgarian League at the end of that season and folded shortly afterwards.

MOST RED CARDS IN A SOCCER MATCH

When a mass brawl broke out during an Argentine League Fifth Division match between Claypole and Victoriano Arenas in Buenos Aires on 26 February 2011, flustered referee Damian Rubino showed a record-breaking thirty-six red cards. He sent off all twenty-two players plus substitutes and technical staff, thereby beating the previous world record of twenty from a Paraguayan match played in 1993.

Referee Rubino had struggled to keep control of the players from the outset, with petty scuffles erupting all over the pitch. By the start of the second half, he had already sent off two players, including one for bad behaviour during the interval. As the violence escalated alarmingly towards the end of the game and fans and coaching staff ran onto the pitch and started challenging the players to fights, Rubino waved red cards left, right and centre in the hope of restoring a semblance of order. Having then sent everybody off, it dawned on him that there was no game to officiate. Victoriano Arenas coach Domingo Sganga said he feared for his life and begged police to lock him and his players in the dressing room. Opposing coach Sergio Micieli saw it differently, claiming that the referee was "confused", and that most of those involved in the fight were actually trying to break it up.

LONGEST EXIT BY A SOCCER PLAYER
AFTER BEING SENT OFF

It can be a long, lonely walk for a footballer who has just been sent off, but for Yugoslav Dragan Kovacevic it went on for 1,000 miles. Playing for Sloga in a 1978 Chiswick and District Sunday League match against Shoreditch College Old Boys, Kovacevic was dismissed for violent conduct, behaviour which so incensed the Shoreditch players that they chased him onto the next pitch. When the Yugoslav Embassy in London (where he worked) heard about the incident, they sent him back to his homeland.

LONGEST BAN FOR A SOCCER TEAM
MANAGER WHO HEADBUTTED A PLAYER

Newcastle United manager Alan Pardew was banned for seven matches by the Football Association for headbutting

Hull City player David Meyler during the game between the two teams on 1 March 2014. Pardew had been angered when Meyler brushed past him in an attempt to retrieve the ball and take a throw-in. Pardew said afterwards that he was simply trying to "push him away with my head".

MOST SOCCER SENDINGS OFF IN A PROFESSIONAL CAREER

Playing for Independiente Santa Fe on 23 September 2012, thirty-six-year-old Colombian international defender Gerardo Bedoya picked up the forty-first red card of his career for elbowing Jhonny Ramirez and then kicking him in the head as he lay on the ground during the Bogota derby against Millonarios. Despite a disciplinary record which would shame Jack the Ripper, Bedoya insists he is misunderstood and "not like that". The Colombian football authorities disagreed and handed him a fifteen-match ban following that particular indiscretion. Somewhat belatedly he vowed to clean up his act, but once he returned to action he wasted little time in taking his sendings-off total to an unprecedented forty-three.

RACEHORSE WITH THE LONGEST LOSING SEQUENCE

Blessed with the speed across the ground of a rocking horse, Puerto Rican mare Dona Chepa failed to win a race in 135 starts from 2001 until her inglorious retirement seven years later. She was only placed three times in her career, her finest hour being when, as a five-year-old, she came second in a race in May 2003. More usually she was to be found just out of vision range of binoculars, finishing last forty-nine times and at least thirty lengths behind the winner on fifty-one occasions. Yet ironically she came from a distinguished line of champion racehorses, her grandmother having won the Kentucky Derby. Somehow the genes skipped a generation with Dona Chepa. Her winless streak saw her stable painted with the words "prolongada mala suerte" meaning "prolonged bad luck", although to attribute her woeful record to bad luck would be charitable in the extreme. Her owner, Rafael Ruiz, claimed that he raced her only for fun, but Puerto Rican trainers and many members of the public felt that Dona Chepa's continued presence devalued the sport. On more than one occasion her trainer was asked: "Why don't you just kill Dona Chepa?" However, her connections realized that although she was far too slow ever to win a race, she could still repay a little of their investment by finishing fifth in small fields. That way she was able to retire with career earnings of $14,028 – none too shabby for the worst racehorse in history.

FIRST DEAD JOCKEY TO WIN A HORSE RACE

When 20–1 outsider Sweet Kiss crossed the finish line first in a steeplechase at Belmont Park, Long Island, on 4 June 1923, observers noticed that the jockey, American Frank Hayes, appeared extremely relaxed in the saddle for such an unexpected victory. Moments later, Hayes fell off the horse, but it was only when the owner, Miss A.M. Frayling, and race officials went to congratulate him that they discovered he was not so much relaxed as dead. He had suffered a fatal heart attack during the race, shortly after Sweet Kiss had taken the lead. The New York Times speculated that it had been caused by a combination of extreme training to make the weight and the excitement of winning his first race at the age of thirty-five. In fact, it was Hayes's only race. He was a longtime stableman who had cared for the horse and had managed to persuade the trainer and owner that he was finally ready to ride in public. Hayes was buried three days later, dressed in his colourful racing silks, and in light of the tragedy Belmont's Jockey Club made a one-off decision to ignore the rule about jockeys having to weigh in after a race and declared his win official. From then on, superstitious jockeys refused to ride the horse, who became known as Sweet Kiss of Death and was retired.

FIRST CRICKET MATCH TO BE
HELD UP BY AN IGUANA

In the first recorded case of "iguana stops play", the First Test between Young Sri Lanka and Young England in 1987 was halted when a large lizard crept ominously across the square at the Colombo Cricket Club ground.

FIRST CRICKET MATCH TO BE ABANDONED
BECAUSE OF CREMATORIUM SMOKE

The Wisden Cricketers' Almanack, the Bible of the game, reported that a village cricket match at Boddington, Oxfordshire, in 1995 had to be abandoned because the pitch was engulfed by smoke emanating from the Companion's Rest animal crematorium at nearby Elmstone Hardwicke.

FIRST BATSMAN TO BE RUN OUT WHILE ON FIRE

Batting at Kalgoorlie, Australia, in the 1970s, cricketer Stan Dawson was hit by a quick delivery that immediately ignited a box of matches which he kept in his hip pocket. With his pants on fire, Dawson frantically hopped around the crease trying to beat down the flames with his bare hands, but the opposing team cruelly exploited his misfortune by running him out.

FASTEST "PAIR" AT CRICKET

Batting for Glamorgan against India at Cardiff Arms Park in 1946, Peter Judge had the unenviable distinction of twice being dismissed for nought in the space of two minutes – the fastest "pair" in cricket history. Last man in for the county, Judge was bowled first ball by India's Chandu Sarwate to end Glamorgan's first innings, forcing them to follow on. As a considerable amount of time had been lost to rain and because cricket lovers had been starved of action during World War II, the captains agreed to forego the usual ten-minute break between innings and decided that rather than waste time swapping batsmen, the same two men should open the second innings. So Judge kept his pads on and stayed at the crease to open the second innings . . . and was promptly clean bowled again by Sarwate's first ball.

FIRST BASEBALL SPECTATOR TO BE HIT TWICE BY THE SAME PLAYER IN THE SAME GAME

During a game against the New York Giants on 17 August 1957, Richie Ashburn of the Philadelphia Phillies hit spectator Alice Roth, the wife of *Philadelphia Bulletin* sports editor Earl Roth, with a foul ball, breaking her nose. As she was being carried off the field on a stretcher, Ashburn hit her with another foul ball, this time breaking a bone in her knee.

FIRST MOTHER TO GET HIT WHILE HER SON WAS PITCHING ON MOTHER'S DAY

On Mother's Day, 14 May 1939, while the Cleveland Indians' Bob Feller was pitching and his mother Lena was cheering him on from the stands near the visitors' dugout at Comiskey Park, Chicago, a foul ball was hit by the White Sox's Marv Owen into the spectator area where it smacked the unfortunate Mrs Feller just above the right eye, causing an injury that required seven stitches.

BASEBALL PLAYER HIT BY MOST PITCHES

Between 1891 and 1903, the fearless Hughie Jennings was hit by a record 287 pitches, including fifty-one times in a single season (1896) for the Baltimore Orioles, which set another record. During an 1897 clash with the New York Giants,

Jennings was hit on the head by a fastball from Amos Rusie in the third inning but managed to hang on until the end of the game, whereupon he collapsed and spent the next three days in a coma. More recently, Craig Biggio of the Houston Astros had been hit by 285 pitches by the end of the 2007 season, when he decided the only way to avoid breaking Jennings's century-old record was to retire.

MOST NFL FUMBLES IN A SEASON

Kerry Collins, a quarterback for the New York Giants, set the benchmark for fumbles by recording twenty-three in 2001, only for his record to be equalled the following year by Daunte Culpepper of the Minnesota Vikings. However, when it comes to the most fumbles in a game, Len Dawson is out there on his own thanks to seven "butterfingers" moments while playing for the Kansas City Chiefs against the San Diego Chargers on 15 November 1964.

LONGEST HOCKEY SUSPENSION

The Boston Bruins' Canadian defenceman Billy Coutu was suspended for life for punching referee Jerry Laflamme and knocking him down, tackling the other referee Billy Bell as he went to his colleague's aid and starting a mass brawl on the ice during a Stanley Cup finals game against the Ottawa Senators on 13 April 1927. His ban was commuted after two-and-a-half years but he never played in the NHL again. In his first practice with the Bruins, Coutu had body-slammed team-mate Eddie Shore with such force that Shore's ear was severed. Not that Shore was exactly a shrinking violet. Refusing an anaesthetic, he used a mirror to watch doctors reattach the ear to his satisfaction and by the end of his career boasted over 600 stitch marks on his body from various injuries, including nineteen scars on his scalp alone.

FIRST HOCKEY PLAYER TO BE
KILLED DURING A GAME

On 24 February 1905, nineteen-year-old Alcide Laurin, who played for an ice hockey team based in Alexandria, Ontario, was clubbed to death during a game in Canada with bitter local rivals Maxwell. The fatal blow to his left temple was delivered by the stick of Maxwell's Allan Loney, who was subsequently charged with murder before the charge was reduced to manslaughter. At his trial Loney claimed self-defence (Laurin had broken his nose earlier in the scuffle) and was acquitted.

FIRST ATHLETICS TRACK TO BE BUILT
WITH RIGHT-ANGLED CORNERS

A unique athletics track opened in China's Tonghe County, Heilongjiang Province, in 2014 – one that was virtually impossible to run around at speed because it had replaced the conventional curves with sharp ninety-degree corners. It seems the distinctive track painting, with every lane featuring four right-angled corners per lap, came about after Communist Party leaders announced a last-minute visit to the stadium, prompting a hasty makeover during which painting right angles was considered easier and faster than painting curves. A local reporter sent to test the rectangular track admitted: "I felt a bit strange at the turn." Meanwhile, a woman who tried unsuccessfully to negotiate the corners moaned: "Normally curves speed people up but these corners slow you down. It is quite inconvenient."

SHORTEST BOXING MATCH

The briefest excursion into the boxing ring was that of Ralph Walton against Al Couture at Lewiston, Maine, on 23 September 1946. Walton was still adjusting his gum shield in his corner when Couture knocked him out. The fight officially ended after ten-and-a-half seconds – and that included the ten-second count.

SHORTEST BOXING CAREER OF A WORLD TITLE CONTENDER

The professional career of little-known Mexican boxer Arturo Mayan lasted just nineteen seconds. He was the first man selected to challenge Puerto Rico's mini flyweight world champion Alex Sanchez, on 7 January 1994, in Mallorca, Spain, but from the first bell it was obvious that he was hopelessly out of his depth. He decided his best tactic was to turn his back on his opponent, forcing referee Ismael Fernandez to stop the "fight" after a minute and a half. In the aftermath, Mayan claimed to have had three previous professional fights, none of which could be substantiated. He never boxed again.

FIRST BOXER TO KNOCK HIMSELF OUT

Irish boxer Jack Doyle was a hot favourite to win his heavyweight bout against Eddie Phillips at Harringay, London, in September 1938, but instead a sudden rush of blood brought about an ignominious defeat. In round two, Doyle, sensing victory, went for the kill and charged at his opponent, only to miss him completely and sail through the ropes and out of the ring. When the hapless Doyle failed to get back into the ring before the count of ten, the referee counted him out and declared Phillips the unexpected winner.

FIRST WORLD TITLE FIGHT TO BE ABANDONED DUE TO TIDE

It must have sounded like a boxing promoter's dream to stage a world title fight on the seafront, but it was to turn into something of a nightmare because nobody had taken into consideration the incoming tide. The world middleweight title fight between challenger Johnny Reagan and champion "Nonpareil" Jack Dempsey had already been postponed once for fog when the pair reconvened on the waterfront at Huntington, Long Island, on 13 December 1887. The two boxers were soon slugging it out, oblivious to the rising tide, until in the eighth round the ring became completely flooded. With Reagan refusing to fight on sand, the contest was abandoned, and the crowd of twenty-five (itself a record for the smallest audience for a world championship fight) boarded a tug and moved to another spot twenty miles away, where, after a further sixteen rounds, Reagan was too exhausted to continue, leaving Dempsey home and dry.

MOST NASCAR RACES WITHOUT A WIN

Between 1963 and his death in a race at Watkins Glen in 1991, North Carolina-born driver John Delphus "J.D." McDuffie started in 653 NASCAR Grand National/Sprint Cup races without recording a single win. His best finish was a third in 1971. He also held the record for the most last-place NASCAR finishes (thirty-two) until Joe Nemechek claimed that unwanted record in 2014.

MOST FORMULA ONE GRAND PRIX RACES WITHOUT A WIN

Italian driver Andrea de Cesaris competed in 214 Grands Prix between 1980 and 1994 (starting 208) without winning a single race. Nicknamed "Andrea de Crasheris" following a number of racing mishaps early in his career, he drove for Alfa Romeo, McLaren, Ligier, Minardi, Brabham, Rial, Dallara, Jordan, Tyrrell and Sauber but mustered just five podium finishes. He also holds the record for the most consecutive non-finishes – eighteen across 1985 and 1986.

SHORTEST FORMULA ONE CAREER

The Formula One career of Japan's Masami Kuwashima lasted just one day. After gaining valuable experience in the Japanese lower formulae, he sought a drive at the 1976 Japanese Grand Prix at Mount Fuji and was given the opportunity by the struggling Wolf/Williams team. He drove in the first practice session for the race but proved decidedly slow, more than five seconds off the eventual pole position time but nevertheless quicker than two other cars, including fellow countryman Noritake Takahara in a Surtees. However, when Kuwashima's sponsors withdrew their financial backing for the Williams deal a few hours later, team boss Frank Williams promptly replaced him with Austrian driver Hans Binder for the second practice session and the actual race. Kuwashima never returned to Formula One, having found to his cost that in motor racing money talks.

FASTEST FAILURE OF A DRIVING TEST

In the early 1970s, Mrs Helen Ireland, of Auburn, California, failed her driving test in the first second when, after starting the engine, she immediately mistook the accelerator for the clutch and shot straight through the wall of the driving test centre.

MOST DRIVING TEST FAILURES

Sixty-nine-year-old Cha Sa-soon from South Korea finally passed her driving test in 2010 at the 960th attempt. She actually passed the driving section of the test at the tenth try, but only after 949 failures in the written exam, which she had taken almost every day for four-and-a-half years.

LARGEST PARKING FINE

Jennifer Fitzgerald racked up $105,000 in fines by collecting more than 670 tickets when a 1999 Chevrolet registered in her name sat in a parking garage at Chicago's O'Hare International Airport for three years. In response she claimed that her former boyfriend had registered the car in her name without her permission before abandoning it at the airport, and that as she had no access to the vehicle she was not liable for the fines. After the usual legal wrangling, in 2013 she was ordered to pay a reduced bill of $4,470, a portion of which would be paid by the ex-boyfriend.

LONGEST TRAFFIC JAM

On 16 February 1980, a combination of congestion and inclement weather caused a 109-mile traffic jam on the French highway between Lyon and Paris, a situation that produced even more Gallic shrugs than normal. This was nearly surpassed in August 2010 when a 62-mile jam on National Expressway 110 between Beijing and Inner Mongolia, caused partly by roadworks, lasted for more than two weeks. Many drivers, some of whom were trapped in their vehicles for five days, passed the time by playing cards, while local traders capitalized on the captive custom by setting up roadside stalls selling their wares at extortionate prices. Those selling bottled water fared considerably better than those selling copies of *What's On In Mongolia*.

MOST EXPENSIVE CAR CRASH

A multi-car pile-up on a freeway in Shimonoseki, Japan, in December 2011 involved eight Ferraris, a Lamborghini and a Mercedes-Benz, and caused damage estimated at $4 million. The chain-reaction smash occurred when the Ferrari driver at the head of the convoy of luxury sports cars, which were on their way to a supercar event in Hiroshima, lost control and those behind failed to brake in time.

LONGEST TIME FOR A MAJOR ARTWORK TO BE HUNG THE WRONG WAY UP

On 18 October 1961, New York's Museum of Modern Art proudly opened an exhibition titled "The Last Works of Henri Matisse", displaying a number of paintings by the celebrated French artist. Among them was "Le Bateau" ("The Boat"), a painting which measured 56 inches by 44 inches, and which was greatly admired over the next forty-seven days by 116,000 visitors, none of whom spotted that it had been accidentally hung upside down. Even the artist's son, dealer Pierre Matisse, had failed to notice the error. It was not until almost the end of the exhibition, on 4 December, that stockbroker Genevieve Habert finally spotted the mistake and notified a guard.

MOST HAUNTED VILLAGE

With up to sixteen ghosts on call at any one time – making them easier to find than electricians, plumbers or builders – the village of Pluckley in Kent is reputed to be the most haunted in the UK and almost certainly the world. With a population of just 1,050, it means there is a ghost for every sixty-five residents. If that ghost-per-head ratio were applied to New York City, there would be almost 154,000 phantoms haunting the Big Apple. Among the local apparitions you might hope not to see in Pluckley are:

- Lady Dering, "The Red Lady", who died in the twentieth century but continues to haunt the graveyard in search of her stillborn child.
- A screaming workman who was smothered to death when a wall of clay fell on him at the local brickworks.
- A highwayman, Robert du Bois, who, while lurking in his favourite hiding place, was himself ambushed by villagers, run through with a sword and pinned to a tree in what is now known as Fright Corner.

- An elderly gypsy woman who made a living selling watercress but died when a spark from the pipe she was smoking ignited the whisky she was drinking and burned her alive. An alternative version says that the pipe set fire to her clothes while she was sleeping. Either way, her tale is confirmation that smoking is dangerous.
- A nineteenth-century headmaster who was found hanging from a tree. His ghost can be seen today in the school grounds wearing his favourite green blazer and striped trousers.
- A colonel who hanged himself in nearby Park Wood. His ghost is seen marching through the trees in full military uniform.
- The ghost who haunts the old ruined windmill, which closed in 1930 and was later destroyed by lightning. Seen as a completely black silhouette, he is usually spotted immediately before a storm.
- A ghostly monk who haunts the grounds of a house called Greystones.
- The Lady of Rose Court who killed herself by drinking the juice of poisonous berries. Thought to be a mistress of one of the Dering family, she may have been involved in a love triangle featuring the phantom monk of Greystones. She haunts the house and gardens only between the hours of 4 p.m. and 5 p.m. and is said to be heard calling her two dogs.
- A phantom coach drawn by four ghostly horses.
- And, of course, the obligatory lady in white.

BIGGEST BALL OF FAT IN A CITY SEWER

Using high-powered water jets, a heroic team of workers took three weeks to clear a fifteen-ton "fatberg" – a toxic ball of congealed fat the size of a double-decker bus – that had built up in a London sewer in the summer of 2013 and was threatening to turn the streets of Kingston upon Thames into a cesspit. The first sign of trouble came when local residents reported difficulty flushing their toilets, and upon investigation Gordon Hailwood and his merry band of sewage workers found a giant ball of solidified grease and oil blocking 95 per cent of an eight-foot-diameter brick sewer pipe. Thames Water spokesman Simon Evans made no attempt to underplay the severity of the situation. "I have witnessed a fatberg," he said. "It's a heaving, sick-smelling, rotting mass of filth and faeces. It hits the back of your throat, it's gross. Hailwood and his team certainly saved Kingston from a terrible fate. We have recorded greater volumes of fat in the past, but we don't believe there's ever been a single congealed lump of lard matching this one." He didn't say whether or not he would be applying to Guinness World Records.

MOST DEAD PIGS FOUND FLOATING IN A RIVER

Shanghai's Huangpu River claimed this record in March 2013 when 16,000 dead pigs were found floating in it. As if that bald statistic were not disconcerting enough, it is the river that supplies drinking water to most of the city's twenty-six million residents. It is thought the pigs were dumped there following a sickness epidemic, so that farmers could avoid having to pay for the carcasses to be disposed of properly.

COW CARRIED FARTHEST BY A TORNADO

When a fierce tornado struck a rural area sixty miles north of Little Rock, Arkansas, in January 2008, it picked up one of the Killins family's cows, carried it through the air and dumped the animal unharmed three-quarters-of-a-mile away.

LARGEST NUMBER OF FATALITIES IN A TV STUDIO

On 8 February 1990, a major fire broke out on the Mysore studio set of the sixty-part Indian historical drama series *The*

Sword of Tipu Sultan and eventually claimed sixty-two lives. Among those badly burned was the show's producer, co-director and star, Sanjay Khan, who had to spend thirteen months in hospital and undergo seventy-two surgeries.

MOST PEOPLE KILLED BY EXPLODING MOLASSES

The world's worst ever molasses disaster took place in Boston, Massachusetts, on 15 January 1919, when a tank holding more than two million gallons of the stuff exploded and sent a forty-foot-high sticky wave roaring through the streets at 35 mph, killing 21 people and injuring 150. The force of the wave destroyed buildings, buckled the girders of a railroad bridge, derailing a train, and hurled a truck into Boston Harbor. People in the wave's path were picked up and tossed through the air, the unlucky ones being crushed or drowned in the sea of molasses. The *Boston Post* reported that "horses died like so many flies on sticky fly-paper. The more they struggled, the deeper in the mess they were ensnared." The Boston Molasses Disaster, as it became known, was caused by structural defects in the tank combined with unseasonably warm weather which led to a sudden increase in the internal pressure. For decades afterwards, local residents claimed that on hot summer days the area still smelled of molasses.

MOST TOASTERS RECEIVED AS A WEDDING PRESENT

When Mike and Victoria Seymour opened their wedding presents at their Nottingham reception in February 2014, they discovered that two-thirds of them – twenty-seven in total – were toasters. The couple had decided not to send out a wedding list beforehand because they wanted guests to choose their own gift, but the tactic left them vulnerable to a prank by best man Rob Kanok. The groom said: "When we saw the table loaded with presents, we did notice that they all looked similar shapes, they were all rectangular and around the same size, but we didn't think anything of it." They finally realized what was going on when Kanok stood up and said: "Please raise your glasses for a toaster to the happy couple." Their experience broke the record of twenty-four toasters set by Claire and Stuart Linley, from East Yorkshire, in 2009. They, too, were the victims of an organized joke.

LONGEST TIME CELEBRATING THE WRONG BIRTHDAY

In the build-up to her centenary, Evelyn Frost, from Tamworth, Staffordshire, learned that she had been celebrating the wrong birthday for the past ninety-nine years. The blunder was discovered after she applied for her birth certificate to register for her congratulatory letter from the Queen. She had never had a birth certificate before and was shocked to see that it listed her date of birth as 16 April 1914 instead of 17 April, which she had always thought was her birthday.

HEAVIEST TUMOUR REMOVED
FROM THE HUMAN BODY

A 303-pound tumour was removed in six-hour surgery from an unnamed female patient by Professor Katharine O'Hanlan at Stanford Hospital in Palo Alto, California, in October 1991. The patient weighed 210 pounds after the operation and left the theatre on one stretcher while her ovarian cyst left on another.

LARGEST SCROTUM

Until it was surgically removed in 2013, the scrotum of the late Wesley Warren, Jr, from Las Vegas, Nevada, weighed 132 pounds and was so big it hung down between his ankles. His problems first arose in 2008 when he accidentally struck his testicles while sleeping. The pain was intense and by the following morning he noticed that his scrotum had swollen "to the size of a soccer ball". He was diagnosed as suffering from scrotal lymphedema, a debilitating condition where fluid builds up inside the scrotum, causing a swelling so severe that the patient finds it difficult to walk, urinate or have sex. To keep his scrotum covered, he resorted to wearing a hooded sweatshirt upside down as a pair of pants, with his legs in the sleeves. If he travelled on a bus, he had to take along a milk crate or a cushion on which to rest his scrotum during the journey. At one stage he became so desperate that he considered selling his engorged scrotum on eBay to raise money to pay for surgery. When it was finally cut away in a thirteen-hour operation, surgeons found his penis buried twelve inches deep inside his testicle sac. Indeed, despite being relieved of his unsightly burden, Warren was initially unhappy because he claimed the surgery had left him with a one-inch penis.

LONGEST TIME FOR SURGICAL TWEEZERS TO BE ACCIDENTALLY LEFT IN A PERSON'S BODY

In 1997, doctors in Bogota, Colombia, noticed a pair of surgical tweezers in a stomach X-ray of sixty-seven-year-old Silvio Jimenez. They had been accidentally left there during a previous operation in 1950 – forty-seven years earlier.

BIGGEST HUMAN HAIRBALL

The New England Journal of Medicine reported in 2007 on the case of an eighteen-year-old woman who had gone to Rush University Medical Center in Chicago complaining that for the past five months she had suffered pain and swelling in her abdomen, vomiting after eating, and that she had lost an alarming 40 pounds in weight. A scan of her abdomen showed a large mass covering almost her entire stomach, and the subsequent surgery removed a 10-pound hairball, measuring 15 inches by 7 inches by 7 inches. When questioned about it, the woman admitted that for many years she had been eating her own hair.

BIGGEST CAT HAIRBALL

Cats routinely cough up hairballs – often into their owner's discarded slippers to create that nice warm feeling – but when Ty, a 400-pound tiger living at an animal rescue centre in Florida, produced a hairball in May 2013 it was so big it had to be removed by surgery. Having noticed that Ty was off his food, staff sent him for an X-ray which revealed a hairball the size of a basketball, and when it was eventually removed it weighed a fraction over four pounds.

MOST GOLF BALLS SWALLOWED BY A DOG

When Max, a nine-year-old Rottweiler-kelpie cross, started vomiting and shaking in 2013, his owner Tina Ross sent him for X-rays, where doctors discovered fourteen golf balls in his stomach. It so happened that Max's favourite park, near the family home in Melbourne, Australia, was situated next to a golf driving range. Max snatched the record from Oscar, a black Labrador, who, in 2008, was found to have thirteen golf balls rattling around in his stomach, including one ball that had been in there for so long it had turned black. Oscar's owner, Chris Morrison, regularly took him for walks on Pitreavie golf course near Dunfermline, Fife. He said: "He hunts golf balls down like truffles. He finds them in all sorts of places where golfers lose them." Veterinarian Bob Hesketh was alarmed by the find. "When I went into his stomach I was expecting one or two balls, but they just kept coming!"

MOST GOLF BALLS SWALLOWED BY A PYTHON

In 2008, a twenty-eight-inch-long carpet python swallowed four golf balls that had been put in a New South Wales henhouse to encourage a hen to lay eggs. Mistaking them for real eggs, the snake eagerly devoured the balls, which were later extracted from its gut and sold on eBay for $1,401.

LONGEST TIME SITTING ON THE TOILET

Pam Babcock, of Ness County, Kansas, spent at least a month sitting on the toilet of the mobile home she shared with her boyfriend because she had a phobia about leaving the bathroom. By the time the thirty-five-year-old was discovered by police, in February 2008, her body had become stuck to the seat. Sheriff Bryan Whipple said it appeared that the woman's skin had grown around the seat. "We prised the toilet seat off with a bar, and the seat went with her to hospital. The hospital removed it. She was not glued. She was not tied. She was just physically stuck by her body. It is hard to imagine."

LONGEST WAIT ON A HOSPITAL TROLLEY

After contracting a virus, forty-year-old Tony Collins was taken to the Princess Margaret Hospital in Swindon, Wiltshire, on the afternoon of Saturday 24 February 2001. As no bed was available at the time, he was left on a trolley in the corridor outside the washrooms . . . for the next three days. Finally, after spending 77 hours 30 minutes on the trolley he was found a proper bed. He said afterwards that he had no privacy and the experience had left him with a bad back. Two years later, he was admitted to the town's Great Western Hospital (which had replaced the now closed Princess Margaret Hospital), where he again had to wait 60 hours on a trolley. He was just relieved not to have broken his record.

LARGEST INSECT REMOVED FROM A PERSON'S EAR

When Australian warehouse supervisor Hendrik Helmer woke at about 2.30 a.m. on 8 January 2014 with a sharp pain in his right ear, his first thought was that some type of insect may have crawled in while he was asleep. Worried that the intruder could be a venomous spider, he first tried to suck it out with a vacuum cleaner and then to flush it out with tap water, but when both attempts proved unsuccessful and the pain was intensifying by the minute, he decided to present himself at hospital in Darwin. There, a doctor poured olive oil into his ear canal, but that merely caused the insect to burrow in deeper. Finally, after ten long minutes, the creature began to drown. Helmer recalled: "He suddenly started to stop burrowing but he was still in the throes of death-twitching." At that point, the doctor produced a pair of forceps and pulled out the dead culprit – a two-centimetre-long cockroach. "The doctor told me, 'You know how I said a little cockroach? That may have been an underestimate!'" Afterwards Helmer was philosophical about the incident, but friends told him they were so freaked out by his experience that they had started to sleep wearing headphones or earplugs.

MOST METAL ITEMS REMOVED FROM A PERSON'S STOMACH

When doctors in Chhattisgarh, India, opened up the stomach of twenty-eight-year-old Kuleshwar Singh in November 2011, they found that he had swallowed a grand total of 640 metal objects – 421 coins, 197 fishnet pellets, 3 keys and 19 bolts of a bicycle chain. Unsurprisingly, he had been suffering recurring abdominal pains for three months. The head surgeon said: "We were astonished to find almost 6kg of iron objects, most of which seem to have rusted, in his stomach." The good news was that the patient was expected to make a full recovery; the even better news was that the retrieved coins probably paid for the hospital staff's Christmas drinks.

MOST PIECES OF CUTLERY REMOVED
FROM A PERSON'S STOMACH

In the 1970s, surgeons in Rotterdam, the Netherlands, were "flabbergasted" when they found and removed seventy-eight pieces of cutlery from the stomach of fifty-two-year-old Margaret Daalman, a secretary at a local estate agent. She was said to have been suffering from a rare personality disorder that caused her to eat cutlery whenever she sat down for a meal. "I don't know why but I felt an urge to eat the silverware," she said. "I could not help myself." Bizarrely, she only ate spoons and forks and never touched knives. There's nothing worse than a picky eater.

LONGEST TAPEWORM EXTRACTED
FROM A LIVING HUMAN

The star specimen at the Meguro Parasitological Museum in Tokyo, Japan, is a twenty-nine-foot-long tapeworm that was taken from the body of a forty-year-old man and was apparently caused by the patient eating too much sushi. Interestingly, the museum is a popular venue for young dating couples, presumably because nothing says "I love you" like a near thirty-foot tapeworm.

LONGEST TIME FOR SEX TOY TO BE
LEFT INSIDE THE HUMAN BODY

When a thirty-eight-year-old Scottish woman turned up at Aberdeen Royal Infirmary complaining of severe weight loss, shaking, lethargy and mild incontinence, doctors were surprised to find a five-inch-long sex toy protruding into her bladder from her vagina. What alarmed them even more was that the woman said it must have been there for ten years without her knowing. She told them that she and her boyfriend had used it while she was drunk a decade ago and said she couldn't remember taking it out afterwards. As reported in a 2014 issue of the *Journal of Sexual Medicine,* the doctors managed to remove the toy, repair the damage and discharge the woman who, it was said, had a perfectly normal IQ. Perhaps it was a good thing that she was not named because it's probably not a world record she would want to boast about.

MOST KIDNEY STONES PASSED

Don Winfield, of Caledonia, Ontario, Canada, passed 6,504 kidney stones by the age of sixty, ranging in size from a grain of sand to a dried pea. His problems began in 1986 and at his most productive he passed twenty-four stones in a single day.

LONGEST OPERATION

From 4 to 8 February 1951, fifty-eight-year-old Gertrude Levandowski, of Burnips, Michigan, underwent a ninety-six-hour operation in Chicago, Illinois, for the removal of a huge ovarian cyst. The reason the surgery took so long was because instead of just cutting out the cyst, Dr M.S. Roberts opted to drain the fluid from it gradually, like slowly deflating a balloon. During her four days in theatre, Mrs Levandowski's body shrunk by 312 pounds. Four months later, she had a second operation that removed 50 pounds of excess skin.

MOST OPERATIONS ENDURED

Between 1954 and 1994, Charles Jensen, of Chester, South Dakota, underwent 970 operations to remove facial tumours. His tally would have appealed to Englishman William McIlroy who, suffering from Munchausen's Syndrome – an extreme desire for medical attention – had more than 400 operations in 100 hospitals between 1930 and 1979, using twenty-two aliases. He finally gave up, saying: "I'm sick of hospitals."

LONGEST BOUT OF HICCUPS

Charles Osborne, from Anthon, Iowa, hiccuped continuously for sixty-eight years. He began hiccuping in 1922 after a 350-pound hog collapsed on top of him while he was preparing it for slaughter. It is thought that he either pulled a muscle in his abdomen or that a blood vessel in his brain burst and destroyed the part of the brain stem that restricts hiccups. For the first few decades he hiccuped as often as forty times a minute, later cutting down to twenty a minute. All attempts to find a cure proved unsuccessful until the hiccups finally stopped in 1990, by which time Osborne was ninety-seven. Alas he had little time to enjoy his new-found freedom as he died the following year.

LONGEST SNEEZING FIT

Donna Griffiths, from Worcestershire, England, started her marathon sneezing fit on 13 January 1981 when she was twelve and finished it 978 days later on 16 September 1983. Although nobody was actually counting, it was estimated that she sneezed more than a million times in the first year alone. Her sneezes initially came at one-minute intervals before eventually slowing down to five minutes. Kleenex must have announced record profits for that two-and-a-half-year period.

MOST BONES BROKEN IN A LIFETIME

If Robert Knievel had wanted to lead a quiet life, he could have remained in his job as an insurance salesman. Instead he changed his first name to Evel and began flying over lines of cars on speeding motorbikes – a career for which, ironically, he was virtually uninsurable. The writing was on the hospital wall at an early stage. In only his third performance he was thrown fifteen feet into the air and ended up in a California infirmary. Four months later, on 19 June 1966, he attempted to jump twelve cars and a cargo van in Missoula, Montana, but his back wheel hit the top of the van and he suffered a broken arm and several broken ribs. The American public had become captivated by his exploits and with each successful jump they urged him to add one more car. So on 28 July 1967, in Graham, Washington, he tried to leap sixteen cars, only to sustain serious concussion in a crashing fall. Three weeks later, he had been discharged from hospital and was back in Graham to show how the jump should be done. This time he broke his left wrist, right knee and two ribs. Further pelvic, hip, wrist, back, ankle, foot, collarbone and head injuries followed, until by the end of 1975 he had suffered 433 broken bones, his consolation being an entry into the Guinness World Records for the most bones broken in a lifetime. The following winter he broke both arms and sustained brain concussion in a spectacular crash while attempting to jump a tank full of sharks in Chicago, but it was an injury to a cameraman, who lost an eye when the bike ploughed into him, that convinced Knievel it might finally be a good idea to retire while he was almost in one piece.

MOST COMPLAINTS TO A COUNCIL

Spanning four decades, Steve Bradbury has made an estimated 10,000 complaints – in the form of letters, phone calls and personal visits – to Kirklees Council in West Yorkshire. His grouse began in 1988 when his household garbage was not collected and has escalated to the point where the council says it spends around £11,000 ($17,000) a year just dealing with his complaints. An unrepentant Bradbury says: "They're just so incompetent that they answer one complaint and create half a dozen more." In 2011, the council actually banned him from visiting its offices because staff said they found him intimidating.

UNLUCKIEST PRODUCTION OF *MACBETH*

The curse of Shakespeare's *Macbeth* dates from its very first performance, 7 August 1606, when Hal Berridge, the boy actor hired to play Lady Macbeth, died from a fever halfway through the piece. Since then, it has been considered bad luck to mention the play by name. Instead, superstitious theatricals insist on referring to it as "The Scottish Play". There have been many instances of misfortune associated with *Macbeth* over the centuries, but the November 1937 production at London's Old Vic theatre starring Laurence Olivier and Judith Anderson must rank as the unluckiest. Just before the scheduled opening night, theatre director Lilian Baylis's favourite dog, Snoo, died, and the next day, Miss Baylis herself, having learned that the opening night was to be postponed, died of a heart attack. In the finest traditions of the theatre, the show went on, but Olivier was nearly killed by a falling 25-pound stage weight, which missed him by inches. Then in the final battle scene, which was unwisely fought with real swords, the tip of Olivier's weapon broke off and flew into the audience, hitting a man and causing him to have a heart attack.

The runner-up in this category is probably the 1934 production at the Old Vic where no fewer than four different actors played the title role in the space of a week. Malcolm Keen lost his voice, Alastair Sim went down with a bad chill, and Marius Goring was sacked by the director, leaving John Laurie to finish the run. The 1938 Stratford Festival opened with a production of *Macbeth*, which also appeared cursed. An old man broke both his legs when he was hit by his own car in the car park, Lady Macbeth drove her car into a shop window and Macduff fell off his horse and had to be replaced by an understudy for several days.

Just to prove that the curse is still going strong, Jonathan Slinger, who was playing Macbeth in a 2011 Royal Shakespeare Company production, broke his arm after being knocked off his bike in the street, and then in 2013 an actor appearing in Sir Kenneth Branagh's production of *Macbeth* in

Manchester was rushed to hospital after being injured by a sword in the opening battle scene.

FIRST ACTOR TO DIE IN HIS OWN PLAY

Noted French playwright Molière collapsed on stage with a violent coughing fit towards the end of a Parisian performance of his ironically titled comedy *Le Malade Imaginaire* (The Hypochondriac) on 17 February 1673. As the scene continued around him, the audience thought it was all part of the action, but after the curtain was lowered the stricken dramatist was taken home, where he died a few hours later.

FIRST ACTOR TO DIE DURING A LIVE TV SHOW

During a live broadcast of *Underground*, part of ITV's *Armchair Theatre* series, on 30 November 1958, thirty-three-year-old Welsh actor Gareth Jones suffered a fatal heart attack between scenes. Coincidentally his character, a businessman trapped by falling masonry in a subway station, was also scheduled to have had a heart attack later in the play.

FIRST SINGER TO SCORE "NUL POINTS" IN THE EUROVISION SONG CONTEST

Since its inception in 1956, the Eurovision Song Contest has offered such unforgettable titles as "Pump Pump" (Finland, 1976), "Boum Badaboum" (Monaco, 1967), "Boom Bang-a-Bang" (UK, 1969) and "Boom Boom Boomerang" (Austria, 1977), while the various subject matters have covered everything from a jolly arrangement of a Lapp reindeer-herding call to a little number about the construction of a hydroelectric power station. Yet the first song to receive zero points (or "nul points", as it is known in Eurovision-land) from all the other participating nations was "Mil Etter Mil" (Mile After

Mile), performed by Norway's Jahn Teigen at the 1978 contest in Paris. Nineteen voting juries, from Germany to Greece, France to Finland and Ireland to Italy, totally ignored the Norway song, with the result that it finished 157 points behind the winning song, Israel's "A-Ba-Ni-Bi". Far from being downcast by the result, the eccentric Teigen sensed that it could give his career a timely boost and, sure enough, "Mil Etter Mil" reached number one in the Norwegian charts and stayed in the top ten there for over four months, although this may say more about the state of Norwegian pop music than any lack of judgement from the Eurovision voting juries.

BIGGEST SINGLE-WEEK DOWNWARD MOVEMENT ON THE BILLBOARD CHARTS

Those who believe that TV "talent" shows are ruining the music business can take comfort from the fate which befell Javier Colon, the first winner of the US version of *The Voice*. His single "Stitch by Stitch" plummeted an unprecedented seventy-nine positions from seventeen to ninety-six on the Billboard chart in the week of 23 July 2011 – an unwanted record in more respects than one.

SHORTEST CELEBRITY MARRIAGE

Rudolph Valentino's marriage to Jean Acker on 6 November 1919 was just six hours old when she angrily locked him out of their honeymoon suite at the Hollywood Hotel immediately after the reception had ended. After knocking on the door for twenty minutes, "The Latin Lover" sensed she was not going to change her mind and headed home. However, the divorce was not finalized until 1922 with Acker claiming that the union was never consummated, which was hardly surprising considering the groom could not get past the bedroom door.

Britney Spears and childhood friend Jason Alexander fared

little better after getting married on impulse in Las Vegas at 5.30 a.m. on 3 January 2004. The bride wore white – well, a white baseball cap teamed with ripped jeans – but just fifty-five hours later they were granted an annulment on the grounds that Spears "lacked understanding of her actions, to the extent that she was incapable of agreeing to the marriage". She later described the short-lived union as "me being silly, being rebellious".

SMALLEST CONCERT AUDIENCE

Romanian folk singer Joan Melu set a record of sorts by attracting an audience of zero for a concert at the 2,200-seater Capitol Theatre in Melbourne, Australia, in August 1980. Undeterred by the lack of audience response, he proceeded to give a two-hour show, complete with an interval and encores, ultimately overrunning by thirty minutes. Performing as if real people were present, at one point he shouted out: "Hey everybody, do you want to hear my new one?" He interpreted the ensuing silence as a sign of approval (it was better than being booed) and said afterwards that he felt very satisfied with the way the show had gone. The previous week, he had hired the Sydney Opera House and pulled in an audience of eighteen, most of whom left before the interval. Word had obviously spread.

SHORTEST THEATRICAL RUN

The first and last performance of Lord Lytton's play, *The Lady of Lyons*, at London's Shaftesbury Theatre took place on 26 December 1888. After waiting for an hour, the audience was sent home because nobody was able to raise the safety curtain. In 1983, an Edinburgh Festival Fringe production of *Ubu Roi* by the Freie Theateranstalt company from West Berlin closed after just fifteen minutes of its solitary performance. The show's director and star, Hermann van

Harten, had intended the cast to include a pig plus several parrots and cockatoos, but he had forgotten about quarantine restrictions. Since the pig played Ubu Roi's wife, it was a key character, so van Harten had to resort to acquiring an understudy porker from the nearby East Lothian city farm. Alas, the replacement proved a veritable ham actor, and after a quarter of an hour van Harten decided to abandon the rest of the show and refund the audience.

LONGEST TIME SPENT FIGHTING AFTER A WAR HAS ENDED

Hiroo Onoda, a second lieutenant in the Japanese army, carried on waging a one-man war on imaginary enemy forces for twenty-nine years after the end of World War II. As a twenty-three-year-old, Onoda was posted to Lubang Island in the Philippines in 1944 to perform guerrilla and intelligence duties, with orders to continue fighting even if his unit was wiped out. Onoda obeyed the orders to the letter – and insisted on fighting the war long after his fellow countrymen had surrendered. He refused to believe stories that the war was over, convinced that they were merely US propaganda. Leaflets confirming Japan's surrender and signed by his chief of staff were dropped on the island but Onoda dismissed them as a trick. Friends, relatives and old comrades made loudspeaker attempts to persuade him to come out of hiding but these, too, proved fruitless, and when search parties and Japanese police officers were dispatched to Lubang, Onoda greeted them with a hail of bullets.

To avoid detection, the resourceful soldier switched hideouts and, as the years passed, took care to conserve his ammunition, but still found time to kill as many as thirty islanders in a series of skirmishes. The Suez Crisis, JFK, the Beatles, miniskirts and flower power all came and went, but Onoda remained steadfastly defiant until in 1974 he stumbled across Norio Suzuki, a Japanese student on a camping holiday. Onoda was about to shoot the hapless tourist but Suzuki said he knew of Onoda's story and told him how concerned the Emperor and the people of Japan were for his safety. Onoda replied that he would only lay down his arms if ordered to do so by his commanding officer. So it was that Major Yoshimi Taniguchi temporarily left his job as a bookseller to fly to Lubang, where, at 3 p.m. on 10 March 1974, Hiroo Onoda was finally persuaded to stop fighting. It was Onoda's fifty-second birthday. "I became an officer and I received an order," he explained before his death in 2014. "If I could not carry it out, I would feel shame. I am very competitive."

FARTHEST DISTANCE ON A ZIP WIRE
BY PONYTAIL (POSTHUMOUS)

In March 2011 at Rajasthan, India, Sailendra Nath Roy travelled 270 feet (82.5 metres) along a zip wire to which he was attached solely by his hair tied into a ponytail. Two years later, while attempting to smash his own record, the forty-eight-year-old suffered a fatal heart attack at a height of more than sixty feet above the Teesta River. He was left hanging there for forty-five minutes before he was finally brought down. The good news was that before his untimely demise he had covered a new world record distance of 295 feet (90 metres).

Sources

Ripley's Believe It or Not! annuals
The Wisden Cricketers' Almanack

www.alternativerecords.co.uk
www.goldenbookofrecords.com
www.guinnessworldrecords.com
www.indiabookofrecords.in
www.limcabookofrecords.in
www.recordholders.org
www.recordholdersrepublic.co.uk
www.recordsetter.com
www.singaporerecords.com
www.thelongestlistofthelongeststuffatthelongestdomain
　　nameatlonglast.com
www.uniqueworldrecords.com
www.worldrecordacademy.com